PERFUME ON THE PAGE IN NINETEENTH-CENTURY FRANCE

Despite long-standing assertions that languages, including French and English, cannot sufficiently communicate the experience of smell, much of France's nineteenth-century literature has gained praise for its memorable evocation of odours. As French perfume was industrialized, democratized, cosmeticized, and feminized in the nineteenth century, stories of fragrant scent trails aligned perfume with toxic behaviour and viewed a woman's scent as something alluring, but also something to be controlled.

Drawing on a wealth of resources, *Perfume on the Page in Nineteenth-Century France* explores how fiction and related writing on olfaction meet, permeate, and illuminate one another. The book examines medical tracts, letters, manuscripts, posters, print advertisements, magazine articles, perfume manuals, etiquette books, interviews, and encounters with fragrant materials themselves. Cheryl Krueger explores how the olfactory language of a novel or poem conveys the distinctiveness of a text, its unique relationship to language, its style, and its ways of engaging the reader: its signature scent. Shedding light on the French perfume culture that we know today, *Perfume on the Page in Nineteenth-Century France* follows the scent trails that ultimately challenge us to read perfume and literature in new ways.

(University of Toronto Romance Series)

CHERYL KRUEGER is an associate professor in the Department of French at the University of Virginia.

Perfume on the Page in Nineteenth-Century France

CHERYL KRUEGER

UNIVERSITY OF TORONTO PRESS
Toronto Buffalo London

© University of Toronto Press 2023
Toronto Buffalo London
utorontopress.com
Printed in the USA

ISBN 978-1-4875-4655-7 (cloth)   ISBN 978-1-4875-4657-1 (EPUB)
ISBN 978-1-4875-4656-4 (paper)   ISBN 978-1-4875-4658-8 (PDF)

University of Toronto Romance Series

Publication cataloguing information is available from Library and Archives Canada.

Cover design: Val Cooke
Cover image: Alphonse Mucha, Lance-Parfum Rodo (Paris: F. Champenois, 1896).
Image Source: The Mucha Foundation

We wish to acknowledge the land on which the University of Toronto Press
operates. This land is the traditional territory of the Wendat, the Anishnaabeg, the
Haudenosaunee, the Métis, and the Mississaugas of the Credit First Nation.

This book has been published with the assistance of the University of
Virginia Department of French and Dean's Office of the College and
Graduate School of Arts and Sciences.

University of Toronto Press acknowledges the financial support of the Government
of Canada, the Canada Council for the Arts, and the Ontario Arts Council, an agency
of the Government of Ontario, for its publishing activities.

Canada Council   Conseil des Arts
for the Arts   du Canada

ONTARIO ARTS COUNCIL
CONSEIL DES ARTS DE L'ONTARIO
an Ontario government agency
un organisme du gouvernement de l'Ontario

Funded by the   Financé par le
Government   gouvernement
of Canada   du Canada

Canadä

For John

Contents

Illustrations

Preface and Acknowledgments

Every perfume tells a story. What initially motivated my research for this book was the desire to better understand the stories of fragrance, suggested or elaborated, that waft from the pages of nineteenth-century books, to observe how these aromas mingle with plots and poetics, and to understand how readers of the era would have sensed and interpreted them. The perfumes of now classic works like Flaubert's *Madame Bovary* and Baudelaire's "Correspondances" reveal facets of form and meaning that were always there, though I had passed them by, again and again, before I began following literary scent trails. I first encountered Baudelaire's influential "Correspondances," a sonnet built on the lush notes of musk, amber, benzoin, and incense, in an undergraduate French literature course. As we analysed the poem line by line, a classmate asked what benzoin (*benjoin*) smelled like. The query seemed unusual in the critical context of a linguistic turn that shaped our discussions at the time, an approach that did not readily invite sensorial connections to the words we read. The reply, offered by a diligent student who had taken the time to investigate, was that it smells like *tar*. No one expressed surprise. I hardly gave it a thought. After all, Baudelaire mentions *goudron* alongside *musc* and *huile de coco* in the verse poem "La Chevelure" and its prose cousin, "Un Hémisphère dans une chevelure." But what if benzoin does not smell like tar? How would knowing the smell of benzoin influence the experience of reading Baudelaire's poem, or the direction of scholarly inquiry?

As I learned much later in my olfactory fieldwork for this book, benzoin smells to me nothing like tar. I suspect the earlier misidentification was caused by a dictionary consultation that led to an inadvertent *correspondance*: a confusion of benzene (a hydrocarbon found in coal tar) and the sticky *styrax benzoin*, a tree ooze recommended in nineteenth-century perfume manuals (along with ambergris, tolu, storax, and other materials), as fragrant fixatives to stabilize more volatile floral and citrus notes. Decades unfolded before I finally discovered the sweet, smooth, almost-vanilla, almost-almond resin delight that is benzoin, a dulcet note still humming in perfume blends today. Now that I have inhaled musk, ambergris, benzoin, and incense in many iterations, I both feel and think about the poem differently. The scent of benzoin brought Baudelaire's time, his experience, his contemporary readers, and his poetics closer to my mind and body. Today I get distracted if I read an odour I cannot identify. Smell words taunt me until I hunt them down, breathe them in, and learn their story. The aroma of benzoin opened Baudelaire's sonnet, revealing its deep texture, materiality, and cultural significance. The poem's aromas sparked my curiosity about scent studies in general, and above all, about the meeting of perfume and words. After consulting specialized literature on olfaction, meeting with perfumers, and sniffing my way through hundreds of fragrance samples, I found myself reading familiar novels and poems with deeper intellectual and emotional engagement, noticing passages that had hardly caught my attention before, understanding more clearly the personal and cultural impact of fragrant episodes.

For a long time, though, my personal fascination with scent seemed to have nothing to do with my deep interest in French literature. Like the nineteenth-century examples I explore in the chapters to follow, my own story of perfume shows olfactive encounters to be a blend of aromas, language, imagination, and human connection. It began with Oh! de London, a bottle I coveted for the image, the idea, the promise, and the wordplay, more than the scent. The advertising campaign featured a flower-framed photograph of Olivia Hussey, the Juliet of Franco Zeffirelli's Shakespeare adaptation, who seemed effortlessly stunning to girls like me, in the depths of their awkward stage. In high school, a friend's parents brought back from Paris a gorgeous flacon of l'Air du Temps. It was the first *serious* perfume I had truly noticed, unlike anything I had smelled before, or will smell again, since decades of reformulations have both diluted and sharpened it. In college I frequented a soap shop whose owners were willing to custom blend a white musk in my favourite body lotion, even though they insisted the fragrance was too light to hold up. As an *assistante d'anglais* in Nice, France, I would stop in a perfume shop on the way home from work, where I chatted with a patient sales associate who never pressured me to buy and always had me sample a maximum of three perfumes per visit, in the interest of staving off olfactory fatigue. Little did I know that one day my fieldwork would include hours of conversation and sampling at fragrance counters, museums, workshops, and perfumers' offices, along with consultation of document archives and libraries in Europe and the United States. Most of the illustrations in this book come from my growing collection of original nineteenth-century print advertisements, inspired by the hours I spent exploring the archives of Lubin perfumes. I have also built up my own collection of nineteenth-century perfume, beauty, etiquette, and hygiene manuals, and a vast library of liquid fragrances, many of which provided olfactory information and inspiration as I wrote.

My eventual exploration of the written word in relation to perfume culture called for research materials which were new to me, and which often led to fortuitous finds. Some of these *trouvailles* steered the course of my project, while others informed my thinking in a more embodied way. The reason I requested Huysmans's manuscript of *À rebours* at the BnF was to find out how the pages smelled – an intention I did not share with librarians who were already rather unconvinced that I needed to handle a manuscript that had been so beautifully digitized. It was only by perusing these – alas! – nearly odourless pages, that I discovered Huysmans's olfactory vocabulary notes in the margins. Chatting with curators for the Mucha Foundation, I was able to get a sense of what it was like to break the seal of a Lance-Parfum Rodo tube. While discussing the Baudelairean inspiration for Charogne perfume, I was treated to a sampling of fragrance materials, including a recently acquired chunk of ambergris. At the Musée international de la parfumerie in Grasse, I leafed through issues of the monthly trade manual *Revue des marques de la parfumerie et la savonnerie* dating to the 1930s, seeing and carefully touching the beautiful perfume labels affixed to their manufacturers' advertisements, and gently opening small, clear envelopes to inhale paper infused with samples of eugenol or vanilla concentrate, synthetic odour molecules first manufactured in the late nineteenth century. Later, when issues of *La parfumerie moderne* dating from 1910 to 1917 arrived at my doorstep, I was delighted to discover that the entire batch smelled of oakmoss, the fragrant soul of classic chypre perfume blends. It struck me that if I had been able to find digitized copies of these materials, I would have missed the thrill of encountering perfume on the page in such unexpected, multisensorial ways.

As I followed literary scent trails in French fiction, I spoke quite often, casually and formally, about my work. In so doing, I discovered that indeed, every perfume tells a story – and everyone has a perfume story to tell. Never has a research topic opened so many conversations for me, with librarians, with colleagues, with professional perfumers, with sales associates, with archivists, with family, with friends, with complete strangers. Like a scent trigger, the very mention of a fragrance jostles memories and leads to storytelling. Even those who dislike perfume have tales to share: of the co-worker who left a cloud of heavy-hitting gardenia in the conference room; of the opera lover who gave up on a season subscription because of the overly spritzed woman seated in front of her at every performance; of a lecture hall redolent of a patchouli that failed to mask its wearer's cannabis sillage. More often, though, people fondly remembered perfumes that marked stages of their lives, and they sought the right words to name, describe, and preserve the elusive essence of those scent memories. One friend hosting a dinner brought a favorite bottle to the table and asked if I could identify its haunting base (guaiac wood). Another sent me a signed copy of his latest book, the pages scented with a delicious vintage tobacco fragrance we both loved. I now know the signature scents of not only many colleagues, but their mothers, too. At home, guests have asked to sample and discuss a few perfumes from my stash over digestifs. In recent years, when the venue allowed it, I distributed illustrative scent samples when delivering conference papers. Unlike a projected image, which draws all eyes to the screen for a tidy group viewing, the experience of smelling test strips involves fumbling, touching, moving, breathing (more often than not with eyes closed), and a solitary, yet public, sensorial encounter, even when several people are sampling the same fragrance at the same time. Participants sometimes asked if they might keep the *mouillettes* I'd passed around. The answer was always *yes*. I imagine those scent strips, still diffusing a bit of now-subdued fragrance, nestled as markers between the pages of a book.

I could not have completed this project without the help of librarians, archivists, and perfumers, in France, the United States, and the United Kingdom, who found materials to view, read, and sniff, and who generously shared their knowledge and expertise. At the Osmothèque in Versailles, Jean Kerléo and Isabelle Chazot met with me to discuss and experience a range of perfumes related to the writers and works I discuss in this book. In Paris, Gilles Thévenin opened the doors to the beautiful office of Lubin perfumes, where I spent many days combing through countless nineteenth-century print materials, from books, advertisements, and perfume labels to order forms for Empress Joséphine's scented gloves. Etienne de Swardt passed around fragrant materials and gave me a sneak preview of an upcoming fragrance release, as he explained the literary inspiration for some of État Libre d'Orange's fragrances. I also benefited from skilled librarians at the Bibliothèque nationale de France (François-Mittérand and Richelieu branches, and online services), the Musée des arts décoratifs, and the Bibliothèque Forney. The staff at l'Eau de Cassis assembled an abundant selection of scents for a presentation I gave in Cassis, France. Along with archivist Tomoko Sato, Sarah Mucha took the time to meet in London to discuss Alphonse Mucha's designs for perfume posters and labels. She has also graciously found and shared images belonging to the Mucha Foundation. Margaret Khoury, general manager at Michael Edwards, sent me useful statistics on perfume sales. University of Virginia librarian Miguel Valladares-Llata tracked down difficult-to-find published works in every format imaginable, and Chloé Fargier gathered materials for me at the Centre de documentation du Musée international de la Parfumerie in Grasse.

I thank the Camargo Foundation, whose residency program provided a stunningly beautiful and fragrant place to work, in the company of an inspiring group of scholars and artists. Executive Director Julie Chénot and her wonderful staff came to the rescue in ways I could never have predicted. I also thank the University of Virginia, who supported this project with funding from the Dean's Office of the College and Graduate School of Arts and Sciences and the Department of French, as well an International Studies Faculty Travel Grant, a Summer Research Grant, and a Sesquicentennial Research Associateship.

As I researched and drafted this book, I spoke regularly at annual conferences of the Nineteenth Century French Studies Association (NCFS) and Society of Dix-neuviémistes (SDN). Discussions with colleagues at those meetings were central to shaping my thoughts and to deepening connections with fellow scholars. I cannot name every colleague who followed up by sending me links to articles on perfume over the years, but I sincerely thank each of you.

I am deeply grateful to the following friends and colleagues who generously took the time to read the entire manuscript or to read versions of various chapters along the way, to discuss the book in depth, who listened, added suggestions, and guided me in countless ways: Antoine Guibal, Melanie Hawthorne, Susan Hiner, Janet Horne, Edward Kaplan, Claire Lyu, Amy Ogden, Timothy Scheie, Richard Stamelman, and Rosalynn Voaden. I wish I could thank Ross Chambers and Priscilla Ferguson one more time for the kind support that led to completion of this project.

I thank Érika Wicky, who is always able to answer the most arcane questions about perfume in nineteenth-century France and who, along with Alice Camus and Jean-Alexandre Perras, has been instrumental in bringing together scholars from around the world and across disciplines to share their research in scent studies. I am also grateful to Holly Dugan, who early on included me in a lively forum for scent scholars. Before this project grew from an article to a book, I wrote book reviews for the blog *Now Smell This*. I thank founder and editor Robin Krug for that opportunity to connect with fragrant readers and perfume enthusiasts.

Heartfelt thanks to Nigel Harkness and Alexandra Wettlaufer, who organized and spoke on many panels with me over the past years and who were subjected to more conversations about this book than they could possibly have wanted. I am also grateful to those who answered questions, shared information, and offered invaluable advice: Janet Beizer, Masha Belenky, Nadia Berenstein, Sophie-Valentine Borloz, Aimée Boutin, Stacey Katz Bourns, Heidi Brevik-Zender, Sima Godfrey, Andrea Goulet, Richard Holway, Marni Kessler, Kevin Kopelson, Philippa Lewis, John Lyons, Mary McKinley, Rachel Mesch, François Proulx, Loren Ringer, Paul Sammak, and Holly Tucker.

Mark Thompson at University of Toronto Press guided this project and immediately sent the manuscript to three incredibly attentive and knowledgeable peer reviewers. I am indebted to those anonymous readers who shared brilliant comments, made important suggestions, and asked insightful questions. Thanks also to Elizabeth Ferguson, Lisa Jemison, Deborah Kopka, Virginia Ling, and Stephanie Mazza for helping to shape my manuscript into a book.

My history of perfume sniffing with Heidi Erickson, my sister, is decades long. I thank her and faithful fellow fragrance samplers Chrissy Angrick and Madeline Spring for their steadfast encouragement and morale boosting. My parents, Patricia and Richard Krueger, and sister Karie Pollard provided sustenance, often in sniffable and comestible form. I also thank Melissa Bradner, Jaquelin Crebbs, Jeannene Krone, Elise Leahy, Sarah Nelson, Rebecca Saunders, Kathy Suchenski, Nancy Virtue, and Dolly Weber for their community of support near and far.

John Urbach was with me every step of the way along these scent trails. I am grateful for his patience, wisdom, love, and encouragement, and his sharp editorial eye. I thank him for reading the manuscript and discussing it with me, for revising itineraries in North America, Europe, and New Zealand to include fragrant detours, and for learning more about nineteenth-century fiction and perfume than he had ever planned.

Notes on Translations, Sources, and Previously Published Material

All translations are mine unless otherwise attributed. I try to stay close to the original French syntax when possible.

Some perfume materials have alternative names (*orris*, *iris root*) in English and French. I maintain the terminology used in the original when I translate quoted text but try to stick to one spelling or term in my own prose. When, in the context of perfumery, French terms are usually carried over to English, I too use the French.

I cite medical tracts, perfumers' manuals, and books on etiquette, health, and beauty that were published in many editions in the nineteenth through early twentieth centuries. On rare occasions I have had to use the only edition available to me, but generally I try to quote the edition published closest to the time of related texts I am discussing.

Except where noted, illustrations come from my collection of French print advertisements and are in the public domain. They are not meant to represent a carefully balanced sampling from various perfume houses or publications, but to provide examples of how some perfume houses targeted their marketing by showing how perfumed products could be used, by whom, and what image or message such products might convey.

Sections of Chapter 2 previously appeared in the article "The Scent Trail of 'Une Charogne.'" *French Forum* 38, nos. 1–2 (2013): 51–68. I thank *French Forum* for allowing me to reprint parts of this article.

Chapter 5 is an expansion of the article "Lettres parfumées, correspondances fatales," *Littérature* 185, no. 1 (2017): 39–54. I thank *Littérature* for allowing me to reuse content from this article.

Chapter 7 is an expansion of "Decadent Perfume: Under the Skin and through the Page," *Modern Languages Open* (October 2014): 33p. I thank *Modern Languages Open* for allowing me to reprint much of this article.

PERFUME ON THE PAGE IN
NINETEENTH-CENTURY FRANCE

Something in the Air

In a 1905 treatise reporting the effect of cosmetic fragrances on neurotic and hysterical patients, Dr. Antoine Combe bemoaned the ubiquity of perfumed Parisiennes scenting the city streets. According to Combe, women of all classes were wearing enough perfume to immerse the innocent urban bystander in an odiferous *sillage.*"[1] This new usage of a familiar word gained traction sometime during the late nineteenth century, primarily in relation to women's scent trails.[2] *Sillage* translates as *wake* or *trail*: the visible trace on the water of a phenomenon (motion) and of the object (a boat) that produced it. There is no single-word English equivalent in the context of fragrance. To this day, perfumers borrow the term and its pronunciation [sē'äZH] from French.

Unlike aroma escaping an opened bottle of perfume, the sillage that Combe detected relies on a human carrier. Sillage is the fragrance that wafts from the clothing, accessories, hair, or skin of a passerby. It is a marker of both presence and absence, the fragrance trail that lingers after a perfume-wearer has left the room. Sillage expands personal space as it narrows social distance. At once the condensed and displaced essence of an individual, sillage represents the intimacy of an olfactory signature, even as it mingles with the air and the objects it touches. The experience of sillage engages the bodies of both the person inhaling and the one radiating fragrance. Through accident or intention, the sensorial experience of sillage communicates meaning once the scent is perceived, perhaps identified, and consciously or unconsciously read.

Today, sillage carries positive connotations for perfumers and fragrance lovers. Advertisements refer to a perfume's subtle, tenacious, floral, or rare sillage. It appears in product naming as well: the California-based company House of Sillage (founded in 2012), Dusita's Le Sillage Blanc eau de parfum (2016), and the historical recreation of one of Marie Antoinette's signature scents, M.A. Sillage de la Reine

(2005).[3] Perfumers differentiate between a product's sillage, its longevity, and its strength. Sillage indicates how a scent lives and moves in relation to the body and the space around it, the fragrance's presence, its projection, and its diffusion. The effect is temporal as well as spatial: like a visible wake on water, fragrant sillage will eventually disappear. Its fleeting character links to time and memory as well as to person and place. A perfume like M.A. Sillage de la Reine recaptures a fragrance Marie Antoinette reportedly wore, while just as importantly reviving and coexisting with, via its name and aroma, her time, her surroundings, her tastes, her body, and her being. Similarly, the figurative phrase *dans le sillage de* (*in the wake of, in the footsteps of, influenced by*), when attributed to artists or their works, conjures the uncanny coexistence of absence and presence, past and present, a temporal phenomenon associated with memories and remembering. Both the expanded usage of the word sillage and the interactive, olfactory phenomenon it signifies, evoke a set of social practices which together characterize a dynamic culture of modern French perfume, written on paper and in the air.

This book examines a convergence of literary production, medical writing, fashion trends, and social practices during a century that saw the rise of modern French perfume culture. The topic is motivated by the observation of two seemingly paradoxical phenomena revealed in fiction and extraliterary discourse, including Combe's treatise, regarding the implications of infusing the skin, the air, and the page with perfume. First, despite ongoing concern that languages, including French and English, cannot sufficiently communicate the experience of smell, much of France's best-known nineteenth-century literature has earned acclaim or infamy in part for its striking evocation of odours. Second, published works of the era dealing with women and olfaction, whether fiction, medical tracts, or books of etiquette, show that fragrance products sparked deep suspicion, even as their popularity soared. Although the increased demand for scented toiletries in the nineteenth century is often interpreted as evidence of heightened attention to cleanliness, I find a persistent, ambivalent counter-discourse in novels, poems, and non-fiction works that allies fragrance with more toxic airborne substances. It is as if suspicion of perfume supplanted the fear of miasma as an olfactory indicator of hygienic and social danger.

These two observations may seem at first only tenuously or coincidentally related. Yet, as the example of *sillage* demonstrates, both the language and the practices relevant to perfume use were in a constant, often symbiotic state of scrutinized self-invention. As a result, works of fiction that showcase the presence of fragrance not only reflect a cultural phenomenon, its emerging language, and its semiotics, they co-construct them; and writers of fiction convey their individual style via evocations of aroma in verse and prose. Dr. Combe's commentary on perfumed women is but one example of how scented products drew criticism as they became trendier. The era's interdependent, smell-focused discourses express a conflicted fascination with, and fear of, scented women. The newly mobilized bourgeoise shopper, the prostitute, the homemaker, the exotic other, the marriageable daughter, the femme fatale – these are the usual fragrance-diffusing protagonists of nineteenth-century novels, and the "characters" in medical narratives of extreme and unusual perfuming.

Modern perfume culture was feminized to a great extent by men, who were writing its origin story in the prefaces of their perfume manuals and medical treatises, buoyed by their fiction-writing brothers. The result of such textual attention to the smell of women is the olfactory equivalent of a male gaze,[4] for which there is no adequate term, though I think of it as the male sniff. Like the male gaze, the male sniff represents a perspective that women, too, both adopt and experience. Voices of authority in the nineteenth century who sought to define and control the smell of women within a heteronormative framework included male medical doctors and perfumers, along with women who wrote etiquette books and advice columns targeting female readers. Such writers show that the more obtainable and feminized perfume became, the more toxic and symptomatic its portrayal. A growing wariness of perfume, and vigilance to its implementation and proximity to the body, coincide with a likelihood that women of all classes might leave their scent trail in spaces beyond the privacy of the boudoir. As French perfume was industrialized, democratized, cosmeticized, and feminized, stories of fragrant sillage grouped it, intentionally or not, with other invisible threats to the individual and the environment. The very language used to evoke the dangers of cosmetic scent borrows heavily from the lexicon of disease, contamination, and airborne toxins. Sillage became the new miasma, something in the air, something contagious, something to be controlled.

Every Fragrance Tells a Story

Examples of the fragrant materials that grace the pages of nineteenth-century novels and poems read like the index of a perfumer's manual: ambergris, benzoin, chypre, frangipane, incense, jasmine, musk, opoponax, orris, rose, storax, styrax, tobacco, Tonka. Such scents are emitted, perceived, judged, identified, compared, and classified; their emotional, biological, and social effect on characters clearly signalled.

Though they contribute to the scaffolding of descriptive passages, fragrances themselves do not always enjoy the detailed attention that ekphrasis lends to works of art, or that the Balzacian verbal portrait brings to textual ecosystems linking characters to their habitats. Unembellished mentions of odour create an ambiguous descriptive register for any reader who, olfactorily speaking, has no point of reference. Recognizable as signs of authenticity or verisimilitude, smell words at times serve as partial, or would-be descriptors, a version of Barthes's *l'effet de réel* determined by reader response (or lack thereof). When neither sniffed nor sniffed out, the multitude of odours in nineteenth-century fiction may indeed read as a *luxe de narration*, signalling only the concept of realism itself. Yet the remarkable presence of scented bodies, objects, and spaces in the era's fiction represent a phenomenon more complex than a realist reflection of arbitrary true-to-life details in fictional prose, and more expansive than the textual residue Barthes attributed to the reality effect.

Nineteenth-century French literature offers innumerable encounters with a lexicon of aromas. Yet the most basic denotations and more nuanced connotations of such words may not be evident to readers today. The titular protagonists of Balzac's *Honorine* (1843) and Zola's *Nana* (1880), women who seem otherwise to have little in common, both radiate violet fragrance. Balzac and Proust mention (three times each) rooms that smell of iris in *Le curé de Tours* (1832) and *À la recherche du temps perdu* (1913–27) respectively. Huysmans's decadent protagonist Jean Floressas des Esseintes (*À rebours*, 1884) suffers from olfactory hallucinations of frangipane, and Goncourt's *Chérie* (1884) swoons to the scent of heliotrope. What would Balzac's contemporaries have understood when, in *La cousine Bette* (1846), a servant describes women at a housewarming as smelling heavily of patchouli? The suggestion of odour evokes the physicality and social significance of novelistic encounters as it enhances plot and character development. Passages rich in aroma express in various ways (depending on the author, the work, the aesthetic inclination) a convergence of mind, body, language, and culture, concentrated in olfactory perception. A perfumed letter from her husband's mistress is believed to damage a mother's milk in Balzac's *Beatrix* (1839). The smell of apricots delivered with a note from her lover provokes *Madame Bovary* to consider throwing herself from a window (1857). Learning to "read" the smell of iris (his mistress's signature scent) proves a confusing lesson in the *Sentimental Education* of Flaubert's protagonist Frédéric Moreau (1869). For Huysmans's *Marthe* (1876), the stench of musk and patchouli rising from her own body rouses the prostitute's consciousness of her deprivation.

In works of fiction, fragrances seduce, linger, betray, and forebode. They twist plots, stir memories, and signal social status. Moreover, representations of odour reinforce stylistic innovations and aesthetic experimentation. Literary scent trails mark the way to deeper understanding of the individual works and their aesthetic context. Evocations of odour and perfume in novels and poems accompany transformational junctures in the evolution of literary aesthetics. When perfumers and medical doctors of the nineteenth century argued the merits and dangers of synthetic fragrance molecules, they were grappling with a tension between nature and artifice, humans and the environment, that also characterized aesthetic movements across the century. Smells stir memories and are themselves memorable, as are their written representations. Smells, especially disturbing ones, are what many readers – critics and fans alike – tend to recall about a text, and as such, are essential to the distinct signature of a given author or work. In some decadent novels, for example, hyperbolic passages on peculiar perfuming practices feature full page enumerations of arcane smell substances, with commentary and descriptive elaboration emphasizing their effects and their materiality. Charles Baudelaire, on the other hand, offers a spare, almost generic vocabulary of smell (*perfume, flower, miasma*), and grammatically unembellished mentions of scented matter (*amber, musk, benzoin, incense*) in multisensorial poems that blend physical experience with transcendence (*Fleurs du mal*, 1857). Such divergent approaches to writing about smells compel the reader to grapple with the dynamics and rhetorical strategies necessary to create language–smell correlations and to understand the cultural implications embedded in references to olfaction. But like Flaubert's fictional Moreau, who cannot immediately decipher the meaning of odours he encounters in Paris, readers today may initially overlook the semiotics of unfamiliar aromas in writings of another age. Once unleashed, these fragrances contribute to an understanding of plot, rhetoric, style, and the cultural framework of the text's production. The evolving language and status of perfume provide a supple lexicon, both familiar and strange enough to showcase a writer's individual aesthetics and poetics, in dialogue with the larger context of a dynamic smell culture. For while scents belong to an intimate network of perception, reception, and interpretation that includes biological process and phenomenological immediacy, the experience of olfaction is both mediated by cultural and societal factors and mitigated by individual attitudes and experiences.[5] A close reading of specific texts leads to the larger question of how modern French perfumery and modern French fiction informed one another, owing to what I see as a dynamic relationship between perfume culture and creative written production in the nineteenth century.

To uncover the social messages signalled by scented bodies, objects, and spaces in literary works, I turn to other fragrance-centred writing of the era, including medical treatises, magazine articles, etiquette books, and manuals of beauty, hygiene, and chemistry. Such works articulate a history and vocabulary of modern French perfume co-evolving with experimental modes of expression in modern French fiction and poetry. In perfume culture as in literary culture of this era, one finds a tremendous outpouring of energy related to self-definition. In countless manifestos, prefaces, newspaper articles, and in arguments over coffee, wine, opium, and other substances, writers debate the nature and the purpose of their literary production: What is a poem? What is a prose poem? Should art imitate nature or embellish it? Is language purely intellectual or sense-related? Similar sorts of manifestos – though not defined as such – appear in the prefaces to most non-fiction works on fragrance and olfaction, presented in relation to beauty, hygiene, medicine, and the human body. Perfumers are determining whether and when to call themselves chemists. They contemplate the stakes of defining perfumery as a craft, an art, or an industry. They debate the value of perfume as a necessity versus a luxury good. They question the value of synthetic fragrances, all the while exploiting them.

Like fiction and poetry of the nineteenth century, perfumery is in a constant state of invention, always revising and retelling its story, as its story is read and critiqued within and outside fields of expertise. Perfume and literature are related in another more obvious way: novels recycle paragraphs from perfume manuals, and perfumers quote poets and novelists. Perhaps more strikingly, medical doctors who wrote about olfaction cited fiction writers (especially Baudelaire, Maupassant, and Zola, but many others as well) to justify their diagnoses. One of the characterizing features of nineteenth-century perfume writing is a keen awareness of olfaction as a growing subject of interest, bolstered in part by the very works that make such claims. "C'est en vain … que vous chercherez jusqu'au siècle dernier l'expression des émotions olfactives dans la littérature" ("It is in vain … that you will seek out, until the last century, the expression of olfactive emotions in literature"; 10) claims, inaccurately, André Monéry in his 1924 *L'âme des parfums: essai de psychologie olfactive*. Though Monéry seems to have overlooked earlier, noteworthy olfactive writing, he is correct in observing that smell references abound in literature of the nineteenth century.

The Architecture of a Fragrance, the Structure of This Book

This book focuses on a convergence of fiction and non-literary storytelling, related to the rise of an increasingly democratized and feminized perfume culture in modern France. I follow the scent trails in selected works of the long nineteenth century (1789–1914), particularly the era Alain Corbin dubbed the "golden age of osphresiology" (1821–85).[6] Due to the significant cross-pollination of olfactory knowledge during this era, I also consider some works published in England and the United States. My research shows that the surge of French fragrance production, and the persistent presence of aroma in concurrent literary works, are deeply intertwined through mutually reinforcing discourses on the social and literary implications of permeating the skin, the air, and the page with perfume. The incorporation of fiction and poetry into extra-literary texts on olfaction and perfume demonstrates a collaborative history of French perfumery in the making. An era eager to develop catalogues, monuments, and museums did not create commemorative spaces for perfume, or cultivate a prevailing centre of knowledge for perfume culture; nor did any single, dominant discourse confirm its status as an art, a science, or a consumer good. Yet the history of modern French perfume culture was being written in the air and on the page, in the words of perfumers and poets, and in the sillage of French women.

Across the chapters to follow, I uncover places where fiction and related discourse on olfaction inevitably meet, permeate, and illuminate one another as they shape a language and culture of modern perfume. I show how scents tell stories in French fiction, and French fiction tells a story of an emerging modern perfume culture. Embedded in this collective history of perfume, its pleasures, and its perceived dangers, is a story of women, their bodies, and their occupation of private and public space. It is an incomplete story, recounted in overlapping, sometimes interlocking fragments, told by multiple voices, using new words, and deeply related to the cultural relativity of medical diagnosis, as evidenced by case studies of olfactory symptoms attributed to neurosis and hysteria.

In classic perfumery, the three-tiered fragrance pyramid provides a visual translation of a given blend's structure and dimension (Figure 0.1).[7] The top or head notes (often citrus, herbal, or green) dominate in a first spray. Composed of weaker or lighter molecules, headnotes can modulate or in some cases disappear quickly, making more discernible the middle or heart notes, the flowers, spices, fruits, and other elements that give the composition its distinct character. The more persistent, yet sometimes less familiar, base notes – often animalic (musk, civet),

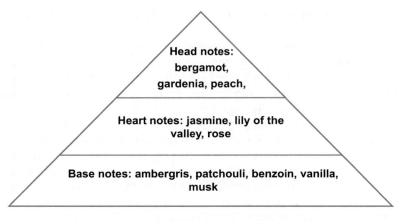

0.1. A perfume pyramid

woody (cedar, guaiac) or resinous (benzoin, opoponax) – anchor the blend and make it last. They serve as fixatives, enhancing the tenacity and expansion of a perfume's more volatile elements. On their own, some base notes can be overpowering. Natural tinctures of musk and civet smell pungent, often fecal, in their raw state. Once mixed, they may figure among a perfume's most appealing and memorable notes. Most importantly, all three layers of the pyramid commingle from the very first splash or spritz, but their relative proportions shift as the fragrance moves through time and space.

Like the layers of the fragrance pyramid, the main ideas linking the chapters of this book coexist and combine, though one may assert its presence over the other in a given chapter. The first theme, the head notes of this analogy, involves the allegedly precarious, paradoxical relationship between odour and words. A tremendous concern, even anxiety, over the limits of smell language is expressed across disciplines to this day, particularly in anthropology, linguistics, and cognitive science. Yet there is overwhelming evidence of written and verbal communication about smell across the ages. In fact, some smells have expanded the vocabulary of French and English through linguistic innovation, appropriation, or repurposing. In 1964, scientists Isabel Bear and Richard Thomas created a name for the "argillaceous odor" that had long been perceived – the pleasant smell of earth after rain – *petrichor*.[8] The words *ambre* or *ambré* were adapted to describe not ambergris or amber resin, but a fragrance blend (or accord, now also known as a category or family[9] of perfumes) born in the late nineteenth century, a scent that is not representational in that it does not imitate a known substance.[10] Perfumer Jean-Claude Ellena notes that the amber accord (built on labdanum and vanillin) was "the first abstract smell in perfumery and appeared at the end of the nineteenth century with the invention of vanillin" (*The Diary of a Nose*, in the section "A Summary of Smells," n.p.). Earlier in the book, Ellena posits that the amber/*ambre* was so named for its colour. He compares the invention of this non-referential fragrance to the invented flavour of Coca-Cola (94).[11] The innovative repurposing of *sillage* to evoke the relationship of perfume to the body and its environment facilitates communication about a fleeting phenomenon and expands the meaning of the word itself. Like *ambre*, *sillage* is an adapted, hybrid term. Like petrichor, sillage was perceived and described long before it was named.

While most scholarship on olfaction acknowledges an ongoing debate about the shortfalls of smell language, some researchers dismiss the topic, since Baudelaire, Huysmans, Proust, Zola, and so many others did successfully produce evocative scent writing. Literary studies do not tend to examine whether or how nineteenth-century writers perceived the alleged smell–language gap. My first chapters lead with questions about the language, lexicon, and semiotics of perfume. They deal overtly with writers of medical tracts, perfume manuals, novels, and poetry who not only recognized the challenge of writing about odours, but devised terminology and distinctive methods for dealing with it. Words like *sui generis* and *confused* appear again and again in these works, be it to celebrate or condemn olfactory language.

The "heart notes" of my study are women, a newly mobilized consumer base for perfumed products. While women are present in my earlier, more language-focused chapters, they are the central focus of chapters 5 through 7. Whether or not they knew it, women played a crucial role in the production and diffusion of knowledge, superstition, and fiction related to perfume. Like novels of the era, perfume manuals, etiquette books, health treatises, and titillating works of medical vulgarization,[12] are filled with stories – some of them case studies, some of them casual anecdotes – about women, the natural scent that their bodies exhale, their fragrant microcosm, and their use and misuse of perfume. If the sections on women were removed from these books, they would be slim volumes indeed. The lack of confidence in women's taste and judgment when it comes to wearing fragrance relates to the larger concern, particularly during the Third Republic when, as Lisa Tiersten shows, the prodigious growth of a consumer marketplace both "catapulted the bourgeoisie to new heights of economic power" and "fanned the flames of marketplace individualism" (2). Women were increasingly criticized for their shopping behaviour, which "seemed to unleash their private persona in the public domain" (5). Moreover, bourgeois women were the targeted buyers of knock-offs and mass-produced goods that threatened the prestige of handcrafted, luxury items associated with France. As the perfume industry rapidly grew across the century, perfumers were in the enviable position of being able to build their brands by deciding to focus on affordable wares with broad distribution, to cultivate a narrower market for more exclusive boutiques, or to develop both high- and lower-end lines.[13] Particularly as the discovery of synthetic molecules made fragrance production easier and less costly, the French perfume industry consciously carved out a double identity for itself, using many of the same materials to manufacture accessibly priced scented cosmetic and luxury items. As a result, the scent of perfumed women became less decipherable as a signal of class and taste.

Despite obvious efforts on the part of medical doctors and beauty mavens alike to create a system of social meaning or a semiology of cosmetic perfumes, by associating some fragrances with innocence and modesty, others with vulgarity and overt sexuality, it would be short-sighted to assume that all women followed the rules of hygiene and fashion or read the staging of perfumes in works of fiction as cautionary tales. Such stories did, however, contribute to a narrative of fragrance culture in the making that to some extent both reflected and defined the history of modern French perfume. By the nineteenth century, perfume had been, and remained, a product fashioned for both women and men. Royal parfumer Simon Barbe called Louis XIV "le roi le plus doux fleurant" ("the sweetest smelling king"; Le Guérer, *Le parfum des origines à nos jours*, 132–3). Louis XV and his "perfumed court,"[14] the Directory–era Muscadins (noted for the pomanders they carried and their musky scent trails [Feydeau 1003–4]), and Napoleon I, a heavy user of eau de cologne at home and on the battlefield,[15] are among France's most recognized fragrance eccentrics. As Jean-Alexandre Perras demonstrates in his discussion of gun powder versus hair powder, from the time of the French Revolution, perfumed powder for men became both more available and more disparaged. Powder was a go-to motif for earnest and satirical condemnations of softened masculinity, while de-powdering signalled strength and rusticity.[16] The social codes of perfuming for men continued to shift in the nineteenth century along with evolving constructs of masculinity.

Histories of perfume summarized in prefaces of books on olfaction often label male users and abusers of perfume as effeminate or

eccentric. Similarly, in medical literature, men with psychological disorders related to olfaction are deemed neurotic or feminized as hysterical (despite their lack of a womb, wandering or stable). Nonetheless,
men did continue to use perfume in the nineteenth century, though,
if they were following advice administered in the popular press, less
abundantly than in the past.[17] Images of bourgeois men appear in
print advertising of the late nineteenth and early twentieth centuries,
but they are often seen offering perfumes as gifts, or appreciating,
rather than wearing, fragrance. For example, a 1911 advertisement for
Lubin's "Bouquet Greuze, Pampres d'or, etc." depicts a man on a couch
breathing in and apparently appreciating the fragrance of a letter he
has opened. The text reads, "Ce qui, dans PARFUMS LUBIN, a de tout
temps séduit les connaisseurs, c'est leur extrême distinction" ("What, in
LUBIN PERFUMES, has always attracted connoisseurs, is their extreme
distinction") (see Figure 0.2). Upon inspection, it seems the target client
here is not necessarily, or not only, the letter reader, but those whose
Lubin-scented letters will convey to recipients the writer's good taste
and distinction.

The nineteenth-century sartorial extremes that Margaret Waller
has identified as "Old Regime exhibitionism and modern understatement" (117) characterize fragrance-wearing as well, with the redolent
dandy on one end of the spectrum and the less showy bourgeois on
the other. Marketing and fashion trends contributed to the feminiza-
tion of scented products, but the relationships between hygiene, fashion, sexuality, and a drive to construct a mainstream masculinity were
also subject to the dominant discourse of the male sniff.[18] In a chapter
mocking current suspicious, hypocritical attitudes about perfume and
floral scents, Grandville's 1847 *Les fleurs animées* declares that while
men may still wash their hands and groom their beards with perfumed
soap, "[a]ujourd'hui un homme n'ose pas avoué qu'il met de la pommade à ses cheveux.... Il suffit d'humecter son mouchoir de quelques
gouttes d'eau de senteur pour se donner le vernis du petit maître ou
d'homme efféminé.... Voilà pour l'homme!" ("[t]oday a man does not
dare put pomade in his hair.... Just dampening his handkerchief with a
few drops of scented water is enough to give him the veneer of a dandy
or an effeminate man.... That's it for men!"; vol. 2, 292).[19] As Rosalind
H. Williams has shown, the very notion of dandyism was democratized and "tainted by consumerism" in the nineteenth century, with
vulgar acts of shopping seemingly at odds with dandyism's spiritual
superiority (119–20). Williams refers specifically to how materialism
and excessive consumption gradually became signs of dandyism, a
phenomenon dramatized in Joris-Karl Huysmans's *À rebours* (further

0.2. A 1911 full-page print advertisement for Lubin perfumes shows a man sensing a scented letter.

discussed in chapter 4). But the idea and the figure of the dandy were also eventually exploited to promote democratized luxury goods, as the marketing and the very name of Parfums d'Orsay's Le Dandy fragrance demonstrate.[20] A 1926 print advertisement for the fragrance seems to embrace this double, or perhaps more fluid, gender appeal. While its illustration of a dapper man (with top hat, cane, and cravat), framed in flowers and holding the perfume bottle, could indicate that the product was designed for men, the text promises that "she" ("celle") who uses the perfume and "they" (the masculine "ceux") who breathe in her sillage will experience a light, poetic, and "fairied" ("féerisée") intoxication (see Figure 0.3). For today's viewer, the consumer identification suggested in the play of image and text seems to push against more traditional gender binaries upheld in marketing of the era.[21] But it is likely the perfume producers were primarily motivated to cast a wide consumer net. According to Groom, the fragrance was launched in 1923 for men, but soon become popular among young flappers (96).

As reported and satirized in the popular press, in the nineteenth century, the balance of attention to perfume use in popular culture gradually shifted to women, a newly mobilized customer base (Corbin 260–6). This fluctuation in consumer practices is reflected in two French novels, set against a backdrop of evolving cosmetic sales tactics in Paris. Balzac's 1837 *Histoire de la grandeur et de la décadence de César Birotteau*, a novel that pays surprisingly little attention to smell, given its subject,[22] tells the story of a perfume-shop owner who markets scented hair oil to men. Zola's 1883 *Au bonheur des dames*[23] depicts the rise of an unstoppable department-store machine whose labyrinth aisles lure women shoppers in droves.[24] The *parfumerie* department at Bonheur des dames has been strategically placed near the store's reading room and popular buffet, where its penetrating aromas reach prospective clients throughout the gallery, beckoning them to join the crush of eager hands vying for the department store's signature soaps. At the centre of a stunning display rests a silver fountain featuring a shepherdess standing in an abundance of flowers. The female shoppers dip their handkerchiefs into the fountain's violet water as they pass (479–80). On a larger scale, a fountain whose waters cascaded over natural flowers and plants would later dazzle visitors to the French perfume section at the 1900 World's Fair. The *Paris Exposition, 1900: Guide pratique du visiteur de Paris et de l'exposition* spotlights the luxurious decor of the perfume pavilions, the grace and delicacy of both the products and the clients, and its unique, utterly feminine style (280–1). The exhibit owed its distinct appeal in part to walls adorned with decorative depictions of women symbolizing flowers (Piver 1900, 5–6).

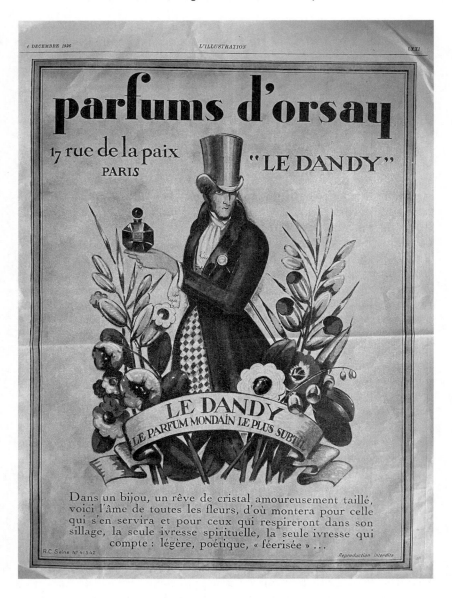

0.3. A 1926 print advertisement for "Le Dandy" by Parfums d'Orsay.

But women's interactions with perfume were not always portrayed in a light or flattering way. Studies in social history and literary criticism reveal a symbiosis between nineteenth-century medical depictions of hysterical women and comparable iterations in literature and the visual arts.[25] Medical case studies of hysteria, often with an emphasis on the afflicted woman's sensitivity to smells and other sensory stimuli, constitute one of many narrative threads that contribute to the incomplete story of perfume and women's bodies. A proliferation of nineteenth-century fiction showcasing fragrance and odour perception converge with disparate sources of non-fiction writing to co-construct the intertwined culture and poetics of perfume, which by the end of the century pathologized women who smell too much.

The "base notes" permeating the chapters of my book are the scents and fragrant materials themselves, perfume as a substance, as matter to be touched, seen, and smelled, as an object, an object of desire, a product, a personal statement, and a memory trigger. In every chapter, I pause to better understand the history of the scented matter mentioned in novels, poems, and non-fiction works, how it smelled, and how readers of the era might have encountered it in their lives. Every fragrance tells a story; these stories provide the keys to interpreting scents that may be less accessible in the twenty-first century than they were in the nineteenth.

Using one of the nineteenth century's most enduringly popular fragrances as a case study, Chapter 1, "In a Violet Sillage," sets the stage for the chapters to come, with an overview that situates Dr. Antoine Combe's pejorative use of *sillage* in the context of evolving practices and attitudes related to women and concerns since early in the century over their abuse of perfumes. Writers develop a semiology of fragrances like violet and musk to articulate the social and literary construct of the *jeune fille* (a morally upright, marriageable young woman), versus her fallen sister, the *fille* (prostitute). Yet depictions of young women as violet flowers and devotees of violet fragrance link ostensibly unrelated individuals: the demure heroine of Bernardin de Saint-Pierre's 1788 *Paul et Virginie*, the nonconformist poet and "Muse aux Violettes" Renée Vivien (1877–1909), and the members of an eccentric elite deemed "violet maniacs" who, at the turn of the century, purportedly injected perfume for recreational and cosmetic thrills. Tracking references to violet sillage and *violettomanie* from the 1820s to 1905, I show that while voices of authority attempted to demarcate limits of taste and class by defining a social semiotics of fragrance, some women nonetheless expressed themselves in a language of perfume that broke the rules.

Chapter 2, "The Language of Flowers and Silent Things," takes its title from Baudelaire's poem "Élévation," in which the poet rises high above the Earth's "morbid miasmas," for: "Happy is he …/ Who understands with ease/The language of flowers and silent things." This chapter spotlights ongoing debates about if and how language conveys the presence of odours and the experience of smell. What remains to be explored, though, is whether writers of scent and smell specialists of the nineteenth century were concerned about the limits of an olfactory vocabulary; and if so, how did they express this concern or work around the perceived problem? This is the first of three chapters that explore these questions, beginning with an overview of the olfactory-lexicon debate from the perspectives of anthropologists, linguists, historians, cognitive scientists, and literary scholars. I then look more closely at how Baudelaire incorporates the lexicon of odour in his scented poetry, focusing on "Correspondances" (the synesthetic sonnet evoked for its *benjoin*/benzoin in this prologue), and on what I see as a closely related poem, "Une charogne" ("A Carrion"). My analysis of the poems shows that the solipsistic or *sui generis* correlation of objects and smell words discussed earlier in the chapter belies a dynamic process of sensorial reading in Baudelaire, sparked by even the most generic lexicon. Similarly, the power and mobility of smell words in the final stanza of "Correspondances" give dimension to a seemingly linear enumeration, through a linguistic *sillage* that stirs the senses, the memory, and the imagination. I argue that the intensity of what Baudelaire called "dangerous perfumes" lies as much in his simple but synesthetic "confused words" as in his dramatization of perfumed encounters.

Chapter 3, "Confused Words?", expands my examination of the danger and confusion attributed to an insufficient olfactory lexicon, by centring on the way writers grappled with smell language in three types of nineteenth-century texts, written for very different audiences: medical treatises by Dr. Jean-Joseph Brieude and Dr. Ernest Monin, dedicated to the promotion of olfaction as a medical diagnostic tool; manuals by and for perfumers (Pradal, Piesse, Poncelet, and Rimmel) seeking a common language of odour classification; and passages from a novel that borrowed heavily from those perfume manuals, J.-K. Huysmans's 1884 *À rebours*. The works discussed in this chapter reveal a keen awareness of the smell lexicon, along with efforts to vary a vocabulary that writers found to be deficient.

Chapter 4, "The Osmazome of Literature," discusses in depth the now iconic "perfume chapter" of Huysmans's *À rebours*, focusing on the metaphorical relationship between written and olfactory composition, sustained through descriptions of decadent protagonist Jean Floressas des Esseintes's perfume appreciation and practice. Consulting Huysmans's handwritten manuscript of the novel, I discovered word lists and edits in the margins that reveal the author's careful attention to diversifying the lexicon of olfaction and fragrance in his prose, traces of the author's research and writing process. Within the novel, Des Esseintes works on a sort of smell classification system in reverse, characterizing works of fiction according to the odours their words and syntax evoke for him. The prose poem is his favourite of all literary genres because it represents the *concrete juice*, the *osmazome* of literature, the essential oil of art. Like essential oil, concrete is a perfumer's term, referring to a fragrance in the form of a highly condensed, sometimes waxy paste. Osmazome (from the Greek *smell* and *bouillon*) is what gives meat its *sui generis* smell and flavour, its signature scent. In episodes on perfume and reading, the evocation of real fragrance released into the air from Des Esseintes's vast perfume collection enhances the materiality of words and images, while abstracted aromas written on the page stir the senses. The actions of words on perfume, and of perfume on words, are reciprocal, as texts and smells merge to become correspondingly tangible and readable. At the same time, the language of perfume, its syntax and phrasing, is incorporated in the structure of the "perfume chapter" itself.

Chapter 5, "Perfumed Letters," turns from the abstract idea of perfume on the page, to the materiality of fragrant letters in Balzac's *Béatrix* (1839) and Flaubert's *Madame Bovary* (1857), contextualizing those aromas within social attitudes and practices of perfuming various home goods and accessories in the nineteenth century. The practice extended to Balzac's perfumed correspondence with Madame Hanska, Gustave Flaubert's fragrance-enhanced readings of Louise Colet's letters, and George Sand's letters to Musset. Like scented clothing and accessories, the fragrance of writing paper signals levels of taste, or *distinction*, related to both physical and moral cleanliness. An apprehension over perfume and the women who use it, serves as both cultural and discursive intertext to the staging of Balzac and Flaubert's fictional, scented letters.

Chapter 6, "Smelling (of) Iris," considers the social, material, and sensory implications of people and places described as *sentant l'iris* in fiction of the era, most notably, *Madame Bovary*, whose changing fragrance proclivities correlate to her moral and physical downfall. I discuss the novel's keen attention to the protagonist's skin and fragrance preferences, in light of attitudes about hygiene, bathing, and fears of contaminating the body by penetrating it with liquids and odours of all kinds. Iris (the flower or the root) and its fragrance (an air freshener or an elegant perfume material) offers a complex example of the equivocal olfactory codes readers and sniffers of the era encountered.

Chapter 7, "Decadent Perfuming," investigates the true stories that stoked sensationalistic reports of perfume abuse, and similarly pathological representations of perfume in novels. Such examples were presented as signs of moral corruption, especially for female protagonists in naturalist and post-naturalist works. The story of Goncourt's fragrance-crazed *Chérie* (1884) reads as an absurd culmination of the physical, psychological, and moral degeneration of the *jeune fille*, foreshadowed in the story of *Paul et Virginie*, and developed in the works of naturalist writers. The perfume-abusing woman fictionalized in the character Chérie, and most likely embellished in newspaper reports of women's injection parties, may also have been the target buyer of the Lance-parfum Rodo (1896), now best remembered from a poster by Alphonse Mucha. Goncourt's *Chérie*, Alphonse Mucha's advertisement poster for the Rodo, and the surprisingly hazardous product itself, place women at the nexus of discourse on the risky social and literary implications of fragrant indulgences.

The "Epilogue: Cooked Apples and Exotic Perfume" considers the future of past perfumes, the enduring yet ever-transmuting sillage of nineteenth-century French fragrances. First, I read Rachilde's counter-naturalist olfactory discourse in *Monsieur Vénus* (1884) as a response to the *jeune fille* literary theme that so fascinated writers including Zola and Goncourt. Rachilde's resistance to her era's dominant, binary perspective on gender and social practices, including perfume use, serves as a reminder that not all writers and fragrance-wearers bought into the increasingly dominant discourse on perfume that persisted well into the twentieth century, and that in many ways characterizes the semiotics of perfume today. While the gendering of specific scents has been called into question over the decades, particularly by perfume houses replacing (or, more often, supplementing) their catalogues of perfume for men and women with unisex offerings, other aspects of nineteenth-century perfume culture have become engrained, most obviously in the enduring Western legacy of exotic perfumes.

Although an exhaustive chronicle of references to perfume in nineteenth-century French literature would be a useful research tool, it is not my intention to create one here. Nor do I use examples from literary passages solely to illustrate cultural practices, though I point out when they do. Instead, I investigate olfactory cues as markers of linguistic, aesthetic, and social codes. Informed by studies of olfaction in anthropology, cognitive science, cultural history, literary criticism, and psychology, I review the relationship of selected literary texts to concurrent popular and specialized writing on olfaction. This approach allows us to recognize how such texts define, archive, and construct communications about smell, and in particular, fragrance. Across modern French fiction, odour articulates class differences, as well as crossings of moral, psychological, and geographical borders. An emphasis on smell (as metaphor, as narrative device, as poetic figure, as cultural referent) links disparate works of fiction and poetry, yet highlights stylistic differences, and blurs conventional boundaries: between the sacred and the profane, body and spirit, self and other, past and present. Reading works of literature alongside related historical documents, I demonstrate how this hybrid archive of experience and imagination, revealed in stories of perfume, provides a foundation for the French perfume culture we know today.

Chapter One

In a Violet Sillage

Despite widespread acceptance today of the word *sillage* among fragrance experts and aficionados, it is difficult to pin down modern French perfumery's first use of the term. Manuals by the influential perfumers Septimus Piesse and Eugene Rimmel[1] do not mention sillage by name; nor do self-help beauty experts Madame Celnart or the Baronne Staffe, both of whom dispensed wisdom and warnings about the intensity and diffusion of one's personal scent aura. The 1835 *Dictionnaire de l'Académie Française* (vol. 2, 735), the *Grand dictionnaire universel du XIXe siècle, 1866–1877* (vol. 14, 723), and Émile Littré's 1875 *Dictionnaire de la langue Française* (vol. 4, 1943) include only the analogous nautical definition (a ship's visible *wake* on water), with related technical and figurative usages (23).[2] Yet the fragrance term does surface in other places. This expansion of olfactory expression seems to have come to light not because the phenomenon of sillage had never existed before, but rather, because it was experienced differently, with renewed attention that fuelled a desire to name it, define it, and control it.

Before the noun *sillage* was adapted to the context of smell, encounters with active, invasive fragrances, seductive or foul, were (and still are) described in other multisensorial ways, often as physical contact between the perceiver's body and an aroma, its transmission supplemented by sensations of touch (odours in the air colliding with or layering on one another, smells brushing against the skin), or sight (rays of light and colour), or sound (the rustle of fabric). A loud opening and closing of doors signals a release of odours, for example, in the theatre where Zola's titular protagonist Nana (1880) performs: "un vacarme de portes dont les continuels battements lâchaient des senteurs de femme, le musc des fards mêlé à la rudesse fauve des chevelures" ("a din of doors whose continuous slamming released the smells of women,

the musk of makeup mingling with the harsh, animal odour of hair";
1206).[3] The smells of soaps and perfumes drift down from the dressing
rooms, temporarily cutting off the more toxic bouquet of gas, glue, dank
corners, and the chorus girls' dubious undergarments (1206). Wending
his way up the theatre's odiferous staircase, Nana's increasingly light-
headed suitor, Count Muffat, also senses the presence of smells on his
skin: "le comte avait senti de nouveau un souffle ardent lui tomber sur
la nuque, cette odeur de femmes descendue des loges, dans un flot de
lumière et de bruit" ("the count felt [or smelled] again a burning blast
on the back of his neck, that odour of women wafting down from dressing rooms, on a wave of light and noise"; 1222).

Fiction and extra-literary texts rely heavily on verbs, some more
inviting than others, to convey the diffusion of cosmetic perfume and
the relationship of personal fragrance to the body and its surroundings.
Along with their adjectival forms, the verbs *exhaler* (to exhale), *imprégner*
(to impregnate, soak, permeate), *répandre* (to diffuse, or spread), *envahir*
(to invade), and *pénétrer* (to penetrate or enter) mark the spatial presence and effect of a perfume (or a stench) on environments and people.
Their extreme reactions, *griserie* (intoxication, excitation) and *évanouisse-
ment* (swooning, fainting), link smell sensitivity to physical reactions,
medical conditions, and substance abuse. Zola pairs the verb *pénétrer*
with *parfum* in the description of the dressing room in Nana's second-
floor apartment on boulevard Haussmann, where visitors encounter
a blend of odours wafting from cosmetics and floral bouquets radiating, "un parfum pénétrant et fort; tandis que, dans l'air moite, dans la
fadeur exhalée des cuvettes, trainait par instants une odeur plus aiguë,
quelques brins de patchouli sec brises menus au fond d'une coupe" ("a
penetrating and strong perfume; while, through the dampish air, in the
vapidity exhaled by the washstands, there occasionally wafted a more
pungent odour, some grains of patchouli ground to a fine powder in the
bottom of a cup"; 1137).

Though not yet widely used in print media, the word *sillage* did
appear in discussions of women and fashion by the turn of the century.
In August of 1902, an article in the literary and fashion review *Les modes*
reporting on a trend for soft, wavy, odorous hair announces that perfumes are becoming quite a craze ("une vraie folie") as "toute femme
évolue dans un sillage embaumé" ("every woman moves in a fragrant
[embalmed] sillage"; 22)[4] (Figure 1.1). Several years later, Renée Vivi-
en's collection of thirty-six poems was published as *Sillages* (1908), a
title which, in concert with the works themselves, evokes the temporal,
spatial, visual, and olfactory associations of the phenomenon.[5] Most of
the volume's verse, dedicated to Natalie Clifford Barney,[6] deals with

café, de la cigarette... et des conquêtes. A propos de robes décolletées, dirai-je que « tous les genres sont de mode, hormis le genre laid » (ô poète, pardon !) : des fourreaux princesse en tulle ou en cluny incrusté de guipure d'Irlande, du flou comme cette fine silhouette drapée de chiffon de soie que nous donnons ici, ou de la fantaisie comme cette robe de tulle rayée de pastilles de velours d'une si heureuse disposition dégradée du bas de la jupe à la taille. Très en vogue, les pastilles comme les pois qui en ont été les inspirateurs : pois gros ou petits, en semis ou irréguliers, on leur prédit un gros succès, que nos gravures font aisément comprendre. Comme formes générales, apparition des doubles jupes ou tuniques, vers lesquelles la mode paraît s'orienter (comme dans cette toilette à pois), puis toujours beaucoup de volants en forme, la tête dissimulée sous des broderies; des jupes superposées faisant volants-pèlerines pour les costumes tailleur.

Comme tissus, après que nous aurons dit adieu au foulard et à l'éolienne — qui ont encore quelques semaines de règne — nous oscillerons entre le drap souple et les lainages bourrus, le sanglier et la zibeline ; actuellement, c'est le drap qui nous fournit nos plus jolis manteaux de voiture ou de casino : un tout simple et ravissant est une sorte de collet Aiglon, la première pèlerine très longue, la seconde venant aux hanches, et une troisième, faite d'un énorme col en grosse guipure en drap pastel avec le col revers brodé d'or, rabattant sur la guipure, l'effet est charmant.

Avec les séjours dans les châteaux, voici venir le triomphe de la tea-gown ; la place me manque pour y insister aujourd'hui, mais je livre aux méditations de mes lectrices ces deux exquises reproductions, où la grâce du modèle lutte avec l'élégance de la toilette : rien ne surpasse la séduction de ces ajustements caractéristiques de la vie la plus luxueusement raffinée.

Pour finir, un mot du panama (toujours !) en feutre blanc comme équivalent du canotier d'automne : mais cette fois il ne reste plus du panama que le nom et la forme : j'avouerai même que la souplesse du feutre communique une certaine grâce aux cabossages savants qui le constituent, et, noué d'une grosse cravate de surah blanc ou de teinte vive, l'ensemble devient seyant à un joli minois jeune, aux cheveux très souples, ondulés, odorants (les parfums deviennent une vraie folie, et toute femme évolue dans un sillage embaumé), bichonnés à souhait ; car, n'oublions jamais que plus une mode est négligée, plus il faut l'entourer de raffinements qui la distinguent du vulgaire !

SYBIL DE LANCEY.

LAFERRIÈRE.   ROBE DE DINER   Cliché Reutlinger.

1.1 An article from the fashion and literary magazine
Les modes no. 20 (9 August 1902), 22, in which wavy hair and soft,
flowing fabric suggest the flow of a woman's fragrant sillage.

Image source: gallica.bnf.fr / BnF.

remembering, forgetting, lost love, and lost time. These memories are steeped in the odours of jasmine, violet, iris, amber, and many unspecified, perhaps metaphorical fragrances, including "un nostalgique parfum" ("a nostalgic perfume"; 126). Though the titular sillage does not reappear in the individual works, its presence transpires in poems like "La demeure du passé" ("The Dwelling Place of the Past"), when the poet urges her lover to return to the "maison aérienne / du songe et du passé: ("the ethereal house/of dream and of the past"). Throughout the poem, this intangible, lost time materializes in solid structures and visible spaces (the bedroom, the floor, the foyer), which still recall the absent lover's physical being, in familiar objects left behind (forgotten books, aromatic sachets, necklaces), and in fragrant sillage: "Reconnais ton odeur d'ambre mêlé d'iris... / Toute chose dans la demeure de jadis/Porte ta chère empreinte" ("Recognize your odour of ambergris mixed with iris... / Everything in the dwelling of yesteryear / Bears your beloved imprint"; 127).

Less tender was Dr. Antoine Combe's reference to the sillage of Parisian women three years earlier. His foreword to *Influence des parfums et des odeurs sur les névropathes et les hystériques*, like much olfaction-focused writing of the time, serves up a brief history of perfume practices from antiquity to modern France, including several cautionary tales of excess and abuse, with a dash of moralizing. Combe laments in particular the recent rise of synthetic perfumes and the concurrent democratization of fragrance-wearing among women:

Depuis que les chimistes, par de savants procédés de synthèse, ont jeté à bas l'industrie des parfums faits avec des fleurs, les différentes essences les plus variées, les plus fortes comme les plus suaves, se multiplient et deviennent à la portée de tous. On se parfume, et à outrance. Il suffit de sortir un instant sur nos grandes avenues pour être aussitôt dans le sillage odoriférant d'une femme du grand ou du demi-monde.

Since chemists, using the learned processes of synthesis, have brought down the industry of perfumes made of flowers, different and more varied essences, the strongest and the most agreeable alike, have multiplied and become available to all. One perfumes oneself, and excessively. One instant on our grand avenues is all it takes to be immediately in the odiferous sillage of a society woman or a woman of the *demimonde*. (13)

Here *sillage* is modified (as *odoriférant/odiferous*), indicating perhaps that Combe knows his lexical usage is unconventional or relatively new. Or is he mocking an emerging, trendy expression? The fact that Guerlain

1.2. An interior photograph of the Maison Guerlain boutique
at 15 rue de la Paix, where Sillage was among the newest
fragrances sold in 1909.

Image source: *La ville lumière: anecdotes et documents historiques,
ethnographiques, littéraires, artistiques, commerciaux et encyclopédiques*
(Paris Direction et Administration, 1909), 160.

filed a trademark for a perfume called Le Sillage one year later[7] suggests that the neologistic meaning was in the air. In its tour of the 11th
Arrondissement, *La ville lumière*'s illustrated write-up on the Maison
Guerlain (see Figure 1.2) identifies the newest fragrances as Jicky, Après
l'Ondée, and Sillage as being "à la mode aujourdhui" ("in fashion
today"; 162).[8]

By the mid-twentieth century, the term appears regularly in advertising and articles about fragrance in France.[9] *Sillage* in its new usage conveys the unfolding, contingent nature of both the language and experience of fragrance in modern France. Stories of fragrant sillage ally it
at times with taste and elegance, but also with the more contagious

"something" in the air, miasma. This contradictory view is but a microcosm of the generally mixed messages about perfume and women that flourished in the nineteenth century. The suspicion is pervasive enough to represent more than a fringe reaction. It is a defining feature of modern perfume culture.

The Grandeur and Decadence of Perfume Use

Perfume (and sillage) have been a part of human life for millennia in cultures across the world. The Latin meaning, "in smoke,"[10] conveys the early use of fragrant plants and resins burned in sacred rituals. France perfected the craft of perfume production over centuries, from the Renaissance through the era of Louis XV's perfumed court. Although France has a long tradition of fragrance production, the dawn of modern perfumery dates to the Napoleonic era, an age that saw both the expansion of scented products and dogged efforts at hygiene reform. After the Revolution of 1789 the manufacture of fragrance commodities escalated. As mass production, new models of commerce and advertising, and the fabrication of synthetic scents contributed to ever-widening distribution of perfume and related accessories,[11] the production of books and articles on perfume accelerated as well.

The foundation story of France's now world-famous industry, reiterated in hygiene manuals, novels, and medical tracts, maps the rise of perfume culture as a progressive, civilizing journey from the temples of ancient Egypt to the dressing tables of modern Paris. "L'histoire des parfums est, en quelque sorte, celle de la civilisation" ("The history of perfumes is, in a way, the history of civilization"), says perfumer Eugène Rimmel in his 1870 *Livre des parfums* (7).[12] Yet his contemporaries warn that such cultural advancement can easily lead to excess and degeneration. The Industrie chimique's perfume section in the international jury report for the 1900 World's Fair similarly presents progress in perfumery in the context of the rise and decay of a civilizing force. Not unlike Combe's introduction to medical experiments, the jury report notes that the use of fragrances originated in religious rites and ceremonies, but in due course, perfume functioned primarily as an embellishment, notably for women: "Il constitue un art véritable dans lequel la femme règne en maîtresse" ("It constitutes a true art in which woman is the reigning mistress"; Piver 10). According to the report, all cultures follow this path of development from the sacred to the practical to the frivolous, perfume use inevitably leading to excess and abuses (10).

As the fragrance industry expanded, etiquette manuals offered perfume advice that was at best ambiguous, and too often confusing. Women should wear perfume but they should smell natural. Perfume threatens the physical and moral health of its wearer as well as those who encounter her scented aura. Nonetheless, women should develop a personal, olfactory identity through their selection of a signature scent. Women were crucial to the success of the perfume industry and the diffusion of fragrance products. Increasingly mobilized in the public sphere, both physically and economically, women purchased perfume, they wore it, and by the end of the century, images of perfume-loving women adorned print advertisements and posters. Beauty mavens discussed why, where, and when to apply fragrance. Poets celebrated the abstract and material power of aromas, and novelists perfumed their plots. Commercial and fine art depicted the seductive movement of fragrances in the air. At the same time, in an abundance of published case studies and anecdotes, medical doctors, early sexologists, and social critics concentrated on evaluating, classifying, and regulating the scent of women.[13]

A drive to contain the seemingly uncontrollable smell of women is dramatized to a pathological degree in Patrick Süskind's well-known 1985 novel *Perfume: The Story of a Murder*, set in late eighteenth-century France.[14] Here protagonist and perfume apprentice Grenouille applies the scent extraction technique of enfleurage[15] to women's bodies, capturing their odour in oiled fabric in order to distil their natural perfume. Though medical science does not seem to have gone to such an extreme, an 1877 study conducted by Dr. William Hammond in New York, discussed later in this chapter, resonates with Grenouille's macabre practice, echoing a combined fascination and fear of the female body revealed in nineteenth-century olfactory discourse of all kinds. As more women impose their microclimates on social spaces, they leave a scent in the air that does not function as an antidote to miasma. Instead, it threatens the health of the wearer and those infected by her. It is miasma's sister, something for which there is no precise name, but that would eventually be called *sillage*.

Perfume Goes Viral

The miasmic theory of contagion held that disease was spread by fetid air emanating from filth, stagnation, and decomposing bodies. Since noxious odours signalled tainted air, treatment of those odours might cure the polluted atmosphere. Aromatic fumigations had been among the arsenal of weapons deployed to protect the environment from miasmic assault. Early personal protective equipment like the doctors' plague masks (including long beaks filled with aromatic herbs)[16] were believed to create an odour shield against contagions (see Figure 1.3).

Habit des Medecins, et autres personnes qui visitent les Pestiferés, Il est de marroquin de levant, le masque a les yeux de cristal, et un long nez rempli de parfums.

Cette gravure avait déjà paru dans le *Traité de Peste* de MANGET, Genève, 1721.

1.3. Engraving made in 1721 of a doctor wearing a plague mask, reprinted as a curiosity in many medical treatises of the nineteenth century, found here in Ferdinand Chavant, *La peste à Grenoble 1410–1643* (Lyon: Storck, 1903), 58.

Image source: gallica.bnf.fr / BnF.

The salubrious effect of perfuming foul air was largely discredited in the nineteenth century, as a mere masking device; yet traditional views of smell-related contamination persevered long after research on microorganisms and germ theory had deflated the belief that epidemic disease was spread by odour (see Barnes 2006). Still, pollution, putrefaction, effluvia, and miasma had been associated with corrupted air and its attendant smells for so long that it must have been difficult to renounce the concern that odour itself was a vehicle for contagion.

Though the hygienic practice of aromatic fumigation declined in the nineteenth century, use of fragrance products for the home, as for personal grooming, was on the rise. To assure that scented accessories were not simply frivolous, proponents now presented them, if not as a prescribed antidote, then as a pleasant, personal shield from the assault of mephitic air. Portable scent delivery devices, including artificial corsages

1.4. An 1895 Viville advertisement featuring the handkerchief, a popular vehicle for perfume. The text reads: "Oh! quel parfum exquis que cette Violette Reine!" ("Oh! What an exquisite perfume is this Violette Reine!").

Image source: gallica.bnf.fr / BnF.

and nosegays, handkerchiefs, gloves, bookmarks, pincushions, vinegar bottles dangling from chatelaines (*armoires* or *escarelles* in French, affixed to a belt), and an assortment of clever perfume dispensers, might mitigate the unpleasant and potentially dangerous intrusion of stifling indoor air or pungent city streets, but they were also used proactively, especially by women, as a fashion statement, a readable sign of individual taste and attention to grooming (see Figures 1.4 and 1.5).

1.5. A 1911 print advertisement showing a woman echoing the gesture of lifting to the nose odour shields such as pomanders, handkerchiefs, and bouquets. Here she holds a bouquet of violets in her right hand, a perfume bottle in her left, as if to compare them. The tagline reads: "C'est exactement la fleur!" ("It's exactly the flower").

It stands to reason that the golden age of osphresiology,[17] with its renewed interest in the physiology of smell and the chemistry of odors, unfolded in tandem with the rise of modern French perfumery. Between 1810 and 1912, the French perfume trade soared from 2 million to 100 million francs, and the number of perfume houses in Paris expanded from 139 in 1807, to at least 346 in 1914 (Briot 2011, 275–6).[18] Formerly an artisanal craft, perfumery became a science and an industry. The 1791 abolishment of a restrictive guild system[19] allowed perfumers to expand their product lines in the interest of attracting new buyers. Innovative technologies for extracting scent, the use of steam power, mass-production techniques, and the development of synthetic compounds allowed perfumers to create products more rapidly and at lower cost. This expansion, a boon to be sure, also proved a sort of existential crisis for perfumers who consciously attempted to define their work as art or industry, luxury or necessity, hygiene or cosmetics.

As early as 1801, Jean-Louis Fargeon, personal perfumer to Marie Antoinette, called perfumery the application of chemistry to modern arts (2).[20] By the 1860s, authors of perfume manuals listed their credentials as *parfumeur-chimiste*, as they pitched their books simultaneously to *chimiste-fabricants* and do-it-yourselfers. Aware that their field was rapidly changing in ways that might confuse the consumer, perfumers addressed the question of safety in their writing on chemicals and synthetics. Louis Claye, then director of the luxury perfume house Violet, presented his 1861 *Les talismans de la beauté* as a modest book devised to help women make wise decisions in choosing safe and authentic scents.[21] His discussion of the history and manufacturing of perfume rests on two fundamental principles: first, that quality perfume is not just an industrial product serving the whims of fashion; rather, it is an essential element of both health and beauty regimes. Second, quality perfume is distinctly French, specifically, Parisian. Though Claye's book follows the generic tradition of presenting a chapter on the geographical origins of perfume materials (43–70), he makes clear that some products formerly obtained abroad are now cultivated on French soil. The scent of roses that used to be imported from the Orient (Constantinople and Smyrna), he claims, is inferior to that of the more refined rose cultivated in Grasse (55–6). Going further, Claye indicates that France is an exporter of perfume, conceding that the majority of the materials essential to French perfume production are not grown in France, with little to no commentary on the role colonial enterprise plays in this market (39–41).[22] He does not go so far as to point out an irony that business historian Geoffrey Jones later articulated, that "the growing vitality of the Parisian fragrance industry ... rested on the role of colonialism in making available new raw materials," and depended on resources and labor in Asia and Africa (*Beauty Imagined* 22). Instead, Claye emphasizes that it is "le génie national, le sentiment artistique, plein d'élégance et de bon goût que Paris sait mettre dans tous ses produits qui ont fait nôtre cette industrie" ("the national genius, the artistic sentiment, filled with elegance and good taste that Paris knows how to put into its products that have made this industry ours"; 40). Throughout the book, Claye carefully reinforces the importance of balancing science and craftsmanship while underlining the significance of Parisian perfume as a source of national pride and identity that will continue to characterize the industry for centuries to come:

> De vastes magasins, des manufactures, des usines considérables ont remplacé les modestes laboratoires où travaillait le parfumeur des anciennes époques. Notre génie et le goût parisien se sont emparés de cet art créé pour le luxe et pour le plaisir; Paris fournit aujourd'hui des parfumeries au monde entier.

> Vast stores, workshops, extensive factories, have replaced the modest laboratories where the perfumer worked in former times. Our genius and Parisian taste have seized upon this art created for luxury and pleasure; Paris today supplies the perfume shops of the entire world. (35–6)

Instead of arguing for or against the now inevitable place of chemistry in the art of perfumery, Claye analogizes perfumery to the emerging field of pharmacy: "La parfumerie est, en effet, à la cosmétique, – ou l'art de conserver la beauté, – ce que la pharmacie est à la médecine. Elle repose sur les sciences anatomiques, physiologiques et thérapeutiques, aussi bien que sur les découvertes de la chimie organique et de l'histoire naturelle" ("Perfumery is, indeed, to cosmetics, – or the art of conserving beauty, – what pharmacy is to medicine. It relies on anatomical, physiological, and therapeutic sciences, as well as the discoveries of organic chemistry and natural history"; 1). Claye endorses a distinction between high-quality products, respectable everyday fragrances, and cheap counterfeits,[23] in the interest of preserving one's natural beauty. Touting the progress France has brought to perfume production, Claye credits his era and his nation for harmoniously binding the potentially dichotomous axes of health and fashion: "Hygiène et élégance, double résultat qui ne pouvait guère être obtenu qu'à notre époque" ("Hygiene and elegance, a double result that could hardly have been attained until our era"; 34). Though couched in a positive message about the perfume industry, his argument addresses a growing counter-discourse that shines a more sceptical light on the relation between perfume, physical well-being, and mental stability.

Claye's sometimes defensive tone responds to at least two threats to the luxury perfume market. First, it was indeed easier to produce less expensive approximations of more expensive perfumes. As new materials and technologies facilitated expansion of the fragrance market, manufacturers had to justify offering both high-end and more accessible products, and to point out their differences.[24] Second, while the pleasures and merits of cosmetic fragrances were vaunted in print advertising, product labels, catalogues, and perfume manuals, the perils of perfume abuse had become a topic of growing interest, evidenced especially in newspaper articles, hygiene manuals, and medical treatises that commingled the language of disease and contamination with that of fragrance. Even some of the most celebratory evocations of fragrance in poetry and fiction of the era suggest, insidiously or overtly, a looming danger associated with the smell of something in the air, even when that something is perfume.

It is true, as Combe observed, that many perfumes popular at the end of the century owed their success in part to synthetics.[25] Houbigant's 1884 Fougère Royale, which launched a now classic family of woody fragrances,[26] was the first to use a synthetic coumarin molecule (Nicolaï, 1137).[27] Guerlain's Jicky (1889) famously featured coumarin as well, along with vanillin. In his 1903 Les odeurs du corps humain, Dr. Ernest Monin similarly bundles concerns about the rise of synthetic perfumes with a threat to France's national identity, and the precarious control that women, as consumers, now have over this realm: "Hélas! Il faut, de plus en plus, démocratiser même les industries aristocratiques.... Nos femmes françaises devraient bien joindre à leur bon goût naturel un peu de patriotisme protectionniste, pour réagir contre ces apports incessants de la chimie allemande, dont les conquêtes compromettent peu à peu notre commerce national d'essences naturelles." ("Alas! One must, increasingly, democratize even the aristocratic industries.... Our French women should join to their good taste a bit of protectionist patriotism, in order to react against the incessant contributions of German chemistry, whose conquests are compromising little by little our national commerce of natural essences"; 46–8). The same year, in more positive terms, perfumer Septimus Piesse cites Justin Dupont's defence of synthetic fragrances which have boosted the production of natural ingredients by expanding sales in general:

> Grâce aux produits chimiques, le parfumeur et le savonnier ont pu établir des articles à pris très abaissés qui ont trouvé immédiatement une clientèle neuve…. L'emploi de l'eau de Cologne, de vinaigres aromatiques, des eaux de toilette, des extraits de mouchoir s'est généralisé. Cet accroissement de production s'est effectué grâce à l'emploi de produits artificiels qui, pour un prix modique, mettent à la disposions du parfumeur une puissante odorante considérable.

> Thanks to chemical products, the perfumer and the soap-maker have been able to make items at lower prices that have immediately found a new clientele…. The use of eau de Cologne, aromatic vinegars, eaux de toilette, and extracts for the handkerchief has become widespread. This growth in production took place thanks to the use of artificial products, that, for a moderate price, has made significant fragrance power available to the perfumer. (*Chimie des parfums* 1903, 193)

Though Maryan and Béal's 1896 *Le fond et la forme: le savoir-vivre pour les jeunes filles* does not specifically mention that many of the synthetic fragrances now essential to the French perfume industry had been developed in Germany, it too links fragrance selection to national identity, though in a more visceral way. Readers are warned that musk is to be shunned, not only because it is strong enough to linger indoors for years and loud enough to spread in a thirty-foot radius. For the readers' parents and grandparents, musk would awaken the memory of "odious contact" with Prussian conquerors of 1870, soldiers who smelled strongly of the musk they wore to kill parasites, and whose horrible presence on French soil and in French houses would forever be conjured by the smell (108–9). To conclude their lesson in reading musk, the authors urge those who did not experience this olfactory assault first-hand to remember the story and to let the smell always serve as a reminder of how it is used on the other side of the Rhine.

A Superfluous Necessity

In her postumous essay "Parfums," writer, performer, scent enthusiast, and eventual cosmetics seller Colette[28] uses the oxymoron "un superflu nécessaire" (a necessary superfluity; 179) to summarize her enthusiastic but qualified appreciation of fragrance. The expression foreshadows a lengthier contemplation of the simultaneous joys and caveats of perfume-wearing. Her cautious approach to both synthetics and sillage reveals an awareness of a more general, growing anti-fragrance sentiment. Colette loved freely, but promoted fidelity when it came to perfume, pointing out that she has worn the same scent for over forty years. Drawn to the mystery and tenacity of white flowers, she described her go-to fragrance as rich in the pulpy, fragrant-by-night, lightly fetid-by-day lushness of jasmine. She described her signature blend as bold, with a base of white flowers combined with her own natural scent. Though Colette announced her presence and marked her territory in signature scent, she lamented that between 1900 and 1935, "[l]es femmes emportaient dans leur sillage, au restaurant et au théâtre, des fragrances capables de couper l'appétit et d'ôter à l'écran ou à la scène tout intérêt" ("[w]omen carried in their sillage, to the restaurant and the theater, fragrances capable of ruining the appetite and eliminating any interest in the scene or on the screen"; "Parfum," 150). The witty meditation on perfume closes with a dialogue between Colette and a perfumer whom she sniffs out on a tram, the suave, mixed, floral scent he radiates (s'exhaler), providing much needed respite from the olfactory assault of the other passengers carrying freshly caught river fish, balancing quarter wheels of Roquefort on their heads, or exuding a strong human odour of "hope," sweat, or cigarette smoke (154). When the more pleasantly fragrant passenger reveals himself to be a chemical engineer (here signifying "perfumer"), Colette voices her fragrance preferences and suspicion of chemically produced scent, cleverly reprising the tagline for Gabilla's *Violette* perfume print advertisements (see Figure 1.7): "Quand je respire un parfum vanillé, je veux croire bonnement que vous y mettez de la vanille; j'espère que la violette sent la violette" ("When I inhale a vanilla perfume, I simply want to believe you put vanilla in it; I hope that violet smells of violets"; 155) (Figure 1.6).

Monsieur le chimiste (who indeed works for Gabilla)[29] soon allays her worries about artificial ingredients, explaining that perfumery is the poetry of hygiene (156) and that natural and fabricated fragrances complement one another. Synthetics stabilize the otherwise "vagabond" vegetal materials, and the latter poeticize more brutal manufactured notes. Only a poorly made perfume announces its pharmaceutical lineage by smelling of vanillin, ionone, and other artificial ingredients (156). Colette's playful dialogue and Gabilla's reassuring print advertisement confirm that by the early twentieth century, non-specialist fragrance shoppers knew that artificial ingredients were widely used in perfumes, and that suspicion of synthetics was another potential perfume danger to be assuaged in marketing campaigns.

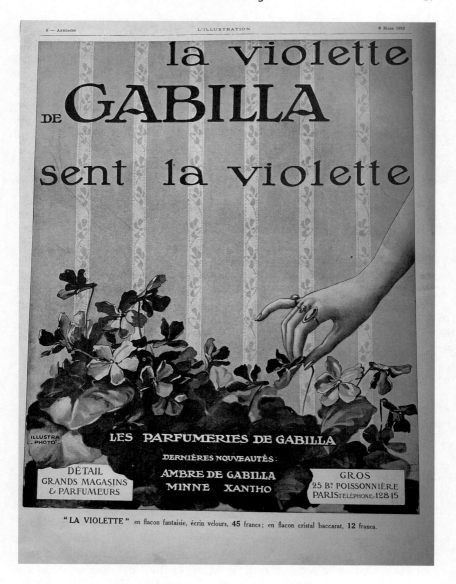

1.6. A 1913 print advertisement for Gabilla violette perfume showing a woman's hand plucking a violet flower. The tagline reads: *la violette de GABILLA sent la violette* ("Gabilla's violet smells like violets").

In reaction to overt and implied criticisms, perfumers had for decades tauted the superior quality and safety of their fragrance products, their wholesome value, and their practical utility. Piesse argues in his 1857 *The Art of Perfumery* that music, the visual arts, and fine fabrics are signs of the senses evolving in civilized and refined people; smell is most enjoyed in the forest and garden; perfume raises smell to the level of the other senses. Piesse also reminds his readers that perfumes have medicinal qualities: "Pathologically considered, the use of perfume is in the highest degree prophylactic; the refreshing qualities of citrine odors to an invalid is well known. Health has often been restored when life and death trembled in the balance, by the mere sprinkling of cedrat[30] in the sick chamber" (x).

Similarly, in 1895, Pradal devotes a section his *Nouveau manuel complet du parfumeur* to the antiseptic properties of perfume (vol. 1, 27–32). In 1882, Rimmel continues to support the refuted premise that perfume was an antidote to miasma. Rimmel makes a case for the practice of fighting illness and miasma with fragrant fumigations, in direct response to what he calls a war, waged by medical doctors and other "enemies of perfumes":

Et cependant nous voyons certains médecins faire une guerre acharnée aux parfums en disant qu'ils sont nuisibles à la santé. Nous prétendons, au contraire, que leur usage dans certaines proportions est bien faisant et surtout éminemment prophylactique, et nous croyons l'avoir prouvé.

And nevertheless we see certain doctors waging a relentless war on perfumes by saying they are harmful to health. We contend, on the contrary, that their usage in specific proportions is beneficial and above all prophylactic, and we believe we have proven it. (22)

Rimmel cites a hypothesis from an article published "a while ago" that claims the odour of flowers is anti-pestilential: "Pourquoi le PARFUM ne serait-il pas le contre-poison du miasme?… Il faut prouver que le parfum n'est pas destiné seulement à masquer l'odeur désagréable du miasme, mais à le réduire radicalement, et qu'il est non un objet de luxe, mais un objet d'utilité et un des vrais gardiens de la santé" ("Why would PERFUME not be an antidote to miasma?… One needs to prove that perfume is not destined only to mask disagreeable odour, but to reduce it radically, and that it is not a luxury object, but an object of use and one of the true guardians of health"; 19–20). On a lighter note, when Piesse describes the novelty *bague à jet d'odeur* (a fountain finger-ring)

Fig. 61. Bague à jet d'odeur.

1.7. The Fountain Finger-Ring (*bague à jet d'odeur*) described as both useful and ornamental in Septimus Piesse's *Des odeurs des parfums et des cosmétiques* (1865, 279).

Image source: gallica.bnf.fr / BnF.

in his popular *Des odeurs, des parfums, et des cosmétques*, he is careful to acknowledge that: "C'est à la fois un objet de luxe et d'utilité" ("It is at once an object of luxury and utility"; 279), always on the hand when a refreshing spray is needed, be it at a ball, a concert, or in a sick person's bedroom. (See Figure 1.7.)

Reading Perfume

As the alleged hygienic utility of fragrance proved less convincing, and its cosmetic use more affordable, perfume became an increasingly complicated, readable, yet polysemic sign. Encouraged to wear a single, recognizable perfume, women could make an entrance and leave a scent trail, with a fragrant signature or olfactory identity that would mark their presence in time and space. That presence might be interpreted as modest, coy, seductive, unhealthy, or threatening, depending on the smell literacy of those caught in her odiferous sillage.

While nineteenth-century writers like Baudelaire and Huysmans explored the rhetorical and sensorial implications of "dangerous perfumes,"[31] health experts warned against the physical, emotional, moral, and psychological perils of hazardous scents. And as modern perfumers created readable classification systems for fragrance components like heliotrope, iris, jasmine, musk, patchouli, and violet,[32] doctors and self-appointed specialists communicated their own less methodical rankings of risky odours. Generally speaking, natural materials were perceived as more wholesome than synthetics, floral scents were deemed more tasteful than the animalic civet or musk, and single-note scents (soliflores) were recommended over mixtures (bouquets). Within these guidelines further distinctions contributed to an unofficial semiotics of scent, informed more by social norms than by science.[33]

The social semiotics of cosmetic perfume, reinforced in a gamut of serious and pseudo-medical tracts, provided fiction writers a multi-layered strategy for showing how characters, knowingly or not, were read and misread by those who encountered their scent. A lack of explanation about the perfumes named in many novels suggests that readers were presumed to be attuned to the social messages conveyed in fragrance. For example, in Balzac's *La cousine Bette* (1846), when a maid knowingly mentions women who smell of patchouli, it is unlikely that she has detected a liquid perfume. Patchouli would have been blended with other ingredients but was usually not worn as a solo scent, its aroma considered strong and rather mossy. In the nineteenth century, the French smelled patchouli that was used as an insect repellent in fabrics imported from India, and on fashionable shawls in particular. In fact, French knock-offs of the sought-after Indian shawls could be identified by their lack of the signature patchouli aroma, that is, until the counterfeiters caught on.[34] Contemporary readers in the know would have attributed the patchouli sillage in Balzac's scene as wafting from women's shawls, a known luxury accessory, and a desirable gift, offered to wives and lovers alike.[35]

Patchouli remained (and remains) a staple of perfume composition, though it was not recommended as a stand-alone scent. In 1857, Piesse warned that patchouli must be carefully blended and applied with a light hand: "Its odor is the most powerful of any derived from the botanic kingdom: hence, if mixed in proportion of measure for measure, it completely covers the smell of all other bodies" (49). He added that "the essence of patchouly [sic] thus made is that which is found in the perfumers' shops of Paris and London. Although few perfumes have had such a fashionable run, yet when smelled at in its pure state, it is far from agreeable, having a kind of mossy or musty odor, analogous to Lycopodium, or, as some say, it smells of 'old coats'" (50).

The social and moral messaging of fragrant cosmetics was articulated in health and beauty manuals and in medical treatises that placed lighter, floral fragrances on one end of the hygienic spectrum, and heavier, animalic[36] fragrances at the other. Due to its peculiarity and tenacity, patchouli was grouped with the latter. When, in their 1896 etiquette book for young women (*jeunes filles*), Maryan and Béal offer advice on tastefully perfuming writing paper, they reinforce advice that women had been receiving since early in the century:

> Il n'est certes pas de mauvais goût de glisser un sachet dans sa boîte, mais ce doit être un parfum extrêmement léger et discret, tel que la violette ou l'iris, et jamais une de ces odeurs qui peuvent causer de la répugnance par leur exagération ou leur essence, comme le musc ou le patchouli, et en particulier le musc, qui est un parfum des plus mal portés, et causant à certaines personnes un véritable malaise.

> It is certainly not in bad taste to slip a sachet into one's box [of writing paper], but this must be a very light and discrete perfume, such as violet or iris, and never one of these odours that can cause repugnance due to the exaggeration of their essence, like musk or patchouli, particularly musk, which is one of the most improperly worn, and causes true discomfort in some people. (252)

That the scent of patchouli rising from women's shawls can be read as a sign of luxury earlier in the century, while its wafting from the body or other accessories such as writing paper communicates bad taste by the 1890s, is to some extent an example of shifting clothing and fragrance fashion; neither the shawls nor their patchouli were in style.[37] But such fragrance trends did not change quite as quickly as they do today.[38] This divergent messaging reveals that the social codes of fragrance use, while appearing to fall neatly into a binary scale distinguishing clean from dirty, floral from animal, innocent from corrupt, natural from synthetic, distinction from bad taste, are in fact nuanced and contextual.

The Chaste Violet

One of the most enduringly popular and socially acceptable fragrances of the century was violet, a scent characterized as light, discreet, and elegant.[39] Books on the language of flowers,[40] like the "botanique des dames" of the era, provided, as Susan Hiner states, "a way of imparting sexual knowledge to innocent girls without apparently doing so" (Hiner, "From *pudeur* to *plaisir*," 510). In her 1810 *La botanique historique et litté-raire*, Madame de Genlis attributes a "modestie raisonnée" ("calculated modesty"; 222), to the violet flower, for it knows to hide in its foliage. In her 1827 *Manuel des dames*, Madame Celnart recommends violet as a handkerchief perfume (56) and urges women to use only rarely cos-metic products with penetrating aromas (carnation, vanilla, cinnamon), to banish entirely ambergris and musk from their homes and to opt instead for the softer scent of iris, heliotrope, mignonette, and violet (58). Almost seventy years later, an etiquette manual for young women reiterates that when it comes to perfume, the less worn the better, but a drop of demure violet on one's handkerchief never hurts.[41] Nonethe-less, others perceived danger even in these relatively prim floral notes. In the 1826 *Dictionnaire de la beauté ou la toilette sans danger*, César Gar-deton[42] warns readers (identified in his preface as the "sexe aimable," the "beau sexe," and "mesdames") that even the most suave odours are not innocent; roses, jasmine, and violets emit mephitic air and can trig-ger anxiety, headaches, convulsions, and fainting.

Such cautions aside, within the language of flowers the innocent violet symbolized modesty and hidden merit,[43] qualities suggested in written and visual personifications of the flower. Grandville and Karr's *Fleurs animées* characterizes the violet as having a beauty "qui ne sau-tait point aux yeux, mais se trahissait par son parfum" ("does not leap out at you [before your eyes], but reveals itself in its perfume"; vol. 1, 142), and as being "la violette timide, ce doux symbole de la discrétion et de la modesite" ("the timid violet, that sweet symbol of discretion and modesty" and "the chaste violet"; vol. 2, 48); "les chastes violettes" ("chaste violets") bring harmony to the concert of floral fragrances (vol. 2, 130–1). The illustration shows three identical violet women hud-dled together under their leaves in what Susan Hiner has called "an exagerrated representation of female domesticity" (56–7),[44] since the composition recalls fashion plates of the era that show women together reading or working on needlepoint (see Figure 1.8). As Hiner points out, particularly in its illustrations, Grandville's *Fleurs animées* satrizes the mainstream depictions of feminine modesty and domesticity shown in flower books and fashion plates, and meant to promote a certain image of the idealized woman: "*Les Fleurs animées* contests the supremacy of feminine *pudeur* and endorses feminine pleasure as its counterpoint" (49). There is indeed a subversive element in what at first appears to be no more than a whimsical representation of female modesty drama-tized by Grandville's three hidden flowers. Rather than shrinking from society, the violets seem to be enjoying, in private, a pleasant fragrance

VIOLETTE

1.8. Grandville's personified hidden violet, whose beauty "ne sautait point aux yeux, mais se trahissait par son parfum" (J.J. Grandville and Aphonse Karr's *Les fleurs animées*, Vol.1 (Paris: Garnier frères, 1867), n.p.

Image source: gallica.bnf.fr / BnF.

that is not the natural sillage of their petals but, instead, the more contrived and staged perfume wafting from little perfume burners.

More ernest than Grandville's animated flowers, the "Dictionnaire des plantes avec leur langage" that closes Auguste Debay's 1861 *Les parfums et les fleurs* associates the violet flower, depending on its variety, with modesty, candour, a pure soul, fecundity, reciprocal friendship, perfect beauty, and hidden love (287). Applying the characteristics of the natural flower to cosmetic perfume, hygienists and beauty advisors generally included violet on their short lists of safe, tasteful fragrances, neither too strong nor too showy, safer than most for innocent young women.[45] Though scents fall in and out of fashion, particularly as innovative scents like new mown hay[46] are developed, the general code

of perfume holds true through the end of century, its message popular-
ized in magazines and newspapers:

> Une femme de goût se trahit par son parfum. Silencieuse et réservée, quelques
> gouttes d'huile antique à l'extrait de violette lui suffiront; fière, un peu cra-
> vachante, elle aimera le tzinniah [sic] hautain; blonde et caressante, et languis-
> sante et troublée, elle s'annoncera telle par l'héliotrope blanc; mûre, encore
> sensuelle, un peu massive, elle aura de l'inclination pour le patchouli, ardem-
> ment; âprement voluptueuse, ses favoris seront le stephanotis, le chypre,
> l'opulent opopanax[47]; simple, franche, le foin coupé imprégnera son mouchoir.

> A woman with good taste gives herself away with her perfume. Quiet and
> reserved, a few drops of violet scented *huile antique*[48] will do; proud and
> driven, she will like haughty zinnia; blond and caressing, and languid and
> agitated [or aroused], she will announce herself as such with white helio-
> trope; mature, still sensual, a little heavy, she will have an inclination for
> patchouli, ardently; bitterly voluptuous, her favorites will be stephanotis,
> chypre, the opulent opoponax; simple, frank, new mown hay will soak her
> handkerchief. (René Fleury, "L'art des parfums," 1900, 43)[49]

Fleury shows confidence in the readability of women's sillage:
"Comme toute société féminine s'adonne à une certaine famille de parfums qui disent fidèlement ses mœurs et son esprit, dans chaque société
chaque mondaine se laisse lire par son parfum. Et cette lecture n'est
pas trompeuse, car si défiante et si rusée qu'elle soit partout ailleurs, la
femme est sincère devant ce qui lui plaît et court d'instinct à l'odeur la
mieux seyante" ("As every feminine society indulges in a certain family
of perfumes that faithfully reveals its morals and disposition, in every
society every fashionable woman allows herself to be read according
to her perfume. And this reading is not deceptive, for as defiant and as
cunning as she may otherwise be, woman is sincere in the face of what
pleases her, and instinctively runs to the most becoming odour"; 43).
Yet, if women were indeed so naturally destined to select the perfume
that best complements or, better, reveals their character, would they
need over a century's worth of advice on how to select an appropriate
signature scent? Surely if women did not challenge social scent codes,
beauty and hygiene manuals could devote fewer pages to steering
proper women and *jeunes filles* away from perilous fragrance choices.

Violet was marketed through the end of the century as a prestige
fragrance associated with innate elegance[50] and good taste, though its
availability at various price points made it a widespread success. The
manufacture of violet "dupes" (use of other flower blends and ingredients such as iris root to imitate the smell) and the eventual discovery of

the ionone molecule in 1893, were key to the tremendous distribution of violet-scented products at the end of the century.[51] An 1898 *Washington Post* article credits the "vogue of violet" in London to the availability of artificial fragrance formerly extracted from flowers in Grasse,[52] and Piesse notes in 1905 that rose and violet, two of Marie-Antoinette's favourite scents, remain fashionable (*Histoire des parfums*, 1905, 25). *La mode illustrée* (14 June 1896) reports that the most distinguished women have a marked predilection for violet, which has replaced the muskier fragrances, since it is infinietely finer, more delicate and better suited for the "femmes comme il faut" ("respectable women"; 161).[53]

In step with other fashion writers of the decade, *La revue illustrée's* Le Masque de Velours affirms the elegance of violet perfume. The article "La vie mondaine: le vernissage au salon des Champs-Élysées" (1 June 1893) includes a drawing of a fashionable Madame Pelletier-Vidal "toilette de Derby" made complete with parfum Oriza à la violette du Czar de L. Legrand, identified in the description of the illustation, along with the dress and hat (404) (see Figure 1.9).[54] In December

Toilette de Derby de Mme Pelletier-Vidal.
Chapeau de Virot.
Parfum Oriza à la violette du Czar de L. Legrand.

1.9. The fashionable Mme. Pelletier-Vidal derby outfit is complemented with violet perfume. *La revue illustrée* (1 June 1893), 404.

Image source: gallica.bnf.fr / BnF.

of 1890, the "Carnet mondain" section of *La revue nouvelle* includes a lengthy commentary on the semiotics of violet perfume, seemingly funded (like the examples above) by the L. Legrand perfume house, whose Parfumerie Oriza was located on Place de la Madeleine:

> Deux personnes, aujourd'hui n'ont pas besoin d'être présentées l'une l'autre pour savoir à quelle société elles appartiennent, le parfum qu'elles portent dit suffisamment qui elles sont. Et je n'en sache pas de plus fin, ni de plus discret, que celui de la violette…. Le bon ton, chacun sait ça, n'admet pas le mélange des parfums; or puisque la Violette du Czar est le dernier mot de la distinction parfaite et sa spécialité, la parfumerie Oriza est parvenu non seulement à emprisonner ce parfum subtil et savoureux dans une essence pour le mouchoir, le savon et la poudre de riz mais par un vrai tour de force, elle est également arrivée à en parfumer aussi l'eau de Cologne.

> Two people, today do not have to be introduced to one another, the perfume they wear sufficiently says who they are. And I know of none finer, none more discreet, than that of violet…. Good taste, everyone knows, does not allow mixing perfumes; now since la Violette du Czar is the last word in perfect distinction and its specialty Oriza perfume has managed to not only capture this subtle and savory perfume in an essence for the handkerchief, soap, and rice powder; but a true tour de force, it has also managed to perfume eau de Cologne. (440)[55]

The article further links the taste for violet perfume with elegance and distinction by parenthetically suggesting that the discerning buyer who shops for violet cosmetics at the Parfumerie Oriza will rub elbows with the titled elite: "Mais tandis que vous êtes là, Madame, à vous enivrer de parfums à côté de la baronne de R., ou la marquise de B." ("But while you are there, Madame, getting intoxicated by perfumes next to the baronness of R., or the marquise of B."; 440). The growing popularity of perfume challenged the centuries-old association of innocent, young women with fresh and natural flowers; thus the language of (natural) flowers was for the most part adapted to cosmetic fragraces.[56]

Despite a preponderance of not-so-subtle violet messaging, not all women who chose this scent identified with respectable bourgeois fashion plates. Violets were, for example, the signature flower of Renée Vivien. Raised in London and Paris, Vivien published in French, and is known both for her literary talent and for her turbulent life and eccentricities (did she, as Colette suggested, drink or cover her breath with perfume?[57]), stoked at times by self-mythologizing.[58] Hardly a shrinking violet, her candid, unapologetic approach to lesbianism in her life and in her works inspired contemporaries and subsequent generations of writers. Vivien was known as "The Muse of the Violets," for her love of both the flower (which appears in so many of her poems) and the colour (with which she penned her name).[59] Her attachment to violets has been traced to the association with her childhood friend Violet (also called Violette) Shillito, who died in 1901, fictionalized as *Ione* (from the Greek *Iona*, or *violet*) in Vivien's novel *Une femme m'apparut*.[60] The violets featured in Renée Vivien's poetry (and home décor) are no longer emblems of modesty or self-effacement, but link the flower to both pleasure and death, and most likely to virginity as well, revalued as a positive rejection of heterosexuality, since Vivien "criticized heterosexuality, rejected marriage, celebrated infertility and virginity" (Pious 1). After a visit in 1908, Marcelle Tinayre recalls bouquets of wilted violets contributing to the tomb-like ambiance of Renée Vivien's apartment.[61] Louise Faure-Fauvier, who describes Vivien's drawing room as smelling of too much incense and too many flowers, mentions the poet's "elegant letters written on vellum bordered with garlands of violets and sealed with gold wax" (14–15). According to Faure-Favier, in 1908, when Vivien attempted suicide by drinking laudanum, she "stretched herself on one of those divans 'deep as a tomb' which were affected by the Baudelairean cult in puritanic England. With a bouquet of violets over her heart, she hoped to go to sleep forever" (18).[62] After her death in 1910, "loving hands kept her grave blossoming constantly with her favorite violets" (20).[63]

Book publishers and bloggers have underscored the relationship between Vivien and violets in their iconography, illustrating book jackets and home pages with the flower. But more than that, the words *violette* and *violet* (singular and plural) appear frequently in Vivien's poems. "Dans un chemin de violettes" (in *Sillages*) indeed evokes "[d]ans l'air la merveilleuse odeur de violettes" ("[i]n the air the marvelous odour of violettes"), but as Nicole G. Albert has argued, in Vivien's richly layered, perfume-infused poetry, the odour of flowers is frequently associated with death.[64] The connection between death and flowers may have been a familiar trope in Decadent and Symbolist imagery, but Vivien goes further, to cultivate an association of violet flowers and smells with the women in her works.[65] Vivien's violet-infused verse resists the status quo by destabilizing the familiar connotations of the flower and its fragrance, and by pushing against the mainstream's binary oppositions of moral versus immoral. If the social code of fragrance-wearing could be written, read, and interpreted, it could also be borrowed, appropriated, reinvented, even undermined, in the interest of self-expression.

From Animated Flower to Still Life

The image of Vivien lying with a violet bouquet over her heart recalls the suicide episode of Zola's *La faute de l'abbé Mouret* (1875), where Albine stretches out on her deathbed of flowers, hands over her heart, with violets arranged close enough to be inhaled. Throughout the novel, Zola highlights odours (human, animal, and vegetal), showing them to merge in the character of Albine, whom Serge perceives as "un grand bouquet d'une odeur forte" ("a big bouquet with a strong odour"; 1245). Albine's characterization as a living (and, eventually, dying) flower is enhanced by a sumptuous backdrop of personified blooms who appear at times to be as closely attuned to human biology and society as Albine is to botanical nature: flowers have skin and lips, they are adorned with cosmetics (*poudre de riz*), they wear muslin and lace; they are laughing, loving, graceful, shy, impudent; some are sultanas, others coquettes, bourgeoises, or aristocrats (1340–1). When convalescing, smell-sensitive Serge is overcome by a mixed vapour of present and recalled pestilential stench (an asphyxiating gust composed of mown hay, human sweat, church incense perverted by the smell of greasy-haired girls, musty cemetery, manure, and the suffocating fermentations of animal germs). The memory of Albine, like a natural flower leaping from her stem towards his mouth, serves as a fumigant, "en le parfumant de son long rire" ("perfuming him with her long ripple of laugher"; 1309–11).

While the dozens of plants and flowers mentioned in this novel merit attention,[66] the progressively overpowering odour of violet stands out as it undergoes a narrative metamorphosis, the fragrance signalling at first freshness and innocence, then sensual pleasure; at first fragility and modesty, and then the power of seduction, temptation, and death. Modulations in the narrative staging of violets show them becoming more pervasive and invasive relative to Albine's physical proximity to Serge, and then to the memory of that lost intimacy. As the not-yet lovers Serge and Albine first encounter their *locus amœnus*, the lush, abandoned Paradou garden and grotto, they cautiously encounter fresh, sweet, fragile violets: "un champ voisin de violettes, si douces qu'ils tremblaient d'en meurtrir la moindre touffe…; puis … n'ayant plus que des violettes autour d'eux, ils étaient forcés de s'en aller à pas discrets sur cette fraîcheur embaumée, au milieu de l'haleine même du printemps ("a field of violets, so delicate that [Albine and Serge] trembled at the

thought of bruising the slighest clump...; then ... with nothing but violets surrounding them, they were forced to continue with discreet steps
on this fragrant freshness, in the very center of springtime's breath";
1348). But the sea of violets soon becomes excessive and encroaching,
leaving their fragrant mark on the couple's feet: "Et cétaient les violettes
qui revenaient toujours, une mer de violettes coulant partout, leur ver-
sant sur les pieds des odeurs précieuses, les accompagnant du souffle
de leurs fleurs cachées sous les feuilles" ("And it was the violets that
always reappeared, a sea of violets flowing everywhere, shedding their
precious odour on their feet, accompanying them with the breath of their
leaf-hidden flowers"; 1348). Eventually, as they play a more prominent
role in the garden's seduction, the violets' odour is described as musky
("des violettes musquées"; 1353), though in the semiotics of fragrance,
musk was normally positioned opposite the modest violet. It is not the
first time the couple encounters a blend of clean and musky odours;
earlier, when Albine wears a white dress, a second skin revealing the
form of her knees, chest, and arms underneath, Serge compares her to
a "fleur musquée, d'une odeur propre" (a musky flower with a clean
odour"; 1340). And under the branches of the tree whose "fraicheur
musquée" (musky freshness), suggestive of ripe fruit, in concert with
the fruity taste (le goût d'un fruit) and the floral scent in the air, lulls the
couple into succumbing to temptation (1405).

The violet odour is at times penetrating, disquieting, and displaced.
Entering Serge's bedroom, its suffocating effect and ghostly location
at the head of his bed foreshadow the blooms that will adorn Albine's
deathbed: "Et sur le lit lui-même, contre le bois du chevet, Serge pré-
tendait retrouver l'empreinte d'une petite main, qui avait laissé là son
parfum persistant de violette" ("And on the bed itself, on the wooden
headboard, Serge claimed to find a little handprint, which had left
there its persistent violet perfume"; 1396). Violet is one of the voluptuous scents that overwhelms Serge and Albine, leading to the illicit
consummation of their love: "Du parterre, arrivaient des odeurs de
fleurs pâmées, un long chuchotement, qui contait les noces des roses,
les voluptés des violettes" ("from the flowerbeds, arose the odours of
swooning flowers, a long whisper, which told of the nuptials of roses,
the sensual pleasure of violets"; 1407). Albine chooses violets to complete the synesthetic bed of flowers which will lull her to death with
their whispering, singing, melodious, brazen, and above all, suffocating
fragrance: "Enfin, elle songea au lit. Elle roula près du chevet une petite
table, sur laquelle elle dressa un tas énorme de violettes" ("Finally, she
thought of the bed. She brought close to the headboard a little table,
on which she arranged an enormous pile of violets"; 1514). The violets

contribute "de petites notes musquées" ("musky little notes"; 1516), singing of the first charms of her love, the first declarations of love, the first kiss. When she opens her mouth to seek out "le dernier baiser qui devait l'étouffer" ("the final kiss which was to smother her"), a chorus of heady, indolic hyacinth and tuberose takes over, drowning out even the fanfare of roses, and providing the crescendo of scented seduction and danger that allows Albine to die "dans le hoquet suprême des fleurs" ("in the ultimate gasp of the flowers"; 1516). After her death is discovered, Jeanbernat, the uncle who had always fostered her connection with nature, gathers fallen rose blooms from the floor, placing them again one by one on his niece's skirt, accompanying this gesture with a comment that underscores the literal and metaphorical substance of the scene: "[l]es fleurs, ça ne vit qu'un jour" ("[f]lowers, they only live for a day"; 1519).[67] Though it was not her intention, Albine had to kill her beloved blooms in order to orchestrate her own death. The animated floral perfumes may have suffocated her, but she has put an end to their sweet aroma as well. It is the culmination of an extended metaphor that the once fresh and virginal Albine became a plucked flower herself and now represents a final, fading bloom in a lethal bouquet.

While metaphorical and narrative networks linking flowers to sensual pleasure, seduction, and danger suffice to validate the plausibility of Albine's highly symbolic, sensual, sensorial, and performative suicide in the context of this fictional world, medical writing of the decades leading up to Zola's novel also lends credibility to his staging of a lethal floral sillage. In 1821, Hippolyte Cloquet warned readers not to sleep with vases of flowers in their rooms, as the odour might cause syncope, asphyxiation, and death traceable to no other cause. He cites several cases of suffocation reported in medical journals, including that of a young woman who died having kept violettes in her bedroom (92–3). Cloquet clarifes that while highly fragrant flowers are the most dangerous, it is not their odour itself that causes severe illness and death, but rather the carbonic acid gas they release. In the 1840 *Dictionnaire de la médecine* entry on olfaction, P.-H. Bérard similarly argued that it was inaccurate to attribute fatalities caused by flowers to their odour; that it is rather the carbonic acid they release that causes asphyxiation. He compared the phenomenon to that of sickness and death resulting after inhaling the smell of an exhumed corpse: its exhalation of deleterious gases would be fatal even if the person inhaling them suffered from anosmia; though the odours of flowers, musk, and ambergris can be harmful, those odours alone are not deadly (21). Nonetheless, the idea that fragrance itself kills persists in the 1867 article "Alteration de la santé par les odeurs," which recycles and reports several more cases of death due to the "funeste propriété des fleurs" ("deadly property of flowers"): an imprudent woman who died after fatally filling her bedroom, like a greenhouse, with flowers; a couple found dead after their wedding night, their nuptial bedroom filled with flowers; a young wife who poisoned her husband by placing a vase of blooms, including hyacinth, in the bedroom (101–2).[68] Such accounts stated or suggested that the very odour of flowers in a closed room was enough to asphyxiate the bloom-loving slumberer or the innocent victim of a conniving spouse.

As doctors and hygienists repeated such warnings, novelists and painters, too, exploited the theme of death by flowers, before and after *La faute de l'abbé Mouret* was published. Following the book's release, one sceptical reviewer claimed that Zola had pilfered the idea from an earlier novel: "Enfin la conception de l'asphyxie volontaire d'Albine par les fleurs est encore un plagiat" ("Finally the concept of Albine's voluntary asphyxiation by flowers is another plagiarism"; 335).[69] The work in question, Léon Gozlan's *Le notaire de Chantilly* (1836), ends with its heroine enclosing herself in a greenhouse to die: "Son âme est au milieu de ces parfums qui l'ont aspirée. Caroline est morte, asphyxiée par les fleurs; mort douce, douce comme la vie" ("Her soul was amidst those perfumes which had inhaled her. Caroline died, asphyxiated by the flowers; sweet death, sweet like life"; 272). A sardonic comment in the 1847 *Fleurs animées* may have been triggered by this episode of Gozlan's novel as well: "Il y a des romanciers qui ont fait mourir leur héroïne en l'enfermant dans une serre" ("There are novelists who have their heroine die by locking herself in a greenhouse"; vol. 2, 294). According to this account, medical doctors, with their "invention" of nerves, are to blame for vilifying the fragrance of natural flowers and their bottled essence: "On ne l'accepte plus que comme moyen de suicide" ("It is accepted now only as a means of suicide"; vol. 2, 294).

Zola's attention to the seductive power of floral fragrance also seems to have been sparked by a novel he reviewed as literary critic for *L'événement* ("Livres d'aujourd'hui et de demain," 20 March 1866), Louis Ulbach's 1866 *Le jardin du Chanoine*. In his write-up, Zola highlights the story's paradisical garden setting, and the heady floral fragrances it produces.[70] Two years later, Zola mentions floral asphyxiation in his rather breezy "Chronique" column for *L'évenement illustré* (30 April 1868).[71] The wryly pitched essay laments a lack of originality in crime, positing that most criminals are clumsy and unimaginative, that they imitate one another "et se laissent pincer en flagrant délit de plagiat" ("and get caught in the act of plagiarism"; 259).[72] After offering several examples of clumsy and botched crimes, Zola closes his essay with an antithetically clever murder. According to the wise (but unnamed) doctor who certified the death, an English governess called Mary poisoned her lover's wife by leaving heavily scented exotic flowers in the victim's bedroom. While his tone remains droll to the very end, certain elements of the story as Zola tells it resonate with details of Albine's death. Zola calls Mary not a *bouquet* but a somber *bouquetière* (florist, bouquet-maker; 266). Though in a more chilling way, Mary's flowers, like Albine's, seem animated: "on eût dit que ces fleurs avaient des regards de personnes vivantes, des regards lourds qui glaçaient" ("it was like the flowers had the gaze of living humans, a heavy, paralyzing gaze"; 266). The image Zola paints of the asphyxiated wife shows her in the position Albine will later assume, lying on her bed, hands crossed over her breast. Though Zola's novel diverges in plot, message, and mood from earlier books and anecdotes about floral seduction and destruction, he does seem to have been moved to acts of fragrant, but not flagrant, adaptation of such stories.

Since the idea of floral asphyxiation was in the collective imagination long before and after Zola penned *La faute de l'abbé Mouret*,[73] it is likely that what he referred to as Albine's *fleurs mortelles* ("deadly flowers"; 1701) in planning notes may have been perceived by contemporary readers as more than a symbolic threat or poetic image. The visual and verbal motif of a beautiful, young woman succumbing to an excess of floral fragrance plays into "the French concept of *volupté*," sensual pleasure considered by some writers of the era to be "indulged in as result of failing sexual self-restraint or excessive appetite" (Wilson, 339).[74] The sort of *volupté* attributed to Albine's violets turns up in discourse about and depictions of women and perfume abuse across the century. The perfume-crazed swooners of novels and medical treatises share with Albine a proclivity for fragrance excess, and the fascination such indulgence provokes. Zola's novel indeed motivated several artists in France and beyond to portray Albine, dying or already dead, in her bed of flowers. John Collier's painting *The Death of Albine* in particular "attracted much attention" at the Royal Academy, according to *The Graphic* (262), which printed a reproduction of the work on 31 August 1895 (see Figure 1.10). True to the novel, Collier's depiction suggests a peaceful, carefully choreographed scene in which Albine appears fresh and attractive, though dead or dying, like a cut flower in a still life.[75]

Zola specified in his notes that the Albine character was to be a woman in touch with with nature, and that nature would play the role of Satan in the novel's idyllic garden. A temptress, an Eve, Albine has not learned moral or social values, she is rather "la bête humaine

"THE DEATH OF ALBINE" (*from Zola*)
FROM THE PICTURE BY THE HON. JOHN COLLIER, EXHIBITED IN THE ROYAL ACADEMY, 1895

1.10. John Collier's painting *The Death of Albine* "attracted much attention" at the Royal Academy, according to *The Graphic* (262), which printed a reproduction of the work on 31 August 1895.

amoureuse" ("the human beast in love"; 1979). After Serge leaves her, Albine was initially meant to throw herself into books, which would lead her to discover society's rules, recognize her wrongdoing, and eventually kill herself. Zola ended up changing his heroine's name, her age (from twenty to sixteen), and the final chapters of her story, notably leaving out any lingering commentary on shame, remorse, or repentance, while instead reinforcing an ambiguous representation of her connection to nature. As Charles Bernheimer has argued, the novel seems to reverse the Edenic myth, then to confuse that message (56), in part by staging the *faute* (be it sin or human error), in a garden that is not entirely natural, but instead, "an excessive overgrowth of what was initially a sophisticated plan," the grounds and château that still contain statues and paintings, notably of "human and mythological couplings" (57).[76] The novel's complex relationship between the human body and nature, both vegetal and animal, provides another key for understanding the fresh yet musky violet. Zola may have been describing the flower as he perceived it: violet leaf itself has an earthy, musky aroma much appreciated in perfumery today. Breathing in the aroma of a natural violet bed involves a mingling of the earth, the petals, and the leafy aromas. The metaphorical thread linking Albine to flowers brings her especially close to the violet, because both she and the flower naturally give off a fresh yet musky scent. Albine and the violet, two fragrantly related, animated flowers, share a note of human animality that taints their innocence and hints at their destructive power, as it muddies the semiotics of floral fragrance.

Despite its obvious biblical themes and inspiration, *La faute de l'abbé Mouret* in the end portrays Albine as suffering from lost love, not lost innocence. The very name Albine, and the original *Blanche* that Zola had selected for her, signal purity in a way the novel's tone does not render ironic. She is even accorded a Christian burial after committing suicide. What truly disrupts the harmonious, musky-clean blend of sensual humanity and nature established in *La faute de l'abbé Mouret* is the scent of church incense wafting through Serge's physical and inner world. As he tells Albine he must leave her, he likens himself to statues of saints bathed in the scent of incense: "J'ai de l'encens jusque dans le dernier pli de mes organes. C'est cet embaumement qui fait ma sérénité, la mort tranquille de ma chair, la paix que je goûte à ne pas vivre" ("I have incense through the deepest folds of my organs. It is this embalming that gives me serenity, the tranquil death of my flesh, the peace I savor at no longer living"; 1506).

With Albine and Serge buried, one physically, one figuratively, the final episode closes in a gust of sensation, a chorus of human and animal sounds – cackling, bleating, flapping, rustling, laughing – along with the suggestion of odour as Désirée, who has just climbed a manure heap, calls out Serge's name four times and speaks the novel's last words: the cow has given birth to a calf. It is a triumph of the natural world mitigated by humans, since this is a farm, not a wilderness. The fertilizing manure, most likely wafting, perhaps falling from Désirée's hands as she claps to get Serge's attention, contributes the final odour note to the symphony of foul and fragrant emanations that drew critical attention, both positive and negative, at the time of the novel's publication.[77] This final moment reminds the reader that the story of Serge Mouret, which framed the story of Albine, was itself but an episode presented against the backdrop of village life in Les Artaud. Church incense and violet flowers may offer temporary solace or pleasure but they are too volatile to outlast the generative power of manure.

Sillage and the *Jeune Fille*

Like so many *jeune-fille* stories of the nineteenth century, Albine's ends in death once she has lost her viriginity. An in-between, impossible to maintain status serves as a general identifier of the *jeune fille* protagonist in countless nineteenth-century French novels, and the real-life target reader of many nineteenth-century beauty and etiquette manuals.[78] Writers like Madame Celnart upheld the moral implications of floral fragrance selection for young women through the turn of the century, and violet perfume remained one of France's most popular cosmetic scents from around 1860 through 1910.[79] Yet the very fact that warnings against some fragrances existed suggests that less innocent perfumes were available, and even preferred by some women. Similarly, women who controverted advertisers and advice columnists could adapt the language of flowers and fragrance to their own personalities and messaging.

The significance of violet flowers, fragrance, and colour, reinforced by beauty and hygiene experts, also declares itself in fictional characters and real-life writers of the era. To underscore the extent of Charles Baudelaire's idiosyncrasies, writer Champfleury[80] pointed out that the poet preferred dahlias to violets.[81] Violet was, after all, one of the modest scents recommended for the chaste young woman, or *jeune fille* (literally *young girl*, understood as *young woman*). Perfumer Louis Claye characterized it as "[l]a modeste violette, dont les suaves arômes se rapprochent du chaste parfum qu'exhalent les lèvres de l'adolescence" ("[t]he modest violet, whose suave aromas are like the chaste perfume that adolescent lips exhale"; 55).

Not surprisingly, violets are a favourite flower of Bernardin de Saint-Pierre's Virginie (*Paul et Virginie*, 1788), a heroine so virtuous, she essentially dies of modesty. Moments before a hurricane shatters the ship on which she stands, Virginie refuses to jump to the safety of eagerly awaiting rescuers, since this would require taking off her heavy dress. A network of associations links the heroine and the flower, first when the good reputation of Paul, Virginie, and their mothers is described as analogous to that of violets, which exhale the sweetness of their fragrance, though no one sees them: "Ainsi des violettes, sous des buissons épineux, exhalent au loin leurs doux parfums, quoiqu'on ne les voie pas" ("Thus violets, under thorny bushes, exhale far away their fragrance, though no one sees them"; 127). During her stay in France, Virginie sends violet seeds for Paul to plant, along with a letter in which she anthropomorphizes the violet bloom "qui aime à se cacher sous les buissons; mais son charmant parfum l'y fait bientôt découvrir" ("who delights to conceal itself beneath the bushes; but its charming perfume soon gets discovered"; 127). Her would-be lover duly observes that violets and scabious flowers "semblaient avoir quelque analogie avec le caractère et la situation de Virginie" ("seemed to have some sort of analogy with the character and situation of Virginie"; 178). Indeed, as if to foreshadow the tale of Virginie's fatal return from France to her island home, the violet seeds she has sent Paul prove to have spoiled in the voyage and fail to thrive. The reader soon discovers that Virginie herself, after spending time in Europe, will similarly never again bloom in her island home. After the storm, her body washed ashore maintains the pose Virginie struck when she was last seen alive: one hand on the clothing she refused to remove, the other clutching to her heart a little box containing Paul's portrait. Her facial features seem unaltered, but for emerging discoloration: "seulement les pâles violettes de la mort se confondaient sur ses joues avec les roses de la pudeur" ("only the pale violets of death mixed on her cheeks with the roses of modesty"; 211). Though "roses" and "violets" obviously refer here to colour hues, their suggestion of flowers reinforces another message: though Virginie, like her sister-flower the violet, has died, the rose of her chastity remains intact. The lesson of her death, repeated for the benefit of Paul, for others who grieve, and for the reader who may learn something from her story, is that unlike most humans, Virginie has died "heureuse jusqu'au dernier moment" ("happy up to the last moment" 223), and rewarded for her virtue, she is certainly happy now in death (225).

Intermittently popular and always well known,[82] *Paul et Virginie* remained a cultural touchstone throughout the century, its title synonymous with virtuous (and impossible) love, a topic considered by some to be dangerously attractive to easily influenced young women. Balzac, Flaubert, and Goncourt dramatize and problematize the importance of this love story to their female protagonists in *Le curé de village*, *Madame Bovary*, and *Chérie* respectively, relating it to perceived dangers of fiction-reading.[83] The precarious moral equilibrium of the *jeune fille* becomes the object of increased scrutiny as the century moves forward. In a 1907 article, critic Remy de Gourmont explained that the question of the *jeune fille* had become particularly complicated at the turn of the century.[84] What was that question? For Gourmont, it was how to keep the *jeune fille* on a straight and narrow path when, since the Second Empire, women had been postponing marriage, waiting until as late as age twenty-five to settle down with the right man: "C'est de l'espace toujours plus allongé qui s'étend entre nubilité des femmes et leur mariage, qu'est née la question si compliquée de la jeune fille" ("It is of this ever expanding space between nubility and the young woman's marriage that the complicated question of the *jeune fille* is born"; 732).

Expanding, yes, but for the *jeune fille* the space between adolescence and marriage was also, by definition, unsustainable, a liminal state that identified the young woman by what she was not ("no longer a little girl, and not yet a woman"[85]) and what she would presumably become (a virtuous, married woman). Thus, the idea of the *jeune fille* is more complex and culturally dependent than a general biological time frame would suggest. She is understood to be both interested in marrying and marriageable, characteristics that distinguish her from the abject woman she may become if she strays from her wholesome destiny: a *vieille fille* (old maid); a *fille-mère* (a pejorative term for single mother); or a *fille publique* (streetwalker). Thus, all *jeunes filles* will lose their status, be it legitimately (in marriage), through a less socially sanctioned loss of virginity, in the gradual slide into the tragi-comical world of old maids that Balzac so often presented, or by a hard fall into moral corruption. Virginie ironically remains a *jeune fille* to the very end; she dies not long after her sexual desire is awakened, but before her love for Paul can be consummated.

Novelists experimenting in realist and naturalist aesthetics ramped up the presence of odours in descriptions of objects and places to be sure, but also in the social and moral depictions of their characters. Their fragrance portraits both borrowed from and contributed to a code for reading the scent of women. As the title suggests, Zola's *Joie de vivre* (1884)[86] deals with roads to happiness, in this case exploring a spectrum of optimistic and pessimistic characters, with the undaunted Pauline and the angst-ridden Lazare at each extreme. Lazare, presented as an ever-failing, would-be romantic hero,[87] finds himself drawn at different times to two marriageable young women, Pauline and Louise, whose significant differences are distilled in passages referring to their personal odours. Pauline smells of woman, of herself, or of breezy air, while the relatively worldlier, more refined Louise has adopted heliotrope as her signature scent. Louise's choice of heliotrope perfume echoes the popular wisdom on what a woman of her look and character should wear. René Fleury described heliotrope wearers as "blond and cuddly/caressing" (43), terms applied to the catlike Louise in Zola's novel. The more restrained Madame Celnart groups heliotrope with gentle fragrances, including violet, appropriate in small doses for taste-ful women.

Pauline's "odeur de femme"[88] (mentioned three times) is juxtaposed to Louise's "odeur de femme coquette" (184, 195), which provokes in Lazare the sickly (or sick) desire (*désir maladif*), that ultimately lures him away from Pauline. Lazare and Pauline are sensitive, in different ways, to Louise's cosmetic perfume, but only Véronique, the housekeeper who functions as an observer and moral commentator, voices criticism: "Si vous voyiez dans sa chambre tous ses petits pots, des pommades, des liqueurs! Dès qu'on entre, ça vous prend le gosier, tellement ça embaume" ("If you saw, in her room, all the little pots of pomades, of liquids! The moment you enter, it grabs you by the throat, the fragrance is so strong"; 179). Louise's presence, her room, her writing paper, and her gloves give off the warm, intoxicating fragrance noticed by both Pauline and Lazare. During one of Louise's temporary absences, Pau-line catches an emotional Lazare furtively hiding the scented glove that has become his fetish:

> C'était un vieux gant oublié par Louise, et qu'il venait de retrouver derrière une pile de livres. Le gant, en peau de Saxe, avait gardé une odeur forte, cette odeur de fauve particulière, que le parfum préféré de la jeune fille, l'héliotrope, adoucissait d'une pointe vanillée; et, très impressionnable aux senteurs, violemment troublé par ce mélange de fleur et de chair, il était resté éperdu, le gant sur la bouche, buvant la volupté de ses souvenirs.

> It was an old glove forgotten by Louise, and that he'd just found behind a pile of books. The glove, in Saxony leather, had retained a strong odour, that particular, animal odour, that the young woman's preferred per-fume, heliotrope, softened with a hint of vanilla; and, quite susceptible to odours, he had remained distraught, the glove over his mouth, drinking in the sensual pleasure of his memories. (268)

Though he does not identify heliotrope itself as being a lure, Lazare is aware of his attraction to Louise's fragrance, blended with the sugges-tive animal smell of the glove's leather. Pauline, in contrast, reads the fragrance and understands the olfactory power of Louise's signature heliotrope, the dizziness and carnal hallucination it triggers in Lazare (279). When, resigned to never marrying, Pauline stages a reconciliation of Louise and Lazare, she makes sure to leave the two in Louise's room with a closed door to keep the spell-binding heliotrope inside.

La joie de vivre reinforces many of the heavy-handed naturalist tropes for which Zola is famous, as it also dramatizes a progressive undermining of romantic and literary clichés via failures and character flaws, particularly in relation to the young male protagonist, Lazare. In the literary sillage of works like *Paul et Virginie*, Zola's novel reinvents the construct of the *jeune fille*, making Pauline, ever a virgin, a surrogate life-giver and mother. Pauline's animality, which would typically be depicted as a sign of perversion or hypersexuality, has instead been harnessed (or repressed) to bolster her strength and natural wholesomeness, her kindness and loyalty. Similarly, her interest in books, often viewed in other works of the era as a danger to the easily manipulated imagination of the *jeune fille*, proves invaluable. Her aunt may be horrified to discover Pauline's clandestine reading of illustrated anatomy textbooks, but the knowledge Pauline gleans from these pages ultimately helps her save a life, rather than lose her virtue: she successfully assists Louise with a dangerous labour, and gives life through the patient work of breathing into the stillborn baby's lungs. This symbolic virgin birth underscores the fact, mentioned many times over, that despite her good health, ample breasts, and solid, robust hips (91), Pauline will never have her own children. Yet as Louise and Lazare muddle through an unhappy marriage, Pauline, ever single, continues to take care of her sick uncle, as she spreads optimism and good deeds to her neighbours. The end of the story finds Lazare, who does not particularly care for children, even his own (387), seeing himself on a road of boredom and uselessness leading to death. Voicing a key tenet of Zola's naturalist doctrine, he predicts his son will inherit the grandfather's gout, and the father's unhinged nerves: "C'est la loi des dégénérescences!" ("It is the law of degeneration"; 388). Pauline assures him that nurture will prevail: she will make a man of this child. She will never marry, already having "had" this child from Lazare, and she will never be a woman in the social sense. In a reported dialogue of playful chatter between this surrogate mother and baby, Pauline confirms that "elle voulait rester fille afin de travailler à la délivrance universelle" ("she wanted to remain a girl in order to work for universal deliverance"; 389).

La joie de vivre echoes, reframes, and repurposes plot points from *Paul et Virginie*. It situates the central characters, would-be lovers raised like brother and sister in relative isolation, not in the exotic, colonial, island setting of Mauritius, but in the seaside village of Bonneville, which Zola called a "petit pays perdu au bord de l'Océan" ("a little, lost place on the Ocean's shore"; Mitterand 1755).[89] The passage from little girl to *jeune fille* (the onset of puberty, body consciousness, and sexual awakening) represents a pivotal episode in both works, with Zola offering a thorough account of Pauline's first menstruation.[90] However, in Zola's world, there is much work to be done, and pragmatic needs that move society forward are more important than the love triangle that ostensibly centres the plot. Romantic love fizzles. The suicide of Véronique, the maid, is presented as hardly tragic, instead as unremarkable, unmotivated, unjustified, and unintelligent: "Faut-il être bête pour se tuer" ("You have to be stupid to kill yourself"; 390) remarks Lazare's now elderly father, whose complaints of painful gout have been a soundtrack to the novel as constant as the ocean's roar.

In *La joie de vivre*, the sick, the weak, the venal, and the unmotivated need a very human saviour who can rise above the jealousy and petty desires that lead others to resignation, mental distress, and physical decline. As Lazare's inability to compose music, to write plays, to play the piano, to study medicine reveal, there is no room for lofty whims in this novel. The sea is a force to be respected, not tamed, nor is it the stuff of romantic contemplation. It brings destruction and death to Bonneville. Romantic love is fraught, ambiguous, and ultimately not enough to inspire or sustain the individual or society. Louise wears the right perfume and wins a husband, but she soon sees her youth as wasted, her marriage a prison of mutual resentment. This oddly sad tale casts honest work, self-sacrifice, virtue, and good deeds[91] as the ultimate roads to happiness, despite all accompanying hardship. Though Bernardin de Saint-Pierre's Virginie possessed many of these qualities, they were of no benefit to her, her family, or her society. Her impossible love and tragic death are a gift to the idea of virtue. In the intertextual sillage of Virginie, Pauline remains chaste through the end of the novel, and presumably all her life. Since the story ends before her death and before she ages enough to be established as a *vieille fille*, the illusion that a young woman can remain a *jeune fille* is upheld, and in this way, more than any other, Pauline's story echoes Virginie's.

Sillage and the *Fille*

The social and literary construct of the modern *jeune fille* developed in contrast and in deterrent proximity to examples of young women who did not succeed in finding husbands, and to prostitutes of various classes. The *roman de la jeune fille* (novels focused on marriageable young virgins) and the *roman de la fille* (novels focused on prostitutes) co-evolved in both the fragrant and literary sillage of *Paul et Virginie* and were explored with impressive gusto by the naturalist and post-naturalist writers whose work has a reputation for evoking smells, noxious and pleasant. Earlier stories of courtesans penned by Balzac and Dumas would pave the way for grittier naturalist depictions of struggling working-class streetwalkers, who are neither repentant nor reformed.[92] These women, vulnerable in similar ways, fascinated writers to such an extent that they became the source of a generally friendly competition, stoked via private letters and published articles, among novelists including Huysmans, Goncourt, and Zola,[93] whose protagonists, Marthe, Élisa, and Nana, navigate with various degrees of success and ultimate failure the precarious world of prostitution.

Of the three "sister" novels, Joris-Karl Huysmans's *Marthe, histoire d'une fille* was the first published, though not necessarily the first to be penned. Inspired by Balzac's *Illusions perdues* (1837–43),[94] the novel was released in Brussels in 1876; the four hundred copies Huysmans attempted to bring over the border to France were confiscated. He held on to a few, though, and sent one to Goncourt. Huysmans knew that Goncourt was writing his own story of a *fille*. Yet Huysmans insisted, in a rather disingenuous letter, that his own book about a working girl in a licensed brothel had been completed before he heard about his friend's project. Goncourt's *La fille Élisa* hit the bookstores in 1878, and Zola's *Nana*, whose in-progress status had been known as well, came out in 1880. It is tempting to weigh the three works against one another. They were written at the same time, by on-and-off friends who exchanged ideas and who, for a time, together embraced naturalism as an antidote to romantic illusions. Ernest Raynaud in fact made just such a comparison in his article "Les écrivains de filles" (1890), arguing that the three very different treatments of a similar topic reveal the three novelists' disparate temperaments and approaches to writing: "Zola c'est Nana. Il n'est pas jusqu'au nom qu'il n'offre – en sa sonorité dissyllabique de tam-tam – une frappante analogie. Nana, c'est Zola. Pendant dix ans, Zola accapara exclusivement les librairies comme Nana le trottoir" ("Zola is Nana. It isn't only the name that offers – in its dissyllabic tom tom sonority" – a striking analogy. Nana, is Zola.... For ten years, Zola exclusively took over the bookstores the way Nana took over the pavement"; 232). Zola may have done a bit too much "fieldwork" according to Raynaud, who finds that Nana reads like a how-to manual for prostitution.

Raynaud finds Edmond de Goncourt's work superior in its empirical, rational method; the documentary value and social significance of the work; the acuity of analysis; the fact that he improves on Zola by instructing, rather than just entertaining, the reader. Huysmans, on the other hand, attacks the nerves: "*Marthe*, encore qu'elle soit l'aînée, tient de *Nana* et d'*Elisa*, mais elle n'a ni le relief de l'une ni l'intérêt de l'autre" ("*Marthe*, though she is the oldest, takes after *Nana* and *Elisa*, but she has neither the vividness of the former nor the interest of the latter"). He comments on the novel's lack of balance and deficient "santé morale" ("moral health"; 236).

Raynaud expresses his distaste for this literary work in terms of smell. Of *Marthe*, he protests: "Il a des mots ... qui vous soufflent une haleine chaude au visage, vous prennent la main, vous mettent dans l'oreille un chuchotement honteux de coin de rue, déchaînant la bête; et du remuement des pages montant d'accablantes touffeurs, d'empoisonnées fragrances, toute une lourdeur de ciel d'orage qui énerve" ("There are words which breathe hot breath in your face, take you by the hand, put a shameful whisper from a street corner in your ear, unchaining the beast; and from the stirring of the pages rise sweltering heat, poisoned fragrances, all the weight of a stormy sky that gets on your nerves"; 237–8). Raynaud distinguishes the toxic smells of Huysmans's novel from Zola's healthier (though not sweeter) aromas: "Ce n'est pas, comme chez Zola, l'odeur des germes robustes, une exaltation de vie, le travail des fumiers dans les étables. L'effusion d'un trop plein de sève, le rut puissant et sain, non!" ("It is not, as in the case of Zola, the odour of hardy germs, an exaltation of life, the work of manure and stable. The effusion of an excess of sap, a powerful, healthy, rutting, no!"; 238). Perhaps not all readers detected a metaphorical stench, but the three writers indeed imbued their prose with references to often unsavoury odours, among them disturbingly heavy and animalic perfumes.

While Raynaud's critical approach may be outdated, the proximity he detects between the *fille* and her narrator (and her author) is not unfounded, and this textual distance, or closeness, is often evident in the evocation of smell. As the novel's title makes abundantly clear, *La fille Élisa* is about a prostitute, though Goncourt insists in the preface that "la prostitution et la prostituée ce n'est qu'un épisode; la prison et la prisonnière: voilà l'intérêt de mon livre" ("prostitution and the prostitute, that's but an episode; prison and prisoner: there's the subject of my book"; 6). Specifically, Goncourt reveals the cruelty of *silence continu* (the code of silence) along with the *folie pénitentiaire* (prison madness) caused by this extreme form of social isolation.[95] Though one could argue that of the three works, Goncourt's novel shows the most compassion for the prostitute, Élisa's world is no more fragrant than that of Marthe or Nana.

Having, with his brother, done extensive research on the topic,[96] Goncourt characterizes Elisa as an hysteric, carefully tracing the manifestations and the sources, in nature and nurture, of her particular predisposition to prison madness.[97] Her recurring hysterical symptoms include sudden, fleeting, and uncontrollable sensations,

shivering, tingling, torpor, and dizzy spells, and sensitivity to fla-
vours and smells:

> En ses rares sorties, quand elle se trouvait avoir à passer devant la boutique
> d'un épicier, soudain elle descendait du trottoir et traversait de l'autre côté
> de la rue; un jour qu'elle mangeait d'un entremets où se trouvait de la can-
> nelle, elle avait une indigestion avec des espèces de convulsions. C'était,
> continuellement, une succession de petites agitations, de petites inquié-
> tudes, qui ne lui paraissaient pas toujours absolument et tout à fait être
> des souffrances dans son corps, mais parfois lui semblait les vertiges *d'une
> tête en tourment.*

> During her rare outings, when she would find herself passing by the spice
> shop, suddenly she would go down the street and cross to the other side;
> one day when when she was eating a dessert that contained cinnamon,
> she had indigestion along with convulsions. It was, continually, a succes-
> sion of little agitations, little anxieties, which did not always seem to her
> to be absolutely and completely bodily sufferings, but sometimes seemed
> to her to be the vertigos of a *head in torment.* (88–9)

Even Élisa's otherwise spotty recollection of the violent episode that
lands her in prison is sharpened by a clear memory of sweet odours rising around her, resembling the honeyed flavour of the flowering cherry
trees she knows from her country home (125). Fresh, natural scents create an incongruous backdrop for prostitutes who entertain their clients
in the brothel's garden: "Là, parmi la floraison des arbres fruitiers, au
milieu du reverdissement de la terre, sous le bleu du ciel, un peu de
l'innocence de leur enfance revenait chez ces femmes dans la turbulence
d'ébats enfantins. Le plaisir de petites filles qu'elles prenaient à courir,
à jouer, effaçait en elles l'animalité impudique" ("There, amongst the
flowering of fruit trees, amidst the greening of the earth, under the blue
of the sky, a bit of their childhood innocence came back to these women
in the turbulence of childish frolics. The little-girlish pleasure that they
took in running, playing, erased their shameless animality"; 36).
Perfume-wearing is less a focus of Goncourt's olfactory writing in
this novel than it will be in his *Chérie* (discussed in chapter 7), in Huysmans's *Marthe*, or in Zola's *Nana*. When, in prison, Élisa retrieves from
her chignon a yellowed love letter penned in blood by her former lover
Tachon, the soldier she has killed, neither the current scent of her hair,
nor the odour mentioned in the error-laden letter's postscript are identified: "P.S. Met dans tes cheveux l'odeur qui ï était la première fois"
("P.S. Put the odour in your hair that was there the first time"; 117).[98]

Earlier in the novel, however, the narrator had claimed that "leurs cheveux qui sentent le jasmin" ("their hair which smells of jasmine"; 84) are among the lures that draw peasants and soldiers to prostitutes.

The floral opposite of chaste and modest violet, jasmine was associated with passionate love and sensual pleasure (Debay, 282), its heady scent not recommended for the well-bred *jeune fille*:

> Les parfums aromatiques, comme ceux de l'œillet, de la cannelle, de la vanille, doivent être employés rarement, en très-petite quantité, et adoucis par un mélange d'odeurs plus faibles, les odeurs fragrantes, comme celles de lys, de tubéreuse, de jasmin; les odeurs ambrosiaques, comme celles de l'ambre, du musc doivent être complètement bannies de votre personne et de vos appartemens.

> Aromatic perfumes like those of carnation, cinnamon, vanilla must be rarely used, in small quantity and softened by a mix of weaker odours, fragrant odours like those of lily, tuberose, jasmine; ambrosial odours, like those of amber, musk, must be completely banished from your person and your living space. (Celnart, *Manuel des dames*, 1833, 92)

The most obvious trait linking Celnart's fragrances-to-be-avoided is their strength. Violet was deemed softer and more understated in character than white flowers like jasmine, neroli, and tuberose. It was probably perceived as gentler in part because the ionone molecule that gives violet its distinct odour is known to cause nose-blindness, that is, "olfactory fatigue and temporary anosmia" (Billot and Wells 1975, 152). In contrast, jasmine contains the organic compound indole, which conveys a heavier, dirtier (though not necessarily unpleasant) edge. Speaking of the indolic *jasmin sambac* flower, perfumer Jean-Claude Ellena is reported to have called it "animalic and overwhelming," since feces are "full of indoles ... and so are decomposing human bodies.... It's a feminine scent, the smell of death").[99] Death and feces may not be the first things to come to mind when inhaling a jasmine perfume, but their presence in the composition accounts for the complexity, tenacity, sultriness, and seductiveness that translated to some as immodesty.[100] On the scale of innocent to corrupt perfumes, jasmine figures more closely to the animalic musk and amber than to the more sweet and volatile violet. Its mention in *La fille Élisa* operates within a network of language and images reinforcing the animality of prostitutes, be it in prison or in the brothel: "La ruée des femelles dans le salon, où elles se poussaient en se bousculant, montrait quelque chose de l'animalité inquiète et effarée d'un troupeau" ("The stampede of females in the salon, where they pushed and shoved one another, revealed something of the worried, alarmed animality of a herd"; 32).

Élisa's rapid physical and mental degeneration during imprisonment takes the form of a descent from humanity, to both a robotic and animal-like state already apparent earlier in her life, then later excerbated by her time as a prostitute. Her assignment to the shoe repair section of the prison workhouse places her in an atmosphere of dirt and stench: "Une saleté inlavable, qui faisait contraste avec la sévère propreté du reste de la prison, était incrustée dans les murs, mettant une grande tache autour des prisonnières. Et dans l'atmosphère épaisse de ce lieu, les puanteurs du cuir se confondaient avec l'odeur de la crasse d'une humanité qui ne se lave plus" ("An unwashable filth, which contrasted with the rest of the prison's severe cleanliness, had been encrusted in the walls, leaving a great stain all around the prisoners. And in the thick atmosphere of this place, the stench of leather blended with the grimy odour of a humanity that no longer washes itself"; 148). This episode of prison life drives Élisa into an inner world of memories that she will occupy to her death: "Dans la Cordonnerie, Élisa commença à descendre, peu à peu, tous les échelons de l'humanité qui mène une créature intelligente à l'animalité...; enfin, reconnue incapable de tout travail, elle passa ses journées dans une contemplation hébétée et un ruminement grognonnant" ("In the prison shoe repair, Élisa began to descend, little by little, all the echelons of humanity that lead an intelligent creature to animality...; finally, deemed incapable of any work, she spent her days in a dazed contemplation and a grunting rumination"; 151–2). Before her death inside the prison, Élisa's memories take her to the fresh, outdoor spaces of her childhood, filled with trees and blooming white orange blossoms (traditionally used in wedding bouquets), in the open air.

While Huysmans, like Goncourt, portrays the stupefying, zombifying effects of the working girl's existence, his narrative voice and compositional juxtapositions betray an almost brutal detachment from his subject. Marthe is more an alien being than an unfortunate creature of heredity and society. Marthe's story unfolds against a backdrop of stench, including a "pissy" velvet banquette (11), lavatory drains, dank cellars, stale tobacco, manure, horse dung, and garbage. Her lover recoils at her sloppiness and the stench of her cooking. Early in her career as a prostitute, in a rare moment of contemplation, Marthe catches sight of herself in a brothel mirror and becomes keenly aware of her own made-up face, and her noisy, heavily scented surroundings: "Elle ne pouvait croire que cette image fût la sienne.... Et dans ce salon, tout imprégné des odeurs furieuses de l'ambre et du patchouli, c'était un vacarme, un brouhaha, un tohu-bohu..., des roulements d'ignominies et d'ordures

"("She could not believe this image was her own…. And in the salon, completely drenched in the furious odours of amber and patchouli, it was a din, a brouhaha, a hubub…, rumblings of disgraceful behavior and filth"; 22–3).

This is a rare moment in *Marthe*, where the protagonist shifts perspective in order to see herself as part of the vista, the decor, and the sickening scentscape of her brothel. Marthe snaps out of her contemplation when a little bell rings, signalling the arrival of what will be her first client. After that encounter, the narrator again offers Marthe's point of view, and point of smell, the aroma of this private space proving even more sickening: "L'atmosphère de cette chambre, alourdie par les émanations musquées des maquillages, ces fenêtres cadenassées, ces teintures épaisses, tièdes au souffles des charbons encore roses, ce lit démembré et saccagé par le pillage des nuits, le dégoûtèrent jusqu'au vomissement ("the atmosphere of that room, rendered heavy by the musky emanations of makeup, the locked down windows, thick tinctures, warm in the puffs of still rosy coals, this bed, dismembered and trashed by the nights' pillage, disgusted her to the point of vomiting"; 24). The persistence of musky smells indicates the prostitute's failure or refusal to modulate the strength of perfumes that suggest an animality associated with unclean living and uncontrolled sexuality. But more importantly, in the context of this novel, Marthe is able to read her social status as others do, by inhaling the scents that waft around and from her. As Maryan and Béal state in an 1896 book of etiquette for *jeunes filles* that the *fille* Marthe was unlikely to have consulted, "Parmi toutes les odeurs, ayez l'horreur du musc, qui incommode la plupart des gens, et qui n'est ordinairement employé que par des personnes dépourvues de distinction" ("Amongst all the odours, be horrified by musk, which bothers most people and is ordinarily used only by those lacking in distinction"; 108).

Taking into account Debay's caution against overuse of perfume in general, and Piesse's warnings about patchouli in particular, we can conclude that Marthe's musk and patchouli were too strong, not expertly mixed. The smell is dirty both in the sense of its being invasive and in poor taste. During the short time Marthe leaves the brothel to live with her lover, she acquires a different perfume, Chypre; though still heavier and more complicated than violet or rose, Chypre would have been considered more acceptable than musk or patchouli. Years before Coty's 1917 Chypre provided the genetic code for what would become a perfume category, or family, many perfume houses sold Chypre perfumes, though there was not one common formula.[101] In his 1857 *Art of Perfumery*, Piesse offers an idea of what a clean but noticeably perfumed woman would have worn. His blended Chypre smells primarily of one flower, in this case rose: "This is an old-fashioned French perfume, presumed to be derived from *chypre esculentus* by some, and by others to be named after the island of Cyprus; the article sold, however, is made thus" (137). Piesse's rose-centred formula also includes musk, ambergris, vanilla, Tonka bean,[102] and orris, but none of the oakmoss (or oak moss) that defines the chypre accord today.[103] Though the chain linking the island of Cyprus to Chypre perfumes appears broken in some places, this is a case where the evolution of the word and its associations may be as important as the pedigree of its odour. The Romans imported a Chypre from Cyprus, and the island was essential to the early supply chain that brought new resins, herbs, and spices to European perfumers. The name Chypre was already associated with fragrance materials when Medieval monks included oakmoss in their recipe for eau de Chypre, used in glove-making. In the seventeenth and eighteenth centuries, little birds called oiselets de Chypre, moulded of Chypre perfume paste, were placed in decorative cages.[104] Recipes for Chypre hair powder, used by men and women in the eighteenth century, called for orris, oakmoss, and rose water.[105] Though the recipe changes over time, Chypre maintains its status as a product of European breeding with an exotic backstory, which makes it, one could argue, doubly European in concept. Though not always at the height of fashion, more complicated, and in some blends more animalic than the scents favoured for demure *jeunes filles*, Chypre – as a name, as a concept – would not fall into the depth of disapporval reserved for heavier musk and patchouli.

In a description of odours that parallels the visual and olfactory cacophony of the brothel's salon, Marthe's lover observes and inhales the toiletries she has hurriedly left behind: "la cuvette pleine d'eau savonneuse, l'odeur du renfermé, le parfum de l'eau de Botot avec laquelle on s'est rincé les dents, l'arôme fin du Chypre qui fuyait du flacon mal bouché, tout ce tohu-bohu d'objets, tous ces réveils de senteurs lui rappelèrent la fuite qu'il n'avait su prévoir" ("the sink full of soapy water, a stuffy odour, the scent of the the Botot mouthwash she used for her teeth, the fine aroma of Chypre escaping a poorly closed bottle, all of this hubbub, all of these awakenings of scents reminded him of the flight he had been unable to foresee"; 43). Marthe's toiletries may not be tidy, but the soap, mouthwash, and fine fragrance suggest a cleanliness she had not before known, and will not maintain when she returns to street-walking.

Of the three novels, Zola's *Nana* most obviously characterizes its protagonist through her radiating bodily scent and the odours that surround her. In Zola's narrative voice, one senses intimacy with the prostitute, especially in evocations of the senses in Nana's world: the touch of silk and soft skin, the whiff of perfumes, the heavy, warm air of private chambers. Balzac presented the perfumer's world as backdrop for his novel on the speculative, predatory world of high finance (in *César Birotteau*); Zola used the heavily perfumed world of prostitutes to expose the contagious nature of Second-Empire corruption and hypocrisy in *Nana*.[106]

Dangerous Sillage

Though he certainly exaggerated, Dr. Antoine Combe was not alone in lamenting the popular appeal of commercial fragrances, precisely because widespread use made reading the smells of women, and thus classifying them, confusing. Expansion of the perfume industry brought new scents to the market at a range of price brackets. Advertisements for perfumes increasingly graced the pages of illustrated journals and fashion magazines, and though the images and taglines often linked perfume-wearing to well-bred homemakers, there was no guarantee that the same mass-produced scent might not emanate from the skin of a "proper" woman, or mingle with the musky *odeur de femme* of a demi-mondaine like Zola's Nana. For Combe, among many others, the modern French woman's *sillage* was becoming easier to detect but more difficult to read. When Zola's Nana rises in the economic ranks of her profession, acquiring celebrity status as well as a luxurious mansion on the avenue de Villiers, she marks her new prominence with garish decor and a new signature scent, replacing the heavier, muskier, more animalic smells of earlier days, with the cleaner, trendier, more bourgeois violet: "et c'était, dès le vestibule, une odeur de violette ... un parfum de violette, ce parfum troublant de Nana, dont l'hôtel entier, jusqu'à la cour était pénétré" ("and it was, from the vestibule, an odour of violet ... a scent of violet, that disturbing perfume of Nana's, with which the whole house, through the courtyard was penetrated"; 316). A detailed visual description of Nana's comically excessive acquisition of mismatched, lavish home furnishings calls attention to the unshakable smell of violet.[107] This virtual tour of Nana's home engulfs the visitor, and the reader, in Nana's penetrating essence. Within this showy space, even the potentially modest violet fragrance is too loud, an example of Nana's inescapable, humble beginnings and innately poor taste for "vulgar magnificence." More *troublant* perhaps is how, like the displaced hodge-podge of possessions in her rooms, the mainstream, respectable violet fragrance clashes with the lifestyle of its wearer and thus fails to signify what it should about the woman it represents. But there is another possible reading of Nana's new scent. In this chapter we learn that she has become a *femme chic* and a trendsetter, an influencer, that she "donnait le ton, de grandes dames l'imitaient" ("set the fashion, great ladies imitated her"; 1347). Here, Zola's insistence on "her" violet perfume suggests the choice was calculated, perhaps not only to imitate a type of decorous woman, but to shape that mainstream woman, even contaminate her image, by rebranding the innocent violet,[108] and thus revising the social language of fragrance. The prostitute's use of violet scent cleverly manipulates the language of flowers and their bottled essence enough to trouble both the reader of scent and the guests who cross her threshold.

Nana's appropriation of violet perfume, and to some extent Marthe's use of Chypre, serve as reminders that olfactive codes can be rewritten, reinterpreted, and misread. This is the point of Dr. Combe's concerns about artificial fragrance and blurred class distinctions; one can walk into a seemingly innocent scent trail that may mask something more sinister. Underlying this social uneasiness is a fear of physical and moral contamination, and invasion of personal and public space via perfume. An odiferous sillage, after all, moves and lingers. It enters the breath and the body of innocent bystanders. The insidious invasion of sillage, though unseen, can indeed be visualized. Edouard Manet's 1877 painting of the fictional Nana shows a fully dressed male caller observing a partially clothed Nana in the intimate space of her dressing room.[109] Throughout the novel, the Count Muffat de Beauville experiences an array of physical reactions, from heavy perspiration to vertigo, caused by the overpowering odour of "flowers and woman" in spaces associated with Nana (72). Manet suggests Nana's powerful sillage by showing her holding a powder puff and a hidden cosmetic item near her face; and in the depiction of the sofa frame, whose curve gives the illusion of snaking from Nana's torso to just before her caller's face, and of course, his nose (see Figure 1.11). In contrast, an eerily wholesome 1908 print advertisement for three Pinaud perfumes (including Violet, Gênet d'or, and even Corrida) shows young, smiling, clothed girls with flowers in their hair (two of them hold flowers as well), before whom are placed three bottles of perfume, which appear to be tightly sealed, posing no danger of unwanted, unnatural sillage (see Figure 1.12).

1.11. *Nana* (Edouard Manet, 1877). The curve of the sofa frame suggests Nana's sillage, wafting from around her body towards the face of her visitor.

Image source: Wikimedia Commons

1.12. A 1908 print advertisement for Pinaud perfumes, including a "fragrant breeze" of violet.

A Variation on Odiferous Sillage

If perfume has not yet taken over Paris by 1905, it seems to have taken over Combe's research. In his records of patients – most, though not all, of them women – Combe identifies fragrances by their brand names: Guerlain, Viville, Auber, Pinaud. He also mentions perfumes that were fashionable, including Jicky (by Guerlain), and Chypre, Peau d'Espagne, and Violette scents produced by various perfume houses. In fact, Combe focuses on violet fragrance in discussing the titillating reports of perfume injection (subcutaneous and intravenous) that circulated in France and the United States at the fin de siècle, a trend that would cause the skin and the breath to exhale cosmetic fragrance.[110] The perfume-injected body itself would function as a perfume diffuser, emitting its internalized cosmetic sillage. Inspired by the terms *morphinomanes* and *éthéromanes*, Combe calls the perfume-shooting women *violettomanes* (violet maniacs/ addicts), a label that manages to sound at once frivolous and morbid.[111] Though Combe presents several rather surprising case studies of hysterics and perfume, he does not include a case study of *violettomanie*. But a neurologist across the Atlantic had already reported a most unusual, unrelated case of persistent violet sillage.

In 1877, Dr. William A. Hammond, a former military physician who had become a professor of nervous and mental diseases at New York University, read an intriguing paper for the American Neurological Association.[112] At this time, it was not unusual to present visual back-up during a professional talk. But remarkably, instead of charts, graphs, or drawings, Hammond offered an olfactory illustration in the form of a small vial of liquid, which he passed around for his colleagues to sniff. The doctor had manufactured this fragrance himself, by saturating "a perfectly clean cambric handkerchief" in the patient's sweat. He then "placed it [the redolent perspiration] in a glass retort into which [he] introduced four fluid ounces of proof spirit [that is, 50 per cent water, 50 per cent alcohol]" (20). He distilled the mixture at 120° F. The result was a distillate "very strongly impregnated with the perfume of violets" (20). Indeed, in the conference proceedings, colleague Dr. Jewell confirms that "Dr Hammond passed around a small vial containing an alcoholic extract of the odiferous preparation…, which had a distinct violet smell" (xxxii). More surprising than medical doctors spending a session of their conference sniffing violet, is the source of that bottled fragrance. Dr. Hammond's violet perfume was created from the perspiration of his patient. She was,

a young married lady of strong hysterical tendencies, in whom, during a paroxysm, an odor similar to that of violets was exhaled from the body.

This was so powerful as to be distinctly perceptible at a distance of several feet and was noticed by anyone entering the room in which the patient was.... There was nothing at all disagreeable about this exhalation. On the contrary it was decidedly pleasant; nevertheless the patient was exceedingly anxious to get rid of it, even if she had to part with her hysterical manifestations – phenomena which she nursed with assiduous care. (19)

The procedure disconcertingly foreshadows protagonist Grenouille's morbid dabbling in human scent manufacturing and enfleurage in Süskind's *Perfume*. The association with cosmetic perfume is augmented by Hammond's use of not just any cloth to collect the patient's perspiration, but a handkerchief, the traditional vehicle of choice for women's and men's fragrance, reflected in the name of Guerlain's 1904 Mouchoir de monsieur (Gentleman's Handkerchief). At the medical conference, the doctor also distributed a second vial containing a fluid that smelled of pineapple. It was the very same *eau de l'hystérique* to which Hammond had added bicarbonate of soda, and in which he then detected butyric ether, a product he described as being of "very extensive use in perfumery," because it can produce various scents depending on what is added to it.

Hammond eventually freed his patient "from redolent perspiration and from hysterical manifestations of all kinds" by "administration of salicylate of soda in doses of five grains, three times a day, continued for about thirty days" (21). But he did not present this case study to illuminate colleagues on the subject of hysteria, or the fragrant perspiration thereof. Instead, his thesis concerned the odour of sanctity – the phenomenon attributed to saints of the early church, whose living and sometimes dead bodies filled rooms with a sweet aroma, bodies that, much like the ritually burned aromatics at the root of the word perfume (*in smoke*), joined heaven and earth by way of their sweet fragrance.[113] In this study, Hammond wanted to prove that the odour of sanctity was simply a natural phenomenon. Reactions to his paper show that Hammond's demonstration was convincing. Dr. Jewell remarked that it had been interesting from "a scientific as well as a theological point of view" (xxxi), adding, "I think one thing can be said in regard to Dr. Hammond's paper, and that is, it has furnished a new means of disposing of the phrase 'odor of sanctity'" (xxiii).

The American doctor's experiment was subsequently cited in France.[114] Dr. George Dumas expanded on Hammond's conclusions in his 1907 article "L'odeur de sainteté,"[115] accepting the scientific evidence, while defending the integrity of hagiographers. Dumas says one must either admit that doctors like Hammond were fooled by their patients or believe in the possibility of an odour of sanctity in saints, "puisque nous y croyons chez les profanes" ("since we believe it occurs in the profane"; 542). Juxtaposing the ugliness of scientific explanations with the poetic imagination of hagiography, Dumas concludes that, if indeed we can now identify the source of suave odours exhaled by saints, these explanations do not undermine the good will or honesty of witnesses and hagiographers who reported the phenomenon and deemed it miraculous (551–2). Throughout his article, Dumas reveals an attention to the reading of odour that did not concern Hammond. As Dumas points out, the expressions *to live the odour of sanctity* or *to die in the odour of sanctity* had long taken on purely figurative meanings: to live piously, to die in grace. Though it does not make this explicit connection, Dumas's conclusion suggests that the weakness in Hammond's case study resides not in scientific method, but in a cursory interpretation of olfactory signs, and a dismissive reaction to earlier readers of those signs.

Hammond's emphasis on collecting, blending, and bottling fragrant perspiration, then encouraging his colleagues to test-sniff, may reflect showmanship on his part. Yet his presentation implies that smelling of violet perfume, one of the most popular fragrances for women, is both unsaintly and unhealthy. In the ambivalent context of nineteenth-century women's perfume culture, what better way to dispose of the odour and the aura of sanctity than by debunking it with the distilled, violet sillage of an hysterical woman?

In the nineteenth century, health and beauty experts attempted to define the physical and moral meanings of natural and cosmetic aromas, as novelists turned their readers' eyes and noses to female characters at the extremes of decorum. The latter included the innately good yet vulnerable *jeune fille* and the self-sabotaging *fille*, destined by heredity, environment, and a nervous disposition, to inevitable ruin. Within the spectrum of these extremes lived real young women, their stories less dramatic to tell, but their impact on the language and culture of perfume undeniable, written in words and in evanescent sillage. The emergence of sillage as a fragrance term coincided with shifting practices in perfume application, and a desire to name the noticeable presence of cosmetic scent in the air. At its inception, the usage was malleable enough to denote both appreciation and scepticism. Its evolution reveals that social practice and lexical innovation could be closely knit, as perfume culture became more visible, and more sniffable.

Chapter Two

The Language of Flowers and Silent Things

Happy ... is he whose thoughts like larks,
Toward the heavens, in the morning take free flight,
– Who hovers over life and understands without effort
The language of flowers and silent things.[1]

– Charles Baudelaire, "Élévation,"
Fleurs du mal, 1857

Are words and smells incompatible? According to some biologists, chemists, philosophers, and even perfumers, that may be the case. Yet language has remained an immediate, accessible medium for representing smells and smell perception, and writers from Apollinaire to Zola have successfully perfumed their pages with words.[2] Though twentieth-century sociologist Edward Sagarin was neither the first nor the last writer to find odour descriptors deficient both in quality and quantity, his chapter title "A Science in Search of a Language" seems almost defiant, given its appearance in a 232-page book devoted to *The Science and the Art of Perfumery* (1945):[3] "In one respect the story of odor is unlike that of any other science. For scents defy accurate description. There are no exact terms by which a smell can be characterized. This is a science without a language" (137).

Sagarin argues that the accurate naming of specific odour molecules does little to break a tautological cycle of word–smell denotations: "when we say that anise oil smells like licorice, we are really saying that licorice smells like licorice; for it is the oil of anise, or its main ingredient, anethole, that gives this child's candy the odor and taste with which it is identified" (138). If olfaction lacks a language, then nouns and adjectives are to blame. Yet when Sagarin refers to licorice as a child's candy he reveals, inadvertently it seems, that like odour itself, the lexicon of smell activates associated memories and experiences. Anethole, anise oil, and licorice may smell the same, but as a word, only *licorice* stirs memories of childhood's fragrant treat. Likewise, Sagarin's reference to the "story of odor" resonates with a phenomenon that shapes the course of this book: smells may have an unreliable relationship to words and description, but they are impressive generators of stories and narrative.

Though complaints of deficiencies in odour lexicon persist, some scholars of literature find such concerns less than compelling, since evidence of effective writing about smell can be found all around us, especially in fiction and poetry. This observation certainly applies to written works of the nineteenth century, where attention to olfaction is expressed with impressive persistence on the pages of hygiene and beauty manuals, medical tracts, novels, and poetry collections. Intentionally or not, poets, perfumers, and medical doctors of the era were co-creating ways to talk about smells. A question that remains to be explored is whether smell specialists of the nineteenth century were concerned about the limits of an olfactory vocabulary; and if so, how did they express this concern or work around the problem? This chapter considers these questions by opening with an overview of the olfactory-lexicon debate and an examination of the word *parfum*/perfume itself. I then look more closely at *parfum* and other olfactory language in works by Charles Baudelaire, one of the French poets most celebrated for his signature aromas and stench.

How Words Smell

Sagarin was far from alone in finding language in general, words in particular, insufficient for denoting odours. In Western cultures, the relationship between language and olfactory perception has been viewed for centuries as inadequate, vague, and volatile. It is as if odours and olfactory experience were inherently resistant to verbal adaptation. Smells may be perceived, identified, interpreted, liked, or disliked. They trigger responses (pleasure, comfort, disgust). They deliver warnings (something is burning, the milk has gone sour). They announce a recognizable human presence (a friend's signature scent, a loved one's scarf). They suggest levels of taste, cleanliness, and social status (a loud fragrance, a musty room, a cheap perfume). Smells signal disease. Trimethylaminuria (the body's failure to break down trimethylamine) gives off an odour of rotten fish. The genetic condition maple syrup urine disease (MSUD), in which the body cannot process certain amino acids, was so named for the scent it produces. Among the many maladies associated with characteristic smells are scrofula (stale beer), typhoid (freshly baked bread), and yellow fever (an odour of butcher shop).[4] Aromas provide clues to sniffing sleuths, too. In 2007, perfumers

Sylvaine Delacourte (former perfume creative director for Guerlain) and Jean-Michel Duriez (who created perfumes for Patou, Rochas, and many others) were asked to "blind sniff" a jar of bones discovered in 1867, labelled "Restes présumés trouvés sous le bûcher de Jeanne d'Arc, la Pucelle d'Orléans" ("Remains presumed to be found at the stake of Joan of Arc, Maiden of Orleans").[5] The expert noses[6] smelled a fake, thanks to a telltale vanilla fragrance produced by decomposition, not cremation. Further odorous evidence, confirmed by carbon-14 dating, revealed that would-be relics of the saint were in fact ancient Egyptian feline remains, probably sold as mummy powder, an apothecary's panacea for internal and external ailments, popular in the twelfth through seventeenth centuries.[7]

As professional noses, medical doctors, and daily experience confirm, smells are readable. But are they writeable? Today, the long-held premise that "[o]dors are surprisingly difficult to name"[8] motivates a vast range of research focused on language and olfaction. Smell has been called the speechless sense, the silent sense, the mute sense.[9] When linguists Joël Candau and Agnès Jeanjean refer to the "olfactory silence" of modern Western society, they signal both a lack of smell words, and what was, until recent decades, a lack of critical discourse about smell.[10]

Researchers have investigated anatomical explanations of weak odour–language connections, positing that the human brain lacks the infrastructure necessary to pair semantic cues with the experience of smell perception.[11] But as neurolinguistic studies uncover evidence of how the brain processes olfactory language, it seems increasingly clear that perceived deficiencies in smell vocabulary originate in society rather than anatomy. Many languages, including English and French, have simply not developed a copious lexicon of commonly understood adjectives specific to smell. This language gap reflects a cultural bias that accords greater value to other senses, especially sight and hearing.

Olfaction's low rank in the hierarchy of senses has been traced to a Platonic favouring of hearing and sight that continued to inform philosophers of the modern era. As Annick Le Guérer shows in her chapters on the "The Philosophical Nose" (*Scent* 141–203), Fourier, Feuerbach, and Nietzsche did not get much attention for their attempts to "rehabilitate" the sense of smell; and beyond a nod to the fact that olfaction is often ignored, more recent works that focus specifically on phenomenology and the senses (Michel Serres's *Les cinq sens*, Merleau-Ponty's *Phénoménologie de la perception*) say relatively little about the sense of smell.[12] Theories of evolution, too, have played their part in justifying the depreciation of olfaction. Freud (informed by Darwin) noted briefly in *Civilization and Its Discontents*[13] that bipedal creatures rely on visual horizons, not scent trails for safety. Quadrupeds sniff the ground; humans read poetry. To write or speak about smell, then, is to conjoin a mode of communication unique to humans, with a sense considered by many to be an evolutionary throwback. Yet poets do write memorably about smells.

The relatively meagre everyday lexicon of smell descriptors in Western languages is not so much a problem of incapacity as inattention. Acknowledging the historic devaluation of the sense of smell, linguists and anthropologists investigate odour–language correlations related to the valuation of language and olfactory perception in early childhood development, or within the daily life of specific societies. Ethnographic data from non-Western languages such as Maniq (spoken by a nomadic population in southern Thailand) reveal rich semantic fields related to smell, and in so doing, challenge "the widespread view that language cannot encode odors."[14] In their article "Odors are expressible in language, as long as you speak the right language," Asifa Majid and Niclas Burenhult acknowledge that "people find it difficult, if not impossible to name odor," but challenge "the common belief that the experience of a smell is impossible to put into words" (266) by conducting a comparative study of Jahai speakers located in the Malay peninsula and speakers of American English. Unlike the English-speaking participants in their study, the Jahai named odours easily, using a spectrum of commonly understood words. The authors conclude that socio-cultural and ecological niches are responsible for what may be falsely misperceived as an innate inability, or limitation, in olfactory abstraction.

Historical and cultural scholarship of the modern era recognizes, and often calls attention to, a language–odour conundrum. Alain Corbin's groundbreaking work *The Foul and the Fragrant* (1982; English translation 1986) cites "the baffling poverty of the language" (6) as one reason many scientists and philosophers, from the Age of Enlightenment onward, were reluctant to focus on odour perception. In the preface to his 2006 *A Smell Culture Reader*, Jim Drobnick juxtaposes the strong connection between odour and memory to the weak link between odour and language: "Enigmatically lacking a well-defined or extensive vocabulary, odors are unmatched in catalyzing the evocation of distant memories and places" (1). Social historian David S. Barnes shows the potentially high stakes of word shortage when he attributes the difficulty of creating accurate historical documentation of smells, due to a dearth of lexical tools: "Rendering smells in words is nearly always an exercise in analogy – something smells 'like roses,' 'like rotten eggs,' 'like burning rubber.' Few adjectives exist to describe the precise component qualities of odors, beyond vague allusions such as 'bitter' or 'sweet.' In 1880, Parisians abstained even from this amount of description, instead evoking the odors' *effects* ('sickening,' 'nauseating,' 'suffocating') or qualifying them simply as 'foul,' 'disgusting,' and 'horrible.' 'Putrid' and 'fetid,' two adjectives frequently used during the episode, begin to evoke at least a range of olfactory sensations, but the available evidence goes no further" (15–16). The "episode" Barnes discusses occurred between 1880 and 1895, a period framed by two "Great Stinks" in Paris intrusive enough to spark public outcry, political debate, and relentless commentary in the daily papers. His research uncovers no shortage of witnesses who described the shocking stench, but it also reveals a scarcity of nuanced words that would have been needed to communicate precisely how the bad smells smelled.

Comparable observations appear in popular science articles and in books aimed at an audience beyond academia. Boyd Gibbons ("The Intimate Sense of Smell," *National Geographic*) reverses a commonly held cause-and-effect relationship, suggesting that language deficiencies contribute to marginalization of the sense of smell in scientific and social discourse: "What we lack is not a profound sense of smell, but encouragement to talk about intimate odors. And we lack a vivid vocabulary with which to describe all odors. We fall back on simile and metaphor" (328). "Smells are our dearest kin," notes Diane Ackerman (in *A Natural History of the Senses*), "but we cannot remember their names. Instead we tend to describe how they make us feel. Something smells 'disgusting,' 'intoxicating,' 'sickening,' 'pleasurable,' 'delightful,' 'pulse-revving,' 'hypnotic,' or 'revolting'" (7). Gaston Leroux's novel *Le parfum de la dame en noir* (1908) offers countless examples of describing a perfume in this way, in terms of its quality and effect, but not its fragrant ingredients. The novel brings together the physical and figurative acts of sniffing out clues, as reporter Rouletabille follows the scent trail of perfume described as soft, pretty, isolated, personal, discreet, melancolic, tyrannical, extraordinary, and persistent.

If there are indeed so many obstacles to communication about olfactory perception, smells must pose a particular challenge to poets, novelists, and their readers, when literal rather than figurative description is the goal, though simile and metaphor certainly help. Much like Barnes, who shows that an absence of accurate odour words limits the documentary power of historical texts, Hans J. Rindisbacher identifies the lack of nuance and specificity in smell descriptors as a challenge to creating a taxonomy of odour references in literary works: "Whereas we find 'blue' or 'red' or 'green' in a paradigm for 'colors,' the 'smell of coffee,' the 'scent of a rose,' or the 'stench of power' have no such superordinated paradigm" (v). In fact, much like the names of individual colours, the words for individual smells cannot be described adequately, though they may be evoked in examples and comparisons.

Not everyone sees the self-defining nature of a smelly noun's smell, or reliance on simile, metaphor, or metonymy, as lexical limitations. Avery Gilbert contends that, on the contrary, "[t]ar, fish, grapefruit – every smelly thing in the world is a potential adjective. Add to these the names of branded products with iconic scents: Play-Doh, Vicks Vapo-Rub, Dubble Bubble, and WD-40" (126–9). Others argue that despite this plethora of ready-made adjectives, the layman cannot accurately describe the smell of fish, tar, Play-Doh, or WD-40 to someone who has never encountered the odour before: "The very way we talk about smells – the metonymic language denoting the origin of the phenomenon – sends us to as many places in the encyclopedia as there are 'smelly' objects" (Rindisbacher, v).

English and French syntax reflect this means of description-by-identification in structures like: *The room smells of roses*; *The room smells like roses*; *Ça sent la rose*; *Licorice smells like anise*. Rindisbacher sees the unreliable linguistic structure of olfaction as leading to disorder when it comes to making sense on the real-object level (x). Yet, as Boyd Gibbons suggested by saying we "fall back" on metaphors and similes, there are ways to evoke smells in language, even in the absence of rich lexical paradigms for odours. From the perspective of cognitive linguistics, Rémi Digonnet shows that olfactory metaphors serve the double function of expanding representations and shaping our perception of odours.[15] Holly Dugan argues that culturally shaped and shared metaphorical language facilitates communication about the senses, and thus metaphors provide "a historical archive of sensation" (5).[16] She cautions that twenty-first-century scholars should not sell short the quality of smell qualifiers, even in Western culture. In demonstrating that early modern English had a precise lexicon of olfaction largely forgotten today, Dugan also calls into question any history of olfaction that would map the fluctuating language of smell words as a one-way trajectory, from scarcity to abundance or vice versa.

It is true that modern French presents certain limitations and confusions when it comes to the everyday vocabulary of olfaction.[17] In their introduction to a 2011 volume of *Langages* dedicated to a linguistics of odours, George Kleiber and Marcel Vuillaume characterize the study of olfactory language as relatively new and uniquely compelling because, unlike the lexicon of sight and sound, nouns denoting smell (*stench, perfume, effluvia*) lack specificity and defy systematic classification. Groupings of odour words are so contrary to accepted theories of linguistic categorization, so lacking in rigour, and so dependent on the individual speaker's experience and perception, that linguists call them "pseudo-categories."[18] Classen observes that in addition to being limited in quantity, olfactory lexicon is less supple than that of the other senses: olfactory terms borrow from gustatory and tactile words, and to a lesser extent, vision and sound, but olfactory terms rarely carry over to qualify the other senses (*Worlds of Sense*, 55).

To fuzzy categories, generic nouns, and all-purpose adjectives add the problem of ambiguous verbs. Anne Theissen points out that the verb *sentir* (*to smell*) applies just as often to other sensory and abstract phenomena: to sense (physically), to feel (emotionally), to sense (intuitively), to interpret, or to understand. Classen further specifies that the polyvalence of *sentir* (rooted in the Latin *sentire*, the base of the English word *scent*), along with "association of smell and perception in general," may reveal "a certain primacy accorded to the role of smell in sense experience"; or, on the contrary, "because smell was such a difficult sense to pin down, that it ended up being expressed simply as 'feeling'" (53).[19] Theissen's analysis of the "*sentir*-olfactif," shows the strictly olfactory usage of the verb *sentir* to be ambiguous as well.[20] One obvious example is a potential semantic confusion shared by French and English: *sentir/to smell* designates both taking in and giving off an odour, an ambiguity which Érika Wicky embraces in the title of her 2014 article "Ce que sentent les jeunes filles" ("[Of] What Young Women Smell").[21]

Like the odours they designate, smell words penetrate would-be borders, they intermingle, they challenge control. Poor, limited, unstable, imprecise, non-specific, parsimonious, idiosyncratic, tautological, inconsistent, difficult to categorize – these are some of the characteristics that French linguists attribute to the language of olfaction. Yet while the unreliability and underuse of one-to-one word–smell pairings may in some ways hinder communication in everyday language, these linguistic setbacks press us to use language in more expansive, creative, and personal ways, through metaphor and simile, yes, but also anecdote, comparison, circumlocution, and metonymy. We may struggle to describe an aroma or stench, but we can adapt it to poetry. And we can tell its story.

Through Smoke

While it is difficult to convey a specific experience of olfactory perception in precise yet commonly understood words, it would be even more challenging to do so in other media. Smells pose a problem of data entry and storage. We may breathe in countless odours throughout the day, but we cannot photograph, record, or pocket scent molecules to commemorate chance encounters with fragrance and stink. The technologies chemists and perfumers use to capture smell remain too cumbersome for everyday use. Headspace technology, also called living flower technology, involves encapsulating a single flower (or other smelly substance) in a vacuum for six to twelve hours. The captured fragrance is then analysed using gas–liquid chromatography and mass spectrometry.[22] As yet, no pocket-sized version of this laboratory equipment has been marketed for everyday use. Likewise, the sort of identification software that "hears" and names a tune drifting from a café, or "sees" a leaf and recognizes its tree, has not yet been developed for sniffing and tagging odours. Even if the source of a smell (a sprig of rosemary, a cluster of mimosa, a perfumed handkerchief) can be located and pilfered for future examination, its fragrance will soon change, dissipate, or vanish. We can hum a tune, paint from memory, or dictate a portrait to a sketch artist, but we cannot duplicate or imitate our memory of smell with much practical precision in any medium but words. It is paradoxical that the sense most often associated with our animal nature, thus most often dismissed as evolutionary vestige or debris, still ties us closely to language; and paradoxical that many languages provide so few words for non-specialists describing smell.

The French word *parfum* is itself elusive. In his 1895 study of olfactory sensation, Jacques Passy concurs with physician Henri-Etienne Beaunis's distinction between *odeurs* (substances which produce a quick and clean sensory response) and *parfums*, which act more slowly and imprecisely, concluding, however, that most substances are at once *odeurs* and *parfums* (388). This designation was not adopted by his Dutch contemporary Hendrik Zwaardemaker, and it would not likely have been understood by the general public.[23] In a more everyday context, *odeur* applies to both pleasant aromas and stench, while *parfum* is typically used more restrictively.

In common English and French usage, *perfume/parfum* and its derivatives generally designate the palpable, breathable cosmetic product itself: a fragrant cream, paste, or powder; a scented, bottled liquid. The French language (more regularly than English) expands usage beyond this cosmetic context to other pleasant smelling things: the *perfume* of night air, the *perfume* of nearby jasmine blooms, the *perfume* of strawberries.[24] Poetic license allows for broader usage, including ironic and metaphorical constructions (Charles Baudelaire's *dangerous* and *hideous* perfumes, his *perfumes of indifference* and perfume *of haughty virtue*).[25] Without clear contextual cues, then, *parfum* could be understood as the smell of fragrant matter designated for cosmetic or ritual use, the products themselves (even if their odour is sealed in a bottle), or a more generic smell, an odour, an aroma (most likely agreeable). As a result, translating the word *parfum* from French to English can be challenging. The *parfum* of Baudelaire's famous line from "Correspondances," "Les parfums, les couleurs et les sons se respondent" ("Perfumes, colours, and sounds respond to one another") has been translated as *perfumes, fragrances, scents,* and *odours*.[26] It is worth noting, too, that the French *parfum* is a synesthetic noun, as it designates both flavour and scent.[27] Though it is generally read as connotating smell in Baudelaire's sonnet, the term *parfum* subtly mingles the sense of taste within one word in a poem that already more obviously evokes a coalescence of sights, sounds, scents, touch, and movement. Unlike the *fragrances, scents,* or *odours* suggested in some translations, *parfum* lends to the first line's metaphorical *temple* a materiality and visuality that can be otherwise hidden in the poem's forest of symbols. The word *parfum* contributes to an associative network linking ritual perfume burning to the ingredients of cosmetic perfumes featured in the last stanza, thus blurring the sacred and the human as the poem's "man" navigates, but also leaves his mark on, the forest and the temple. Such examples demonstrate that the noun *parfum* adapts ambiguously to English, and just as important, they reveal how the challenge of finding precise words may be complicated by the volatility of intended meaning. As a result, readers play a vital role in the interpretation of written smells.

The etymology of *perfume/parfum* (*per-fumum*: in/through smoke) conveys an image of ephemeral materiality, in words that preserve the memory of perfume's ancient form and function: the sacred ritual of burning aromatic plants and resins, which rise to the sky in smoke, joining earth to the heavens in fleetingly visible fragrance. Along with this cultural memory, the word *parfum* invokes the phenomenon of odours as a presence by suggesting their movement in time and space (*par*), and it reinforces the multi-sensory connections, odoriferous materiality, palpability, and visibility that *fumée* implies. John Singer Sargent's 1880 painting *Fumée d'ambre gris* depicts the movement of odour through smoke rising from a censer towards a woman's face (see Figure 2.1). With the shawl held over her head forming a partial enclosure, the woman creates an intimate space in which to capture the aroma of ambergris, a fragrance she can see, smell, and even feel.[28] Yet the vast, nearly empty, and compositionally open space above and around her reminds the viewer that the smoke cannot be harnessed, that it will spread, dissipate, and disappear from view, touch, and smell.

Visible wafts of liquid, vapour, and fragrant smoke appear in several of *fin-de-siècle* artist Alphonse Mucha's posters.[29] His 1896 lithograph *Salammbô*, incorporated in a Coryn perfume advertisement, appeals to the consumer's fascination with exotic themes and recalls the dozens of perfume-infused descriptions and scenes in Gustave Flaubert's novel, set in Carthage, third century BCE. Mucha's lithograph depicts Salammbô kneeling on a terrace, where in each corner burns a pan[30] of fragrant materials visibly transporting the scent of spikenard, incense, cinnamon, and myrrh, from the earth to the heavens (see Figure 2.2).[31]

2.1. Smoke rising from a censer in
John Singer Sargent's *Fumée d'ambre gris*, 1880.

Image source: © 2009 The Sterling and Francine Clark Art Institute
Williamson, Massachusetts

2.2. Stylized perfumed smoke trails in *Salammbô* show
fragrances rising from burning pans as mentioned in chapter 3
of Gustave Flaubert's novel. Here Alphonse Mucha incorporates
his 1897 lithograph design in an 1898 advertisement
for Coryn Perfume.

Writers too explore the literal and metaphorical perceptibility of perfume via senses beyond smell. Richard Stamelman's readings of Baudelaire show that in lyric poems like "Parfum exotique," "smells make vision – an interior, dream vision – possible" (104). Baudelaire also visualizes and materializes odour in his 1862 prose poem "Le fou et la Vénus" ("The Jester and the Venus"; OC I: 283–4), where he adapts the exotic image of ritual perfume burning to the updated setting of a park sizzling under the "burning eye" of the sun. In this scene, brightly coloured flowers contribute to a "universal ecstasy of things" that "expresses itself without a sound." Rather than utter words, this "silent orgy" transmits fragrance: "la chaleur, rendant visibles les parfums, les fait monter vers l'astre comme des fumées" ("the heat, rendering perfumes [odours] visible, makes them rise toward the celestial body like smoke [fumes/smoke/vapor/dung]"). Both the singular *fumée* and plural *fumeés* have positive or negative connotations. Yet it is worth noting that the *Grand dictionnaire universel du XIX siècle* offers the example of *fumée d'encens* (incense) in the singular (vol. 8, 874), and variously formed *fumées* (animal droppings) in the plural; the latter in a rather lengthy discussion of how hunters describe and distinguish various forms of animal excrement (vol. 8, 874–5). The ambiguity of Baudelaire's *fumées*, like the blending of sacred and profane in "Le fou et la Vénus," is in keeping with the association of opposites cultivated throughout his verse and prose poetry, evident in the very titles *Flowers of Evil* and *Little Prose Poems*,[32] and in sensory echoes that bring together poems as seemingly disparate as "Correspondances" ("Correspondences") and "Une charogne" ("A Carrion").

Pictorial adaptations of fragrance in the works of Sargent and Mucha, like the visualized depiction of smell in Baudelaire's poems, remind us that odours act in a constant state of metamorphosis. They are spatially ordered but not spatially fixed. Their capacity to strengthen, weaken, infiltrate, permeate, and cling was cause for alarm among modern hygienists and moralists. In social spaces, smells impose intimacy between people who would rather keep their distance. The very act of breathing in the smells that surround us is inherently intimate.[33] For perfumers, the dynamic nature of fragrance, or its movement, is as much a distinguishing compositional feature as a scent note (rose, musk, violet). Movement, defined as form or structure in combination with longevity,[34] is both a temporal and a spatial quality.

Whether experienced as shifting, fleeting, invasive, or evasive, the movement of smells in space and time, and how we perceive that phenomenon, have been identified as sources of resistance to verbal description. According to Henri Lefebvre, smells "are not decodable. Nor can they be inventoried, for no inventory of them can have either a beginning or an end" (198). In the context of space, place, and smells-capes, Paul Rodaway observes that the "subject-object dichotomy of everyday language forces our description of olfactory experience into an inappropriate framework" since "smells are not neatly defined objects in the sense of visual objects but experiences of intensities, more like those of pain and joy" (65). If smells are mobile and transient, with no lines of demarcation, yet highly perceptible and experiential, it is not surprising that perfumes and miasmas, so wanting for words in everyday communication, have found a voice in the more capacious time and space of poetic language; or that, in turn, the poetic evocation of odours has provoked such strong positive and negative reactions among readers.

Baudelaire's Wordscapes and Smellscapes

Though the tautological pairing of words to the olfactory phenomena they represent has been cited repeatedly as evidence of deficient language, limited perception, or both, it has not prevented poets from writing about odours. The few critics who have addressed in some depth the question of smell language in Baudelaire's work, reveal a deep connection between smell, the act of reading, and the dynamics of poetic production. For example, Richard Stamelman's analysis of Baudelaire's most perfumed verses further implicates the reader, by showing the very act of reading these poems to be an embodiment of poetics, a form of smelling, thus breathing, the musicality of the verses. In his analysis of the poem "Le parfum," Stamelman shows the movement of poetry – in syllables, words, lines, stanzas, and syntax – as evoking the movement of memory and of perfume itself:

> several words, like "rose," "permeated," "emanated," describe not only the perfumed imagination active in the poem – the reader's memory of perfume, of the smells adhering to places and things, of the real or remembered aromas of love – but also the structural movement and activity of the poem itself. Not only is "Perfume" about perfume; it moves like a perfume as well, each image permeating and then mixing with another: each stanza offering a rich, heady, perhaps even hyperbolic, description of perfume's mobility and its power to create plenitude. (Stamelman, *Perfume*, 109–10)

Looking closely at the function of rhetorical strategies, Jonathan Culler, citing Poe, relates Baudelaire's metonymical poetics to the peculiar language of odours:

> Poe writes in his *Marginalia*, "I believe that odors have an altogether idiosyncratic force, in affecting us through association, a force differing essentially from that of objects addressing the touch, the taste, the sight, or the hearing." Of all sensations, smells are the most inextricably linked with tropological, specifically metonymical operations (the substitution of cause for effect or the naming of something by what is contiguous to it). Other sensations may have literal names. Smells mnemonically generate chains of metonymical associations: to name a smell is metonymically to describe its cause or the circumstances in which one first smelled it (unlike colours, which have names of their own), so that smells hold the attention to reorient it towards what surrounds them – for example, in the poetic (discursive and descriptive) movement evoked in Baudelaire's "La Chevelure," in the prose poem "Un hémisphère dans une chevelure," or in "Parfum exotique." (129)

Culler's observations on smells and poetry suggest that, contrary to popular belief, the limited language of olfaction does not impede communication about smells. Instead, the tenuous lexicon of odours drives poetic creation. Thus, naming a smell "rose" involves a word–object operation more complex than simple identification, since the fragrance of a rose is not the rose itself. The associative chain activated by the smell of rose includes the flower itself, yes, but along with it, related things, spaces, experiences, memories, and emotions in both the poetic cosmos and in the reader's world. Baudelaire, translator of many works by Poe, took the title of his "Mon cœur mis à nu" ("My Heart Laid Bare") from *Marginalia*.[35] Though he did not make written statements like Poe's about the difference between smell and other senses, Baudelaire indeed demonstrated in his poetry how the evocation of odours harmonizes with associative movement in poetic language.

Confused and Corresponding Words

In his notes to the Pléiade edition of *Les fleurs du mal*, Claude Pichois says of "Correspondances:" "De tous les poèmes de Baudelaire, c'est le sonnet qui a suscité le plus de commentaires: on pourrait facilement doubler le nombre des pages du livre de J. Pommier centré autour de ces vers" ("Of all Baudelaire's poems, it is the sonnet that has sparked the most commentary: one could easily double the number of pages by J. Pommier centered on these verses"; 839). Since the 1932 publication of Pommier's book, *La mystique de Baudelaire*, many have read, even memorized, "Correspondances," but in light of post-Benjaminian theories of modernity, Baudelaire's poems about Paris, women, and exoticism have attracted more scholarly attention in recent years. Despite the sonnet's obvious sensory echoes, "Correspondances" does not, in terms of the narrative action or inaction it conveys, seem to fit among those fragrant poems of urban, exotic, or corporeal experience, literally or figuratively conveyed. One encounters no displaced swans, no brushes with strangers, no trysts with bejeweled lovers, no streetwalking, no seafaring.

Still referenced across disciplines for its attention to fragrance, Baudelaire's "Correspondances" is a sonnet recognized as a Baudelairean *ars poetica* that provides "a conceptual bridge between the Romantics' yearning for transcendence in the early years of the nineteenth century and the hermetic theories of the Symbolist generation in its closing decades" (Evans 139). The poem is also widely appreciated as a tribute both to transcendence via the senses and to voluntary, or non-clinical synesthesia.[36] Yet, with the important exception of Stamelman's analysis (*Perfume*, 114–26) the sonnet's relationship to the context of its smell culture has not attracted a great deal of attention in literary scholarship. Perhaps this is because, from an olfactory perspective, the poem seems at first almost too programmatic and accessible, or deceptively simple. We have already "listen[ed] to the warm."[37] We know that some smells are green, that some music is sweet, that some colours are cool, and that adjectives like *sweet* and *warm* and *cool* may qualify colours and sounds as well as smells. To communicate about smell often requires linguistic ingenuity, along with a shared familiarity with scented matter and the ability to remember it. We use rhetorical synesthesia all the time. And yet, though arguably the most obvious, synesthesia is not the only type of olfactory correspondence suggested in Baudelaire's sonnet.

Hardly forgotten, it would be more accurate to say that the sonnet's olfactory connections are sometimes taken for granted, because they so clearly relate to the philosophies of art and beauty Baudelaire expressed elsewhere. "Correspondances" dramatizes Baudelaire's poetics by proclaiming a dynamic, transcendent relationship to sensorial experience. This approach recalls Baudelaire's assertion that all forms of beauty contain both something eternal and something transitory (*Salon de 1846*, OCII, 493), evident in the sort of revelation Baudelaire saw in Delacroix's visual "translation" (*traduction*) of the spirit: "Comme la nature perçue par les nerfs des ultra-sensibles, elle révèle le surnaturalisme" ("Like nature perceived by ultra-sensitive nerves, it reveals supernaturalism"; OCII, "Exposition universelle 1855," 596). Despite its obvious naming of colour, sound, smell, and sensation, "Correspondances" can seem surprisingly intangible, more a celebration of thinking than of feeling, an expression in verse of aesthetic ideals Baudelaire had and would state elsewhere. Its sensory offerings are delivered in declarations, from a chilly narrative distance, charted by an absence of personal pronouns. The inclusive imperatives (*remember! think of it! imagine it! soar!*) of other perfumed *Flowers of Evil* never punctuate these serene affirmations. No reader, real or implied, is beckoned to join this symphony of colour and fragrance, to inhale (much less wear or emit) those corrupt or corrupted perfumes. A rather hermetic discursive style partially explains an interpretation that seems contradictory: that this poem, offered as primary evidence across disciplines of Baudelaire's status as a writer of smells, is often seen by literary critics as a vehicle for abstraction. The reader takes in and blends the poem's sensuality and spirituality to reach an unnamed, unphysical means of communication and transcendence. The *idea* of odour stimulates imagination and memory and leads to a form of perception that is more cerebral than sensate. The senses summoned foster an out-of-body experience.

Other poems like "Le cygne" or "Parfum exotique" that more obviously engage both the mind and the body, also lend themselves to culturally focused commentary. But for many readers, the fragrant materials wafting from the final stanza of "Correspondances" generate rhetorical strategies, not tableaux of women whose perfumes would have contained those ingredients. In its ever-shifting horizontal semantic system, the poem evades progress despite its devotion to transport. The poem eludes mise-en-scène, it embeds associations, it enumerates comparisons, and it offers the infamous seven-time appearance of the word *comme*, which ambiguously either sets up an analogy (like) or itemizes examples (such as).[38]

Perhaps this relatively less poetic use of *comme* has contributed to a tendency in literary criticism to pass by the list of scents, without stopping to breathe them in. Paul de Man, for example, suggests that the best way to understand the sonnet's amber, incense, musk, and benzoin is within their linguistic network: "One wonders if the evil connotations of these corrupt scents do not stem from the syntax rather than the Turkish bath or black mass atmosphere one would otherwise have to conjure up. For what could be more perverse or corruptive for a metaphor aspiring to transcendental totality than remaining stuck in an enumeration that never goes anywhere?" (250). It is true that the poem lacks the obvious, disturbing, dangerous proximity that is a signature of Baudelaire's style, present in many of his more dramatized perfume poems.

Yet even separated from their sensual denotations and cultural connotations, the perfume words themselves reinforce the sonnet's multisensorial theme. Their satisfying phoneme collisions provide mouthfeel, and musicality, too: the low hum of *ambre*, the scratch of *musc*, the smolder and sizzle of *encens*, punctuated, if you choose, by the little spark of a pronounced final "s" (to enrich the rhyme with *sens/encen-s*). Like the base notes that anchor more volatile top notes in a blended perfume, the scent words in the last verse contribute to the poetics of Baudelaire's sonnet by exerting a phonemic and syntactic gravitational pull, so that complete separation from *terra firma* is never possible. It is not an escape from the material that allows for transport, but rather the mingling of matter and abstraction that creates the space of a poetic ideal.

The terms *amber, musk, benzoin*, and *incense* figure prominently in the sonnet's wordscape, and in the nineteenth-century smellscape as well. They conjure fragrant materiality, a combination of smell, shape, and texture. They unite the poem simultaneously with nature, sacred ritual, the human body, and the culture of commodities. Embedded fragrances connect the poem to the consumer culture that so famously provided a backdrop for the poet's urban life, aesthetic contemplation, and *flânerie*. In other poems by Baudelaire, consumer goods mingle with order and beauty on a path to stillness and pleasure. Luxury objects crackle, gleam, rustle, and shine; they furnish rooms, they spread across dressing tables, they adorn the body. Here, valuable scented matter rises from the last stanza as if in smoke or vapour, mingling with the sweet, fresh, and green smells already in the air. These materials were, and are, consumer goods, their names enumerated not only in poems and the pages of novels, but in catalogues and on shipping receipts of the era. Perfume manuals offer classifications, descriptions of properties, and full cosmetic recipes, while emphasizing the exotic pedigrees of the perfumer's raw materials. Amber, musk, benzoin, and incense were imported from great distances, often blended, and repackaged in liquids, powders, lotions, pastes, and pomades. They were used in makeup and other cosmetic products, and they were (and remain) components, often base notes, in fragrance blends.[39] Base notes add strength and longevity to a perfume's more volatile, more lilting, sweeter, and greener head and heart notes; they lend to a blended fragrance both tenacity and expansion. Benzoin, derived from the styrax benzoin tree of Siam, Sumatra, and Singapore, is a sticky, liquid resin. Olibanum, or incense, is found in the Boswellia tree of North India and in parts of the Middle East. Like benzoin, this gooey resin oozes from an incision in the tree trunk. In the nineteenth century, it would be encountered in smoky church rituals. But once marketed, particularly in women's cosmetic and hygienic products, incense would be experienced as liquid, lotion, or paste. By grouping incense with musk, amber, and benzoin, Baudelaire also blends the sacred with hygiene, beauty, and feminized fashion.

Musk comes from an excretory gland of the musk deer. It was sold in the nineteenth-century with fur and tail attached to assure authenticity. According to Rimmel, the raw stench of musk is so strong, that Chinese musk deer hunters had to cover their own noses and mouths to prevent hemorrhaging as they extracted the glands (*Le livre des parfums*, 247–9). Today, musk (and other glandular secretions, such as civet), are usually used only in synthetic form.

Amber (or ambergris), perhaps the most mysterious, elusive, and misunderstood of perfume materials, is an intestinal secretion found in the sea and on the coasts of Australia, Brazil, China, the East Indies, India, Japan, South Africa, New Zealand – anywhere near sperm whale habitats. The waxy substance protects the intestines from sharp irritants such as squid beaks and cuttlefish bones, which the whales ingest, as they do all their food, in gulps – no chewing. Whales cough up or defecate ambergris, or in some cases, the collection of ambergris causes a fatal intestinal rupture (Kemp 2012, 13). After years or decades of tumbling in the ocean's swirling gyres, the substance washes ashore in odorous clumps. Few of us today have smelled natural ambergris, since hunting the whale is illegal nearly everywhere, not to mention a gamble, as there is no guarantee a whale's innards will house this precious, waxy clod.[40] Accidental procurement of ambergris that has washed ashore is a rare and lucrative phenomenon.[41] The lucky person who finds it can make a great deal of money selling ambergris to the perfume industry. "Who would think, then, that such fine ladies and gentlemen should regale themselves with an essence found in the inglorious bowels of a sick whale!" says *Moby Dick*'s Ishmael (304). Raw ambergris is pungent, but not harsh. Blended as a perfume base it adds depth, tenacity, and a rich odour, neither sweet nor bitter. More often than not, perfumers now use the synthetic molecule ambrox/ambroxan to imitate the natural wonder.

Like *parfum*, the word *ambre* invites multiple interpretations. Translators are divided in calling it "amber" or "ambergris." Both are correct. There is no doubt that in the nineteenth century, in reference to odour, the French word *ambre* was synonymous with *ambre gris* or *ambergris* (*grey amber*). This lexical overlap is confirmed in the *Grand dictionnaire universel du XIXe siècle* and in perfume manuals. But in French and English, *ambre*/amber refers in other contexts to different substances. Today, ambergris is often confused with one of seven perfume "families" called the *ambré* (or oriental).[42] Whether floral, spicy, woody, fruity, or some combination thereof, a *parfum ambré*, or *oriental*, does not owe its distinctive character to the aroma of ambergris; it is rather "characterized by the presence of vanillin and labdanum," (Ellena, *The Alchemy of Scent*, 111). This system of categorization had not yet been established in Baudelaire's time, but perfumers of the era do express frustration at the misconception that *ambre* (*gris*) was a boiled down version of the fossilized resin used in jewelry (*ambre jaune*). In 1870, Rimmel claims that such confusion persists, even among perfumers, though Marco Polo correctly identified the source of ambergris in the thirteenth century (384–5). Despite Rimmel's efforts to set the record straight, an 1895 article published in the *Chicago Daily Tribune* once again promises to unravel the "Mystery of Ambergris," via "Curious facts concerning [this] little-known substance" (34).

If the mistaken identity of amber for ambergris further entangles the poem's "confuses paroles," the multiple understandings of the word *amber* (a sticky resin, a rich scent, a warm colour, a gem-like substance, a rare animal product) enrich the sonnet's sensory correspondences within and around the poem. Ambergris is a high-value mainstay of French perfumery that perfume-wearers would have encountered in scented products, as well as in contemporary fiction and poetry. Would poetry-readers and fragrance-sniffers of the era know what ambergris was, how it was procured, how it looked or felt, or even how it smelled? Many would not. Yet most would have understood the name itself, in concert with the three other fragrance materials listed, as associated with the feminine and the exotic, and blended with a scent of familiar religious ritual.

Because of its use in churches, incense was likely the most recognizable word–smell pairing in the group, and one which simultaneously reinforces the poem's evocation of the ideal and the real, the abstract and the material, the sacred (the first line's "temple") and the profane (the last line's fellow secular cosmetic perfume materials – ambergris, benzoin, and musk). Rimmel discusses incense at length in his *Book of Perfumes* (1865), as used in cosmetic practices and sacred rituals of various cultures, in China, India, Tibet, and ancient Greece and Rome. Perfumers and hygienists include incense in their recipes for scented skin toners and wrinkle creams, and for pellets burned in pans (*cassolettes*) to perfume indoor spaces (Bertrand 1809, 103, 188–9, 295; Celnart 1829,

46). Baudelaire concocts a more obvious blend of sacred and sensual fragrance in his later sonnet "Le parfum," (1860), the second piece in the four-part suite "Un fantôme":

> Lecteur, as-tu quelquefois respiré
> Avec ivresse et lente gourmandise
> Ce grain d'encens qui remplit une église
> Ou d'un sachet le musc invétéré?

> Reader, have you sometimes inhaled
> With intoxication and slow greed
> That grain of incense which fills a church,
> Or a sachet containing musk?   (OCI, 39)

This first stanza sets up an olfactory experience to which a different blending of memory and experience will be compared. The rapture of breathing in church incense and musk sachets (both their sensuous proximity and physical consumption reinforced by the rhyme *gourmandise/ église*), links present and past through memory, as does the scent of a lover's body (stanza 2). A shift from the present tense in stanzas one and two, to the continuous past (*imparfait*) in stanzas three and four, shows that these smells – or the verbal evocation of these smells – have indeed stirred memories and facilitated the poet's plunge into the past. The remembered lover's hair (a "living sachet" and "censer of alcoves") and clothing (muslin and velvet), gave off "un parfum de fourrure" ("a fragrance of fur").

In the published poem, a *perfume* of fur replaced an *odour* of fur ("odeur de fourrure") that appeared in the manuscript Baudelaire sent to editor Poulet-Malassis in 1860 (OCI, 902). The choice of *parfum* over *odeur* further strengthens a chain of associations throughout the *Flowers of Evil*, and unites through scent, fragrant churches, sensuous animality, and smelly cats who represent naturally and cosmetically perfumed women.[43] In "Le chat" ("The Cat"), "dangerous perfume" swims around one feline's brown body (OCI, 35). In a longer poem of the same title, the blond and brunette fur of a cat gives off a sweet *perfume* (OCI, 51) that lingers on the poet's hand after just one caress. The final four fragrance words of "Correspondances" – amber, musk, benzoin, and incense – find echo in other poems as well, particularly those more overtly dedicated to women, travel, and displacement. Whether or not the reader knows and recalls the fragrant materials oozing, puffing, and burning from the last stanza, their names alone – then and now – associate the poem with faraway places, passage upon and across the seas, and above all, women's bodies, surpassing nature via their cosmetic embellishment.

With an olfactory bias, it is tempting to read the poem today allegorically, as a commentary on the inadequacy of language dedicated to smell – the forests of symbols and *confuses paroles* being what Baudelaire elsewhere called a "language of flowers and silent things," the scent vapours, the ephemeral miasma which we always traverse, even here, even now, and which we are at odds to describe. Or one might view the entire poem as a classic perfume pyramid, constructed in the form of a sonnet: base notes simmering in the last stanza, below the green heart notes, and sweet head notes, triumphantly corrupting, yet enriching, those fresh aromas as they rise like smoke through the first stanza's metaphorical temple. But such interpretations say more about the reader's connection to the poem than about Baudelaire's relationship to perfume and olfaction. In the context of Baudelaire's era and poetic works, the poem's perfume materials create a reciprocal literary, social, and cultural *sillage* that crosses time and space, and evokes transcendence in the rising smoke of blended thought and sensation, wonder and familiarity. Without illustrating women or their daily perfuming practices, the poem engages with their bodily presence; with other discourse, such as perfume manuals, catalogues, books of receipts, accounts of travel; and with other poems in the collection that, due to their less dulcet aromas, may not initially appear related.

In a more nuanced way, this sonnet, already rich in comparison and analogy, performs a textual phenomenon which fuses it conceptually with the theories of beauty Baudelaire outlined in *Le peintre de la vie moderne*, where fashion is considered a "symptôme du goût de l'idéal," ("symptom of the taste for the ideal"; OCII, 716), and makeup should not cleverly imitate nature but, instead, be worn with candour, to stand out and to stun. Baudelaire sought to recuperate the "art of the toilette" from those "amants équivoques de la nature" ("equivocal lovers of nature"; OCII, 714) who undervalued fashion and adornment (*parure*). Similarly, the final stanza of "Correspondances" infuses a sonnet that announces its subject as Nature, with not just any aromas, but materials used to create fragrant, toiletries, makeup, and fashion accessories. The cosmetic perfume of "Correspondances" manages to bring beauty and transcendence to the poem beyond the obvious textual channelling of synesthesia, in two very different, even contrasting ways. First, perfume materials represent elements of the contingent, transitory, and thus modern world, providing the dose of the real essential to Baudelaire's alchemy of the ideal. At the same time, much as makeup raises humans from their natural, animal state, toward a virtue that is both artificial and supernatural (OCII, 715–17), perfume adorns and lifts the

verses critics have seen as otherwise contingent, allowing then to transcend in a fragrant vapour joining earth to the heavens.

Smelling Flowers of Evil

Charles Baudelaire's status as writer of smells owes as much to neurolo-
gists, psychologists, criminologists, and sexologists, as to literary critics. By the end of the 1800s, a dangerous cluster of aesthetic decadence,
sexual deviance, and hypersensitivity to odours had been ascribed to
artists whose attention to smells exemplified allegedly perilous predi-
lections. The "symptoms" of unhealthy olfactory weaknesses resided
sometimes in biographical anecdotes, but more often in published fiction and poetry, as if scent maladies constituted a contamination of language. When singling out misfit writers who walked a fine line between
genius and degeneration, Cesare Lombroso (1895), Max Nordau (1895),
Havelock Ellis (1905), and many others, branded Baudelaire an *olfactif*.
This nominalization of the French adjective meaning *olfactory* designates
a person with unusual sensitivity to smells. The term and the phenomenon, embraced with pride by writers including Wilde and Symons,
was used pejoratively in much *fin-de-siècle* discourse.[44] In a conference
paper on intellectual superiority and the neurotic presented in 1900
and published in 1903, Dr. Joseph Grasset concluded that Baudelaire
"parait avoir été un olfactif avec perversions sexuelles" ("seems to have
been an *olfactif* with sexual perversions"; *Leçons de clinique*, 694), citing
Bernard who claimed that "[i]l y avait en lui une sorte d'amour maladif des parfums" ("he had a sort of sickly love of perfumes/odours";
694, note 3).[45] Baudelaire's attention to perfume and evocation of stench
were seen as bifurcated manifestations of the same perversion. During
the poet's lifetime and the years shortly thereafter, critics who did not
appreciate his work decried it for being smelly, unhealthy, venomous,
poeticized garbage.[46] By the turn of the century, due in great part to the
poet's olfactory verse, reading Baudelaire and perfuming would eventually be seen as concurrent practices of a decadent mind.

Among evidence presented to justify his diagnosing Baudelaire as suffering from neurosis and insanity (695),[47] were tidbits from the catalogue
of his "sensitive delight and interest in odors" (Havelock Ellis 1905, 76)
that recurred both in Baudelaire's own published work, and the many
biographies and anecdotes that circulated in the decades after his death.

When Marcelin included Baudelaire, who was in the spotlight that
year for his obscenity trial), in a caricature roundup of 1857's notable
fashion, journals, and books, he depicted the poet not only holding but
smelling a "bouquet of Flowers of Evil" (see Figure 2.3). Journalists,

34. *Ch. Baudelaire* respirant un bouquet de *Fleurs du Mal.*

35. *Revenons à nos moutons,* et relisons *les OEuvres complètes d'Arsène Houssaye.*

36. *Charles Monselet* l'accommodant au dernier goût avec le *petit bout de sa lorgnette.*

37. Réimpression de *l'ancien Moniteur,* par *Plon.* 150,000 livraisons 10 centimes. Abonnons-nous vite, la vie est si courte !

38. Apparition du *Monde illustré.* Avantages inouïs offerts aux abonnés : moyennant 18 fr. par an, ils reçoivent, avec le journal, cinqua[...]

39. Depuis qu'il tie[...] accablé de *maux;* ses nouvelles sont trop cru[...] salés.

40. Avez-vous jama[...] de *Saint-Victor,* sur [...] son article sur Angéliq[...]

41. Le principal pe[...] société, intitulée: *Cha[...]*

rtsauf.
remier

isation
guéri-
parfait

)ar les

2.3. Detail from "Revue comique de France 1857" by Émile Marcelin. *Le monde illustré,* 30 January 1858, 72. The image's caption reads "Ch. Baudelaire respirant un bouquet de Fleurs du Mal" ("Ch. Baudelaire inhaling a bouquet of Flowers of Evil").

Image source: gallica.bnf.fr / BnF.

acquaintances, and fans who recongized Baudelaire's smell sensitivity also later contributed to the legend of a forever sniffing Baudelaire
whom others found deviant. In a preface to the 1868 edition of *Les fleurs
du mal*, friend and writer Théophile Gautier described Baudelaire's nose
as fine and delicate, a bit rounded, with quivering nostrils that seem to
detect faraway perfumes (2–3). Charles Toubin also mentioned Baudelaire's well-placed nose, resting on two nostrils, always ready to inflate
themselves (Bandy and Pichois 22). In his droll, yet often poignant
tribute, *Charles Baudelaire intime*, Nadar marvels at Baudelaire's ability
to blend the inspiration of an abominable odour into verbal perfume:
"Par quelle spéciale perversion des sens le poète des *Fleurs du Mal* en
arrivait-il à flairer précisément là pour nous les chanter les aromatiques
effluves du cinname et de la myrrhe?" ("By what special perversion
of the senses did the poet of the *Flowers of Evil* arrive at sniffing precisely there in order to sing for us the aromatic effluvia of cinnamon
and myrrh?"; 20).[48] Nadar later describes the "atmosphères parfumées"
("perfumed atmospheres") of Baudelaire's top-floor flat on the quai
d'Anjou as smelling of musk (40).

Like the cat poems, a much-quoted line from Baudelaire's *Journaux
intimes* provided entertainment for admirers and fodder for those who
found his relationship to smells unwholesome: "Je confondais l'odeur
de la fourrure avec l'odeur de la femme" ("I would confuse the odour
of fur with the odour of women"; OCI, 661). In his 1889 study of smells
in the work of Émile Zola, Léopold Bernard described Baudelaire
as "un autre gourmet d'odeurs" for whom "le monde n'était que miasmes
et senteurs" ("another gourmet of odours" for whom "the world was
nothing but miasmas and fragrances"; 8). Bernard saw Baudelaire as
an olfactory precursor to Zola, stipulating that as a poet, Baudelaire
was always telling his own story, evoking his personal impressions
and emotions, whereas novelist Zola was putting characters in a scene
and explaining their actions and motivations. This tendency to read
poetry as essentially autobiographical was important to the claim that
Baudelaire's relationship to olfaction was unhealthy. When Grasset
(citing Lombroso) reported that Baudelaire preferred stench to the
good odours that "healthy" men enjoy, he claimed that rot, decomposition, and pestilence delighted Baudelaire's nose. Along with "infection," both "rot" and "decomposition" (in adjectival form) appear in
the poem named for decomposing flesh, "Une charogne" (694). Anecdotes about Baudelaire's odour sensitivity were recycled in Europe
and the United States as well. In "Ozolagny" (1922), American psy-
chologist and sexologist James G. Kiernan provides a roundup of publications focused on the diagnostic use of odors in the detection of

degeneracy in the literati. Kiernan defines *ozolagny* or *odor volupty* as a mental state which consists of "sex excitement or satisfaction through odor" (413) and includes Baudelaire among his examples. Grasset also recycled Lombroso's characterization of Baudelaire as having "a very delicate sense of smell" who "perceived the odor of women in dresses" and "could not live in Belgium, he said, because the trees had no fragrance" (28).

The rhetorical synesthesia of Baudelaire's sonnet "Correspondances," widely quoted today in anthropological, medical, cognitive, and literary studies of olfaction, stood as an example of his malady in *fin-de-siècle* studies of an olfactory perversion that tainted the literati, and thus the French language itself. Baudelaire, along with Rimbaud, Huysmans, and most writers considered symbolist or decadent, was held up as an example of a *mattoïde littéraire*[49] who allegedly tinkered with language in order to associate one sense with another through evocation of *audition colorée* (colour audition) and *goût auditif* (auditory taste): "Aux uns, les sons donnent des sensations de couleur…. Les autres entendent des sons là où les pauvres diables comme nous n'éprouvent que des sensations gustatives" ("For some, sounds give a sensation of colour…. The others hear sounds where poor devils like us experience only gustatory sensations") (Grasset 1903, 707–8). Rhetorical synesthesia is, from this perspective, a linguistic regression to animal instinct, and thus an abuse of language. Max Nordau juxtaposed the madness of a poetic language that links words, senses, and emotions, to "cultivated, grammatically articulated language" (139). Lombroso credited Baudelaire as "the first to find new poetic associations in olfactory sense," a symptom of morbid genius, paraphrasing (and embellishing) a line from "Correspondances" as evidence: "perfumes which have the smell of infants' flesh, or of the dawn" (318).[50] Like sense-bending practices, word-blending synesthesia reads as toxic and contagious. Baudelaire's synesthetic writing was, however, eventually praised as a manifestation of his poetic genius, notably in 1832 by Jean Pommier who described Baudelaire's intelligence as penetrating his senses, and his senses as perceiving ideas (*La mystique Baudelaire*, 14–15).[51]

While poems like "Correspondances," "La chevelure," and "Parfum exotique" were key contributors to Baudelaire's unofficial status as "le plus grand poète olfactif de la littérature française" ("the greatest olfactory poet in French literature"; OCI, 846), "Une charogne" fast became a popular hit for its shock value.[52] In an 1859 collection of quips and observations in the "Echos de Paris" section of *Figaro: journal non politique* (6), Alphonse Duchesne identified Baudelaire as the author of "Une charogne" who had just published a poem on the smell of his mistress's hair ("La chevelure"). Duchesne lists the elements of the hair's fragrant "composition" (musk, tar, coconut oil), then wonders – with irony – who would have guessed that Baudelaire had it in him to be a great perfumer and rival of Balzac's fictional César Birotteau. Duchesne suggests that perfumers like Guerlain get together with booksellers to market "Fleurs du mal et le philocome[53] Baudelaire" (*Baudelaire's flowers of evil and hair treatment*).[54]

The Prince of Carrion

Baudelaire knew that the poem "Une charogne" was shaping his notoriety. In a letter to friend and photographer Nadar (14 May 1859) the poet said he was annoyed at being seen as the "Prince des Charognes," when in fact, a good number of his poems smelled of musk and roses.[55] In 1859, Nadar illustrated the visual dimension of Baudelaire's scented atmospheres in "Baudelaire à la charogne" (Figure 2.4), a charcoal and gouache depiction of the poet nearly stumbling upon a rotting animal.[56] The carcass lies legs up, its belly covered in swarms of buzzing flies, wafting fumes, or both, which rise up, blending with the dried leaves of spindly shrubs, then metamorphosing into vertical marks and rejoining to form atmospheric graffiti or sky-writing. Death gives birth to life and words, with the figure of the poet positioned between the carrion-etched "FLEURS DU" looming over his right shoulder, and "MAL" under his left hand. These textual flowers frame the portrait of the Prince of Carrion, simultaneously discovering and orchestrating a synesthetic landscape of decaying flora and fauna; refiguring beauty; representing silent, invisible odour in voiceful, visible words; and turning stench into poetry.

Though Baudelaire did not express an intention to translate perfume into poetry, he did promote a kind of critical synesthesia in the essay "À quoi bon la critique?" (*Salon de 1846*). He urges the art critic to deviate from faithful description or explication when writing about paintings, in favour of a more personal and creative response that today we might call adaptation: "Je crois sincèrement que la meilleure critique est celle qui est amusante et poétique;... Ainsi le meilleur compte rendu d'un tableau pourra être un sonnet ou une élégie. ("I sincerely believe that the best critique is one that is amusing and poetic;... Thus the best review of a painting could be a sonnet or an elegy"; OCII, 418). Nadar's depiction of "Baudelaire à la charogne" offers a similar dynamic of critical reaction, that is, a response to poetry in the form of a caricature. Of course, sonnets and caricatures do not occupy the same register in aesthetic hierarchies, but Baudelaire's chiding ("Tu n'as sans doute pas lu

2.4. *Baudelaire à la charogne.* Nadar, 1859.

Image source: gallica.bnf.fr / BnF.

une foule de choses de moi, qui ne sont que musc et que roses") shows that he did recognize Nadar's gouache as a playful critique via visual interpretation of odour and verse.

Known for his invocation of ambergris, musk, benzoin, incense, flowers, warm skin, tarry hair, fetid exhalations, sulfurous flatulence, and the lingering smell of cat on the hand that caressed it, Baudelaire does not disappoint when it comes to carrion, even if from a purely lexical perspective, the poem contains few smell words. Instead, associative meaning and juxtaposition, connections to other senses, human reactions, and movement, both textual and dramatized, combine to reinforce a looming stench. A monologue in three parts, the poem's first eight stanzas open an invitation to remember, followed by a richly embellished, multi-sensory evocation of a rotting roadside carcass once encountered by the poet and his companion.[57] Like a cosmetic perfume, the story of "Une charogne" unfolds in layers, with the lightness and false sweetness of the first stanza's invitation soon dissipated, eclipsed by the bittersweet description of a strangely beautiful carrion, and anchored in animal rot, the ironic decomposition of *ars poetica*, and the harsh gravity of the last stanza's final line.[58] The rhetorical strategy is familiar. Baudelaire's *memento mori* reads as a sinister adaptation of the poetic seduction tactics recognizable to readers of sixteenth-century *carpe diem* poems, specifically, as many have noted, Ronsard's "Ode à Cassandre" (Tucker 1975; Krause and Martin 1989).

The last four stanzas form a closing argument (more reminiscent of "Quand vous serez bien vieille" than "Mignonne, allons voir"): you will one day be like that carcass, both decomposed and preserved in my verse. "Alors, ô ma beauté! Dites à la vermine / Qui vous mangera de baisers / Que j'ai gardé la forme et l'essence divine / De mes amours décomposés" ("So, my beauty! / Tell the worms who will devour you with kisses / That I preserved the divine form and essence / Of my decomposed loves"; OCI, 32). The poet's pungent words are all the more jarring because of their familiar but disturbing echoes, an uncanny reshaping and revival of Petrarch and Ronsard. The poem's irony resides in the use of a rotting animal carcass to memorialize love, poetry, and their common denominator, beauty. Baudelaire places the poet in a privileged role, as a capable imitator of nature who then goes further, as interpreter, adorner, and transformer, as restorer and guardian of what nature loses, destroys, dissipates, or simply allows to evaporate – life itself and, specifically, life's sensory and sensual experiences.

Baudelaire's use of physical reaction, along with layers of literal and figurative visual cues (including the personified sun and rhetorical flower) seems to be in synchrony with theories of the dominance of vision, and the paucity of scent language. In words, as in Nadar's caricature, smell is captured in a play of sight and images. But this is only part of the story. Scent-memory triggers normally occur in the cause-and-effect order suggested by the term itself: one perceives an odour; the detection of that odour sparks a memory. Here, instead, the poet induces an artificial, voluntary, or more accurately, imposed scent-memory trigger in reverse: he invokes the memory of an odour, and the woman's reaction to it, in his campaign to recreate a malodorous encounter. His invitation, like those of earlier poets, serves as pretext to a temporarily hidden project. In the guise of inviting his companion to share a sensory memory, the poet in fact coerces her to listen to, or to read, his poetic musings on a chance and seemingly mundane event of cosmic, poetic, and philosophical proportions.

The poem's first stanza recalls "Correspondances" in its evocation of interpreting multi-sensorial input, though here it is not *man*, but an individual poetic narrator, making word–smell connections in the context of that most benign of cultivated leisure activities: a couple's morning walk.[59] Despite its dramatization of a recognizable event, this morning stroll has much in common with passing through a forest of symbols. The rotting body, through sight and smell, first shocks then plunges the poet into a contemplation of life, death, and poetry, a contemplation that apparently compels him to revive and share the memory of that shock. Of course, encountering the smell of carcasses on the streets of Paris was not unusual at the time. The Haussmannization of Paris was devised in part to clean up the city, to widen the streets, and to rid them of foul-smelling debris, including excrement and dead animals.[60] Streets roamed by the Second Empire flâneur displayed as much *odorama* as *panorama*. The morbid miasmas of "Élévation" (OCI, 10), the human miasmas of "Le flacon" (OCI, 48), the ooze of a muddy path and foul reek in the shadows of "Au lecteur" (OCI, 1), and all of Baudelaire's more pleasant *parfums exotiques*, made up the smellscape of the poet's Paris.[61] The discovery of a dead animal would probably have had less shock value on the city's streets than in its parks or outskirts, where urbanites who could afford the times sought refuge from such unsavoury sights and smells.[62] It is stumbling upon that carcass outside the throng, then reviving the memory in verse, that – to use Ross Chambers's terms – makes the everyday extraordinary.[63]

Like man's encounter with "forests of symbols" who "observe him with familiar glances" at the beginning of "Correspondances," the initial discovery of carrion is visual: "remember the object that we saw." The startling comparison of the rotting animal to a woman's body, and suggestion of *odor di femina* ("Les jambes en l'air/Comme une femme lubrique"/"Legs in the air like a lubricious woman") leaves precisely what it is that legs so positioned might reveal, to the reader's visual and olfactory imagination. Even the sky was watching (*regardait*) the "superb carcass" blossom (*s'épanouir*) like a flower. The woman's reaction (nearly passing out) attests to, but does not describe, the stench. Only the generic *puanteur* (stink), one of those nouns emblematic of olfactory language's infamous lack of specificity, speaks directly for the smell of "Une charogne," and by a clearly established association, the natural, unperfumed smell of woman. Other words – *pourriture* (rot), *exhalaison* (exhalation/emission), *ventre putride* (putrid belly/

gut), *ordure* (garbage), *infection* (infection), *amours décomposés* (decomposed love/love affairs) and the word *charogne* itself – bespeak offensive odours, and in so doing, link smell to other senses and sensations. Stanzas 5–9, all recounted in a hypnotic *imparfait*, find the poet (and probably not the woman to whom he speaks) immersed in the memory of the carcass: its sound of buzzing flies, which becomes musical; its movement of feasting larvae, which becomes wind and ocean waves; the sight of it, which up close looks like a forgotten sketch on a painter's canvas. The poet's imagination makes art of this rot.

The contradictory nature of the human relationship to odour (the link to animal behaviour, along with the connection to language) suggests Baudelaire's project of finding the beauty in unexpected pairings and intersections, and, as mentioned earlier, the discovery of what Chambers has called, in reference to other poems, the *insolite* in the everyday. Scents are, like human time, fleeting. In "Une charogne," the sight and stench of death transforms a morning walk into a hypnotic contemplation of time and matter. In other poems, too, Baudelaire's allusions to odour mark, then blur, conventional borders: between the sacred and the profane ("Le balcon"); between the self and other ("La chevelure"; "Le flacon"). Odour provides not only temporal and spatial overlaps, but also a merging of sensory experience and abstraction. The most perfumed, most intimate, and exoticist poems also present perfume at the threshold of interpersonal and geographical border-crossings ("Parfum exotique"; "Invitation au voyage"; "La chevelure"; "Le cygne"; "À une malabaraise"). Mapping these scent trails beyond the language of poetry leads to exploration of global France, colonial enterprise, trade, industry, and commerce. The perfume materials themselves (musk, benzoin, ambergris) were not all household words, nor were their origins widely understood, yet whether or not the reader knows and recalls these smells, their names alone – then and now – suggest passage beyond national borders, across and upon the seas. Whether placed at the centre of poems like "La chevelure," more subtly rising from the final stanza of "Correspondances," or incorporated in layers of real and metaphorical carrion, the natural and cosmetic sillage of women facilitates both transport and transcendence via the diffusion of olfactory language and experience in Baudelaire's fragrant verse.

Baudelaire's references to odour push his words to resonate far beyond the space of the poem, and beyond its time and place of composition. At the same time, the near absence of qualification, definition, explanation, or description of scents and scented matters serve to infuse seemingly banal terms with unusual force. In the context of lyric poetry, the repetition of such generic nouns as *parfum* and *fleur*, where more uncommon or specific language could have been used, releases these words from their referents, pulling them from the direction of representative, prosaic meaning to transcendent, poetic evocation. Take, for example, "Élévation," a poem which mentions both good and bad odours, "morbid miasmas" and "superior airs," and celebrates the ability to rise above it all, to understand effortlessly "the language of flowers and silent things" (OCI, 10).

In such poems, fragrances are quiet but powerful and expansive. Perfume speaks for itself but does not explain itself. Transcendence of the poet's soul, like that of the poet's journeying heart in "Le guignon," leads to understanding without translation of this mysterious language: "Mainte fleur épanche à regret / Son parfum doux comme un secret / Dans les solitudes profondes" "Many a flower regretfully pours out / Its perfume like a secret / In profound solitudes"; OCI, 17). But as signifiers of fragrance, Baudelaire's *fleurs* and *parfums* bottle up the scent. Flowers and perfumes speak, even pour out their silent language, yet the words flower and perfume – for all their simplicity – remain mysterious, inscrutable, their fragrance – but not their meaning – understood, but not translated, in the textual dynamics of poetry and in the space of the mind.

As we have seen in "Correspondances," Baudelaire does identify scented matter by name. There are the biblical and cosmetic scents of spikenard, incense, and myrrh in "Le balcon"; the exotic fragrances of musk and Havana tobacco in "Sed non satiata"; and of course, the overtly trans-sensory evocations of amber, musk, benzoin, and incense of "Correspondances." Baudelaire's poems also mention the intimate smells radiating from the human body, breath, and hair ("Tout entière"; "Le parfum"; "Le balcon"). This double invasion of privacy – spreading the smell around and smelling up close – may be what makes some readers squeamish, others ecstatic, about Baudelaire's scented poetry. One could argue that any references to hair and tresses also evoke the idea of perfume, as do objects: bottles, handkerchiefs, gloves, materials like resin, and even mud (which in nineteenth-century Paris was quite smelly).[64] Similarly, the vocabulary of atmosphere and breathing – words like *exhalaison, respirer, vapeur*, and even *air* – link to smell. But like *ordure, miasme*, and *puanteur*, the word *parfum* and its derivatives appear frequently yet somewhat generically throughout the *Fleurs du mal*, seldom qualified, and if so, in ways resistant to literal olfactory translation: *dangerous perfume* ("Le chat"); *the perfume of your blood* ("Le balcon"). Flowers bloom dozens of times but are rarely named. In other words, most of Baudelaire's scented language resists unequivocal olfactory referentiality. Where no allusions to odour occur, the sniffing reader becomes alert to the other senses, particularly to the cold temperature of Baudelaire's poems. The least scented works conjure frosty climates: the snow and avalanche of "Le goût du néant"; the cold kiss of death in "Le revenant"; the frigid cruelty of an icy sun in "De profundis clamavi"; the polar chill of "Chant d'automne" which renders the poet's heart a frozen, red block. "Le goût du néant" also directly identifies the absence of smell: "Le Printemps adorable a perdu son odeur" ("Adorable Springtime has lost its odour"; OC1, 76).

Though, as in "Correspondances," the cultural resonance of olfactory language may not be obvious to all readers, the everyday history of perfume and miasma plays out quite overtly on the pages of other works. The prose poem "À une heure du matin," for example, opens with the narrator's relief at having left crowded, public spaces for the privacy of his home ("Finally! Alone!"), where he seeks distance from the "vapeurs corruptrices du monde" ("corrupting vapors of the word/of others"). The poet notes that he has neglected a basic hygienic safeguard, having shaken dozens of hands, "et cela sans avoir pris la precaution d'acheter des gants" ("and that without having taken the precaution of buying gloves"; OC1, 288).

Scent-related words appear in many of Baudelaire's comparisons, yet those comparisons do not serve as a substitute for description. "There are perfumes/smells dulcet as oboes, green as prairies" ("Correspondances"), but they go unnamed, it could be argued, because the poem is not about those specific smells; it is about the idea of their synesthetic connections. The associative movement in language so often attributed to Baudelaire relies upon the reader's intellectual, sensorial, and experiential connection to smells evoked in poetry. Baudelaire's odour language functions as a sort of literary antimatter, a poetic device with a reverse charge and tremendous energy, ignited in collision with the reader's experience and imagination. With so little olfactory ekphrasis in the *Fleurs du mal*, the reader must supply the scent memories. "Une charogne" is verse built around a smell, yet neither the *charogne* nor its metaphorical flower is described in the terms of odour. Neither serves as a scent-memory trigger in the traditional sense, for the implied reader, or for the woman to whom the poem is addressed. On the other hand, the reader's mind may be transported to Ronsard's rose, or to Desbordes-Valmore's richly scented "Roses de Saadi" (where *sillage* itself serves as proof and a reminder of love), or to Baudelaire's "stinking darkness" in "Au lecteur" (OCI, 5), or to other sensory correspondences in his work, such as the "fabric that speaks a silent language, like flowers, like skies, like setting suns" ("La chambre double"; OCI, 280), and in so doing, communicates with the poems "Élévation" and "Le guignon."

To posit that any reader who has smelled a dead animal in the sun most likely makes an olfactory connection upon reading the title, is not as speculative as one might think. Recent research made possible by advances in neuroimaging suggests that "reading words with strong olfactory associations in their meaning activates olfactory regions of the brain" (González et al. 2006, 908). In a 2006 study, Spanish-speaking subjects silently read two sixty-word groups. One group was made up of olfactory words, that is, "words with strong olfactory associations" (907), while the other word group, with weak olfactory associations (the Spanish words for *coat*, *entourage*, and *needle*, for example), served as a control. Neuroimaging showed that regardless of their "hedonic odour valance" (their being pleasant or unpleasant), reading general terms like *cologne*, *flower*, *perfume*, *rotten*, *stinking*, and more specific words with strong olfactory associations (*armpit*, *cinnamon*, *garlic*, *patchouli*, *sewer*, *trash*), "automatically and immediately activates their semantic networks in the olfactory cortices" (909). Likewise, the processing of metaphorical language has been shown to be "perceptually grounded," that is, the brain responds similarly to literal textural and sensory words ("rough") and their metaphorical doubles (a "rough" day) (Lacey et al. 2012). In other words, the long-perceived division between language and the senses, thus far fairly resistant to erosion by cultural tides, may quickly crumble in light of what the neurologist now sees, and what the poet and reader have perhaps always sensed.

Because of their common yet elusive referentiality, the words *parfum*, *fleur*, and even *miasme* and *puanteur*, play a crucial role in the experience of Baudelaire's poetry, leading the reader to interpret, in mind and body, within a poetic space that joins physicality and the senses with abstraction and transcendence. His writing of basic (and base) olfactory terms accompanies other literary acts associated with the modernity of Baudelaire's work: the flâneur's ability to simultaneously inhabit and interiorize the city, to penetrate and be penetrated by others; the re-composition of traditional generic conventions; the recycling of Petrarchan elements to create a uniquely Baudelairean grotesque. As William Olmsted asserts, "[n]owhere in Baudelaire's poetry perhaps, does the effort to seize the transitory – 'dont les métamorphoses sont si fréquentes' ('whose metamorphoses are so frequent') – achieve greater force and irony than in 'Une charogne'" (62). Olfactory evocations galvanize this poetic effort to seize the transitory, with both irony and force. The repetition of smell-related terms lends them weight. Yet odours themselves are fleeting and resistant to words. Baudelaire's language of olfaction contributes to what Claire Lyu has identified as "the clash between weight and lightness at the core of 'Spleen et Idéal'" (81).

A recurrence of the generic words *fleur* and *parfum*, with emphasis on their silence, paradoxically pulls them out of the ordinary, infuses them with a heady strength, and reinforces an oppositional harmony of abstraction and sensation: the words are grounded and yet they soar. In this way, the *confuses paroles* of odour–language pairings do not always lead to disorientation, disorder, and miscommunication; they also foster mixing, blending, and shared understanding. The ostensibly solipsistic or *sui generis* correlation of objects and smell words belies a dynamic process of sensorial reading sparked by even the most generic lexicon. Similarly, the power and mobility of smell words in the final stanza of "Correspondances" give dimension to a seemingly linear enumeration, through a linguistic *sillage* that stirs the senses, the memory, and the imagination.

Chapter Three

Confused Words?

The much-discussed weakness of word–smell correlations in modern French is intriguing, given that the nineteenth century's burgeoning perfume industry was chronicled and promoted in print, via trade manuals, etiquette books, newspaper articles, and advertisements. These publications developed alongside an abundance of medical writing on smell, and an impressive number of literary works both celebrated and infamous for their evocations of odours on the page. The imprecision and confusion of smell–language pairings were documented by specialists in nineteenth-century France whose work, for reasons practical or aesthetic, depended at least in part on communication about odours.

This chapter focuses on how writers demonstrated attention to olfactory language in three distinct, but interrelated, forms of nineteenth-century discourse: medical treatises dedicated to the promotion of olfaction as a diagnostic tool; manuals for perfumers seeking a common language of odour classification; and a novel that borrowed heavily from those perfume manuals, J.-K. Huysmans's 1884 *À rebours*. These works show that writers of fiction and nonfiction alike were communicating about smell as never before, yet experts in fields from medicine to perfumery were conspicuously, sometimes apologetically, attributing imprecision in their work to difficulty describing odours with words, while relying on one another to find those words.

While medical practitioners in France, England, and the United States had long advocated "the possibility of diagnosticating certain diseases by smells" (Seguin 1877, 3), they also grappled with the elusive language of such diagnoses. As Dr. James Stewart Jewell, president of the American Neurological Association, put it during a discussion at the group's 1877 meeting: "There is one disease, namely *milk sickness*,[1] in which the odor is very remarkable; any one who has ever smelled it will never forget it. Of course, it is impossible to describe it, unless there is some other odor like it, with which we are all familiar" (Seguin 1877, xxxiii). In his six-volume index of medical terms, Dr. H. Sharples expressed a similar, paradoxical loss for words when describing the smell of milk sickness: "The breath has a peculiar odor, which can neither be mistaken nor forgotten, but which is impossible to describe, and this is the symptom most relied on to distinguish milk sickness from all other diseases" (28).[2] A 2011 article, "Advances in Electronic-Nose Technologies Developed for Biomedical Applications" (Wilson et al.), acknowledges "a long history of human odors being used for disease diagnosis" (1109), dating back to Hippocrates (400 BCE), and expanding in nineteenth-century Europe before and during the advancement of germ theory. A table summarizing descriptive aromas used over centuries for diagnostic purposes illustrates the linguistic problem that Ackerman, Barnes, Corbin, Drobnick, Gibbons, Rindisbacher, Rodaway, Sagarin, and so many others have identified.[3]

While it is quite likely that a medical practitioner could perceive the odours, it would be difficult to rely on these somewhat generic qualifiers to sort out specific diseases: *bad, fetid, foul, offensive, putrid, rank, strong, unpleasant.* On the other hand, analogies and comparisons might have made some conditions easily recognizable to those familiar with specific smelly materials: *dried malt or hops, stale beer, over-ripe camembert, butcher shop, fishy, freshly plucked feathers, horsey, newly mown clover.* Other precise qualifiers would be useful only to those who had already acquired specialized knowledge (*dimethyl sulfide*), or who lived when particular diseases were so rampant and untreated that their accompanying odours would have been regularly encountered: *pox stench, gouty odor.*

At least one late eighteenth-century doctor dedicated to sniffing out human emanations was acutely aware of these lexical limitations. In 1790, Jean-Joseph Brieude implored fellow physicians to sniff out diseases. Before delving into the more disagreeable odours of abscess and decay, Brieude's *Mémoire sur les odeurs que nous exhalons, considérées comme signes de la santé et des maladies* (*Memoir on the Odours We Exhale, Considered as Signs of Health and Sickness*) offers a taxonomy of healthy human smells, subject to variables of age, sex, climate, passions, and diet; but he weakens his own argument by concluding that it is impossible to communicate about odours.[4] According to Brieude, consumption of onion and garlic produces the Quercinois's heavy reek, while the dairy-loving Auvergnat radiates an aroma of souring whey. Anger and terror give off a fetid sweat, especially in the armpits; and the wind and stool of frightened individuals are unbearable to smell. Ingestion of foods like asparagus may inflect the odour of urine, just as garlic and truffle reveal themselves in perspiration. Grown men have a strong odour that distinguishes them from women, whose sweat is weaker and sweetish. The elderly, nuns, and convalescents also give off a faint, somewhat sweet fragrance, but if in hospital, they may also smell of lice. One's profession, too, can nuance a normal, healthy body odour. Brieude reminds the reader that anyone can distinguish the odour of a tanner from that of a cow herder from that of a grape harvester. Like the fetid smell of certain corporeal locales – hair, feet, and armpits – these occupationally induced aromas, though often unpleasant, are not cause for alarm. Medical doctors should acquaint themselves with these baseline odours, in order to distinguish them from the dangerous exhalations of sickness and disease, which Brieude sorts out according to their provenance: breath, perspiration, stool, urine, vomit, pus, open wounds, and smells characteristic of specific afflictions, with their variously situated oozes and coughed-up discharges.

Throughout Brieude's painstaking attention to diagnostic acuity, he is palpably aware of lexical limitations. From the beginning he warns: "Personne n'ignore que l'odorat est un sens très-imparfait, et que les sensations qu'il nous transmet sont très-confuses. À l'exception de quelques odeurs très-suaves ou fortes, dont l'impression se grave distinctement dans notre entendement, les notions qui résultent des odeurs mixtes sont très-vagues et peu claires ("Nobody is unaware of the fact that smell is a very imperfect sense, and that the sensations it transmits to us are very confused. With the exception of some very agreeable or very strong odours, the notions that are the result of mixed smells are very vague and hardly clear"; xlvi). Brieude cautions that, although the quantity of distinctive odours associated with the human body is infinite, the words to describe them remain insufficient. Of intestinal festering, he warns: "Ces genres de putridité purulente ont des nuances de l'infini" ("These types of purulent putridness have infinite nuances"; lxi). Yet language is of little use in classifying such dauntingly numerous smells: "En voyant beaucoup de malades, on apprend à connoître [sic] des pus de toutes les odeurs, que l'on sait distinguer sans pouvoir dire comment" ("By seeing many sick patients, one learns to recognize all the odours of pus, and one knows how to distinguish them, without being able to say how"; lxi). It is not vocabulary, but practice, that will engrave each odour in a doctor's imagination.

It may at first seem odd that an argument for the importance of smell in diagnoses would so quickly make concessions to a relatively crude olfactory vocabulary. Brieude apparently gave this linguistic lacuna quite a bit of thought. He justifies his shortage of words by evoking a long-standing lack of interest in smell, an observation that continues to intrigue researchers to this day. After explaining that the sense of smell in humans is not highly refined, Brieude notes what philosophers had been saying for centuries, the very problem his own article seeks to change: "Nous exerçons peu ce sens, et nous analysons très-imparfaitement les perceptions qu'il fait naître en nous" ("We use this sense very little, and we analyse imperfectly the perceptions it engenders in us"; xlvi).

Indifference to smell in daily life is part of the problem; inattention to the language of smell is another. Brieude's characterization of limited olfactory language will be reiterated throughout the nineteenth century and beyond:

> Quand on auroit surmonté tous ces obstacles, et que l'on aurait acquis sur les odeurs des idées claires dont la chaîne seroit liée par habitude, l'on seroit encore très-embarrassé pour se faire entendre, parce que les mots manquent pour les exprimer. La langue française, ainsi que les autres langues vivantes et mortes ont très-peu d'expressions pour ren-dre les sensations de l'odorat…. Il est donc très-difficile de se former une idée claire et distincte de chaque odeur. Il est en même temps presque impossible de pouvoir transmettre aux autres les connoissances que l'on acquiert, par la disette des mots propres à les désigner. Les livres et les maîtres nous instruisent très-peu sur ces matières. Il faut s'exercer soi-même auprès des malades, et il faut avoir passé nombre d'années dans les airs infectes de leurs appartemens, avant d'avoir acquis l'habitude d'un signe aussi utile.

> Once one has surmounted all these obstacles, and has acquired a clear idea of odours whose chain will be linked by practice, one will still have a lot of trouble being understood, because we lack words to express them. The French language, as well as other living and dead languages, has very few expressions for the sensations of smell…. Thus it is very difficult to form a clear and distinct idea of each odour. It is likewise almost impossible to transmit to others the knowledge one acquires, due to the scarcity of suit-able words to designate them. Books and teachers instruct us very little in these matters. One must practice oneself beside the sick, one has to have spent years in the foul air of their living quarters, before being accustomed to reading this useful sign. These are the reasons that prevent me from delivering my ideas with clarity. (Brieude 1789, xlvii)

Despite his insistence on the insufficiency of smell language, Brieude does not advise practitioners to generate a new lexical apparatus. Instead, doctors should develop a nose, so to speak, in order to forge a direct connection between perception and cognition. They should read the wordless language of bodily exhalations and cultivate, in response, a set of embodied diagnostic tools. How, then, does Brieude communicate about smell in his own treatise? He relies on a relatively limited and overlapping selection of adjectives to describe healthy and unhealthy odours alike. Babies give off a *bitter*, *milky*, or *verminous* odour; their feces smells *fetid*. But drunk individuals smell *fetid*, too, and putrid infections smell *bitter*. Each disease has a signature *putrid* smell that Brieude urges doctors to recognize, though he provides limited distinguishing descriptors. Respiration nuanced by pleuritic (*phthisique*) lung discharge or asthmatic spittle differs from the rotten-egg breath of ingestion gone wrong. Acid, acrid, bitter, cadaverous, disagreeable, fetid, foul, putrid – these are the rather generic words recycled in Brieude's catalogue of healthy and harmful human exhalations. He deems the worst smells *insupportables* (intolerable/unbearable), the best *suave* (meaning agreeable, smooth, sweet, dulcet – a term still often used in wine tasting and perfume sampling). Suave, says Brieude, are the pleasant exhalations of adolescents and young women, a fragrance the poets have compared to roses. Unlike the poets, though, Brieude does not rely on a rhetoric of comparison or simile in his own text.[5] He more often adheres to a restricted repertoire of adjectives not specific to smell (lymphatic transudation is *bitter*); adjectives related to comparable smelly matter (the consumptive's stool smells *cadaverous*); and tautological nominal references to smelly matter itself (urine can smell of *asparagus*). Brieude would have attributed the memorability of Marcel Proust's mention of asparagus-scented urine (almost one hundred years later in *Combray*) to the fact that this is a commonly encountered smell, already etched in the reader's mind from first-hand experience.[6] Doctors should similarly commit to memory the many odours of their trade.

Brieude's consciousness-raising mission did not change the minds or habits of medical doctors overnight. Ninety-five years later, Ernest Monin calls his *Odeurs du corps humain dans l'état de santé et dans l'état de maladie* (*Odours of the Human Body in Health and Sickness*) a "nouveau chapitre de séméiologie" ("new chapter in semiology"; 1886, 3). To achieve his goal, "la réhabilitation en médecine de l'observation olfactive, objet du plus injuste discrédit" ("The rehabilitation in medicine of olfactory observation, a practice most unjustly discredited"; 1986, 3 and 9), Monin champions the precision and practicality afforded by scientific observation and clinical attention to odours,[7] without lamenting lexical imprecision. In the prolegomenon to a revised version of his treatise (*Les odeurs du corps humain: causes et traitements*, 1903), Monin refers to odour as a language unto itself: "L'odeur et l'âme de la clinique; son langage éveille, obscurément, dans l'esprit du praticien, la première idée du diagnostic et fouette, en quelque sorte, l'observation intime" ("Odor is the clinic's subtle soul; its language arouses, obscurely, in the spirit of the practitioner, the first diagnostic idea and stirs, as it were, intimate observation"; 1903, 16). He disagrees with Jean-Jacques Rousseau's belief that smell is the sense of imagination (1903, 6), insisting instead that after reading his chapters, practitioners will understand that smell is fact-based, that the information gleaned through smell is no less absolute than that furnished by sound, sight, or touch. Furthermore, Monin accepts the paradoxical nature of olfaction in human beings: "L'odeur est le plus *animal*, mais aussi le plus *suggestif* de nos cinq sens; les impressions qu'ils laisse restent étroitement liés aux circonstances.... Ni le son, ni la vue, ne sont, comme l'odorat, capables d'évoquer l'idée, de ressusciter la connaissance à un dégré comparable" ("Smell is the most *animal* and the most *evocative* of the five senses: the impressions it leaves remain closely connected to its circumstances.... Neither sound nor sight are as capable as smell of evoking ideas, of resuscitating knowledge/awareness"; 1903, 19). For Monin, smell may not be the sense of imagination, but it is the sense of knowledge and ideas.

While Brieude would most likely have concurred with Sagarin's claim that olfaction is a science without a language, Monin was less preoccupied with the alleged shortage or inexactitude of smell descriptors at his disposal. In contrast to Brieude, who consistently focuses on the frustrating inadequacy of smell words, Monin almost joyfully advocates bypassing the problem by reading the language of odour itself. Though he shares Brieude's opinion that practice makes perfect in olfactory diagnosis, his embrace of smell's mystery and intimacy aligns him more with poets than with physicians. Monin asserts that the works of contemporary writers, especially novelists Henry Céard, Alphonse Daudet, Guy de Maupassant, and Émile Zola, reveal the authors as up-to-date on medical discovery. Yet his own prose indicates a two-way street; that medical writing is itself influenced by fiction and poetry: "Avec l'habitude acquise, les narines médicales frémissent sans cesse, cherchant à noter les mystérieuses correspondances et les secrets affinités des symptômes odorants, surpris dans la variété des nuances infinies" ("With the acquired habit, medical nostrils ceaselessly quiver, seeking to note the mysterious correspondences and the secret affinities of odorous symptoms, stunned by their infinite nuances"; 1903, 16). Words like *quiver*, *infinite nuances*, *secret affinities*, and *mysterious correspondences* overlap with language present in works of fiction known for their olfactory references and ekphrasis. Monin in fact sets up a correspondence between his own writing and literature when he invokes a sort of *fleur du mal*, the mating ritual of the foul-smelling conophallus flower. Also called *amorphophallus*, and more commonly known as corpse flower due to its rotten-meat smell, this is one of the plants that protagonist Des Esseintes (*À rebours*, 1884) has delivered to his home for his collection of seemingly artificial flowers.[8] Monin follows the conophallus vignette by invoking a different flower of evil, citing seven perfume-infused lines from "Correspondances," by the "subtle poet" Baudelaire (1903, 6).

Having absorbed poetic language into his medical prose, Monin further quotes fiction writers to reinforce his principles of odour reception and to provide examples of specific diseases, conditions, and odour phenomena. Like other scientists of the time, he uses the term *onde odorante* (odour wave) to describe the presence of smells around us, noting that these waves can be difficult to decipher, especially when they intermingle (1903, 18). His argument, above all, concerns the relationship between smell and intelligence. Invoking lines from the 1832 novel *Louis Lambert*, Monin deems Balzac prescient in connecting a refined sense of smell to acute intelligence. Later, a passage from Zola's *La terre* serves as evidence in Monin's discussion of *spermaphobie*, a feminine neurosis which causes even the most innocent women to perceive the "hypersécrétion spermatique" ("spermatic hyper-secretion") that certain men's entire bodies exhale (1903, 273–4).

How, then, to communicate the qualities of so many smells from doctor to doctor? "Le nez doit faire son éducation soi-même: c'est un anarchiste" ("The nose must educate itself: it is an anarchist"; 1903, 24), claims Monin, conceding that the sensations of smell are difficult to evoke, while still promoting an "olfactory education" as part of the medical curriculum. Here he turns from medicine to perfumery, reprinting a page-long passage from Piesse's *Les odeurs, les parfums, et les cosmétiques*. Monin does not mention it, but in the passage cited, Piesse was making the case for a classification system of notes for perfumers, who had hundreds of smells to memorize, much as Monin was advancing a would-be taxonomy of human odours. Acknowledging Zwaardemaker's quality-based odour classification system,[9] Monin nonetheless follows a schema close to Brieude's. Instead of cataloguing the odours themselves (putrid, sweet, etc.), he organizes his study by corporeal provenance, beginning with baseline "normal" odours of skin, perspiration, and breath (nuanced by age, sex, hair colour, profession, etc.), then moving on to the bodily excretions, conditions, or diseases that modify human aromas.

It would be impractical to reorganize Monin's information according to smell descriptors. Like Brieude, he relies on a pool of familiar adjectives, including *fétide, horrible, infecte, nauséabonde*, and *putride*. But he very often supplements these descriptors of corporeal effluvia with more colourful vocabulary, illustrative examples, and comparisons. The smell of gangrenous expectoration is comparable to that of recently mixed gypsum plaster, its odour "tue littéralement les mouches" ("literally kills flies"; 1903, 177). Poisoning by the œnanthe plant produces vomit with a disagreeable *sui generis* odour, which Monin further qualifies, likening it to grilled celery (1903, 212). Penile growths, ulcerations, and discharge (due to chancres, cancroids, herpes) have a characteristic repellent odour with a variable gamut of intensities, ranging from cooked crayfish to old Roquefort (1903, 299). Still, more often than not, he uses imprecise and relative descriptors such as *désagréable*, reserving his most subjective and condemning assessment – *insupportable* (intolerable) – for the emotionally altered wind and stool of frightened people and hysterics, along with other smells specifically attributed to women. Intolerable are the odours of post-partum vaginal discharge, and the mouldy breath of menstruating women, as noted by a member of the Neurological Society of London, "société qui compte dans son sein beaucoup de femmes" ("a society which has among its members many women"; 1903, 131).

It is not surprising that Monin summons qualifiers associated with disgust and moral judgment when referring to intimate smells, real or imagined, of women. Brieude and Monin were just two among countless medical practitioners and hygiene enthusiasts who took for granted that one's baseline body odour was a readable indicator of age, sex, race, skin[10] and hair colour, and social status, and who thus, in a circular way, used smell to bolster their constructions of social identity.[11] Similarly, the modification of natural or healthy odours could be read as signs of both physical and moral corruption. Thus, smell descriptors for diseases deemed socially repugnant often seem more creative than objective. The syphilitic's nasal exhalation has "une odeur spermatique fade et écœurante, assez comparable à celle du merlan frais" ("an insipid, nauseating spermatic smell comparable to that of fresh whiting fish"; 1903, 119). Vaginal mucus and the overall scent of a woman, or *odor di femina* (a much-discussed topic of the era) are described as highly sensitive to nerves and emotion: "Les affections morales exercent, sur la sécrétion du mucus, une influence analogue à celle que nous signalons pour la peau" ("Moral affectations exert, on the secretion of mucus, an influence on [vaginal] secretions analogous to those we have signaled for skin"; 275). The concern here is not disease per se, but rather coitus and masturbation, which amplify the *odor di femina*, and certain emotional states that render the odour of woman repulsive.

At the time Monin published his treatise, the emerging field of neurology had established strong connections between female sexual abnormalities, neurosis, hysteria, and smells. Fliess and Freud would soon expand on Charcot's study of hysterics, further emphasizing the nose, smells, and smell sensitivity in their diagnosis and treatment, as would pioneering sexologists, including Havelock Ellis. As we will see in further chapters, much of the language of medicine and hygiene associated with odours, women, and contagion will be adapted to discourse on women and perfume when the modern perfume industry takes off in the nineteenth century. As increasing numbers of women could afford to wear perfume, purveyors of health and etiquette advice warned of the physical and moral perils brought on by selection of the wrong fragrance. Misuse and overuse of perfume endangered not only the wearer but also the innocent bystanders contaminated by this new, commercially obtained *odor di femina*. Such hygienic and cosmetic overlap explains in part why Monin devotes several pages to perfume in his book on human bodily odours. His stated intention is to discuss the effect of perfumes on the organism, a topic of increasing interest throughout the century. But he also takes time to summarize (very briefly) the history of perfume, noting that while it originally accompanied religious and death rituals, women eventually started using it to attract men and to mask and purify bad odours. In closing this section on perfume-induced maladies, germ-fighting fragrances, home fumigation, and personal perfuming, Monin laments the rise of the artificial perfume industry, which he sees as a blow to the distinctly French production of natural perfume ingredients (1903, 47–8).

The entire detour into perfumery was possibly motivated by self-interest. A prolific author, Monin had recently published the first edition of his beauty manual (*Hygiène de la beauté*, 1886), in which he deals extensively with perfumes. Since cosmetic perfume was indeed an outgrowth of medicine and hygiene, many medical tracts discussed the use of fragrance products. Advances in nineteenth-century chemistry, medicine, and perfumery are inevitably entwined. More unconsciously perhaps, Monin's attention to perfume reveals a vestigial fear of miasmas, transferred to cosmetic fragrances, especially in the late nineteenth century. Because perfume enters the body through the nose, mouth, and skin, like mephitic effluvia, it might correspondingly unbalance the body and the mind.

Civilizing the Nose

Perfumers, chemists, and medical practitioners of the era all faced similar lexical challenges. In his 1755 treatise on the chemistry of taste and odours, Polycarpe Poncelet outlined his theory of smell harmony, with a plan to sketch out principles of olfactory music. For Poncelet, words for smelly objects (orange blossom, jasmine, rose) were insufficient to characterize basic smells. He sought a reliable system, across ingredients and among sniffers, much like that of the musical scale of notes for musicians. His project was nipped in the bud because, despite an infinite variety of perceptible odour tones, he could find names for only two – sweet and foul. Poncelet attributed the problem to either a dearth of olfactory language or to negligence on the part of physiologists who failed to observe odours (238).

Throughout the nineteenth century, perfumers and chemists continued to seek a common vocabulary for aroma classification.[12] As late as 1895, in his presentation of taxonomical systems for perfumers (*Le nouveau manuel complet du parfumeur*, vol. 1), Pradal observed that experts had still not agreed upon a definitive common language of categorization: "Aucune des classifications proposées n'a été admise d'une façon générale" ("None of these proposed classifications has been generally accepted"; 16). Good and bad smells are rather easy to name: *parfums* or *odeurs suaves* for agreeable smells and *puanteurs* (*stenches*) or *odeurs infectes* (*foul*, *revolting*, though literally, *infected* or *contaminated*) for rank smells. Beyond that, distinctions are more difficult to articulate. Many perfumers at the time were still reverting to the seven categories that Swedish botanist Carolus Linnaeus had developed in 1752: aromatic (violet, nutmeg, vanilla), fragrant (lily, tuberose, jasmine), ambrosial (civet, musk, amber), alliaceous (garlicky), hircine (goaty), repulsive, and nauseating.[13] These groupings, like those of Aristotle, on which they were based (pungent, sweet, harsh, astringent, rich [succulent/savory], fetid), imply a convergence or confusion of taste and smell, inherent in even the most expert vocabulary of olfaction. The lexical blending of different sense modalities long preceded Baudelaire and others, who celebrated the rhetorical fusion now called synesthesia.[14] But Linnaeus, unlike Baudelaire, was not performing a poetic celebration of sensorial blending, exchange, or expansion. Instead, his was a project of organization and control.

Attempts at smell classification by influential perfumers Piesse and Rimmel took into account the movement and dimensionality of smells, as well as their correspondences with other sensorial perceptions (see Figure 3.1).

Piesse ranked agreeable odours according to volatility (their rate of evaporation, thus dissipation when released into the air), a phenomenon he likened to the vibration of sound waves: "Les ondes sonores qui se propagent le plus lentement produisent les sons les plus forts; les ondes odorantes qui se propagent le plus lentement produisent les odeurs les plus puissantes" ("The sound waves that spread the most slowly produce the loudest sounds; the odour waves that spread most slowly produce the strongest odours"; *Les odeurs, les parfums, et les cosmétiques* 1865, 32). Piesse's volatility scale foreshadowed the perfume pyramid that would later be used (and is still used today) to visualize the notes in fragrance blends: head note, heart notes, base notes.[15] Perfumers knew that the heavier notes would last longer and enhance the longevity of the entire blend. Patchouli would at least temporarily anchor citron,[16] a note that alone would burn away more quickly. Piesse's list provided a time-saving device for perfumers, who could consult the chart without opening their scent vials to make sure their blends were balanced.

Rimmel also offered lists and charts that would save the perfumer time in the selection of ingredients for increasingly popular fragrance blends, called *bouquets* (as opposed to single-note floral, or *soliflore*, perfumes). In a system resembling classification of colours, Rimmel categorized pleasant odours under general headings (*séries* or classes), analogized to primary colours (an odour "type"), and to which all other odours were secondary. Jasmine is a primary scent, lily-of-the-valley and ylang-ylang its related secondary scents; acacia and syringa, secondary scents to the primary orange flower. Rose is a primary odour, but geranium, eglantine, and rhodium have similar characteristics. The fruity category includes pineapple, apple, and quince, grouped under pear (see Figure 3.2).

One of the most ambitious and synesthetic smell classification systems was Septimus Piesse's "gamut," also called an "odophone," a virtual smell organ which paired each fragrance note with a musical note, then grouped them in harmonic keys (fa, sol, la, and so on) (see Figure 3.3)[17] Piesse developed this system in light of his belief that the best way to understand odours was to consider them "comme des vibrations particulières qui affectent le système nerveux, comme les couleurs affectent l'œil, comme les sons affectent l'oreille" ("as particular vibrations affecting the nervous system, as colour affects the

Volatilité en puissance des parfums.

Eau..	1.0000
Essence de sureau.	0.2850
Zeste de citron.	0.2480
Zeste de Portugal.	0.2270
Lavande française.	0.0620
Lavande anglaise.	0.0610
Bergamote.	0.0550
Persil..	0.0370
Petit grain.	0.0330
Thym anglais.	0.0220
Lemongrass	0.0170
Géranium d'Espagne..	0.0106
Calamus.	0.0069
Lemon (serpolet)..	0.0062
Foin coupé.	0.0039
Géranium français.	0.0074
Essence de roses de Turquie. . . .	0.0051
— de France.. . . .	0.0038
Girofle.	0.0035
Cèdre..	0.0020
Patchouly..	0.0010

3.1. Septimus Piesse's classification of smells
in order of volatility, 1865, 8.

eye, as sounds affect the ear"; *Des odeurs* 1877, 4). In step with both his
era's synesthetic spirt and fervour for classification, Piesse's approach
to fragrance analogizes odours to sounds, sounds to colours, colours
to odours.[18] Unlike Poncelet, who wanted to assign musical notes to
odour *tones* (sweet, foul), Piesse worked with the names of smelly
objects already familiar to perfumers: *jasmine, rose, orange blossom, civet,*

SÉRIES.	TYPES.	ODEURS SECONDAIRES appartenant à la même série.
Rosée........	Rose.......	Géranium, Églantine, Rhodium, Palissandre.
Jasminée.....	Jasmin......	Muguet, Ihlang-Ihlang.
Orangée.	Fleur d'oranger. .	Acacia, Seringa, Feuille d'oranger.
Tubérosée.....	Tubéreuse.....	Lis, Jonquille, Narcisse, Jacinthe.
Violacée.	Violette.......	Cassie, Iris, Réséda.
Balsamique.....	Vanille......	Baumes du Pérou et de Tolu, Benjoin, Storax, Fève tonka, Héliotrope.
Épicée.	Cinnamome....	Cannelle, Muscade, Macis, Tout-épices.
Caryophillée.	Girofle......	Œillet.
Camphrée.	Camphre......	Romarin, Patchouli.
Santalée.......	Santal.....	Vétiver, Cèdre.
Citrine.	Citron.......	Orange, Bergamote, Cédrat, Limette.
Herbacée.	Lavande.......	Aspic, Thym, Serpolet, Marjolaine.
Menthacée.	Menthe poivrée. .	Menthe sauvage, Basilic, Sauge.
Anisée.	Anis.......	Badiane, Carvi, Aneth, Fenouil, Coriandre.
Amandée......	Amande amère...	Laurier, Noyer, Mirbane.
Musquée......	Musc......	Civette, Ambrette.
Ambrée.......	Ambre gris....	Mousse de chêne.
Fruitée.......	Poire.	Pomme, Ananas, Coing.

3.2. Eugene Rimmel's classification of odours by series and type.

Image source: *Le livre des parfums*, 1870, 15. Public domain.

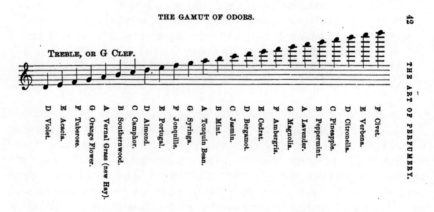

3.3. Translating odours to musical notes. From the 1867 edition of Septimus Piesse's *The Art of Perfumery* (42).

syringa. Inspired by Piesse's odophone classification system, and by other scientific and fiction writings relating sound and smell transmission waves, technologies for performing smell concerts were eventually created.[19] But Piesses's intention was not to revolutionize musical or olfactory performances. Instead, he wanted to help perfumers practise their profession. His creativity obviously made a splash with other experts in smell: Dr. Monin, for one, quoted extensively from this section of Piesses's book:

> Pour le nez "ignorant" toutes les odeurs sont pareilles, mais le nez civilisé par le plaisir ou par l'intérêt devient le plus délicat et le plus sagace des organes.... On a besoin de rappeler les odeurs, et la ténacité avec laquelle celles se fixent dans la mémoire est un fait à remarquer ici.... Dans la gamme ci-dessous, j'ai essayé de placer le nom de chaque odeur dans la position correspondant à son effet sur le sens.... Il y a des odeurs qui n'admettent ni dièzes ni bémols, et il y en a d'autres qui feraient presque une gamme à elles seules, grâce à leurs diverses nuances. La classe d'odeurs qui contient le plus de variétés est celle du citron.

> To the "unlearned" nose, all odours are alike, but when civilized, either for pleasure or profit it becomes the most sensitive and discerning of the organs.... It is necessary to remember odours, and the tenacity with which they fix themselves upon the memory is noteworthy.... In the following gamut I have endeavored to place the name of the odour in its position corresponding to its effect on the sense.... There are odours to which neither sharps nor flats are known, and there are others which would almost form a gamut in themselves, thanks to their diverse nuances. The class of odours that contains the most variety is that of lemon. (*Des odeurs* 1865, 19; 1877, 19–22)

Piesse's gamut would serve perfumers in at least three ways. First, it would provide a system for recalling and keeping track of the hundreds of nuanced smell notes encountered by perfumers and perfume. Having mastered the many notes in his repertoire, the perfumer must then become adept at designing harmonious blends: "Lorsqu'un parfumeur veut faire un bouquet d'odeurs primitives, il doit prendre des odeurs qui s'accordent ensemble; le parfum alors sera harmonieux" ("When a perfumer wants to make a bouquet of primitive odours, he must use odours that harmonize with one another; then the perfume will be harmonious"; 1865, 19; 1877, 22).

In addition to illustrating his musical scales in the keys of G and F, Piesse uses words on the page to provide visual cues for blending complementary notes according to the laws of harmony (see Figure 3.4). A final convenience of Piesse's ingenious and multi-sensorial approach to perfume blending could at first go unnoticed: the gamut allows perfumers to sight-smell the fragrances on the page: "En jetant les yeux sur la gamme, on verra ce que c'est qu'harmonie et discordance en fait d'odeurs" ("In passing the eye down the gamut, one will see what is

44   THE ART OF PERFUMERY.

In making several perfumes for choice they must
be so mixed as to form a contrast when side by side.
The complementary of vanilla is citronella. The
following recipes will give an idea how to make a
bouquet according to the laws of harmony :

Bass.
G   Pergalaria.
G   Sweet Pea.
D   Violet.   } Bouquet of chord G.
F   Tuberose.
G   Orange Flower.
B   Southernwood.
Treble.

Bass.
C   Santal.
C   Geranium.
E   Acacia.   } Bouquet of chord C.
G   Orange Flower.
C   Camphor.
Treble.

Bass.
F   Musk.
C   Rose.
F   Tuberose.
A   Tonquin Bean.   } Bouquet of chord F.
C   Camphor.
F   Jonquil.
Treble.

3.4. Septimus Piesse's compositions for fragrance bouquets
(*Art of Perfumery*, 1867). See also *Des odeurs,
des parfums et des cosmétiques*, 1877, 22–3.

harmony and what is discord in smells"; 22). Using Piesse's charts, perfumers could compose a fragrant blend without actually smelling (or
hearing) anything, by relying instead on the readable scale and the laws
of musical harmony. Piesse's gamut lexicon supports the theory that the
language of smell is one of identification and recognition, that like the
foul smells of disease identified by Brieude, Monin, and others many
sweet fragrances are *sui generis*: a rose smells of rose. But his scales and
chords suggest that to read (and write) smell requires a grammar and
syntax beyond word-to-smell parings; the relative lack of its *words* does
not impede a richness of olfactory *language*.

Though Piesse's classification system may seem esoteric today, it was a welcome novelty among fragrance aficionados of his time, and by the end of the century, the comparison of fragrances to musical notes slipped into light-hearted articles written for a general public.[20] An 1886 volume of the New York publication *The Art Interchange: A Household Journal*[21] discusses Piesse's odophone in relation to making do-it-yourself pot-pourris and air fresheners: "It appeals so strongly not only to the poetic sense, but to common sense, that certain odors, like certain sounds, har-monize with each other, and produce delightful results" (20). The author posits, however, that Piesse's odophone simply revives a wisdom that all grandmothers already possessed: "On Piesse's odophone, santal, geranium, acacia, orange flower and camphor constitute the bouquet chord of C, the heavy sensuous odors representing the low tones, or base, the pungent odors the high tones, or trebles, and the softer more ethereal, the notes between. Be that as it may, we of to-day are reviv-ing an almost lost art practiced by our great-grandmothers, who knew absolutely nothing about odophones, but nevertheless – guided by good sense – composed exquisite harmonies of odors, which they styled rose-jars, spice-jars, scent-jars, pot-pourris, or what-not" (22).

Perfumers would certainly see a difference between do-it-yourself home fragrance blends and artfully composed perfumes. But even the finicky, perfume-obsessed protagonist of Huysmans's *À rebours* con-ceded that, just as the untrained ear may have trouble distinguishing Beethoven from Clapisson, "personne, non plus, ne peut, sans initiation préalable, ne point confondre au premier abord, un bouquet créé par un sincère artiste, avec un pot-pourri fabriqué par un industriel, pour la vente des épiceries et des bazars" ("no one, either, can, without some preliminary instruction, completely avoid at first confusing a fragrance blend created by a true artist with a manufactured potpourri created to be sold at grocery stores and markets"; 670). The *Art Interchange* article does not argue that homemade potpourris smell like professional fra-grance blends. But it does suggest that Piesse's use of lexical "scales" creates a literacy gap between an elite realm of perfume blending and everyday, at-home fragrance crafting. With his carefully composed gamut of scent notes, Piesse had seemingly encoded and fine-tuned a grammatical system for an olfactory language already commonly spo-ken, though rarely documented in writing.

The categories developed by Piesse, Rimmel, and other nineteenth-century perfume experts illustrate how the often solipsistic language of smells tests even the most specialized connoisseurs of fragrance; for Rim-mel, roses smell rosy and, to a certain extent, geraniums smell rosy, too. These music/colour/smell correspondences may function like a Rosetta

Stone of the senses, a key to translating smells, colours, and musical notes, but one that is ultimately readable only to the expert few who already know the smell–word correlations. Clearly, Rimmel and Piesse were perfumer-chemists, not phenomenologists. Their goal was not the exploration of mind–body cognition, nor did they attempt the creation of a specialized vocabulary to communicate about the perception of perfume or the experience of olfaction. As expert noses, they could recognize and name hundreds of smells. Instead, they were grouping fragrances to aid the perfumer in composing balanced blends, or in exchanging one smell for another, without necessarily using their noses at all. In this way, perfumers went beyond translating smells into words: they constructed a language of odour that substituted concepts for sensation, reading for smelling. Thus, they did shape the way we talk about fragrance. Though the classification systems delineated in their perfume manuals were not incorporated in the many cosmetic fragrance recipes featured later in the very same books, terms like *note* and *accord* eventually entered the perfume vernacular where they are still used today, so commonly that one may easily overlook their synesthetic lineage.

In most domains, the absence of a rich, precise, commonly understood stock of smell words might be merely inconvenient. Medical practitioners and perfumers of the nineteenth century were highly motivated, for practical and financial reasons, to pay attention to the way they used words to communicate about smell. For writers and readers of fiction, the stakes of successful or thwarted smell–language associations are less clear or generalizable. Novelists have more complex motives: smells have a function in literary works, but that function varies from movement to movement, aesthetic to aesthetic, author to author, text to text. The expectations, experience, and engagement of fiction readers, too, are more variable than those of Brieude's contemporary medical practitioners, or Piesse's fellow perfumers. And there is no central repository of information on the everyday sensorial experiences that would have shaped the reception and interpretation of nineteenth-century readers' encounters with perfume on the page.

Brieude deems the language of smell insufficient for communication with his fellow physicians because odours transmit sensations that are "confused"; smells are indistinct and unclear because they mix to form a vague impression (xlvi). As a result, he finds himself unable to express his ideas about odours with clarity (xlvii). Words fail him because they too can be confused or intermixed or indistinct. Perhaps it is no coincidence that some of the most celebrated works of nineteenth-century French literature feature smell and that these works were considered dangerous in their time. Confusion itself, as in mingling together, but also as perplexing or puzzling, plays an important role in nineteenth-century literary genres (the prose poem, for example) and aesthetics (grotesque, realist, and decadent amalgamations; the hermetic character of symbolist poetry). The "confuses paroles" ("confused words") of Baudelaire's perfume-heavy "Correspondances," belong to a larger synesthetic phenomenon celebrated, not lamented, in the sonnet, but deemed morbid by psychologists and criminologists of the late nineteenth century, who judged the mixing of senses via words to be a sign of mental imbalance. Olfactory writing blends two things *fin-de-siècle* naysayers found toxic: over-sensitivity to smell, and over-manipulation of language. According to Joseph Grasset, Cesare Lombroso, and others, an unhealthy need to create new ways of using language, including "des sensations associées bizarres" ("bizarre associated senses") were examples of "literary madness."[22] Though such danger alerts did not withstand the test of time, smell language in literary works remains inconvenient, and often overlooked, due perhaps to a combination of cultural, temporal, and sensorial distance. Yet it is worth lingering on the confused sensations and language, the concomitant denotations and connotations produced by smell words in those literary works notorious for their perfumed pages.

Huysmans's "Confused" Words

Nineteenth-century smell experts borrowed from fiction writers to justify their theories, quoting poets and novelists to make their point. Brieude, Monin, Piesse, Rimmel, Baudelaire, and Huysmans shared access to a pool of olfactory terms that have different values and functions in the context of their work. Today, if vigilant readers of nineteenth-century literature stop to look up words for arcane clothing and *bibelots*, they may find almost instant visual gratification in paper and digital reference works. Access to analogous representations of unfamiliar smells would require a more specialized, somewhat cumbersome set of tools. Take, for example, Huysmans's famously redolent 1884 novel *À rebours*.[23] The 2005 Laffont edition glosses an impressive number of fragrant materials mentioned in the perfume-heavy tenth chapter, including: *ambre, ayapana, champaka, gutta-percha, musc-tonkin, opopanax, patchouli, seringa, spika-nard*, and *styrax*. Generous footnotes incorporate information from the 1977 Fumaroli and 1997 Mortier editions, bolstered by relevant passages from the original references Huysmans consulted to build his perfume vocabulary: most often Septimus Piesse's 1877 edition of *Des odeurs, des parfums et des cosmétiques* and Maison Violet's catalogue.[24]

Despite a wealth of olfactory glossing, readers who have not already encountered the named smell materials will remain largely anosmic to the precise fragrances in protagonist Jean Floressas des Esseintes's impressive collection. The problem is not lack of description, elaboration, comparison, or metaphorical language within the novel, or its many subsequently published footnotes. For example, a pellet of styrax rubbed and warmed between Des Esseintes's fingers releases "une très bizarre odeur ... une odeur tout à la fois répugnante et exquise, tenant de la délicieuse senteur de la jonquille et l'immonde puanteur de la gutta-percha et de l'huile de houille" ("a very strange odour ... an odour which was both nauseating and exquisite, evoking the delicious scent of the jonquil and the foul stench of gutta-percha and coal tar"; 676, 98).[25] Brunel, citing Mortier, notes that styrax is a tropical plant which furnishes resins such as benzoin, and that, according to Fumaroli, Huysmans borrowed his description of styrax from Piesse, whose words indeed bring us full circle to the description of styrax:

> L'odeur du styrax est, comme disait feu le professeur Johnston, de regrettable mémoire, le trait d'union entre celles qui déplaisent et celles qui plaisent. Le styrax joint l'arôme de la jonquille à l'odeur désagréable de l'huile de houille, odeur devenue familière depuis que les essences extraites des goudrons de cette substance servent à dissoudre la gutta-percha. Or, cette odeur et certainement du nombre qui nous déplaisent, et cependant le styrax lui ressemble à s'y méprendre, quand il est en grande quantité. Mais, divisé en particules impalpables, comme celles qui doivent exhaler des fleurs fraiches, le styrax rappelle le délicieux parfum de la jonquille.

> The odour of styrax is, as the late and lamented Professor Johnston said, the liaison between pleasing and displeasing odours. Styrax joins the aroma of the jonquil with the disagreeable odour of coal oil, an odour that has become familiar since essences extracted from the tars of this substance serve to dissolve gutta-percha. Now, this odour is certainly among those that displease, and yet styrax resembles it enough to be mistaken for it, when in large quantity. However, divided into impalpably small particles, like those that flowers exhale, styrax recalls the delightful perfume of jonquil. (*Des odeurs, des parfums et des cosmétiques*, 1877, 192–3)

Readers may recognize the aromas of tar and jonquil, but the delicate proportional balance described by Piesse, then Huysmans, would be easier to sniff out first-hand than to imagine via these words. That does not mean Piesse has failed to describe styrax. On the contrary, he has narrated the complexity of its aroma, and in so doing, touched upon an important key to the smell–language puzzle, and its relationship to poetics. Word-to-scent pairings are, at their logical limits, blunt and tautological (jonquil smells of jonquil, and styrax smells of jonquil in a way, but jonquil does not necessarily smell of styrax). A strict adherence to word–odour replacements – such as the musical notes in Piesse's perfume organ – opens communication among experts but offers a language too condensed for the average interlocutor. The prose of Piesse's styrax passage, in contrast, treats smell as a story whose words, syntax, and sentences unfold in time and space, much like a perfume released into the air from an uncorked flacon. Piesse acknowledges, then absorbs, chemist James Johnston's words into his own prose, which was then translated and altered in the 1877 edition of his book.[26] Huysmans subsequently further dilutes, embellishes, and reabsorbs these words, leaving out the brief obituary that adds memory and poignancy to Piesse's otherwise impersonal narrative; the novelist has a different story to tell. The movement of words from Johnston to Piesse to Huysmans reminds us that word–object, or word–experience pairings are never as tidy as we might like them to be. Words, language, prose, and stories are changeable and changing, fusing and compounding, distilling and dissipating; they mutate, they dissipate, they spread, they linger, they leave traces.

Piesse's entry on styrax includes background on the history, provenance, and professional use of this resin. "Les prêtres et les parfumeurs ont de grandes obligations à cette famille de plantes" ("Priests and perfumers are greatly indebted to this family of plants"; 192), used both in church incense and to perfume the home. True styrax comes from Asia Minor, where it once served as a fumigation to fight disease. Since the containment of the plague, its use greatly diminished (191–2). These details, unmentioned in the novel, nonetheless resonate with the conditions under which Des Esseintes fondles his pellet of styrax. He is in the process of creating a hallucinatory smellscape, for which styrax serves as a base note to an ever-changing, increasingly exotic perfume blend. And what has prompted this perfuming binge is a fumigation of sorts – the need to drown out the smell of *frangipane*.[27]

Each of the fragrant materials mentioned in Huysmans's chapter has a similarly deep backstory, with roots in chemistry, botany, foreign and colonial trade, medicine, hygiene, contemporary and earlier cultural practices, perceptions of gender, and Huysmans's own stylistic innovations. Not all are qualified within the novel to the same extent as styrax, but subsequent critical editions provide explanatory notes. To compose "une légère pluie d'essences humaines et quasi-félines, sentant la jupe, annonçant la femme poudrée et fardée" ("a light mist of human, half-feline essences, redolent of skirts, heralding the appearance of powdered and rouged womankind"; 675, 97), Des Esseintes adds a dash of *seringa*, bringing "un fleur naturel de rire en sueur" ("a natural smell of laughter in sweat"; 675). In his 1880 *Croquis parisiens* (*Parisian Sketches*), Huysmans included an entry on the exquisite and divine smells of city women's underarms. When filtered through fabric, he found that: "nul arôme n'a plus de nuances; c'est une gamme parcourant tout le clavier de l'odorat, touchant aux entêtantes senteurs du seringat [another word for seringa, or syringa] et du sureau rappelant parfois le doux parfum des doigts qu'on frotte après y avoir tenu et fumé une cigarette" ("no aroma has more nuances; its gamut traverses the keyboard of the sense of smell, sometimes hinting at the heady scents of seringa and elderflower, sometimes recalling the soft perfume of fingers rubbed together after having held and smoked a cigarette"; 127). Havelock Ellis quoted extensively from this Parisian sketch in his *Studies in the Psychology of Sex*, not to condemn Huysmans for his pathological emphasis on smell (Max Nordau would do a good job of that in *Degeneration*), but to introduce the topic of armpit fetishism. Just as Monin invoked Balzac and Baudelaire to justify scientific theory, Havelock Ellis used Huysmans's prose vignette, because "this very exact description corresponds at various points with the remarks of more scientific observers" (81).

The reader unfamiliar with *seringa* may consult Piesse, who characterizes its scent as strong and similar to orange blossom.[28] This comparison may engage the memory of readers who have encountered and can still recall the latter scent. Those who cannot might pause to seek out samples of orange blossom or *syringa*, or their bottled facsimiles. Others may assume – incorrectly – that *syringa* and orange blossom both smell like oranges. Many readers, of course, will not loiter on such details. Instead, they will exercise the selective slackening of attention that Roland Barthes attributed to "diluted tmesis,"[29] quickly skimming scent words whose precise meaning is not crucial to understanding this episode of Des Esseintes's eccentricity, nor the parallel unfolding (or unravelling) of his character.

Is something lost when a reader hurries through references to specific fragrant matter (styrax, musk, amber, benzoin), knowing neither how it smells, nor how that smell would have been interpreted in its day? As the *syringa* example in *À rebours* shows, characters react to, interpret, contemplate, and opine on smells, as do some intrusive narrators,[30] and readers may follow their cues. The poetic or narrative functions of fragrances come to light, even when the words themselves –

amber, ambergris, storax, styrax – remain unfamiliar, confused, or confusing. This is true not only in narrative fiction, but also in poetry, where individual words more obviously invite the lingering on sound and a contemplation of slower, closer reading. When the sensory and material dimensions of smell words remain muted, it is not necessarily to the detriment of their rhetorical expansion. Readers sensitized to the physical dangers of miasmas and mephitic effluvia, or to how the poet addresses mystery, danger, or corruption in other works, could certainly understand the metaphorical power of Baudelaire's references to *corrupt*, *rich*, and *triumphant* perfumes; to *singular* perfumes, *mysterious* perfumes, *dangereux parfums* and *parfums dangereux*. Yet sharing the smell experience that a writer and contemporary readers would have known creates a temporal proximity and an intimacy with the text that is otherwise difficult to achieve.

Pausing over references to smell in works of poetry and fiction allows us to recognize how and what that language communicates, and what is lost if such passages are chalked up to textual embellishment or to local colour. Like the *sui generis* smells of the human body identified by Brieude and Monin, or the singular perfume notes classified by Piesse and Rimmel, the olfactory language of a novel or poem bespeaks the distinctiveness of a text, its unique relationship to language, its style, and its ways of engaging the reader: its signature scent. Odours enhance the dimensionality of literary pieces, as they function simultaneously within linguistic and cultural domains, blending the two, and thereby contributing to the individual poetics of a given work. They also reinforce the interconnected nature of aesthetics, written expression, social interaction, and sensory awareness in perfume culture.

Chapter Four

The Osmazome of Literature

"[L]a littérature contemporaine se préoccupe des sensations olfactives; … jamais les mots fragrance, fleur (pour odeur), émanations, effluences, senteurs, relent, remugle, troublants effluves, sans compter *odor di femina*, jamais ces mots n'ont été si fréquemment employés que ces dernières années; on en abuse même un peu."

"Contemporary literature is preoccupied with olfactory sensations; … never were the words flower (for odor),[1] emanations, effluences, scents, stench, reek, unsettling effluvia, not to mention *odor di femina*, so frequently used as in recent years; they even overuse [abuse] it a bit."

"Le Paris des Parisiens: l'art des parfums (I),"
Maurice de Fleury, *Le Figaro*, 15 March 1890

Like the works of Charles Baudelaire and Gustave Flaubert that paved the way to fin-de-siècle aesthetics, French fiction and poetry of the late nineteenth century often depicts personae with an uncommonly attuned sense of smell and a proclivity for perfume. Naturalist and decadent novels, now iconic, were disparaged for their emphasis on odoriferous materials and smell perception, attributed to an unhealthy excess of lexical and syntactical experimentation. As the nineteenth century drew to an end, medical literature continued to correlate sexual excitement and disturbances, including neurosis, hysteria, and "insanity," to odour sensitivity and olfactory hallucination, both present in Joris-Karl Huysmans's infamous 1884 novel *À rebours*. Social critics read smell language itself as a cause, a symptom, a contaminant, or a vehicle for transmission of toxic psychological disorders. In his 1892 *Degeneration*, Max Nordau seized upon novelistic evidence of an "unhealthy predominance of the sensations of smell" and "a perversion of the olfactory sense" (502) to fuel his diatribe against various modern writers (naturalists, symbolists, and decadents), citing Baudelaire, Goncourt, Huysmans, and Zola as chief offenders. Huysmans's "breviary" for worshippers of decadent art (Symons 1916, 294) offered much fodder for those, like Nordau, who railed against symptoms of degeneration in art and literature. Huysmans was held up as an example of decadent writers who, like Baudelaire before him, disrupted the natural order of language in order to associate one sense with another, via *audition colorée* (colour audition) and *goût auditif* (auditory taste). Synesthetic rhetoric was viewed by detractors as a precarious emotional state passed on like a disease, through tainted language, from one writer to the next. For Nordau, the language of Huysmans's perfumed prose was as objectionable as its content. He saw protagonist Jean Floressas des Esseintes as "the Decadent with all his instincts perverted, *i.e.*, the complete Baudelairian" (310), who "possesses a nasal picture gallery" and "sniffs also the color of perfumes" (305). The passages are too long ("an endless description of tones associated with colors"; 306); and Huysmans's "drivel about tea, liqueurs, and perfumes" shows evidence of "ransacking technical dictionaries," like the Parnassians before him (305). Such critics see in Huysmans's work a profusion of smell and indulgent sniffing, related to an equally noxious abundance of words and wordplay, made possible by the strains of literary perversion he has contracted.

But not everyone found olfactory language toxic. In 1890, *Le Figaro* ran a piece called "Le Paris des Parisiens: l'art des parfums" (see the epigraph above) by doctor and man of letters Maurice de Fleury,[2] who commended contemporary perfumers, scientists, and novelists for raising smell in the hierarchy of senses, thanks to their excellent writing on perfume.[3] Fleury rejected the view that mass production and synthetics had turned the traditional craft of perfumery into a crass industry. Instead, he saw such innovations leading to the threshold of an art and predicted that in ten years, just as people now say, "Have you read the latest novel by Maupassant," they would be asking: "Vous connaissez la dernière œuvre de Lubin? ... un chef-d'œuvre, mon cher! Et quel artiste...!" ("Do you know the latest work by Lubin? A masterpiece, my dear! ... and what an artist...!"; 42). Fleury praised Huysmans (among other "sensitive novelists")[4] for having rehabilitated "cet art négligé, dédaigné, mis arbitrairement tout en bas de la classification, non loin de l'art du cuisinier" ("this neglected, disdained art, arbitrarily placed at the very bottom of classification, not far from the art of the chef"; 41). Fleury's generally positive commentary does also concede that many olfactory words (flower [meaning odour], emanations, effluences, scents, stench, reek, unsettling effluvia, *odor di femina*), have been overused or abused in works of literature. Both Nordau's condemnation and Fleury's praise indicate that, while olfactory physiology (or pathology) was a topic of contention in the late nineteenth century, its language became a constituent factor in debates over the moral, practical, and aesthetic value of smells.

Decadent Smell, Decadent Style

Joris-Karl Huysmans's 1884 À rebours is among the works of French literature best known for an almost pathological attention to odours and cosmetic perfume, especially in chapter 10, which features a rich and esoteric lexicon of fragrance materials, mastered by the eccentric autodidact protagonist Jean Des Esseintes. Huysmans's À rebours was what Arthur Symons called "the quintessence of contemporary Decadence" and "a breviary for its worshippers" (Figures [1892], 273 and 294). Symons admired the novel's "perverse charm of the sordid, the perverse charm of the artificial" (Figures [1892], 298), its dizzying verbal indulgence ("this audacious and barbaric profusion of words"), and formal deviance (298). Huysmans sent a copy of À rebours to writer and friend Léon Bloy, who famously anthropomorphized the novel's style (expression) as being always armed, and dragging its images by the hair and feet, "up and down the worm-eaten stairway of terrified Syntax" (20). Oscar Wilde similarly underscored the importance of lexicon and style to the novel's toxic, invasive decadence (likened to an odour that enters the body and lasts), with a fictionalized depiction of À rebours ("the yellow book") in The Picture of Dorian Gray:

> It was a novel without a plot and with only one character.... The style in which it was written was that curious jewelled style, vivid and obscure at once, full of argot and of archaisms, of technical expressions and of elaborate paraphrases, that characterizes the work of some of the finest artists of the French school of Symbolistes. There were in it metaphors as monstrous as orchids and as subtle in colour.... It was a poisonous book. The heavy odour of incense seemed to cling about its pages and to trouble the brain. (104)

Georges Veysset, without condemning Huysmans's literary experimentations as noxious, nonetheless diagnosed the author's eccentricities as having been passed on like a literary virus from Baudelaire, who was seemingly not patient zero (Huysmans et la médecine 1950). Veysset identifies perfume as a sensorial conduit for seen and unseen symptoms, the smoke swirls of fragrance ("les volutes des parfums"; 49) visibly feeding Des Esseintes's delirium, nightmares, and neuroses (49).

A fervent admirer of both the man and his work, Veysset rejects the belief that Huysmans was cyclothymic,[5] or that his psychology was abnormal in any pejorative sense of the term. He is, on the contrary, the talented victim of a literary disease. In a chapter devoted to Des Esseintes (48–55), a character that only the most refined readers would be able to grasp (50), Veysset views the decadent protagonist's psychology as representing the novelist's own audacity and outrage, symptoms and syndromes (48). Just as fictional Des Esseintes's *névrose* is attributed to biological heredity in the novel's first chapter, Huysmans's *névrose* is portrayed as a literary heredity in Veysset's study, which traces of the novel's literary lineage back to Chateaubriand's romantic protagonist René. Des Esseintes is seen as the older, more neurotic character whom Chateaubriand's oversensitive hero has become. René's morbid, romantic symptoms are aggravated as he ages into naturalism (51). As the novel progresses, Des Esseintes displays the growing pains of his author, shaking off naturalism, and in so doing, contracting "baudelairisme": "Rappelons que depuis sa jeunesse, Huysmans était imprégné de Baudelaire avec qui sa parenté intellectuelle et sensuelle est ici très évidente" ("Let us remember that from his youth on, Huysmans was permeated with Baudelaire with whom his intellectual and sensual kinship is quite evident here [in *À rebours*]"; 51). Even in this rehabilitation of Huysmans's image, reading and writing, like perfume, do "impregnate" and contaminate the novelist and his protagonist, especially at turning points in their aesthetic thinking.

À rebours has maintained its status as a peculiar, sometimes shocking work that exemplifies the decadent break from naturalism in its rejection of conformity, both in style and content. Des Esseintes's unusual proclivities, his reputation for self-consciously cultivated eccentricity, and his withdrawal from society, are echoed in the stillness of the novel's structure, its constantly undermined plot progression, and its surfeit of lexically rich arcana.[6] Huysmans confirms his intention to make a clean break from naturalism in his "Préface écrite vingt ans après le roman" ("Preface written twenty years after the novel"; 561–77, 183–97),[7] likening his desire to destroy the boundaries of traditional novelistic intrigue, to the act of opening windows to escape a suffocating atmosphere, something he says Zola could not understand (71, 193). Yet *À rebours* is not as immunized from the miasmic air of Flaubert and Zola, nor from the earlier works of Huysmans himself, as the novel's preface would suggest. Christopher Lloyd argues that Huysmans's characteristic "maniacal lexical curiosity, his penchant for neologisms, archaisms, slang and rare synonyms," and "the notorious disrupted rhythm of his sentences," are also characteristic of Zola's writing (39).[8]

As Charles Bernheimer has shown, the aesthetic move in literature from naturalism to decadence involves a recalibration more than a rupture; a maintenance of the "intimate connection between certain fundamental premises of naturalism and certain strategies of decadent creativity" (58).[9] This stylistic compatibility characterizes the language and dramatization of perfume encounters in what has been seen as Huysmans's most decadent novel.

Everyday Decadence

À rebours reveals a simultaneous tension and connection between naturalist and decadent aesthetics, evident across passages related to fragrance, insalubrious odours, poor air quality, hygienic concerns, symptoms of illness, and medical treatments.[10] In one episode, quickly evolving but ever inclement weather threatens over a two-day period, bringing squalls, chilly fogs, blazing heat, steaming rains, and heavy air (713, 134). In another, Des Esseintes opens the window of his study halfway to release the indoor "effluvia" of burning logs (618, 38). Few other than the doctor and Des Esseintes's loyal servants cross the threshold of his fragrantly named home, Fontenay-aux-Roses. The protagonist himself, cleansed inside and out with hydrotherapeutic showers (661, 9) and, eventually, a varied menu of nourishing enemas (753, 171), eschews music performances, as "afin de la déguster, il eût fallu se mêler à cet invariable public qui regorge dans les théâtres ... dans une atmosphère de lavoir" ("to enjoy it, he would have been forced to mingle with the unvarying audience that fills the theaters to overflowing ... in a stifling [washhouse] atmosphere]"[11]; 748, 166). As if in response to the first line of Baudelaire's prose poem "Les foules," ("Il n'est pas donné à chacun de prendre un bain de multitude"/"Not everyone can take a bath in the multitude"), the narrator reveals that Des Esseintes "n'avait pas eu le courage de se plonger dans ce bain de multitude" ("had never felt up to plunging into this mob [bath of the multitude]"; 749, 166).

Des Esseintes's self-imposed isolation to some extent offers a shield from the fetid air, filthy crowds, and rank spaces lingering beyond the protective walls of his dwelling, yet the seal is never airtight. Alone, as he savours just one of the "keys" from his mouth organ (a collection of cordials from which he sips to silently play and compose taste symphonies), the smoky flavour and aroma of Irish whiskey recall the sensation memory of creosote used for tooth pain. Before his retreat from society, the recluse had to leave his home to have a tooth pulled by a "popular dentist" who takes walk-ins. The foul stairway to the office leaves Des Esseintes "épouvanté par les larges crachats rouges qu'il apercevait collés sur les marches" ("terror-struck by the big blood-red gobs of spittle he saw plastering the stairs"; 622, 41).

The recluse does, however, make important exceptions to his sequestration, breaking the would-be hermetic seal of his home for visits from the doctor, and to select or receive the delivery of goods. Related to his urge to collect is Des Esseintes's compulsion to shop, which often places him on the streets of Paris. Perhaps the nineteenth-century protagonist least likely to be called a flâneur, it is nonetheless while "wandering haphazardly through the city streets" (614, 35), that Des Esseintes finds his soon-to-be-jewel-encrusted tortoise displayed in the window of the Palais-Royal restaurant Chevet. A place long known for its seductive odours and crowd-pleasing displays,[12] Chevet was a popular meeting place and a window-shopper's delight, according to an entry on the best shops for gourmands in *La vie Parisienne à travers le dix-neuvième siècle* (Simond 1900). Food critic Grimod de La Reynière's write-up in "Promenade d'un gourmand au Palais-Royal" mentions that Chevet was not the most well-lit or tidy shop, but it enticed plenty of customers with its tempting alimentary aromas and its impressive array of comestibles:

> ce petit trou ne désemplit point d'acheteurs, alléchés par le fumet admirable des marchandises entassées dans cet étroit garde-manger. Des daims tout entiers pendent à sa porte et lui servent d'enseigne…. On s'étouffe dans cette petite boutique, le maître ne sait à qui répondre.

> this little hole-in-the wall is always crowded with buyers, enticed by the aroma of merchandise stacked up in this narrow pantry. Whole deer hang at its doorway and serve as its sign…. You suffocate in this little boutique, the owner does not know whom to reply to first. (Simond 1900, 50)

Chevet serves as a benchmark of aromatic edibles in 1828, when in a write-up of François Marquis's shop in the Passage des Panoramas, the reader is invited to contemplate "le beau magasin de thés, tenus par le Marquis, où le chocolat subit tant de métamorphoses; puis respirons l'odeur des truffes, doux parfum ministériel qui s'exhale de l'intéressante boutique de ce marchand de comestibles, le *Chevet* des Panoramas" ("the beautiful tea shop, owned by Marquis, where chocolate undergoes so many metamorphoses; then let us inhale the truffle odour, the sweet, ministerial perfume exhaled from the interesting boutique of this comestibles merchant, the *Chevet* of the Panoramas"; Simond 1900, 556).[13] In 1858, *The National Magazine* offered a brief history of the renowned Maison Chevet, including the mention of turtles in the window display:

> The shop in the Palais Royal became the *entrepôt* of artistic cheer for all European *gourmands,* and its extensive kitchens dispensed the cream of culinary perfection to half the courts and diplomatic dinners of Europe. In the windows of the former, through which a crowd is always gazing from one end of the year to the other, you behold every species of fish, swimming in tanks or prepared for cooking; turtles crawling lazily in and among stones and streams of water. Hams of every nature and shape. ("A Dynasty not mentioned in History," 175)[14]

The enormous turtle that Des Esseintes happened to see displayed in Chevet's window was destined for a dinner table, not home décor. In episodes such as this, which predate Des Esseintes's self-quarantine, it is clear that the secluded protagonist has at one time shared the sights, sounds, and smells of the crowd that he so disdained. His acquisition of the tortoise and curation of bottled perfume represent the novel's many amalgamations of the effete and the everyday, via both bodily intake (inhaling, ingesting, flushing) and the impulse to purchase and collect. The turtle, displayed in a shop window as a culinary lure, becomes under Des Esseintes's supervision, the canvas on which to create animated home décor, as a gilded, then jewel-encrusted treasure. In a similar transformation of alimentary necessity and luxury, Des Esseintes reads his prescription for a new *lavage* (of cod-liver oil, beef tea, burgundy, and egg yolk) as if consulting a restaurant menu, and dreams of subverting the boring, vulgar, natural burden of eating, by taking three meals a day through enemas.

The Grammar and Syntax of Aromas

When Huysmans looks back on *À rebours* twenty years later, he contrasts the painful and disillusioning task of reading one's own words to the more pleasant act of opening a bottle of wine. While wine improves with age, decanted sentences settle to the bottom of the book. Chapters oxidize and their "bouquet" dissipates (561, 183). Attention to decanting words and odours in equal proportion characterizes the tenth chapter of *À rebours*, where, suffering from "olfactory hallucinations" (669, 92), Des Esseintes reflects upon his acquired knowledge of everything pertaining to the history, production, and blending of perfume. The heady vapours emanating from his collection's countless open bottles, mingled with the weight of memories and a creeping, initially "imaginary aroma" (670, 92) of *frangipane*, eventually make him swoon. From the medical perspective of the era, Des Esseintes's olfactory hallucination is not only an eccentricity, but a symptom. In his influential 1859 study of hysteria, Dr. Jules Briquet reported that: "il existe chez un certain nombre d'hystériques, des altérations dans la faculté de sentir qui ne peuvent être rapportées qu'a une perversion" ("There exist in a certain number of hysterics alteration in the faculty of smelling that can only be related to a perversion"; 307).[15] Such warnings appear in studies of neurosis and hysteria throughout the century, which continue to identify hysterical symptoms as including "la perception illusoire d'odeurs et de saveurs absentes" ("the illusory perception of absent odours and flavors"; Axenfeld 1883, 988).

To demonstrate Des Esseintes's impressive knowledge of perfume history and blending, Huysmans relied heavily upon Septimus Piesse's *The Art of Perfumery*, first published in London in 1857. Huysmans used the second French edition, *Des odeurs, des parfums et des cosmétiques*, published in 1877 with the participation of Chardin-Hadancourt and Henri Massignon, both of whom Piesse credits for providing new information on French perfumery (vii).[16] Like perfumers Piesse and Rimmel, who go beyond naming smells to contextualizing them within a readable structure analogous to a grammar, Huysmans not only presents an impressive gamut of perfume notes and scented products in the novel, but depicts Des Esseintes as a composer of smell, reading and writing in "cet idiome des fluides" ("idiom of fluids"; 671, 94). Des Esseintes is "habile dans la science du flair" ("skilled in the science of smell"; 670, 92) in part because he can decipher "cette langue, variée, aussi insinuante que celle de la littérature" ("its language, which was as rich and devious [insinuating] as that of literature"; 672, 93). His olfactory analyses of perfumes are described as textual exegeses (672, 95). Des Esseintes tackles the blending of his own perfume with joy and trepidation, as a writer might approach the blank page, overcoming "ce moment d'hésitation bien connus des écrivains, qui, après un mois de repos, s'apprête à recommencer une nouvelle œuvre" ("that moment of hesitation well known to writers who, after a month off, prepare themselves to begin a new work"; 673, 95). In the spirit of Balzac, who filled pages with practice writing in order to compose novels, Des Esseintes dabbles in composing less important perfumes before moving on to a larger project.

A metaphorical relationship between written and fragrant expression continues throughout the chapter, elaborated and expanded to include vocabulary, grammar, syntax, the history of French language and literary currents, and the act of reading. To achieve his level of proficiency,

Des Esseintes studies the "dialect" of perfumes blended by the masters. His goal is to disassemble and reconstruct the "sentences" of smell, to weigh the proportion of their words and the arrangement of their historical phases (671, 94). Des Esseintes sees the advancement of classic (French) perfumery as following, step by step, "celle de notre langage" ("that of our language"; 671, 94). Thus, the seventeenth-century fashion for orris-powder, musk, civet, and myrtle water captured the rakish, somewhat crude colours of Louis XIII's time, as did the sonnets of Saint-Amant (671, 94). Des Esseintes traces the overlapping aesthetics of *orientalisme* and perfume (an amalgamation that characterizes the Western perfume industry to this day) directly to the exoticist writings of Victor Hugo and Théophile Gautier (671–2, 94–5). For Des Esseintes, the history of Western perfume constitutes one language unfolding within another, each in constant evolution.

The abundant odours of *À rebours,* and Des Esseintes's active focus on perfume (contemplating, studying, identifying, sorting, categorizing, blending), attest to a cultivation of liquid and lexical rarities, for both the protagonist and the author. References, some lengthy, to perfume materials and production techniques substantiate Huysmans's research in preparing the complex arrangement of subtle and overt intertexts throughout the book. The chapter contributes to a "logbook of aesthetic experimentation and perverse pleasures" for which *À rebours* is known (Cevasco 2001, 79). It also illustrates Huysmans's predilection for using catalogues of words as a way to push the limits of narrative prose.[17] Lexical enumeration itself communicates the din of accumulated arcana in Des Esseintes's mind, enhanced by the visual and olfactory noise of opened bottles and mingled, wafting smells in his study. Just as important, though, is the way in which the composition of perfume informs the very composition of the chapter.

Layers of smell–language associations, suggested by the deciphering of perfume and texts throughout the novel, presage the structure of the tenth chapter. It opens with the idea of a perfume (Des Esseintes's perceived, imagined, or hallucinated *frangipane* blend) and closes with Des Esseintes's creation of a fragrant bouquet that very much recalls *frangipane* perfume formulae of the era. The chapter could be seen as having five sections, though the division is hardly clean, since linear plot movement repeatedly stalls in a series of temporal, spatial, and narrative interruptions, with constant mingling and unfolding of embedded memories, triggered by smells. The first part, composed of eight paragraphs, takes place in Des Esseintes's home, where the present "action" of the chapter involves the latest of his maladies: olfactory hallucination. Besieged by the pervasive, outdated cosmetic smell of *frangipane*, Des Esseintes decides to combat the hallucination with "nasal homeopathy," or immersion in his own fragrance concoctions. He begins sorting perfume flacons on his dressing table in a linear order of complexity, starting with single notes and moving to mixtures, or bouquets. The second section, devoted to Des Esseintes's knowledge and blending of perfumes, consists of what might be called, in a more classic work of fiction, a lengthy narrative intervention (fourteen paragraphs). Yet the story time is so often sublimated to the discourse time, or paused for lengthy recollections, the omniscient narrator so often voices Des Esseintes's thoughts, and there is so little action in the present, that much of the novel reads as narrative intervention. The third part of the chapter (nineteen paragraphs) returns to the scene of Des Esseintes in his study, now engaged in fragrant mixology and a series of contemplations, again spatially and temporally augmented by narrative commentary. The fourth section, a text within a text, is followed by a return to the narrative time and place of the chapter, with Des Esseintes reacting to an invasive heliotrope aroma.

In the long, third section, one of many passages pairing perfume and the written word, we learn that in the past, Des Esseintes used the rhythmic architecture of Baudelaire's poems "Le balcon" and "L'irréparable" (where the last line of each five-line stanza is the same as the first) to structure his perfume blending. Aromatic phrases follow the rhythm of Baudelaire's stanzas, wafting in and fading away, only to return, bringing Des Esseintes's mind back to the original scent motif. In this "odorant orchestration du poème" ("fragrant orchestration of the poème"; 675, 96–7), the syntax of poetry informs the structure and composition of perfume. In so doing, it renders material and multi-sensory (through smell, musicality, and the haptic embodiment of rhythm) the otherwise abstract, metaphorical relationship between language and odours. Though not mentioned in the novel, each of these poems refers to smell in one of its key repeated lines: "Ce pauvre agonisant que déjà le loup flaire!" ("This poor dying man, whose scent the wolf has already picked up"; in "L'irréparable"). The final stanza of "Le balcon" opens with "Ces serments, ces parfums, ces baisers infinis"/"These vows, these perfumes, these infinite kisses"), and closes with this transformation: "Ô serments ! ô parfums ! ô baisers infinis!" ("O vows! O perfumes! O infinite kisses"), as if the last words had been filtered through the stanza, and slightly altered in the process. Or one could interpret the repeated words of the last verse as components extracted from the phrase in which they were blended, like the individual notes of a perfume composition, dissected by the expert nose.

The memory of his long-ago poetry-to-perfume adaptations moves Des Esseintes to compose a new orchestral fragrance blend, based on a structure of recurring "phrases," whose opening motif is an ever-morphing and expanding countryside vista, an extract of meadow blossoms, featuring lavender, sweet pea, linden, and lilacs. With the help of fans, he wafts in and fades out "essences humaines et quasi-félines" ("human, half-feline essences"; 675, 97), the scent of petticoats and made-up women (stephanotis, ayapana, opoponax, chypre, champaka). Then industrial smells take over, a foul-smelling chemical odour mixed with nature's sweet effluvia (released by the styrax in Des Esseintes's collection), which serve as base notes to natural, summery smells, such as new mown hay (a very popular perfume of the era).[18] Finally he unleashes a strong mix of countless exotic perfumes, whose blend becomes "un parfum général, innommé, imprévu, étrange, dans lequel reparaissait, comme un obstiné refrain, la phrase décorative du commencement, l'odeur du grand pré éventé par les lilas et les tilleuls" ("a collective perfume, nameless, unexpected, and strange, in which there reappeared, like a persistent refrain, the ornamental opening phrase, the scent of the great meadow fanned by the lilacs and lime trees"; 676–7, 98).

Smitten with a perfume-induced headache, Des Esseintes finds himself back at his dressing table, contemplating his collection of make-up and toiletry articles, a confusion of bottles and jars containing pastes, lotions, and creams, and of powder puffs, back-scratchers, tweezers, and files. The accumulation of words emulates the accumulation of objects and demonstrates again Huysmans's mastery of both lexical arcana and consumer trends. The dressing-table mirror offers literal and figurative reflection (a view of the street outdoors and a conduit to memory). The mirror's presence also echoes the chapter's narrative mise-en-abîme, accentuated by the choice of words "abîmé dans un songe" ("plunged into reverie"; 227, *my translation*). At this moment, as at the beginning of the chapter, Des Esseintes returns to a contemplation of "de vieilles idées et d'anciens parfums" ("old ideas and ancient perfumes"; 678, 99).

Sights and sounds from the past compel Des Esseintes to repeat (aloud or in his mind – the passage is set off in quotation marks) his own written composition about a rainy day in Pantin, the industrial outskirts of Paris that housed the Saint-James and Pinaud perfumeries. In this text within a text (the fourth section of the chapter), torrential rain and humidity cause dung to marinate in puddles, walls to ooze black sweat, ventilators to exhale fetid air. Like the sequential, interwoven smell phrases he recently orchestrated at home, the foul and filthy odours of outdoor Pantin are counterbalanced by the nearby perfume factories' fragrant emissions. Artificial spring air wafts through window joints, scenting what turns out to be a *trompe-nez* basket of flowers. The aroma of benzoin, geranium, and vetiver seemingly exhaled by these taffeta flowers is, in fact, second-hand industrial perfume. The sight of artificial flowers, complemented by second-hand aroma, marks a shift in the metaphorical relationship between perfumes and floral bouquets. The benzoin, geranium, and vetiver lending aroma to taffeta flowers are classic notes blended to create perfumes. Here perfume does not imitate the smell of flowers, but flowers appear to imitate the smell of perfume. Throughout the chapter, the term *bouquet* is used in its commercial sense: a scented product made up of multiple notes.

Des Esseintes's essay then proposes that the artificial air offered by perfumes could be used in the service of moral and medical hygiene: die-hard Parisians might benefit from artificial fresh air without leaving the city; libertines might enjoy boudoirs and brothels platonically, by inhaling the "languissantes émanations féminines évaporées par les fabriques" ("the languid feminine emanations issuing from the perfume factories"; 679, 101). In Des Esseintes's modern dystopia, the sacred, ritual act of burning aromatic resins has been displaced by mass production. Factories exhale synthetic perfume, filling the air with an olfactory illusion devised not to transcend reality, but to obviate the need for transportation.

At once intertextual and metatextual, this quoted portion of the chapter reprises nearly word for word a "Croquis parisien" ("Parisian Sketch") Huysmans wrote for the *Revue littéraire et artistique*, 15 September 1881 (465). Though an extreme example, this is not the only instance of other published perfume texts slipping into Des Esseintes's fictional world. Des Esseintes's theory of odour waves (which operate like sound waves and light rays), and his valorization of the sense of smell, paraphrase portions of Piesse's chapter "De l'odorat et des odeurs" ("The Sense of Smell and Odors"; *Des odeurs, des parfums et des cosmétqiues* 1877, 1–35).

The Pantin passage also illustrates an aspect of Des Esseintes's perfume appreciation mentioned early in the chapter: "Dans cet art des parfums, un côté l'avait, entre tout, séduit, celui de la précision factrice…. Presque jamais, en effet, les parfums ne sont issus des fleurs dont ils portent le nom" ("In this art of perfumes, one aspect among all of them had seduced him, that of artificial precision…. Almost never do perfumes come from the flowers that carry their names"; 670, 93). The chapter unveils examples of perfumery's compositional deceptions, emphasizing that it takes a certain knowledge of blending to sniff them out. For instance, when Des Esseintes sets out to fabricate heliotrope from a concoction of other fragrance notes, it is not only for the pleasure of olfactory subterfuge. As Piesse and other perfumers of the era indicate in their recipes for heliotrope products (in this case a sachet): "il a si parfaitement l'odeur de la fleur à laquelle il emprunte son nom, que ceux qui n'en connaissent pas la composition ne voudraient jamais croire que ce n'est pas réellement de l'héliotrope" ("its odour is so perfectly that of the flower from which it gets its name, that those who do not know the composition would never believe it was not real heliotrope"; *Des odeurs*, 309).[19] Although by the end of the century perfumers had the option of using artificial heliotropin (discovered in 1869), heliotrope dupes could still be concocted with the right balance of natural ingredients. Piesse's heliotrope formula contains iris, rose, Tonka, vanilla, musk, and almond. Debay, who confirms that "on imite facilement cette odeur" ("This odour is easily imitated"; 311), prescribes vanilla, balsam of Peru,[20] and jasmine.[21]

Like the first and last lines of Baudelaire's stanzas in "Le balcon" and "L'irréparable," and like the first and last "phrases" of the perfumed compositions that Des Esseintes structures on that model, the first and last sections of Huysmans's chapter echo and absorb one another. The fifth and final segment of the chapter (two paragraphs) marks a return to the narrative frame and its smell of *frangipane*. No longer transported in time and space by olfactory hallucination, Des Esseintes moves from his dressing room to his study, where he opens the window to "prendre un bain d'air" ("take a bath of air"; 680, 101), only to realize slowly that the odour wafting into his room is once again the dreaded *frangipane* that triggered the chapter's action and contemplations. With its layers of embedded texts and fragrances, unfolding and overlapping like a blended perfume, the chapter's structure follows what Des Esseintes reads as a syntax of both poetry and perfume.

Huysmans's Word List

Des Esseintes's attention to the manufacture and history of perfume is established throughout the chapter, particularly in the second and third sections. He owns a daunting collection of cosmetics and perfume-making materials, with which he skilfully concocts his own liquid bouquets. Because Huysmans was a meticulous collector of words, much of the vocabulary for fragrance materials on the pages of this chapter derives from catalogues and professional manuals published in the nineteenth century. Like his protagonist, Huysmans consulted the works of perfumers, including Atkinson, Lubin, Chardin, Violet, and Piesse (and likely many others as well). For an author like Huysmans,

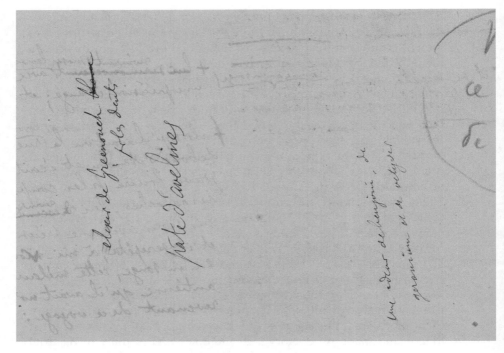

4.1. Page 65r of Huysmans's manuscript *À rebours*, with *pâte d'avelines* written vertically on the left, and "une odeur de benjoin, de géranium et de vétyver" on the right.

Image source: gallica.bnf.fr / BnF.

who famously sought out arcane vocabulary, smells were an excellent place to turn, since the perfume industry was growing, and with it, the number of published books for professional and amateur perfumers. Des Esseintes's mastery of perfume arcana often finds narrative illustration in the enumeration of objects, places, or materials related to perfume.

Marginal notes and edits in Huysmans's hand-written book manuscript[22] also suggest that the author weighed, expanded, revised, or hesitated over the products, or at least their lexicon, in Des Esseintes's collection of perfume-making materials and related cosmetics. "Pâte d'avelines" (a hazelnut paste used for cosmetic gloves and pomades),[23] noted almost vertically on the free space at the left of manuscript page 65r (Figure 4.1), would eventually be added to a detailed portrait of Des

Esseintes's cosmetics table, along with several Orientalist embellishments: "pots pleins de pâte d'aveline, de serkis du harem,[24] d'émulsines au lys de kachemyr" ("pots full of pâte d'aveline, of serkis du harem, of Kasmir-lily emulsions"; 677).

In addition to providing a catalogue of perfume materials, the tenth chapter of *À rebours* describes the smells themselves in a variety of ways, as images, entire vignettes, or personifications. The pervasive scent of *frangipane* [25] that triggers the outpouring of commentary on perfume throughout the chapter is anthropomorphized in terms of its action ("le chuchotement de cette astucieuse frangipane qui faufilait encore dans sa pièce"/"the whispering of that wily frangipani, which was still sneaking stealthily around his room"; 674, 96) and its effect on Des Esseintes ("l'importune frangipane"/"the intrusive frangipani"; 670, 92). *Frangipane* and *maréchale*[26] are interpreted early in the chapter as representing the languid and erudite grace of society under Louis XV (672, 94). But *frangipane* is never qualified in olfactory language.

Nineteenth-century readers who paid attention to perfume would most likely have recognized the scent of *frangipane*, though they may have attributed it to the wrong source. *Frangipane* was (and still is) the name for two very different fragrances (as well as a pastry). Newspaper articles and trade manuals of the time suggest there was some confusion as to what *frangipane* perfume was and how it smelled. As Marie Gacon-Dufour explains in her 1825 *Manuel du parfumer* (51–5), both the word and the smell of *frangipane* were easily misunderstood. Some believe the name comes from the fragrant flower of the tropical *frangipanier* (plumeria tree), and that soaps and pomades bearing the name imitate the tropical flower scent. However, she continues, Frangipani was the family name of an Italian who created a perfume blend for gloves; that scent was later used in pomades, powders, and scented waters. According to Gacon-Dufour, *pommade à la frangipane* means *pommade aux différentes essences* (pomade of mixed essences). Seemingly ready to agree to disagree with anyone who claims *frangipane* is a soliflore fragrance, she proceeds to her recipe: "Avec qui ce soit, de l'homme ou de l'arbre, que l'on doive son nom, sans vouloir pousser plus loin dans les recherches, voici comme se compose la pommade à la frangipane, qu'il serait plus naturel de nommer pommade *au pot pourri*" ("To whomever it owes its name, the man or the tree, without pushing further the research, here is how *frangipane* pomade is made, which it would be more natural to call *potpourri pomade*"; 53). The last phrase of course betrays Gacon-Dufour's desire to hang on to her argument, and after offering her formula (orange blossom, rose, cassie,[27] jasmine, vanilla, bergamot, clove, balsam of Peru, ambergris, and musk in a base of filtered beef or veal fat), she returns to the debate. Published recipes for *frangipane*, she points out, "ne parlent en aucune matière de l'eau odorante tirée de la fleur du frangipanier" ("speak in no way at all of scented water taken from the plumeria flower"; 54); "ils ne disent pas un mot du *frangipanier*, ni de ses fleurs, ni de ses feuilles; ils ne semblent même pas se douter qu'on puisse faire entrer son odeur" ("they say not a word about the *tree*, nor its flowers, nor its leaves; they do not even seem to suspect that one might include its odour"; 55). Her final word on the subject? "Alors, ce n'est pas de l'arbre, mais de l'homme, que la dénomination à la frangipane doit être prise" ("Thus, it's not from the tree, but from the man, that the name *frangipane* must have been taken"; 55). The *Rapports du jury international de l'exposition universelle de 1900* dates *frangipane* to the time of Louis XIV and confirms it is a "mélange de tous les aromates connus" ("a mixture of all known aromatics"; 19). A confusing name for a confusion of scent notes.[28]

Piesse places the solifore *frangipane* (*plumera alba/frangipanier*) on his odour scale, in the key of Fa. He remarks that it is the primary note in an "eternal perfume" very much in vogue (*Des odeurs, des parfums, et des cosmétiques* 1865, 106–7). He also devotes a great deal of discussion to the other *frangipane*, the blended *frangipane*, in his chapter on perfumed gloves (xxx–i), attributing the original formula to the Frangipani family name also cited by Gacon-Dufour. The 1862 English edition of his book (*The Art of Perfumery*) offers even more insights into the convoluted story of the perfume's name and popularity. The blend was originally used to scent gloves, pomades, powders, and essences. Products bearing the name were sold well into the eighteenth century, then fell out of fashion, only to be revived in the mid-1800s (22–5). Piesse's *frangipane* sachet formula contains many of the same notes as Gacon-Dufour's: iris, vetiver, sandalwood, neroli, musk, and ambergris. Versions of the *frangipane* formula appear in manuals throughout the century. Madame Celnart's 1845 recipe for *frangipane* pomade includes orange blossom, cassie, rose, jasmine, clove, bergamot, balsam of Peru, vanilla, ambergris, and musk (*Manuel complet*, 51–2). Debay's 1884 *eau à la frangipane* contains jasmine extract, rose, cassie, bergamot, vanilla, Tolu balsam, balsam of Peru, saffron, ambergris, and musk.

Which *frangipane* formulation did Des Esseintes smell? When he opens his window, the invasive odour does not return all at once, but in phases, like the unfolding of odour waves, unfurling in what perfumers now term head, heart, and base notes, beginning with bergamot, jasmine, cassie, and rose water. Like a composed perfume, the odour balance transforms yet persists, amplified and anchored by less volatile notes, an "indécise senteur de teinture de tolu, de baume de Pérou, de

safran, soudés par quelque gouttes d'ambre et de musc" ("vague scent
of tincture of Tolu, balsam of Peru, saffron, held together [soldered]
by a few drops of ambergris and musk"; 680, 101). The bouquet filling
Des Esseintes's room indeed closely resembles Debay's recipe for *frangipane*. Just as the perfumer may read Piesses's published gamut of fragrance notes to create harmonic blends, the novelist may read printed
fragrance recipes to compose tenacious perfumes.[29]

Clearly Huysmans gave serious thought to his vocabulary of
odours. On the last page of his handwritten manuscript, near the "pâte
d'avelines" note (Figure 4.1), appear the words "une odeur de benjoin, de géranium et de vétyver" ("an odour of benzoin, geranium and
vetiver"). A version of the phrase appears in the published novel, to
describe the taffeta flowers, but the generic "odeur" is notably replaced
by a more evocative noun: "une exhalaison de benjoin, de géranium
et de vétyver qui remplit la chambre" ("an exhalation of benzoin, of
geranium, and of vetiver which filled the room"; 227, *my translation*).
In the margin of manuscript page 64v (Figure 4.2), a list of eighteen
single words and word pairings shores up some of the olfactory lexicon
featured in the chapter: *souffle* (breath, or breeze), *baume* (balm/balsam),
haleine (breath or breathing), *souffle* (repeated), *fumet* (aroma specific
to a given substance; also gamey or fishy scent), *aromate* (a [fragrance]
extract), *bouquet* (bouquet, also meaning a perfume composed of several notes), *effluence-émanation* (effluence-émanation), *exhalaison* (exhalation), *flair-fleur* (*sniffing* – *flower* when feminine, or s*mell* when masculine), *fragrance, fumée* (smoke), *haleine-montant* (breath-rising), *odoration*
(odoration), *oler-répandre une odeur* (to smell or to smell of[30] – spread an
odour), *olfactoire-odorant* (a neologism for olfactory or odorous), *vapeur*
(vapour), and *émaner* (exude from).[31] Most, but not all of these words
appear at least once in the chapter, though the list is far from complete.[32]
Some words (*odoration, olfactoire*) are either highly arcane or invented
and do not appear in the novel, though the neologism "fétider" (a verb
formed of the noun *fétide*) does.

The feminine noun flower (*fleur*) appears in the chapter (fifteen times),
but more interestingly so does, only once, the masculine *fleur* ("un fleur
naturel de rires en sueur"/"a natural fragrance of sweat-drenched
laughter"; 675, 97), the seldom-used synonym for odour that Fleury
claims has made a comeback in fin-de siècle writing. A closer look at the
manuscript suggests that Huysmans may have intended to use *un fleur*
more than once in the novel. In the chapter's opening passage, plagued
by the fragrance of *frangipane*, Des Esseintes calls in his servant to see if
he too smells something: "L'autre renifla une prise d'air et déclara ne
respirer *aucune fleur*" ("The man sniffed the air and declared he could not

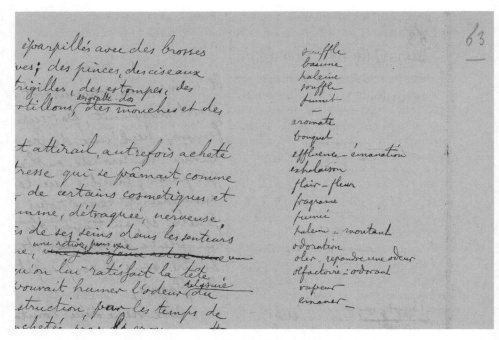

4.2. Manuscript page 64v from chapter 10 of *À rebours* with a
list of smell words in the margin. Image source: gallica.bnf.fr / BnF.

Image source: gallica.bnf.fr / BnF.

smell [inhale] *any kind of flower*"; 699, 92, emphasis mine). Page 60r of the
manuscript shows that Huysmans first wrote *aucune odeur* (no odour),
then crossed out *odeur* and replaced it with *fleur*. Moreover, it appears
Huysmans also deleted the feminine "e" of *aucune*, making *fleur* masculine: *aucun fleur* (an arcane synonym, "no odour") (Figure 4.3).[33] In the
context of the passage, "no odour" seems a better fit than "no flower."
The substitution of *aucun fleur* for *aucune odeur* also lends variation to the
repetitious vocabulary of smell, within a chapter already presenting the
words *odeur* and *odeurs* twelve times.

Some of the words in Huysmans's marginal notes affirm his taste
for esoteric vocabulary, others suggest a basic effort to vary a language
of odour and olfaction. While the names of smelly materials are seemingly infinite (ambergris, cassie, *frangipane*, linden, musk, opoponax,
rose, styrax, syringa, tobacco), the lexicon of smell and smelling per se

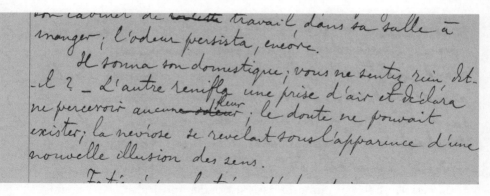

4.3. Manuscript page 60r in chapter 10 of *À rebours* with
aucune odeur replaced with *aucun fleur*.

Image source: gallica.bnf.fr / BnF.

can be repetitious. Some of the listed terms designate types of odours (aromatics, bouquet, fragrance, fumet, odour); others indicate its visible presence (smoke, vapour), or its state of constant, sometimes invasive motion (effluence, emanation, to emanate, to exude, to spread). The movement of air is further voiced in the fricative "f" and "v" of *flair*, *fleur*, *fumet*, *olfactoire*, *souffle vapeur*, etc. A good portion of the vocabulary reflects the human act of smelling, which is inseparable from taking in, consuming, processing smells within the body: breath, breathing, inhalation, exhalation. Such words recall the physical nature of Huysmans's reactions to perfumes, attributed to his nervous condition, and manifesting themselves in physical symptoms such as headaches and fainting.

The Osmazome of Literature

The fragrances released into Des Esseintes's room in chapter 10 recall other episodes in the book, where perfume accompanies his reading of texts or images, activities Des Esseintes pairs with perfume blending. Not surprisingly, these episodes share a lexicon of odours as well. Des Esseintes sees perfume in Gustave Moreau's visual representation of *Salomé*: "des parfums brûlaient, dégorgeant des nuées de vapeur," which immerse the scene in "l'odeur perverse des parfums" ("perverse odour of perfumes"; 624, 45). Later, reading the Latin books he loves, his "nervous brain" grows excitable, enveloped "dans une atmosphère de couvent, dans un parfum d'encens qui lui grisaient la tête, il s'était exalté les nerfs" ("in a convent-like atmosphere, that was scented with the heavy, intoxicating perfume of incense, his nerves had become overwrought"; 645, 65). The smell-sensitive Des Esseintes sees the tetrarch in Moreau's *L'apparition* as crazed by both the sight and smell of Salomé's body: "cette nudité de femme imprégnée de senteurs fauves, roulée dans les baumes, fumée dans les encens et dans les myrrhes" ("crazed by this woman's nudity, soaked in animalic smells, rolled in balsams, smoked in incense and myrrh"; 629, 48). The smell of incense returns in the fifteenth chapter, when sound waves engender smell waves in Des Esseintes's synesthetic hallucinations: "Alors, il sentit son cerveau délirant emporté dans les ondes musicales… Les chants appris chez les jésuites reparurent … répercutant leurs hallucinations aux organes olfactifs et visuels, les voilant de fumée d'encens" "Then, he felt his delirious brain being carried away by musical waves…. The hymns he had learned from the Jesuits came up again,… passing the hallucinations to the olfactory and visual organs, enveloping them in incense smoke"; 745–6, 164). Though primarily olfactory in nature, Des Esseintes's earlier hallucinations, too, gain momentum through other senses. He frequently touches his bottles of perfume and cosmetics, he looks through windows, at mirrors. The perfume adaptations of Baudelaire's poems revoice the musicality of verse, within the language of smell. Certain strings of words that represent smell materials are particularly sonorous, and even haptic, as their pronunciation provides a workout for the lips, the tongue, the jaw: *ayapana, l'opoponax, le chypre, le champaka, le sarcanthus.*

Baudelaire's poems are mentioned often in *À rebours*, [34] yet Des Esseintes engages with them most deeply through the senses, as objects displayed under glass like hothouse flowers (in the novel's chapter 2), and as fragrant orchestrations. The acts of reading and looking seem to conjure the smells he has earlier encountered in books and on canvas, and the works he admires most are comparable to fragrances. Des Esseintes characterizes works of fiction according to the images and odours their language evokes for him, but do not necessarily mention, such as Judith Gautier's 1867 *Livre de jade*, which does not name ginseng or tea, but "dont l'exotique parfum de ginseng et de thé se mêle à l'odorante fraicheur de l'eau qui baille sous un clair de lune, tout au long du livre" ("whose exotic perfume of ginseng and of tea blends with the odorous freshness of water babbling in the moonlight, throughout the book"; 743, 163). Des Esseintes reads Mallarmé's poetry as a fragrant blend of Baudelaire and Poe: "c'était leurs fines et puissantes substances encore distillées et dégageant de nouveaux fumets, de nouvelles ivresses" ("it was their fine and powerful substances distilled again and releas-ing new aromas, new intoxications"; 744, 162). The prose poem is his favourite of all literary genres because it represents "l'état d'of meat [sic] ... le suc concret, l'osmazome de la littérature, l'huile essentielle de l'art" ("beef essence ... the concrete juice, the osmazome of literature, the essential oil of art"; 743–4, 162). Like essential oil, concrete is a per-fumer's term, referring to a fragrance in the form of a highly condensed, sometimes waxy paste. Osmazome (from the Greek *smell* and *bouillon*) is what gives meat its *sui generis* smell and flavour, its signature scent. Here the search for accurate words to convey the experience of smell has been reversed; instead, the evocation of aroma allows Huysmans, via Des Esseintes, to convey not the words but the feeling, the embodi-ment, the experience, the phenomenon of poetics.

In these episodes on perfume and reading, the sensation of real fra-grance in the air enhances the materiality of words and images, while abstracted aromas written on the page stir the senses. Words activate perfume, and perfume acts on words. Texts and smells merge to become correspondingly tangible and readable. The language of perfume, its syntax and phrasing, is incorporated in the structure of the "perfume chapter" itself. The rhythms of Baudelaire's stanzas, which Des Esse-intes knows so well, supply base notes, anchoring and affixing the chapter's layered and embedded pieces within a readable structure, like a blended perfume with a fragrance refrain. Within this structure, too, layers of intertexts, intratexts, and metatexts unleash and absorb one another, forming an alchemy of composition. Its dimensions are as impossible to limit, within the seemingly neat chapter frame, as the uncontrollable fragrance wafting in and out of Des Esseintes's window.

Chapter Five

Perfumed Letters and Signature Scents

*"A young woman was rendered seriously ill by having received a letter heavily perme-
ated with a violent perfume."*

Baronne Staffe, *Usages du monde* (1891)[1]

When *À rebours'* protagonist Des Esseintes refers to a literary text or
genre as a condensed fragrance, or an osmazome, he is portraying a distinctive aesthetic phenomenon in terms of something perceptible, a fragrant, flavourful signature. In a more obvious way, nineteenth-century
novelists attribute to their protagonists' signature scents, that contemporaries would have identified and interpreted both for their aromatic
qualities, and as expressions of social status, temperament, and taste.
Characters in nineteenth-century French novels inhabit a world rich in
objects that readers would have recognized as scented. Handkerchiefs,
fans, and writing paper figured among the era's many recommended
vehicles for projecting a single, discrete, yet recognizable fragrance.
Any self-expression suggested by wearing a signature scent, however, was mitigated by constant warnings from etiquette and hygiene
experts, backed up by medical doctors, that a woman who does not
choose and use her perfume with care puts herself and others at risk.[2]
Cosmetic fragrance, increasingly available at various price points and
steadily marketed to women,[3] clouded distinctions between hygiene
and fashion, utility and ornamentation.[4] An ever-evolving culture of
perfume contributed to what Susan Hiner has called the nineteenth century's "duplicitous ideology of the feminine" (Hiner 2010, 156), a code
of fashion and accessories that could signify, paradoxically, good or
bad taste, modesty, or sexual availability.[5] Though seemingly no more
than a frivolous olfactory accessory, perfume became an ever-changing
social litmus test in a perilous balance of decorum and seduction.

Novelistic missives are important to the development of plot, character, and discursive networks,[6] but this chapter concentrates less on their
written content than on the more elusive smell of fictional letters in
Balzac's *Béatrix* (1839) and Flaubert's *Madame Bovary* (1857). By contextualizing those smells within attitudes and social practices of perfuming in the nineteenth century, we gain a new perspective on character
development, the relationship of the novels to the cultural climate of
their time, and the value of reading odours. In these works, the very
fragrance of letters ignites a hermeneutic engine, driving characters to
action, and plots towards conclusion, while revealing scented gestures
as charged with meaning, as are words on the page. Episodes in *Beatrix*
and *Madame Bovary* portray deviations in the practice of exchanging
perfumed letters, and by linking fragrance to physical and psychological imbalance, they dramatize the stakes of reading and misreading
socially decipherable smells. In *Béatrix*, the perfume transmitted from
a letter to an unfaithful husband is perceived as a physical threat perilous enough to destroy a nursing mother's milk. In *Madame Bovary*, the
self-appointed miasma expert Homais posits that the smell of apricots
(in which Rodolphe's break-up letter to Emma was nestled) is the cause
of Emma Bovary's syncope, paroxysm, and long-term illness (which
would have been attributed to neurosis or hysteria). Though exaggerated, these depictions of pleasant but toxic epistolary aromas reinforce
warnings about the dangers of smells, fetid and perfumed alike, which
circulated throughout the century.

Like the perfumes emanating from other scented objects, the fragrance
of writing paper signals levels of taste, or *distinction*,[7] to use the word
favoured by Balzac and other writers of the era, who recognized that in
a democratized society, individuals could distinguish themselves and
telegraph social value through behaviour and aesthetic choices, including the details of fashion and grooming.[8] But perfume deployment was
a matter of health and hygiene as well. Beauty manuals addressed to
women and marriageable *jeunes filles*, medical writing destined for a
specialized readership, and popular pseudo-medical tracts, refer to *danger* (physical and moral) and *abuse* in their discussions of perfume, sometimes borrowing a lexicon of disease and contagion to drive the point.
The insidious confusion of miasma and cosmetic fragrance reflects and
feeds contradictory attitudes regarding women and perfume. Such language and ambivalence appear in nineteenth-century instructions for
adorning stationery with aroma. The apprehension over perfume and
the women who use it, voiced in mutually reinforcing publications of
the era, serves as both cultural and discursive intertext to the staging of
Balzac and Flaubert's fictional, scented letters.

Perfume on the Page

Perfume and paper are longtime companions. In the first half of the nineteenth century, richly illustrated perfume labels, some etched and hand-coloured, served as eye-catching marketing tools.[9] Advertisements for fragrant cosmetics in newspapers and women's magazines became more visually appealing as the century progressed. While words and images delivered perfume to the page, other sales tactics appealed to the nose as well as the eye. Today's testing strips for sampling (*touches de parfum* or *mouillettes*), and the slim, fold-over margins on magazine pages (opened, then scratched or rubbed to release fragrance) descend from the scented cards, calendars, bookmarks, and fans distributed by perfume houses in the nineteenth century.[10] In 1840, editor Henri de de Villemessant perfumed the cover of the fashion magazine *La sylphide* with sachets provided by Guerlain to promote the house's perfume (Best 2017, 35; Mermet 1879, 374; Stamelman 2006, 66). Later, perfumer Eugene Rimmel published elaborately illustrated scented almanacs at the New Year to promote his products and marketed a scented first edition of his *Book of Perfumes* (1865).[11] While fragrant paper and fabrics were pleasing to both sight and touch, they delivered the added benefit of temporarily preserving the fragrance they advertised.[12]

Then, as now, paper served as a surrogate skin for risk-free fragrance testing. But more intimately, paper figured among the materials imbued with a signature scent, then worn or carried close to the body, to create a woman's distinct atmosphere. Madame Celnart, the author of countless do-it-yourself trade and etiquette manuals, considered scented paper flowers (an adornment for clothing or hair) a "poetic" vehicle for fragrance, a sign of delicate taste, and a desirable personal perfuming medium: "C'est même, selon moi, la meilleure manière de porter des parfums sur soi" ("It is even, in my opinion, the best way to wear perfume"; *Manuel des dames* 1833, 97).[13] Like other beauty and etiquette experts of the time, Celnart guides women to perfume their belongings, including clothing, accessories, books, sealing wax,[14] and writing paper (see Figures 5.1, 5. 2, and 0.2).

Prolific correspondents like Balzac and Flaubert showed attention to the materiality of letters and knew well the pleasure of scented letter reading. As a gift for the still married Madame (Ewelina) Hanska (to whom Balzac famously wrote, "[y]ou exhale, for me, the most heady perfume a woman can have"),[15] he had a box made for securing and perfuming writing paper. He ordered one for himself as well.[16] Flaubert fuelled the composition of steamy missives to Louise Colet by breathing in objects that retained her scent – locks of hair, mittens, slippers, letters – which he fondled and sniffed into the wee hours of the morning.[17] At 11 p.m. on 8 August 1846, Flaubert wrote:

Adieu, je ferme ma lettre. C'est l'heure où, seul et pendant que tout dort, je tire le tiroir où sont mes trésors. Je contemple tes pantoufles, le mouchoir, tes cheveux, le portrait, je relis tes lettres, j'en respire l'odeur musquée. Si tu savais ce que je sens maintenant!… dans la nuit mon cœur se dilate et une rosée d'amour le pénètre. Mille baisers, mille, partout, *partout*!

Adieu! I'm closing my letter. It's the hour when, alone and while everything sleeps, I open the drawer where my treasures are stored. I contemplate your slippers, the handkerchief, your hair, the portrait, I reread your letters, I inhale their musky odour. If you knew what I am smelling now!… in the night my heart dilates and a dewdrop of love penetrates it. A thousand kisses, a thousand, everywhere, *everywhere*! (*Correspondance* I, 280)

An hour later, Flaubert pens a second letter, opening with the smell of night air drifting through his window, and closing with a return to the musky scent of Colet's slippers: "Allons, je vais revoir tes pantoufles.… Celui qui les a faites ne se doutait pas du frémissement de mes mains en les touchant, je les respire et, elles sentent la verveine, et une odeur de toi qui me gonfle l'âme" ("Here we go, I'm going to look at your slippers again.… The person who made them had no idea of the trembling of my hands when I touch them, I inhale them, and, they smell of verbena and an odour of you that swells my soul"; 284).

Perfume, Contagion, and Writing Paper

The perfumers and beauty experts who discussed scented stationery in the nineteenth century often, consciously or not, analogized skin to paper. Carefully selected paper could suggest the writer's fragrant presence without implicating her skin; and other skin (animal, not human), was a preferred vehicle for lending scent to writing paper. According to chemist-perfumer Septimus Piesse, Peau d'Espagne (or Spanish Skin), a scented leather no longer in fashion for gloves by mid-century, nonetheless remained in considerable demand for perfuming stationery (Piesse, *Des odeurs* 1865, 289).[18] In his hygienically inspired advice on contact between Peau d'Espagne and paper, Piesse acknowledges the importance of *indirect* transmission of perfume to paper, to avoid dampening and staining. Piesse's use of the term "contagion" strengthens

5.1. A 1911 print advertisement for Lubin perfumes depicting a woman reading letters. The slogan: "Par les Parfums Lubin les bons moments de la vie sont rendus meilleurs encore" ("The good moments of life are made even better by Lubin Perfumes").

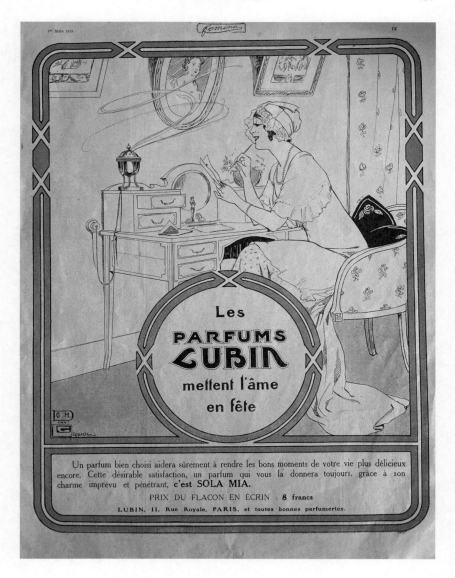

5.2. A 1913 print advertisement for Lubin perfumes depicting a woman holding a pen and letter as a perfume burner unleashes visible wafts of fragrance in the air.

this perceived affiliation of body and paper, while implying a fine line between cosmetic fragrance and miasmic contamination:

> Si l'on met un morceau de peau d'Espagne en contact avec du papier, celui-ci absorbera assez d'odeur pour pouvoir être considéré comme 'parfumé." Il va sans dire que, pour qu'on puisse écrire sur le papier, il ne faut pas qu'aucune des teintures ou essences odorantes le touche car ces substances altéreraient la fluidité de l'encre et gêneraient le mouvement de la plume; ce n'est donc qu'au moyen de cette sorte de contagion qu'il est possible de parfumer avec avantage le papier à lettres.

> If one places a piece of peau d'Espagne in contact with paper the latter will absorb enough odour to be considered "perfumed." It goes without saying that so that one may write on the paper, no scented dye or perfume essences should touch it, for these substances alter the fluidity of ink and upset the movement of the pen; thus is only by means of this sort of contagion that it is possible to perfume writing paper. (*Les odeurs* 1865, 289)

Piesse recommends comparable precautions in his discussion of civet, a penetrating, animal-derived perfume material.[19] His reference to transmission via contact and proximity links what is communicational to what is communicable:

> L'odeur de la civette est excellente, non pas transmise par un contact immédiat, mais placée dans le voisinage des objets qui doivent l'absorber. Ainsi, étendue sur de la peau, et mise dans un pupitre, elle parfume on ne peut plus doucement le papier et les enveloppes, si bien même que ces objets conservent l'odeur après avoir été jetés à la poste. C'est ainsi que sont parfumées les lettres de Saint-Valentin.

> The odour of civet is excellent, not transmitted by direct contact, but placed near the objects that should absorb it. Thus, spread on a skin, and placed in a desk drawer, it perfumes paper and envelopes ever so softly, so well in fact that these objects retain the odour after being dropped in the post. That is how letters for Valentine's Day are scented. (*Des odeurs et des parfums* 1865, 206)

While reinforcing the skin–paper analogy, this insistence on quasi-hygienic precaution also harmonizes with a tendency throughout the century to treat fashion and well-being, beauty and hygiene, as overlapping subjects.

Later in the century, Henry Havelock Ellis, who cites Piesse's *The Art of Perfumery* for his discussion of sexually stimulating smells, deems Peau d'Espagne a "highly complex and luxurious perfume," and "of all perfumes that which most nearly approaches the odor of a woman's skin; whether it also suggests the odor of leather is not so clear" (99–100). Nonetheless, by the turn of the century Peau d'Espagne was produced as bottled perfume by houses including Pinard, and has since been considered a cornerstone of leather scents. Its name is an enduring reminder of the constant connections between perfume, body, and skin.[20]

The meeting of perfume and paper, like the meeting of perfume and human skin, was a union to be arbitrated. In the tradition of Piesse and other perfumers, the Baronne Staffe (who clearly defined her target readers as women), advised scenting paper indirectly, and one might say, *safely*, as one would perfume the body. Staffe recommends, for her do-it-yourself readership, hand-sewn sachets strategically placed in desk drawers: "Le papier ne peut être parfumé que très légèrement, d'une vague senteur d'iris ou de violette, par exemple" ("The paper can only be very lightly perfumed, with a vague scent of iris or violet, for example"; *La correspondance dans toutes les circonstances de la vie* 1895, 21).[21] Paper should be neatly folded. Its colour must not fatigue the eventual reader. Shades of light blue, pearl, pale mauve, Nile green, cream, and white are the only colours used by "le grand monde." Pink is not favoured by les "gens de goût" ("people of taste"). For colour as for scent, fidelity matters; it is best to choose one and stick to it (21).

Signature Scents

Since scented handkerchiefs, flowers, fans, and writing paper facilitated the creation of a breathable, bodily signature (Figure 5.3), it was important to monitor fragrance selection and dosage. Madame Celnart evokes the spectre of contagion to make her readers aware of the physical, moral, and social dangers of cosmetic fragrances. Women who wear strong perfume court trouble because "beaucoup de gens fuient les dames ambrées et musquées comme des pestiférées" ("many people flee from ambered and musked ladies as from the plague-stricken"; *Manuel des dames*, 2nd ed., 1833, 92).[22] Later in the century, Ernest Feydeau similarly advises (though in a more wry tone) that: "[i]l faut éviter le musc et le patchouli comme la peste" ("one must avoid musk like the plague"; 156). Unlike Feydeau, who insists in his aptly named *L'art de plaire* (*The Art of Pleasing*) (1873) that perfume is a woman's

5.3. A 1911 print advertisement for Legrand's Parfum d'Éventail
showing application of perfume to a fan.

indispensable complement, or as he says, "condiment," necessary to complete her seductive allure (150), the more earnest and hygienically focused Celnart promotes perfume use neither as a tool of seduction, nor a frivolous fashion accessory. She cites pallor, weight loss, dark circles under the eyes, and nervous shivering as symptoms of perfume overdose (1833, 91).

If fragrance overload was to be dodged, that did not mean women should eschew perfume entirely. On the contrary, "l'absence totale d'odeurs est une privation inutile, et quelquefois même désavantageuse" ("the complete absence of odours is a useless deprivation, and sometimes even disadvantageous"; 92). Celnart justifies fragrance-wearing for the sake of hygiene and a happy marriage, since: "malgré la plus grande propriété, le corps humain est sujet à tant d'exhalaisons désagréables, générales ou particulières, que l'on ne doit point négliger ces précautions, surtout lorsqu'on a un mari dont l'odorat est très-susceptible" ("despite the greatest cleanliness, the human body is subject to so many disagreeable exhalations, general and particular, that one must not neglect precautions, especially if one has a husband whose sense of smell is quite sensitive"; 92). For Celnart, as for many medical doctors and hygienists of the time, personal perfuming is a delicate balancing act, contingent on taste and moderation.

The Baronne Staffe overtly links the importance of perfume to the construction of a readable feminine identity. In her 1897 *Cabinet de toilette*, she urges women to line their dresser drawers and armoires with sachets in order to scent gloves, handkerchiefs, lace, silk hosiery, linens, suits, dresses, skirts, coats, hat boxes, sleeves, hems, and corsets with one chosen perfume:

> Quand elle approche, on la devine avant de l'avoir vue. Avant d'avoir reconnu son écriture, à la senteur qu'exhale son papier, on sait de qui est la lettre. Prête-t-elle un livre, le parfum dont il est imprégné rappelle qu'il faut le lui rendre … ou vous poursuit comme un remords.

> When she approaches, you sense it is she before seeing her. Before recognizing her handwriting, from the scent it exhales, you know who the letter is from. When she lends a book, the perfume which impregnates it reminds you that that you must return it to her … or it follows you like a regret. (303)

Staffe issues a familiar caveat about dosage, all the while promoting perfume-wearing for pleasure and to please: "Sans se parfumer à outrance, ce qui est une faute, il est donc bon d'imprégner son linge, et tous ses vêtements d'un parfum léger et délicat – unique aussi – depuis la pointe des bottines jusqu'à la racine des cheveux; cela ajoute de l'élégance" ("Without overdoing it, which is a mistake, it is good to imbue one's linens, and all one's clothing with a perfume that is light and delicate – just one – from the tip of one's boots to the hairline; this adds elegance"; 298). Her main concern is that women remain true to one scent. No mixing. A woman should wear her chosen fragrance, faithfully, as an aromatic signature:

> Nous disons que chaque femme doit repousser le mélange des odeurs. Elle choisira un parfum et y restera fidèle. Tout ce qui lui appartient, ses livres, son papier à lettres, son salon intime, les coussins de sa voiture ... ses vêtements, les moindres objets dont elle se sert exhaleront le même et très doux parfum.

> We say that every woman should reject the blending of odours. She will choose one perfume and remain faithful to it. Everything that belongs to her, her books, her writing paper, her personal salon, the cushions of her car ... her clothing, every single object she uses will exhale the same sweet perfume. (298–9)

Though the Baronne Staffe's advice is quite light-hearted compared to that of the more fragrance-conservative Madame Celnart (whose books were still widely circulated at the turn of the century), the words "remain faithful" recall the moral and social gravitas of an item as seemingly frivolous as perfume. Later, in her *Le cabinet de toilette d'une honnête femme*, the Comtesse de Gencé further specifies that decorum prohibits the well-bred woman from wearing the signature perfume of another.[23]

If fragrance is a readable sign of socially constructed femininity, an expression of conformity to standards of taste, yet also an expression of individuality, then the stakes of misusing or misreading it are potentially high. Women who consulted beauty and etiquette manuals in the nineteenth century must have noticed the contradictory messages embedded in personal perfuming advice. Women should wear perfume, but they should smell natural. Perfume threatens the physical and moral health of the wearer as well as those who encounter her scented wake; nonetheless women should develop a personal, olfactory identity through their selection of perfume. Thus, choosing a perfume was no simple task. Dr. Ernest Monin warned that "[i]l faut bien dire (entre nous) qu'une femme *qui sait se parfumer* est aussi rare que celle *qui sait s'habiller*" ("it has to be said (just between us) that a woman *who knows how to perfume herself* is as rare as one *who knows how to dress herself*"; 1890, 244). Monin maintains that the ability to select the right perfume is neither an acquired taste nor a question of following fashion trends. His concept of good taste illustrates a distinction Bourdieu would later study and define as a social construct, masked as something genuine and innate (1979).

In 1882, perfumer Eugène Rimmel showed more confidence than Monin in a woman's ability to select her fragrance. Women were, after all, his potential clients: "Le choix d'un parfum de mouchoir est une telle affaire d'appréciation que nous ne nous permettrons pas plus d'indiquer à une dame celui qu'elle doit prendre, que nous ne recommanderions à un épicurien quel vin il doit boire" ("The choice of a handkerchief perfume is such a matter of judgment, that we would no more permit ourselves to tell a lady what perfume to select than we would recommend to an epicurean what wine he must drink"; 1870, 370–1). Echoing the advice of Madame Celnart, Rimmel warns women with delicate nerves to take it easy with perfume: "Nous nous bornerons donc à cette simple observation: les personnes nerveuses doivent éviter les bouquets composés; les simples extraits de fleurs leur conviennent mieux. Il faut se garder des parfums communs; mieux vaut s'en passer" ("Thus we will limit ourselves to this simple observation: nervous persons must avoid composed bouquets; simple floral extracts are better for them. One has to beware of common perfumes; it is better to do without them"; Rimmel 1870, 371).[24]

Rimmel does concur that women should wear one signature scent, but without going so far as to deny the force of fashion: "chaque femme doit avoir son parfum qui lui soit propre, si elle désire être *autre*" ("every lady must have a perfume of her own, if she wishes *to distinguish herself*"; 371). By suggesting that women can distinguish themselves – become *other* – through their selection of perfume, Rimmel takes a stand on the function of perfume, which was in a constant state of redefinition in the nineteenth century. Perfumers justified simultaneously the chemistry and the art of their trade, hygienists focused on the tonic and therapeutic benefits of fragrant products, and even beauty experts promoted the utility of scented cosmetics. But underlying this discourse on women and fragrance was the fact that, as Rimmel understood, perfume had become a fashion accessory. Rimmel's appeal to distinction, to being *autre* via the selection of fragrance, underscores fashion's central paradox: that it is simultaneously an expression of imitation and of singularity.[25]

Troubling Toilettes

The complicated, often contradictory social messages prevalent in extra-literary writing on odours and perfume also make their way to the pages of novels, sometimes in brief mentions, but often at key moments. Noun, the maid transplanted from l'Île Bourbon to France in George Sand's 1833

Indiana, though uninstructed in the rules of language and spelling, did have enough "style in her heart" to pen a letter to her lover, Raymond, on glossy paper, sealed with scented wax. The stationery was, however, that of her mistress, Indiana, now the object of her lover's desire (Sand 76–7). The narrator's interpretive comments in this passage pertain to Noun's poor writing, not her choice of fragrance, yet Raymond's well-established sensitivity to the perfume that "emanates from" Indiana (180) suggests that he may have perceived the displaced scent. The ability to communicate properly with fragrance, as with words, is a form of social literacy that not all women are shown to achieve.

Flaubert's protagonist Frédéric Moreau (*L'éducation sentimentale*) receives a poorly written, perfumed letter from his soon-to-be mistress Rosanette, just when he has vowed to push the unattainable Madame Arnoux from his mind. Only a portion of the eight-page missive is revealed to the reader; Frédéric himself skips over most of it at first, "l'écriture était si abominable" ("the handwriting was so abominable"; 232).[26] After noticing an invitation to meet at the very end, Frédéric rereads the letter attentively, puzzling over its meaning: "Que signifiait cette invitation?" ("What did this invitation mean?"; 232). It is in part the few words Frédéric manages to decipher, prose more flowery than Rosanette's usual expression, but also the materiality of the letter that captures Frédéric's attention and moves him to action: "Il garda longtemps les feuilles entre ses doigts. Elles sentaient l'iris; et il y avait, dans la forme des caractères et l'espacement irrégulier des lignes, comme un désordre de toilette qui le troubla" ("He kept the sheets of paper between his fingers for a long time. They smelled of iris; and there was, in the form of the characters and the irregular spacing of the lines, something like a disorderly *toilette* that stirred him"; 232).

Frédéric does not seem to make a conscious connection between the perfumed letter and an earlier sighting of Rosanette, dancing at the Alhambra, where her lopsided wig and heavily applied powder fling iris scent into the air all around her (151). Nor does he realize that what is stirring about the smell of lingering iris is its connection to his first furtive glimpse of a different woman, Mme. Dambreuse, whom he only saw from the back as she sprang into a carriage. Looking inside the passing vehicles, still unable to catch a glimpse of the woman's face, Frédéric perceives her clothing and fragrance, both of which fill the coach. Emanating from within is "un parfum d'iris, et comme une vague senteur d'élégances féminines" (an iris perfume, and a sort of vague fragrance of feminine elegance; 51–2).[27]

The iris scents of Rosanette and Madame Dambreuse create an unconscious overlap for Frédéric, a perceptible juxtaposition of these women to the unattainable Madame Arnoux, whose unnamed fragrance Frédéric stealthily inhales from her handkerchief. The fetishization of her handkerchief and other scented possessions (gloves, comb, rings) fortifies a passion, that is in turn compared to a perfume powerful enough to infiltrate and transform his very being: "La contemplation de cette femme l'énervait, comme l'usage d'un parfum trop fort. Cela descendit dans les profondeurs de son tempérament, et devenait presque une manière générale de sentir, un mode nouveau d'exister" ("The contemplation of this woman enervated him like the use of a too-strong perfume. It penetrated into the very depths of his temperament, and became almost a general way of sensing, a new mode of existence"; 99–100). Rosanette's scented cosmetics and writing paper reverse this comparison of all-consuming emotion to strong perfume: they materialize in smellable, tangible paper, an inner turmoil Frédéric experiences but never manages to articulate in words.

That Lethal Paper

Balzac's *Béatrix* dramatizes both the dangers that await readers of perfumed letters, and the strategic social advantage of characters perceptive enough to decipher aromatic messages. The telling episode appears relatively late in a novel that has steadily established connections between characters and odours, affixing the significance of such relationships to dichotomies of wholesomeness and infection, close-knit provincial life and the corruptive forces of the city. Early on, the omniscient narrator casts Paris and its worldly dwellers as alluring menaces to which, through gradual seduction or lack of savvy, provincial innocents succumb. The fall (sometimes temporary) of certain characters is proportional to their degree of drift from the fresh, salty air of protagonist Calyste du Guénic's Breton home. Guérande, where the story begins, is portrayed as a village "complètement en dehors du mouvement social" ("completely outside of social movement"; 637),[28] geographically isolated from modern France for lack of "communications vives et soutenues avec Paris" ("lively and regular communications with Paris"; 638).

In the novel's opening pages, a lengthy, detailed, often humorous portrayal of Guérande's isolation in time and space reveals that "communication" with Paris signifies the process of imparting and sharing information (as suggested by the novel's heavy use of epistolary passages), along with the noxious transmission of mephitic language, books, ideas, habits, and eventually, perfume. Silent, private, unchanging, hard to reach, socially impenetrable, self-absorbed, and stubbornly resistant to influence from the outside, Guérande has remained for centuries in social quarantine, threatened now by an androgynous local woman writer (Félicité des Touches, a.k.a. Camille Maupin), who spends time in Paris, brings her urban friends to town, and thus jeopardizes the innocent, marriageable protagonist Calyste.

The tension between, and would-be separation of, provincial and urban life is reinforced by a narrative structure that situates the story first in Guérande (parts 1 and 2), then in Paris (part 3).[29] As Madeleine Ambrière observes, this geographical division reveals "une tentative de pénétration de l'une par l'autre, dont le jeune héros, Calyste du Guénic, est l'agent" ("an attempt at penetrating one side with the other, of which the young hero, Calyste de Guénic, is the agent"; 601). For instance, Guérande's hermetic seal is broken when Calyste succumbs to invasive Parisian influences on his home turf. "[J]'ai mordu la pomme parisienne!" ("[I] have bitten the Parisian apple!"; 730). Indeed, in the novel's third section, Calyste, his wife, and their baby are keeping house in Paris.

With this backdrop of penetrated spaces, Balzac presents other diametric oppositions, subject to constant infiltration, or infection. Gender ambiguity is frequently mentioned in narrative commentary and dialogue regarding Camille Maupin's masculine characteristics. Duly noted are her cigarette smoking and trouser wearing. And Calyste, though he wears pants and has Herculean strength, "ressemblât assez à une jeune fille déguisée en homme" ("looked a bit like a young woman dressed as a man"; 681). Equally evocative of the infiltration essential to the novel's dramatic tension are the moments when fragrance, representative of insalubrious, outside influences, seductively mingles with wholesome Breton air and bodies. In two such instances, fragrance accompanies the words of written letters.

Calyste encounters Béatrix via a verbal portrait delivered in a briefly interrupted monologue by Camille, followed by the presentation of a letter written in Béatrix's hand. Camille sets the stage for this tease by filling the air with the pungent odour of patchouli:

Camille Maupin, qui partageait le goût oriental de l'illustre écrivain de son sexe, alla prendre un magnifique narghilé persan que lui avait donné un ambassadeur; elle chargea le cheminée de patchouli, nettoya le *bochettino*, parfuma le tuyau de plume.

Camille Maupin, who shared the Oriental taste of the illustrious author of the same sex, took out a magnificent Persian narghile that an ambassador had given her; she filled the bowl with patchouli, cleaned the *bochettino*, perfumed the quill. (712)

The "illustrious author of the same sex," George Sand, is doubly present in the novel. She does not interact with the fictional characters, but is acknowledged by name as Camille's friendly rival, and "her brother Cain." Balzac made no secret of having modelled Camille after Sand.[30] Perhaps less obviously than smoking and trouser wearing, Camille's choice of patchouli reinforces the connection. Among the practical favours Sand asked of Musset when she was in Venice, was the delivery of gloves, comfortable shoes, and patchouli, to be purchased from a designated vendor at a specific price.[31]

The hookah and the scent of patchouli in Camille Maupin's room signal urban exoticism and express her "Oriental taste." In the early nineteenth century, the French smelled patchouli on expensive shawls made in India, where the plant leaves served as insect repellent for storage and shipping. Since patchouli-scented shawls from India could be sold at extravagant prices, French knockoffs were similarly scented but reportedly never had quite the same fragrance as the authentic Indian fabric.[32]

In step with fellow perfumers and hygienists, Rimmel describes the smell of patchouli as particularly strong: "C'est une odeur très particulière, aussi agréable aux uns qu'elle est désagréable aux autres" ("It is a very particular odour, as agreeable to some as it is disagreeable to others"; 259). An important note in perfume blends, in pure form it could smell musty, and was considered too strong and harsh for tasteful women. Though still blended in scores of cosmetic products, patchouli seems to have gone out of style by 1865, when Piesse warned it could give off a musty smell of old clothing (154). In nineteenth-century novels, the recognizable smell of patchouli is frequently associated with women of compromised virtue: the odour of actress and mistress Héloïse Brisetout's shawl in Balzac's *Cousine Bette* (1846); the smell of disenchanted prostitutes and their clothing in Husymans's 1876 *Marthe*; the sharp odour standing out among others on the titular prostitute's dressing table in Zola's *Nana* (1880).[33] Sheltered and inexperienced, Calyste may not know how to read the cultural subtleties wafting in the pungent smoke of burned patchouli, but the layering of Camille's words and fragrance prove to be successful lures.

Though Calyste's eventual pursuit of Béatrix does not end well, her own unnamed perfume proves memorable and recognizable to him. The fragrance also creates an olfactory bridge from the first to the last section of the novel. Living in Paris with his young wife and baby, Calyste happens upon Béatrix at the opera, and against his own good judgment, agrees to meet with her the next day. A savvy wearer of signature scent, Béatrix snares Calyste with the synesthetic overload of her carefully orchestrated toilette: "Par un hasard cherché peut-être …

Béatrix exhalait le parfum dont elle se servait aux Touches lors de sa rencontre avec Calyste. La première aspiration de cette odeur, le contact de cette robe,… tout fit perdre la tête à Calyste" ("Due to a planned coincidence, perhaps … Béatrix radiated [exhaled] the perfume she wore at Des Touches when she met Calyste. The first inhalation of that odour, the contact of that dress,… it all made Calyste lose his head"; 869). Calyste excuses himself from dinner with his wife Sabine via a letter both dictated by Béatrix and written on her stationery. Sabine does not fail to notice the infidelity revealed by the letter's perfume: "Tu m'a cependant écrit sur du papier de femme, il sentait une odeur féminine" ("However, you wrote to me on a woman's paper; it had a feminine odour"; 872). Nevertheless, Calyste dares to visit Béatrix again that very day, apparently having not understood the significance of perfume traces, since upon his return, Sabine again detects the telltale fragrance:

> Tout à coup, comme mordue par une vipère, elle quitta Calyste, alla se jeter sur un divan, et s'y évanouit…. En tenant ainsi Calyste, en plongeant le nez dans sa cravate, abandonnée qu'elle était à sa joie, elle avait senti l'odeur du papier de la lettre!… Une autre tête de femme, avait roulé là, dont les cheveux et la figure laissait une odeur adultère. Elle venait de baiser la place où les baisers de sa rivale étaient encore chauds!… "Allez chercher mon médecin et mon accoucheur, tous deux! Oui, j'ai, je le sens, une révolution de lait."

> Suddenly, as if bitten by a viper, she let go of Calyste, threw herself on the divan, and fainted…. By holding Calyste like that, by plunging her nose in his cravat, abandoned to joy as she was, she had smelled the odour of that letter's paper!… Another woman's head had lain there, whose hair and face left an adulterous odour. She had just kissed the spot where her rival's kisses were still warm!… "Go fetch my doctor and my midwife, both of them! Yes, I feel it, my milk is turning." (874–5)

Sabine has not revealed that she sniffed out Calyste's lie. Instead, as the narrator indicates, she initially invents the breast-milk crisis either to cover for her behaviour or to get Calyste out of the house while she investigates his alibi. However, she soon genuinely experiences the physical symptoms of a nervous attack that the narrator will call a "paroxysme de folie" ("paroxysm of madness"; 876):

> La crise qu'elle avait annoncée comme prétexte eut lieu. Ses cheveux devinrent dans sa tête autant d'aiguilles rougies au feu des névroses. Son sang bouillonnant lui parut à la fois se mêler à ses nerfs et vouloir sortir par ses pores! Elle fut aveugle pendant un moment. Elle cria: "Je meurs!"

The crisis that she had used as a pretext took place. The hairs of her head became so many red needles heated by the fire of neurosis. Her boiling blood seemed to mingle with her nerves and to try to issue from her pores. She went blind for a moment. She cried: "I'm dying!" (875)

Later, having recovered, she again mentions to a friend the damage to her breast milk: "Heureusement, le petit est sevré, mon lait l'eût empoisonné!" ("Happily, the baby is weaned, my milk would have poisoned him"; 877).

Despite the hyperbolic tone of narrator and characters alike, the possibility of a physical crisis provoked by perfume was more than a literary trope. Balzac's fictional attack is justified by publications devoted to the link between smell sensitivity and illness, particularly in women. For example, "sans parler des parfums très-odorants, comme le musc" ("never mind strong smelling perfumes like musk"), Dr. Alphée Cazenave alerts readers to odours that provoke "syncope, la tuméfaction de la face, etc." ("syncope, swelling of the face and so on"; 279–80). In nineteenth-century chronicles of miasma's effects, the soured milk of livestock provides material evidence of contaminated air (Barnes 18–19). The 1790 *Encyclopédie méthodique: médecine* offers advice on how to manage nursing, when (human) maternal milk has been infected by miasmas (vol. 2, 10), and the 1865 *Dictionnaire encyclopédique des sciences médicales* reports an observation which "tend à prouver que le lait d'une nourrice peut servir de véhicule au miasme" ("suggests that a wet nurse's milk can serve as a vehicle for miasma") though "rien ne dit que la transmission à l'enfant s'est faite par le lait plutôt que par une autre voie" ("it is not clear that the transmission to the child was caused by the milk rather than by another means"; vol. 3, 258). In his tellingly subtitled *Dictionnaire de la beauté, ou la toilette sans dangers* (*Dictionary of Beauty, or the Toilette without Danger*; 1826), César Gardeton calls out the extreme imprudence of perfumed women who visit women in labour, thus exposing the latter to "odeurs perfidies" ("hazardous odours"; 160). If the characters in *Béatrix* believe that inhaling the perfume of a shirt collar or a letter could destroy a mother's breast milk, it is because a presumed correlation between the danger of mephitic air and the danger of cosmetic perfume had been well nurtured. Moreover, the provenance of the perfume in question, its belonging to a corrupted and corruptive *Parisienne*, resonates with warnings delivered to young women of the era: that the dangers of perfume are social and moral.

In order to spare the young wife, Sabine's mother and her friend Ursule Portenduère make a concerted effort to get Sabine off the trail of this *lettre fatale* ("lethal letter"; 877). When the women identify the stationery as coming from the Jockey Club,[34] Calyste goes along with the story. But once away from his family, he chides Béatrix for having left her telltale perfume on the letter:

> Ce fatal papier sur lequel vous m'avez fait écrire.... Le chiffre heureuse-ment, votre B., était effacé par hasard. Mais le parfum que vous avez laissé sur moi, mais les mensonges dans lesquels je me suis entortillé comme un sot ont trahi mon bonheur. Sabine a failli mourir, le lait est monté à la tête, elle a un érysipèle, peut-être en portera-t-elle les marques pendant toute sa vie.

> The lethal paper on which you had me write.... The initial fortunately, your B., was accidently erased. But the perfume that you left on me, but the lies in which I involved myself like a fool, have betrayed my happi-ness. Sabine nearly died, her milk went to her head, she has erysipelas, and she may bear the marks for the rest of her life. (879)

Neither the perceived fatality of the letter, nor the threat of Sabine's permanent disfigurement by a bacterial skin rash, are enough to keep Calyste away from Béatrix and her fragrant stationery. Nor does the subterfuge of her well-meaning mother keep Sabine from sniffing out the truth: "Elle chercha le fatal parfum et le sentit. Enfin elle ne se confia plus ni à son amie, ni à sa mère qui l'avaient si charitablement trompé" ("She searched for the lethal perfume, and she smelled it. This time she no longer confided in her friend or her mother, who had so charita-bly duped her"; 881). When the next letter from Béatrix arrives, Sabine hands it to Calyste, declaring in a voice that reveals what she knows: "Mon ami, cette lettre vient du Jockey-Club.... Je reconnais l'odeur et le papier" ("My friend, the letter is from the Jockey Club.... I recognize the odour and the paper"; 882).

The true name of Béatrix's signature scent is never divulged, yet like handwriting, it is identifiable. Had Calyste himself noticed the perfume on his ascot, on the writing paper? Seemingly not. Such an oversight confirms his characterization as an easily manipulated, inexperienced provincial. Though Béatrix successfully employed her signature scent to bait Calyste, his inattention to the traces of that scent on clothing and letters betrays a social gullibility that even time in Paris could not erase. Instead, it is Sabine who learns to read per-fume, and whose olfactory literacy allows her to control the future of their marriage.

Maybe It Was the Apricots

Unlike Calyste's duplicitous message to Sabine, Rodolphe Boulanger's disingenuous break-up letter to Emma Bovary is not imbued with cosmetic perfume. But it does arrive scented. Having rather abruptly talked himself out of a plan to run off with Madame Bovary, Rodolphe decides to apprise his lover of this change of heart in writing. Pen in hand, he encounters writer's block; his memory of Emma (whom he has seen just minutes ago) has already faded. Flaubert uses what Vladimir Nabokov called *counterpoint method* [35] to present the content of the letter as it is penned, interspersed with running commentary (the narrator's and Rodolphe's). Counterpoint will once again structure exposition in the tragicomic scene where Emma receives the letter. There, narrative depiction of her suffering and near suicide parallels a dialogue between pontificating pharmacist Homais, and Emma's oblivious husband, Charles.

The scenes of the missive's composition and delivery each take place against olfactory circumstances related to the materiality of the letter, and its readability as an object. For Rodolphe, the process begins with the failure of odour to trigger memory:

> Afin de ressaisir quelque chose d'elle, il alla chercher dans l'armoire, au chevet de son lit, une vieille boîte à biscuits de Reims où il enfermait d'habitude ses lettres de femmes, et il s'en échappa une odeur de poussière de roses humides et de roses flétries. D'abord, il aperçut un mouchoir de poche couvert de gouttelettes pâles. C'était un mouchoir à elle, une fois qu'elle avait saigné du nez, en promenade; il ne s'en souvenait pas.

> To bring back to mind something about her, he fetched from the armoire an old Rheims biscuit box in which he usually kept letters from women, and from which escaped an odour of damp dust and withered roses. First, he noticed a pocket handkerchief covered with pale little spots. It was one of her handkerchiefs, one time she had had a nosebleed, taking a walk. He no longer remembered it. (475)[36]

To find the long letters Emma had written him early in their liaison, Rodolphe plumbs the depths of his biscuit box, rummaging through messages, bouquets, a garter, hair pins, and locks of hair (both blond and brown), some of which get caught on the box's hinges and break. Mechanically "flânant parmi ses souvenirs" ("wandering among his souvenirs"; 509), Rodolphe's hands jostle mementos in a failed attempt to stir memories, eventually skimming through, and aerating, some saved letters: "À propos d'un mot, il se rappelait des visages, de certains gestes, un son de voix: quelquefois, pourtant, il ne se rappelait rien…. Prenant donc une poignée de lettres, confondues, il s'amusa à faire tomber en cascades de sa main droite à sa main gauche" ("A word recalled faces, certain gestures, the sound of a voice; sometimes, however, he recalled nothing…. Taking a handful of mixed up letters, he entertained himself by making [the letters] fall in a cascade from his right hand to his left"; 509). This passage is one of many in which Flaubert concretizes ideas through the depiction of objects and physical animation, rather than through verbal comparison and metaphors (though he often does that too).[37] Here he presents descriptions that unfold literally and metonymically at the same time, as in the early portrayals of Charles's hat in his school days, Emma's wedding cake, or her burning wedding bouquet. The careless and mechanical handling of love tokens leaves Rodolphe "ennuyé et assoupi" ("bored and numb"; 509), as did his dalliance with Emma. The comically dubious depths of Rodolphe's biscuit box rival the shallowness of his sentiments.

Emma's sensitivity to odours and their power to stir both memories and imagination are reinforced throughout the novel, as is her use of pomades, pastilles, and *eau de colo*gne (see chapter 6). After the ball at la Vaubyessard, Emma stores in her armoire, suggestively tucked within the folds of her linens, a cigar case found along the road. She removes the case time and again in order to breathe in its aroma of tobacco and verbena, and to conjure dreams of a different life (377). It is the fragrance of Rodolphe's beard, vanilla and verbena like that of the Viscount, that makes Emma give in to his advances (459). There is reason to believe, too, that Emma's bloodstained handkerchief was once perfumed, not only because this was a fashion of the time (liquid perfume was called handkerchief perfume – *parfum de mouchoir*). The suave odour of monogrammed handkerchiefs is something Emma notices at la Vaubyessard (371), and later incorporates as a tool of seduction: "C'était pour lui [Rodolphe] … qu'il n'y avait jamais assez de *cold cream* sur sa peau, ni de patchouli dans ses mouchoirs" ("It was for him [Rodolphe] … that there was never enough cold cream on her skin, or patchouli on her handkerchiefs"; 496).[38]

Of the over twenty handkerchiefs mentioned in *Madame Bovary*, nearly all correlate to their owner's level of physical or social grace at a given moment. Handkerchiefs wipe mouths, mop brows, cool temples, muffle tears, catch vomit, and blot stained gowns. Emma's father-in-law douses his own *foulards* with Emma's entire supply of eau de cologne (407), while the cloddish country priest uses his teeth to unfold his (428). Seeing Emma after having stood her up three times,

Rodolphe "eut l'air de ne point remarquer ses soupirs mélancoliques, ni de le mouchoir qu'elle tirait" ("seemed/pretended not to notice her melancholy sighs, nor the handkerchief she took out"; 484). Later, in preparation for a tryst with Emma, Léon "répondit dans son mouchoir tout ce qu'il possédait de senteurs" ("poured into his handkerchief all the fragrance he owned"; 543).

In her best-selling *Usages du monde* (1891), Baronne Staffe presents the pocket handkerchief as a mainstay of civilization: "Il a fallu une civilisation avancée pour nous doter du mouchoir de poche.... Le mouchoir, que la civilisation a mis dans notre poche, devait nous servir à dissimuler notre imperfection physique" ("It took an advanced civilization to bestow upon us the pocket handkerchief.... The handkerchief, which civilization has placed in our pocket, was meant to dissimulate our physical imperfection"; 338–9). Staffe looks fondly on the good old days when a woman carried one handkerchief for show and stored another in her pocket for more vulgar uses (339). Fin-de-siècle print advertisements for perfume often depict women holding, shaking, or inhaling the scent of a perfumed handkerchief, an olfactory accessory which remained in fashion through the early twentieth century (see Figure 5.4).

The cruel irony of Emma's handkerchief, stained and musty smelling at best, lost in a confusion of other women's belongings in a repurposed biscuit tin, finds parallel in the circumstances of its delivery. Rodolphe hides his callously composed break-up letter under some vine leaves in a basket of freshly picked apricots, to be delivered by his ploughman Girard, who in turn wraps the apricots in his own handkerchief. Girard's practical manoeuvre undermines the potential sentimentality of exchanging fragrant letters. The tragi-comic scene following delivery of the apricots centres on the drama of Emma's reaction, undercut by husband Charles Bovary's doltish response, made even more absurd by pharmacist Homais's pontificating interventions.

Emma immediately recognizes the fruit basket is a means of communication from her lover, for, as the narrator explains, Rodolphe had often nestled his *billets doux* in seasonal fruit and game (512). A few moments later, having read and reread the letter, Emma finds herself in the attic, leaning on the window frame, asking herself why she shouldn't end it all (513). Charles interrupts this would-be theatrical ending by calling Emma to the dinner table. There, in one of one of his least empathic moments, Charles bites into an apricot, pronounces it perfect, and offers the whole basket to Emma, attempting to whet her appetite with its aroma: "'Sens donc: quelle odeur!' fit-il en la lui passant sous le nez à plusieurs reprises" ("'Smell then! What an odour' he said, as he waved it under her nose again and again"; 514). Though Emma protests that she is suffocating,

5.4. A 1910 Lubin perfume advertisement showing women smelling perfume on a handkerchief, with the tag line "Ça vient de chez Lubin" ("It comes from Lubin").

Charles continues to savour the fatal fruit, spitting the pits into his hand.[39] When a blue tilbury passes by the house, Emma understands that it carries Rodolphe, who is leaving town without her. She faints.

The version of this episode that Charles recounts just moments later to Homais (who temporarily revives Emma with aromatic vinegar), conveys not only his inauspiciously limited perspective (the reader is privy to quite a bit more information than he), but also his risibly limited powers of observation: "Charles répondit que cela l'avait saisie tout à coup, pendant qu'elle mangeait des abricots" ("Charles replied that it happened to her suddenly, as she was eating apricots"; 515). Homais, as always, weighs in, attributing Emma's syncope to the smell of apricots. It is not the first time the pharmacist has commented on dangerous effluvia in this novel, where vapours and smells persistently define the atmosphere in which its characters wander. When Emma and Léon first meet, their flirtatious exchange of romantic clichés (the poetry of lakes, sunsets, German music, solitary contemplation of the sea) is cross-cut with, and thus undercut by, Homais's pronouncements on air quality, insalubrious river vapours, and poor hygiene (398–400). Later, he declares himself well versed on analysis of gases and the influence of miasmas (447).[40] Just after Emma has died, it is Homais who arrives with camphor, benzoin, and aromatic herbs, and chlorine to banish miasmas (628).

It is as easy for current readers as for characters in the novel to tune out the white noise of Homais's seemingly endless, know-it-all monologues,[41] including his commentary on odours. As is often the case, his ill-timed lectures represent a pastiche of contemporary medical wisdom:

> Mais il se pourrait que les abricots eussent occasionné la syncope! Il y a des natures si impressionnables à l'encontre de certaines odeurs! et ce serait même une belle question à étudier, tant sous le rapport pathologique que sous le rapport physiologique. Les prêtres en connaissent l'importance, eux qui ont toujours mêlé des aromates à leurs cérémonies. C'est pour vous stupéfier l'entendement et provoquer les extases, chose d'ailleurs facile à obtenir chez les personnes du sexe, qui sont plus délicates que les autres. On en cite qui s'évanouissent à l'odeur de la corne brûlée, du pain tendre.

> It is possible that the apricots caused the syncope! There are natures so sensitive to certain odours! And this would in fact be a good question to study, both in relation to pathology and physiology. The priests know its importance, they who have always mixed aromatics with their ceremonies. It is to stupefy your reason and provoke ecstasy, a thing incidentally easy to achieve with persons of the [weaker] sex, who are more delicate than others. Cases have been cited of fainting at the smell of burnt hartshorn,[42] of fresh bread. (516–17)

Indeed, cases of syncope (and worse)[43] provoked by odours had been noted in studies of olfaction, and would continue to be cited as etiologies of hysteria were shaped in the eighteenth and nineteenth centuries. In his 1760 volume on health and hygiene during pregnancy,[44] obstetrician André Levret identifies suave odours as well as musk and ambergris, as particularly dangerous to women in labour (73–4).[45]

Dr. Samuel-Auguste Tissot's 1790 *Traité des nerfs et de leurs maladies*, reprinted and cited throughout the following century, reports the case of a woman who fainted at the smell of lavender (312). In his 1821 treatise on osphresiology, Hippolyte Cloquet warns that smells can excite violent spasms in hysterical women (115), and that even "[d]es douces odeurs, chez certaines personnes nerveuses, produisent la syncope ou la cessation des mouvements du cœur" ("gentle odours, for some people, produce syncope and cessation of the heart's movements"; 340). Cloquet also reports that menstruating, pregnant, or anemic women can experience a sort of olfactory pica, evident in their perceived "perversion" of pleasant odours, which they find repulsive, and exaltation of fetid or unpleasant odours, including hartshorn. As we saw earlier, Cazenave alerted readers in 1867 to syncope and comparably severe reactions to smells. In his 1889 *Le parfum de la femme et le sens olfactif das l'amour*, Galopin also warns that musk can "provoque la syncope avec tout son cortège d'accidents et d'ennuis chez certaines personnes" ("provoke syncope along with its entire procession of medical incidents and problems in certain people"; 139). The relationship between Emma Bovary's symptoms throughout the novel, and etiologies of hysteria circulating at the time, has been well established, and as Janet Beizer has shown, medical writers often found their "evidence" in Flaubert's novel.[46] When later in the century Cazenave (282) or Combe (25) repeat a version of Cloquet's comments on odours and syncope, it is quite possible that Homais's pronouncement on apricots contributed to that chain of medical lore.[47]

For the reader who knows the letter's story from composition to delivery, Homais's assertion, that the smell of apricots caused Emma to faint, provides one of many examples of how the narrative, in both the story and its telling, taints Emma's romantic dreams. Her sensitivity to perfume, potentially a sign of a delicate nature and good taste, has instead been relegated to the realm of the pathological and the ridiculous. The devaluation of Emma's physical and emotional state is exacerbated when Homais pragmatizes the olfactory, first by reviving Emma with the smell of vinegar, then by offering up his apricot-odour theory to diagnose her. Rodolphe's letter, too, bundled with a servant's handkerchief, and scented with apricots, undermines the sentimental gesture of exchanging perfumed letters.

The catalytic placement of letters and their accompanying smells at turning points in the lives of Sabine and Emma attests to the symbiotic relationship between novels and nonfiction discourse, particularly when it comes to perfume. It is true that, as Septimus Piesse and the Baronne Staffe would have it, the fragrance of the letters we have just read (or smelled) neither alters the fluidity of the ink, nor disturbs the movement of the pen. Yet it does nuance, expand, and gloss the written word, within the framework of the novel, and the larger context of modern perfumery in the making. In *Béatrix* and *Madame Bovary*, the perfumed letter contributes to a narrative network of physical, psychological and moral contamination, reinforced within and outside the novel, among the interdependent domains of osphresiology, medicine, hygiene, beauty, and etiquette. A metonymical extension of the writer's hand (and thus the body and the mind), the perfumed letter also functions as a metaphorical stand-in for the skin, the body, and its exhalations, contaminated by, and contaminating with, their signature scent.

Chapter Six

Smelling (of) Iris

In a passage from *Madame Bovary* considered racy enough to be cited in the obscenity trial against Flaubert, lovestruck newlywed Charles Bovary wonders if his wife's fresh fragrance radiates from her skin, or from the chemise that covers it. The fact that Charles conflates the smell of his wife's skin with her scented undergarment shows Emma to be a clever fragrance wearer, mindful of etiquette rules stipulating that a proper woman use modest scents, sparingly enough to suggest her own body's naturally sweet sillage. The *trompe nez* effect of Emma's fresh odour (Is it her skin's natural smell? Is it her scented clothing?) attests to her cleanliness, her attention to cosmetic trends, her good taste, and her moderation. But what was her fragrance?

Foreshadowing suggests that Emma Bovary's linens smelled of iris, a scent presented from Charles's perspective, in a description of the kitchen where he and Emma have their first conversation. The episode begins with a depiction of the farm as Charles would have approached it, the exterior lined with oozing mounds of manure. Though he encounters an unidentified Emma Rouault in a blue merino dress at the farmhouse threshold, it is only after tending to Emma's father, who is sweating profusely under his sheets, that Charles moves to the kitchen, where he and Emma chat in a waft of clean linens: "On sentait une odeur d'iris et de draps humides, qui s'échappait de la haute armoire en bois de chêne faisant face à la fenêtre" ("You could smell an odour of iris and damp sheets escaping the tall oak armoire facing the window"; 339).

Usually the oozing dunghill, not the clean iris, stands out in this novel that earned a reputation for being dirty before it was published.[1] In the 1857 obscenity trial, prosecutor Ernest Pinard argued that the book was an offence to decency in both content and purpose: it painted otherwise innocent scenes with a lascivious brush, and it was an example of an unrestrained, artless realism, with no redeeming moral lesson.[2] Like Baudelaire's *Fleurs du mal*, also the subject of obscenity charges that year,[3] Flaubert's novel brings together clashing words and images (a dung heap and iris-scented sheets), disquieting stylistic techniques (abrupt shifts in perspective, blended narrative voices,[4] ironic juxtaposition), and on a larger scale, the oppositional aesthetics of romanticism and realism. Details loosely defined as realist stand out,[5] but more subtly, the very blending of genres perceived to be antithetical, the penetration of romanticism by realism, is a more insidious contamination that, recognized or not, can get under the skin of some readers. This aesthetic conflict is dramatized throughout the tribulations of Emma Bovary, a romantic dreamer constantly subjected to crudeness and indignities within the plot, and in Flaubert's ironic, deflating orchestration of dialogue and narrative voice. This tension is also reinforced in an impressive array of odours which infuse the novel's atmosphere with both perfume and dung.

Unpleasant sights and smells abound in the novel where, after the initial description of the Rouault farm, manure will be mentioned several times more.[6] *Manure* is one of those words, like *rot*, *carrion*, and *perfume*, that does not need adjectival qualification to read as odorous. The noun itself, *fumier*, shares enough phonemes with *fumée* (smoke) and *parfumer* (to perfume), to suggest odour circulating in the air.[7] But *Madame Bovary* is also rich in passing references to pleasantly scented things. Though these appealing fragrances were not identified as objectionable during the trial, they emanate from many of the passages Pinard cited for more obvious indecencies, including evocations of adultery, irreverent depictions of religious scenes, and references to undergarments and bare skin. Pinard quoted the priest's pronouncement of extreme unction at Emma's deathbed, for example, which deviates from the liturgical text, referring to, among other things, Emma's nostrils, greedy for warm breezes and amorous odours.

Read in light of the era's hygiene and beauty norms, the presence of fragrant products in *Madame Bovary* reinforces ambiguities at the heart of an uneasiness elicited by the novel. To understand the significance of Emma's fresh sillage and her subsequent perfume choices, it is helpful to consider how health and beauty experts viewed the delicate relationship between skin and perfume, where the smell of iris fit into their reasoning, and what it meant to smell of iris.

The Dangers of Bathing and Perfuming

"From a hygienic perspective, one may promote perfumes for their stimulant and refreshing properties but one must never overindulge."[8] So demands the balanced duo of health and good taste, according to the Baronne Staffe in her 1891 *Cabinet de toilette* (297–8), an etiquette manual directed towards women which features, despite this caveat, dozens of recipes for scented skin toners, soaps, pastes, pomades, sachets, and cold creams, along with advice on how to perfume everything from books to shoes. Deferral to hygiene and discernment in the context of fragrance recommendations was not unusual at the time. Scented products in the nineteenth and early twentieth centuries aroused ambivalence, even as their popularity soared. Advertisements reinforced the double identity of fragrance products, promising both hygienic practicality and cosmetic pleasure. A turn-of-the-century print ad for Lubin Eau de Cologne shows a woman at her dressing table mirror, joyfully washing with cologne-infused water (see Figure 6.1), splashing her hands and face, both areas of great concern for skin care and beauty specialists. The text targets buyers wise enough to balance the pursuit of health, beauty, and good taste: "Eau de Lubin refreshes and cleans the skin, makes it soft and white and impregnates it with a marvelous and delicate perfume. Thus, in five ways at once, it satisfies the ideal of hygiene and of *coquetterie* that should be yours, since it is that of all refined people."

Staffe's measured guidance on the proper use of perfume echoes apprehensions about its proximity to the body more emphatically expressed by others earlier in the century. In 1857, the publication and trial year of both Baudelaire's *Fleurs du mal* and Flaubert's equally redolent *Madame Bovary*, tasteful women were advised to apply fragrance to hair, clothing, shoes, stationery, even furniture, but not their skin.[9] Though hygiene and etiquette manuals across the century devote considerable attention to perfuming protocol and abuses, their relative silence on the topic of spraying or rubbing in fragrance suggests that, for their readership at least, this was not a practice in great need of regulation.[10] In fact, the perfume advice addressed to women in *manuels de savoir vivre* throughout the century suggests that "wearing" liquid perfume was achieved by exposing clothing and other accessories to fragrant materials. When, near the end of the century, the Comtesse Xila describes "vaporizing" among ways to use fragrance, she explains that this act, carried out by one's chambermaid in the morning, constitutes spraying the clothing to be worn that day (223).[11] Illustrated advertisements suggest that the practice of directly perfuming the skin without hygienic reason, surely a developing trend rather than an overnight phenomenon, emerged sometime in the late nineteenth or early twentieth century (see Figures 6.2 and 6.3). In her 1888 etiquette book, Ermance Dufaux de la Jonchère reminds her readers that only a woman of easy virtue wears perfume *sur elle* (*on herself*),[12] while well-mannered women with good housekeeping skills scent only their linens, using

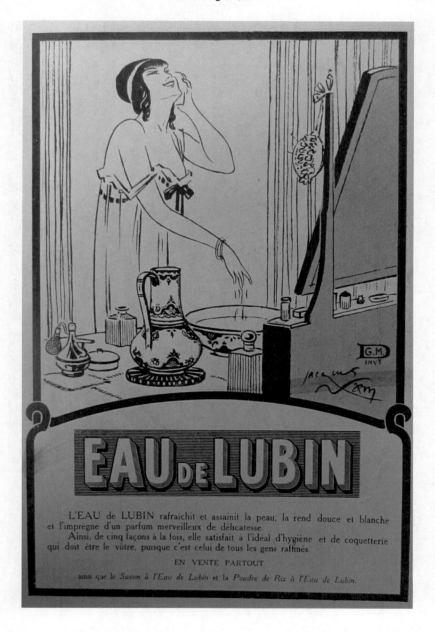

6.1. An early twentieth-century print advertisement for Eau de Lubin offers cleansing and perfuming for both hygiene and *coquetterie*.

6.2. Lubin perfume advertisement showing a woman applying a spray of perfume directly to the skin of her neck, 1912.

6.3. Lubin perfume advertisement showing a woman wearing clothing that another woman is spraying with perfume, 1913.

fresh flowers, such as lavender, muguet bouquets, violet petals, rose, or lily (66). Eau de cologne and scented waters were, throughout most of the nineteenth century, applied to an endless number of accessories, most worn or carried close to the body. Like a second skin, scented linens and undergarments, shawls, handkerchiefs, gloves, and writing paper emitted a woman's fragrance of choice, and suggested the sweet, fresh or animalic presence of her unembellished skin.

This is not to say that a stylish woman's skin would have been unscented. But before fragrance became predominantly an olfactory fashion decoration, its direct contact with the skin of tasteful women was limited, and considered to serve primarily hygienic, not cosmetic, needs. A diluted dose of eau de toilette might be prescribed to treat seborrhea; likewise, pastes, pomades, and lotions (often lightly scented to balance the smell of natural ingredients such as badger fat) were among the arsenal of treatments available for skin conditions of all kinds. Nineteenth-century beauty manuals recommended fragrance-infused waters, lotions, pastes, and vinegars for grooming and skin care, deemphasizing the obvious appeal of such products for superfluous adornment or seduction. Jean-Baptiste Mège affirmed the distinction between health and beauty in the title and chapters of his tremendously popular 1818 *L'allaince d'Hygie et de la Beauté: l'art d'embellir*, a book which, despite the title, advised women to conserve what natural beauty they had rather than adorn it. A review of the book in the *Gazette de France* highlighted the author's mixed messages, pointing out that the crowd of clients eager to buy Mège's new release would be disappointed if they sought secrets to the art of embellishment, rather than discourse on the importance of hygiene over cosmetics.[13] In her 1833 *Manuel des dames*, Madame Celnart is careful to divide fragrance recipes into two functional categories. "Parfums pour la toilette," designated for intimate use, would preserve freshness and combat unpleasant bodily odours. For such purposes, women could lightly perfume their handkerchiefs, undergarments, stockings, hair pomade, and lip balm, or dilute cologne in water for hand and face washing (*Manuel des dames*, 91–2). In addition to these indirect methods of personal perfuming, Celnart recommends fragrance for objects and spaces in the home, including sachets for the armoire and pastilles to be burned as air fresheners (95–9). Never does Celnart recommend wearing perfume rubbed or sprayed on the skin as a fragrant fashion accessory.

The impetus to mediate perfuming of the body was not just a conceit of fashion. Gradually changing beliefs about miasma paralleled cautious modifications of daily skin care rituals. Fear of devitalizing or allowing disease to enter the body by soaking the skin in water remained prevalent for quite some time.[14] As Dr. David Jouysse warned in his 1668 treatise on prevention and treatment of the plague, heating the body with warm water "serait ouvrir les portes au venin de l'air et le boire à pleines coupes" ("would be opening the doors to the air's venom, and drinking it by the cupful").[15] Opening the pores to vapours, mists, and water had long been considered detrimental to the body's equilibrium. Infrequent head washing showed attention to health, not disregard for cleanliness. Bathing remained a topic of delicate concern throughout the century, and skin was the locus of circumspect attention in daily ablutions.[16] By the *fin de siècle*, there was still no unequivocal popular consensus on the risks and benefits of sweating, soaking, and exposing the skin. As a result, etiquette and hygiene manuals devoted attention to fluids of all kinds that came into contact with the skin, from cosmetic and tonic lotions to water and scented baths.[17] In 1855, Auguste Tessereau's *Cours d'hygiène* advised readers to keep footbaths brief, and better still, to reserve them for therapeutic treatments. Otherwise, sponge the feet and apply lotion frequently (262–3). Dr. Augusin Galopin pointed out that a peasant who never takes baths, but sweats every day from the head and feet, may have healthier skin than the woman who takes a full bath daily (1886, 241). As late as 1897, the Baronne Staffe dispensed detailed instructions on general bathing (as opposed to hydrotherapy and other medically prescribed treatments),[18] with attention to water temperature, time limit, depth of the tub, and hour of the day. When in doubt, sponge baths were always sufficient for daily cleanliness and health (24).

To illustrate their point, hygiene manuals usually include a brief history of bathing, presented as a sort of titillating cautionary tale to readers. In the preface to his 1818 *Alliance d'Hygie* [sic] *et de la Beauté, ou l'art d'embellir*,[19] Dr. Mège announces his book as the first to shed light on the dangers of beauty practices that have been recommended out of ignorance and charlatanism, and the first to show the negative influence beauty products can have on both physical and moral health (i). Because "[l]a différence physique fait la différence morale" ("physical difference means moral [emotional, psychological] difference"; 3), Mège directs his advice to women, who, due to their nervous temperament, do not think like men, and are thus more unstable, impressionable, and susceptible to the dangers of beauty products.[20]

Mège situates his beauty advice (at the risk of boring his reader, he admits; 44), in a discussion of cutaneous excretion and absorption. He warns that the skin's ability to soak up fluids and vapours is, with the exception of some medical treatments, nearly always dangerous. Plague, smallpox, measles, and most contagious diseases are caused by respiration or absorption, and mephitic exhalations and deleterious substances absorbed by the skin bring about serious illness. Mège frowns upon at-home baths, to which perfume must be added to mask the putrid smell of skin-softening agents such as calf feet and bouillon of intestines, and considers soaking the skin in general to be so potentially dangerous, that a doctor should be consulted before deciding when, where, how, and how often to bathe (80–2). Less skeptical about baths, Dr. Constantin James nonetheless warns women to beware of scented products like *lait virginal*, which are sometimes saturated with lead (198–9).[21]

Later in the century, despite increased awareness of how diseases were spread,[22] doctors continued to prescribe restraint in bathing. Dr. Ernest Monin's *Hygiène de la beauté* (1890) recommends conditioning with lotion the face, hands, feet, and ano-genital areas twice daily, and a bath every one to two weeks. Aromatic baths (with essence of thyme, wintergreen, benzoin tincture) are acceptable for combating odorous secretions of the skin. In her 1894 beauty manual, the Comtesse Norville calls twice daily boric-acid douches and cleansing of the external genitalia indispensable, but deems full baths necessary only every ten days, for a maximum duration of twenty-five minutes (50). She presents fragrance only in the context of skin treatments, not adornment, warning that perfumed products are absorbed by the skin, and can in extreme cases cause poisoning and death.[23] She is particularly wary of synthetic fragrances: "Comme parfum pour le mouchoir, rien à objecter; mais pour la peau! Par égard pour votre beauté, chères lectrices, n'employez aucun parfum de ce genre" ("As a handkerchief perfume, no objection; but for the skin! Out of consideration for your beauty, dear readers, do not use any perfume of this kind!" 96–7). Baronne Staffe's brief summary of bathing history concedes that, even in times when it was frowned upon, coquettes enjoyed a good bath (25–6). She dispenses practical advice after leading with stories of eccentric celebrity bathers: Nero's second wife Poppaea, who soaked in a blend of ass's milk and strawberry juice; Anne Boleyn, whose lovers drank her bathwater; Diane de Poitiers, who enjoyed daily rainwater baths; and the great women of the eighteenth century whose milk baths contained, among other things, boiled veal. Staffe's section on calming and refreshing baths recognizes that fragrant materials (handfuls of fresh primrose, linden, almond paste, violet) may be used in the interest of toning, refreshing, and softening the skin, and hints at the superfluous pleasure of scent.

Whether or not they insist on a distinction between hygiene and cosmetics, self-help manuals focus a great deal on skin: its freshness, its smoothness, its elasticity; the battle against eruptions, discolouration, and wrinkles; the need to clean the pores and to protect them from pollutants. In so doing, such books offer countless recipes for skin-care products, all of them scented, all of them to be used with great caution. During this time when baths were still recommended guardedly, skin was seen as an essential but permeable threshold between the environment inside and outside the body. To let vapours, water, and effluvia penetrate the skin, or to let the wrong proportion of blood or sweat leak out, was to upset the body's delicate equilibrium, at the risk of physical and mental instability.

Earlier in the century, César Gardeton's tellingly titled *Dictionnaire de la beauté, ou la toilette sans dangers* (1826) reminded readers that it is good to wash the skin from time to time to rid it of ever-looming pollutants: "Je crois qu'il serait nécessaire, lorsqu'on a beaucoup à craindre de l'humidité ou d'autres miasmes qui peuvent s'introduire dans les pores inhalans, de frictionner la peau puis de la frotter avec une éponge imbibée d'huile; car il vaut mieux boucher jusqu'à un certain point les pores que de permettre à des miasmes délétères d'y pénétrer" ("I think it would be necessary, when we have much to fear from humidity, or from other miasmas that can enter in the inhaling pores, to massage the skin, then rub it with an oil-soaked sponge; for it is better to block up the pores to a certain point than to allow poisonous miasmas to penetrate"; 251). Gardeton was writing in 1826, but similar advice for face cleansing was repeated throughout the century. Just as terms like *miasma* (unhealthy, smelly vapours) were closely related to the lexicon of atmospheric conditions, the scientific and lay discussions of the skin's health were expressed in relation to air, atmosphere, humidity, gases, liquids, and temperature. This lexicon of the body's microclimate appears in novels as well, particularly in descriptions of women.

Because cosmetics were so closely related to care of the skin and the body, medical doctors sometimes played the role of beauty and etiquette consultants, though without embracing such titles, in the works they published for non-specialists and "les gens du monde instruits" ("educated readers"; Monin 1883, 1). Ernest Monin was one such medical practitioner. A health inspector, and prolific writer, Monin, in his *Hygiène et traitement des maladies de la peau*, deals specifically with eruptions and diseases of the skin, including eczema, acne, psoriasis, herpes, and scrofula. Monin considered his 1893 book on everyday skin maladies and their treatments as a complement to his *Hygiène de la beauté*, a book that characterizes hygiene as playing a large role in bodily adornment (2), and as representing the true future of medicine, that is, preventative medicine (3). Cosmetics represent a chapter or subcategory of hygiene (2). Monin further distinguishes between the singuler *cosmétique* and the plural *cosmétiques. Les cosmétiques* (cosmetic products), in hygiene, are substances destined for human decoration, while *la cosmétique* (cosmetics) constitute "cette portion de notre art qui s'occupe d'embellir la peau de lui conserver ses qualités, de masquer ses fautes d'orthographe" ("that portion of our art that attends to beautifying the skin and conserving its qualities, masking its spelling mistakes"; 95). Expansive and empirical, *la science cosmétique* (cosmetic science) "se trouve sur la limite incertaine entre l'hygiène et la thérapeutique" ("is situated on the blurred border between hygiene and therapeutics"; 95). One senses in Monin's many, sometimes circuitous attempts to distinguish hygiene from cosmetics, his knowing that the two are already irrevocably entwined. This connection helps to explain an over-determined suspicion of perfume and its dangers to the mind and body, voiced in other discourse of the era. Perfume delivers an ever-changing, culturally coded message about taste and status, but also about the physical and moral cleanliness of its wearer. Perfume is a mutable social signifier, often difficult to read, but it gets under your skin.

Smelling Iris

While some fragrance materials could be sorted easily along the hygienic-to-cosmetic spectrum, most continued to serve both practical and luxury purposes. A potentially confusing example of a multifunctional fragrance is iris, mentioned often in novels of the century which invoke spaces or individuals *sentant l'iris* (smelling of iris), that "vague fragrance of feminine elegance," as Frédéric Moreau perceived it in Flaubert's *Éducation sentimentale* (51–2).[24] The best-known literary example appears in Proust's *Combray*, where the narrator refers to "un petit cabinet sentant l'iris" ("a little room smelling of iris") as a refuge in which, because he was allowed to lock the door, he can pursue solitary occupations: reading, daydreaming, weeping, and voluptuous pleasure. This iris fragrance in Marcel's little room functioned as an air freshener and eventual memory trigger.[25] Earlier, Balzac, too, repeated *sentant l'iris* three times in a single passage of the novella *Le curé de Tours* (1832). Here, the abbot François Birotteau (brother of the perfumer César Birotteau), longs to possess the beautiful library and home furnishings of his friend, l'abbé Chapeloud. Upon his friend's death, having inherited the property he so desired, Birotteau recalls the conversations with Chapeloud that stoked his passion for lush décor and exceptionally good housekeeping:

"Pensez-donc," disait l'abbé Chapeloud à Birotteau, "que pendant douze années consécutives, linge blanc, aubes, surplis, rabats, rien de m'a jamais manqué. Je trouve toujours chaque chose en place, en nombre suffisant, et sentant l'iris."... Birotteau, pour toute réponse, disait: "Sentant l'iris!" Ce *sentant l'iris* le frappait toujours. Les paroles du chanoine accusaient un bonheur fantastique pour le pauvre vicaire.

"Just think," the abbot Chapeloud would say to Birotteau, "that for twelve consecutive years, white linen, albs, surplices, bands, I've had it all, everything in its place, in sufficient number, and smelling of iris."... All Birotteau could say in response was "Smelling of iris!" This *smelling of iris* always struck him. The canon's remarks revealed a fantastic happiness to the poor vicar. (40)

Though the novella was originally published under the title *Les célibataires* (meaning bachelors or celibates), its iris scent is not presented as an accompaniment to solitary pleasure (as it would later be in *Combray*), but Birotteau does invest the appealing scent with the power of orderliness, cleanliness, and attention to detail that are, along with finer things, the objects of his desire.

Things smelling of iris were indeed perceived as fresh and clean, though iris was also a classic ingredient in fine perfumes and make-up. Madame Celnart promotes the use of iris powder for women who sweat profusely from the armpits or hands. In the advice and recipes section of her 1896 *Cabinet de toilette*, Baronne Staffe offers a range of formulas containing iris for freshening clothing cupboards and drawers, cleaning teeth, and combating bad breath. She also identifies iris as an exquisite signature perfume, citing an influential woman who offered this clear juxtaposition: "Satan sent le soufre et moi je sens l'iris" ("Satan smells of sulfur and I smell of iris"; 299). Perfumers describe iris-scented cosmetics as delicate, elegant, and superfine (Pradal 1895, 211). Celnart recommends a bit of iris powder for perfuming artificial violet bouquets (*Manuel des dames*, 73 and 98), and perfumers frequently point out that the scent of iris resembles that of the (nonetheless superior[26]) violet.[27] In what might have been just a slip of the pen, summarizing another doctor's case study of an hysterical patient whose perspiration smelled of violet, Dr. Ernest Monin incorrectly identifies the patient's sweat as smelling of iris (*Les odeurs du corps humain* 1886, 18).[28] The error may be evidence of perceived similarities in the two scents, or perhaps Monin had simply mastered a social code of fragrance that relates iris and violet as modest and gentle fragrances.

6.4. William-Adolphe Bouguereau, *Woman with Iris*, 1895.
Image courtesy of Princeton University Art Museum.

Along with its double olfactory message of cleanliness and elegance, the iris flower offers an image and aroma that do not correlate with the perfumer's iris scent. When Emma Bovary's funeral procession passes thatched rooftops covered in iris (600), the variety that comes to mind is probably the wild blue, or perhaps a bloom like that depicted in William-Adolphe Bouguereau's 1895 *Woman with Iris* (Figure 6.4). This blueish-purple flower with a golden beard and yellow variegation is most likely an *iris pallida*, or the related *iris germanica*, cultivated throughout Europe in the nineteenth century, and by 1922, deemed one of the most common varieties in France.[29] Though many varieties are unscented, irises offer an assortment of pleasant and unusual aromas: ginger, lilac, and even one that has been compared to a garlicky leg of lamb.[30] *Iris pallida* emits a fragrance, sweet but difficult to describe, "more or less pronounced," according to the proceedings of a 1922 iris conference.[31] If the *iris pallida* of the nineteenth and early twentieth century smelled as it does today, that could account for the vague identification of its scent. North Americans describe its fragrance as being like grape candy or grape soda[32] – a smell referent that would not have been familiar in the nineteenth century, as it is not much like natural grape; instead, the scent might have been perceived as similar to gardenia, jasmine, neroli, tuberose, or ylang-ylang.[33] The scent of the flower petals in the garden or depicted in Bouguereau's painting, however, had nothing to do with the fragrance known as iris that was the topic of so many health and beauty manuals.

When objects, spaces, and human bodies are described as *sentant l'iris*, they are radiating the fragrance of the earthy iris root, not the showy flower (Figure 6.5). Orris (another word for iris root) is the rhizome of the *iris florentina*, grown in various parts of Europe, usually Tuscany. The root is cut, dried, and ground to be used in toothpaste, toilet waters, sachets, air fresheners, face powders, and personal perfumes. The era's osphresiologists and perfumers agree that only the root of this iris is scented.[34] Headspace technology makes extraction of scented iris petals possible today,[35] but iris root, not petal, is still the recognizable, signature aroma of most perfumes bearing the name. The flower itself does not appear on Piesse's gamut of fragrances,[36] though in the era's language of flowers, it symbolized good news, trust, and affection.[37] Iris root has a long history of medicinal use,[38] including as an ingredient in tablets prescribed for those who contacted persons infected with plague.[39] Iris of Florence was reported to have been tucked between the breasts of lice-infected women in the seventeenth century,[40] and it was used to deter vermin, such as lice, from the home and body, well into the nineteenth century. Despite its history of masking an impressive array of human stenches, iris root was also known as a refined and very expensive cosmetic perfume ingredient. A scent associated with seventeenth-century taste, iris remained desirable, if a bit old fashioned in the nineteenth century. Piesse finds iris root lacking the stand-alone beauty that made violet such a hit, but of great value when blended in trendier fragrances like Jockey Club.[41]

Ground iris root was arranged and tinted for visual appeal in sachets and room deodorizers like the one in Proust's *petit cabinet*,[42] but the

gnarly rhizome did not lend itself to the visual subject of women smelling flowers, popular in both commercial and fine art.[43] Bouguereau's
portrait of a young woman smelling an iris is compelling in its evocation of both the referential ambiguity of iris fragrance, and the olfactory
objectification and sexual innuendo that often characterize paintings
of women simultaneously smelling and smelling *of* flowers).[44] As Érika
Wicky has shown, women had been compared to flowers for centuries,
but nineteenth-century medical writing reveals a slip from comparison
to attribution. Young virgins, *jeunes filles*, were not just *like* flowers; they
naturally emitted the scent of sweet flowers.[45] French syntax reinforces
this interpretation of the sniffing *jeune fille*. A woman *sentant l'iris*, is
either smelling the flower or smelling like it. Thus, as Wicky demonstrates, paintings that depict a young woman smelling flowers also
transmit a message about her natural, sweet smell.

Bouguereau's portrait, dating from later in his life when he produced
and sold paintings at a rapid pace,[46] shows less blushing skin than some of
his fleshier subjects, yet does suggest an intrusive closeness to the female
subject. The tight frame, absent of contextual or decorative landscape features, creates proximity, while the subject's unrestrained hair and loose
chemise (normally worn as an undergarment or sleeping gown) suggest
intimacy. By 1895, the general subject of the painting may have been a
cliché, and another in a long line of Bouguereau's overly sentimentalized
and rather voyeuristic renditions of women, yet the placement of the portrait's relatively few compositional elements also conveys the intimate
dynamics of taking scent into the body in order to perceive it.

With the woman's nose as a focal point, the position of her hands and
features indicate a cycle of breath. The left hand presses her chemise to
her chest, fingers arranged in a somewhat awkward, yet familiar gesture of modesty.[47] The thumb and three fingers fan in the direction of
the right hand, which holds the iris. The daintily extended little finger
of her right hand points upward, indicating the flower, and the invisible
presence of a scent that reaches visible nostrils. Her downcast, nearly
closed eye leads back to the nose, the hands, and the flower. Though she
may be holding her left hand to her chest in a gesture of modesty, rapture, or both, the compositional emphasis on smelling situates the hand
as much near the lungs as the heart, as the woman inhales, or savours,
or perhaps pauses before exhaling.

Though the focus of the portrait is, by genre definition and in composition, the face, the splay of the fingers draws attention to the left hand
on the chemise. Bouguereau depicted fingers positioned in this way –
the third and fourth together, separated from the index – in a number of
works, including his 1892 *Psyche* (with both similarly positioned hands

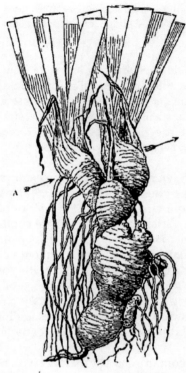

Fig. 20. — Iris Orris Root.

6.5. An illustration of orris/iris root from Septimus Piesse's *Histoire des parfums et hygiene des toilettes* (Paris: Baillière, 1905), 142.

on the heart), and in the 1895 *Abduction of Psyche*. By visual association, the unnamed subject of the portrait resembles the mortal whose beauty rivalled that of Aphrodite in Greek mythology. But another difference here is that some of the fingers push into and draw attention to the thin fabric of the chemise, an everyday, contemporary garment that was often scented.

Iris root was a recommended sachet for linens throughout the century, including the sort of chemise Bouguereau's subject is wearing. As Madame Celnart advised:

> prenez des morceaux de racine d'iris sèche, telle qu'on vend chez les pharmaciens, et renfermez-les dans vos armoires et commodes; ils donneront généralement une légère odeur de violette à tous vos effets. Si vous voulez que le parfum en soit plus fort, vous insérerez un morceau de racine entre

chaque pli de vos chemises, camisoles, jupes, etc.; on en glisse aussi dans les tuyaux des garnitures de de fichus. Rien n'est si doucement suave et si hygiénique en même temps.

Take some pieces of dried iris root, as sold in pharmacies, and store them in your armoires and dresser drawers.; they will generally give a light violet odour to all your things; If you prefer a stronger fragrance, insert a piece of root between each fold of your chemises, camisoles, skirts, etc.; one also slips them into the decorative trim of fichus. Nothing is more gently sweet and hygienic at the same time. (*Manuel des dames* 1829, 53)

The recommendation carries into the twentieth century, for example, when the Comtesse de Gencé advises young women that : "[à] part quelques gouttes d'eau de Cologne qui agrémenteront vos ablutions matinales, un soupçon de violette ou d'iris rendra plus frais le contact de votre lingerie, vous ne devez donc jamais employer de parfum" ("[a]side from a few drops of eau de Cologne which will augment your morning ablutions, a hint of violet or iris will make contact with your lingerie fresher, you then never have to use perfume"; 1909a, 95–6). If violet and iris are similar in their olfactory character and reputation for softness, they also are scents whose natural visual correlatives are hidden: the violet flower, modestly tucked under its own foliage, the iris root covered in earth.

The hands of Bouguereau's young woman, resting in contact with her chemise, allow for a double interpretation of iris scent (both the petals and the rhizome), and a double reading of the woman smelling an iris and smelling *of* iris: *sentant l'iris*. By scenting linens with iris, women might create the illusion of naturally radiating the floral freshness medical writers had already attributed to them. This innocent cultural coding of iris scent breaks down quickly, though, since fresh-smelling virgins were also depicted as the most desirable of women, as hinted in Bouguereau's painting, where the very presence of the thin chemise draws attention to the proximity of bare skin. Is it a play of light, or a flash of rosy flesh peeking through a slit in the fabric near the shoulder, almost parallel to the woman's thumb? The rounded brush strokes resemble those of the flower petals, suggesting a parallel between the open iris and the exposed skin, as both reveal their scent. A lock of hair masks the area of the shoulder where the chemise might be sewn or fastened, covering one of the borders that would distinguish visually, though not olfactorily, skin from fabric. The voyeuristic perspective and implied interruption of privacy complicate the ostensibly straightforward depiction of a woman smelling, or smelling *of*, iris.

Paintings like Bouguereau's contribute to the complex messages that underlie a seemingly obvious semiotics of wholesome versus corrupt smells. As Proust's evocations of iris air fresheners show, the cleanliness of a fragrance can be linked to less innocent memories and experiences. Such is also the case when prosecutor Pinard designates as lewd a passage in which Charles Bovary appreciates his wife's fresh scent. Olfactory allusions, including the smell of iris linens and Emma's skin, provide a powerful undercurrent of sensation, misperception, and atmospheric confusion in Flaubert's *Madame Bovary*. Consciously perceived by the novel's characters, and more insidiously triggering disfavour in the book's more sceptical readers, olfactory moments motivate actions, link episodes, and underscore the novel's keen visual attention to Emma Bovary's skin.

They Smell a Lot in *Madame Bovary*

The emphasis on air quality, vapours, fog, and climate in Flaubert's *Madame Bovary* has been linked to the depiction of Emma's moral and psychological health, particularly in light of etiologies of hysteria that relied in part on fictional characters like Emma Bovary.[48] Closely related to such atmospheric phenomena are Emma's relationship to fragrance, how she reacts to it, and how the novel's ever-observing narrator and characters read her sillage. "On mange beaucoup dans les romans de Flaubert" ("They eat a lot in Flaubert's novels"; 119), Jean-Pierre Richard has famously written, but what stands out even more in *Madame Bovary*, a novel whose protagonist seldom eats, is how much the characters smell.[49]

Readers often find Flaubert's narrator, and Flaubert himself, insensitive or hostile to Emma Bovary, most obviously because of the ultimately catastrophic ignominies of her life. Emma, the admirer of romantic heroines, never becomes one herself, not even when she meets her fate, a death presented as revolting rather than tragic. In several episodes, including that of her demise, irony hovers close to mockery. As damaging as her boredom and failures are the many narrative indignities to which she is subjected: the comic cross-cutting of flirtatious dialogue with concurrent rambling about miasma and manure; the constant undermining of romantic clichés; the rich, meandering metaphors of Emma's inner life, closing with sentences that read like punch lines; and the framing of her own life story within that of Charles, before he meets her and after her death. The opening chapters, dedicated to Charles's education, family life, and first marriage, stage one of the more insidious deflations of romantic tropes, and smells have much to do with that.

Woven into the forever unravelling romantic fabric of Emma Bovary's life is the story of Charles Bovary's tragi-comic failure as a romantic hero. During his medical school days in Rouen, Charles adopts interests and gestures that will later be associated with Emma's disillusionment, including what has come to be seen as Emma's signature body language, leaning on a windowsill. We encounter Charles striking this pose long before Emma enters the scene: "Dans les beaux soirs d'été, à l'heure où les rues tièdes sont vides ... il ouvrait sa fenêtre et s'accoudait" ("On beautiful summer nights, when the warm streets are empty,... he would open the window and lean on his elbows"; 334). During this phase of his student days, Charles develops other physical characteristics that would portray him as brooding romantic: "Il maigrit, sa taille s'allongea, et sa figure prit une sorte d'expression dolente qui la rendit presque intéressante" ("He grew thin, his waistline elongated, and his face took on a sort of sorrowful expression that made him almost interesting"; 334).

What does brooding Charles observe from his fourth-floor window? His mother has set him up on l'Eau-de-Robec, in an apartment owned by a dyer she knows. The nineteenth-century reader would have recognized the problem with this location. Dyers and tanners were among the great urban polluters at the time, the smelly waste of their trades rendering waterways thick with chemicals and debris. Flaubert's narrator accentuates the water's insalubrious presence:

La rivière, qui fait de ce quartier de Rouen comme une ignoble petite Vénise, coulais en bas, sous lui, jaune, violette ou bleue.... Des ouvriers, accroupis au bord, lavaient leurs bras dans l'eau. Et il ouvrait les narines pour aspirer les bonnes odeurs de la campagne, qui ne venaient pas jusqu'ici.... En face, au-delà des toits, le grand ciel pur s'étendait, avec le soleil rouge se couchant. Qu'il devait faire bon là-bas! Quelle fraîcheur sous la hêtrée! Et il ouvrait les narines pour aspirer les bonnes odeurs de la campagne, qui ne venaient pas jusqu'ici.

The river, that makes this quarter of Rouen an ignoble little Venice of sorts, flowed below, beneath him, yellow, violet or blue.... Workers, crouching over the banks, washed their arms in the water.... Opposite, beyond the rooftops, stretched vast, pure sky. How nice it must be there! How fresh under the beech grove! And he opened his nostrils to inhale the good odours of the countryside, that did not reach him. (334)

Later in the century, Flaubert's "ignoble petite Venise" is cited in Eugène Noël's book on the city, *Rouen, rouennais, rouenneries* (Rouen:

Schneider frères, 1894, 2). The chapter on "Pouillerie et Puantuers" ("Filth and Stench"; 168–73) describes the Rouen of "past times" (the 1830s, when the action of *Madame Bovary* takes place) as "infecte" (etymologically related to infection, an adjective signifying vile, revolting, or filthy). Many pollutants must have risen to Charles's window as he contemplated the glowing sunset and imagined fresh air, among them, as Noël specifies: "vidanges, débris de cuisine, eaux de lavage, eaux de teintures, déchets, urines, fumiers, chats, chiens, et rats morts" ("sewage, kitchen garbage, dye water, rubbish, urine, manure, dead cats, dogs, and rats"; 170).

Along with troubling smells, we encounter penetrable skin, and many open nostrils in *Madame Bovary*, beginning with the episodes devoted to young Charles's student life, and following in the early days of marriage. Emma's nostrils are mentioned three times, and her grotesque foil, the beggar, has convulsively sniffing nostrils. Later, when the tax collector Binet is seen working at his lathe, his wide-open nostrils indicate an unenlightened satisfaction with his commonplace hobby (624). And in one of the novel's many book-end-like repetitions, Charles, speaking to Rodolphe after Emma's death, reveals his emotional state in the action of his nostrils: "les narines battaient vite, les lèvres frémissaient" ("his nostrils throbbed, his lips quivered"; 644). Are the hyper-animated nostrils of Flaubert's characters anatomically correct? Perhaps not. But their exaggeration resonates with other references to the precarious opening of the body to dubious elements. Nostrils beat or vibrate, they open wide to take in smells, they release hot air on Emma's neck, they threaten an order that separates personal space from public space through inhalation and exhalation of bad air.

Within the story of Charles lies another framing device, which underscores the vulnerability of the body via its permeable organs, especially the skin. Emma's physical entry into and exit from the novel's diegesis and Charles's life, is marked by the puncturing and leaking of her skin. The first time our doomed heroine's name is mentioned, Emma Rouault is breaking the skin of her fingers with her sewing needle, then sucking the blood. As she packs her belongings to move with Charles from Yonville to Tostes, Emma again pricks her finger, now on a wire in her wedding bouquet, which she immediately throws into the fireplace. Like her dreams, the charred, dead flowers flutter upwards and disappear in the smoke of a now odourless perfume. The last time we see her body before burial, it is Charles, in a loving, would-be romantic, but ultimately awkward gesture (simultaneously recalling the failed surgical procedure on Hippolyte and Emma's earlier sucking blood from her fingertips), who ineptly cuts a lock of Emma's hair, thereby puncturing, more than once, the skin of Emma's temples: "il s'avança lui-même, les ciseaux à la main. Il tremblait si fort, qu'il piqua la peau des tempes en plusieurs places" ("he stepped forward himself, scissors in hand. He was trembling so much that he cut the skin of her temples in several places"; 630).

Between these unusual, somewhat unsettling episodes in which Emma's finger and temple are punctured, the narrator pays remarkably close attention to Emma's skin, and to fragrances and scented accessories that suggest, through their visual and olfactory representation, the presence of her skin. As we have seen, fragrant sillage and mephitic wafts were both in the air and on the minds of many at the time of the novel's setting and composition, and the skin was perceived to be a volatile emitter of smell and a vulnerable shield against it. The novel's focus on medicine, too – practised well or not by its characters – along with frequent mentions of air quality and miasma (one of the topics on which Homais fancies himself an expert) likewise bring attention to the skin. One of the early verbal portraits of Emma Rouault, seen from Charles's perspective, highlights her uncovered and leaking skin: "Entre la fenêtre et le foyer, Emma cousait; elle n'avait point de fichu, on voyait sur ses épaules nues de petites gouttes de sueur" ("Between the window and the foyer, Emma was sewing; she was not wearing a fichu, you could see little droplets of sweat on her nude shoulders"; 435). These oddly seductive yet disturbing close-ups will be echoed in the grotesque depiction of her final days, when with Charles at her bedside, "[d]es gouttes suintaient sur sa figure bleuâtre, qui semblait comme figée dans l'exhalaison d'une vapeur métallique" ("drops of sweat oozed on her bluish face, which seemed frozen in the exhalation of a metallic vapor"; 614).

Typically, much of a middle-class woman's skin was covered in public, for reasons of modesty. As prosecutor Ernest Pinard noted more than once in the selective close reading of the novel on which he built his obscenity case against Flaubert, Emma's revealed skin plays a key role in many of the passages deemed lascivious. In the closing lines of his case, he compares the unregulated art of Flaubert to a woman who would remove all her clothing (6367). Pinard quotes references to Emma's bare feet, to her shoulders, to her lover, Rodolphe, undressing her. Emma's skin is also the focus of many visual portraits, often delivered in uncomfortably extreme close-up, in passages that helped earn Flaubert his (unsolicited) realist badge: her pallor or blush, the lines and flesh around her nostrils and lips, and the many times she shivers and shudders, must have registered with readers who condemned the book as disquieting, disgusting, inappropriate, voluptuous, or all of the above.

Emma frequently finds herself in the company of characters who suffer from maladies. The beggar, staged as her frightful foil, suffers from a condition which Homais diagnoses as scrofula, an affliction he much earlier (in one of his miasma monologues) ascribed to poor hygiene, and one that gives off an odour of stale beer (Monin, *Essai sur les odeurs*, 1886, 26). We later learn that the son of Emma's wet nurse suffers from it, too. For the beggar, Homais prescribes a diet of good wine, beer, and roast beef, no flour or dairy products, exposure to sunlight, a fumigation treatment with the smoke of juniper berries, and an antiphlogistic (anti-inflammatory) pomade of his own creation. When Homais fails to cure the beggar with aromatic remedies, he launches a successful campaign against the vagabond who is put in hospice. In a cruel narrative nod to Emma's sensitivity to perfume and odours,[50] her attentiveness to fragrant hygiene, and to the doppelgänger status of the disfigured beggar, Homais will later administer scented fumigations to combat the miasmic odour of Emma's dead body.

While Pinard does not focus on perfume per se as he builds his argument for the novel's indecency, many of the passages he declares offensive do mention odour and fragrance or are revealed in other episodes to have olfactory significance. The scene of Emma and Léon meeting at the cathedral in Rouen, and the subsequent carriage episode, were both subject to the prosecutor's scrutiny. Seen and smelled from the perspective of Léon (who has drenched his own handkerchief in fragrance for this meeting with Emma), "[L]'église, comme un boudoir gigantesque, se disposait autour d'elle;.... les vitraux resplendissaient pour illuminer son visage, et les encensoirs allaient brûler pour qu'elle apparût comme un ange, dans la fumée des parfums" ("[T]he church, like a gigantic boudoir, spread out around her ;... the stained-glass windows shone and illuminated her face, and the censers were burning in such a way that she looked like an angel, in the smoke of perfumes"; 544).

Fragrant air was among the sensual pleasures of the church that Emma experienced in her childhood, another flaw in Flaubert's fiction, from Pinard's perspective. In the chapel, Emma "s'assoupit doucement à la langueur mystique qui s'exhale des parfums de l'autel" ("was gently lulled by the mystic languor exhaled from the perfumes of the altar"; 357), and during mass, she saw the face of the Virgin "parmi les tourbillons bleuâtres de l'encens qui montait" ("amid the bluish whirls of incense that arose"; 425). During the emotional and physical crisis that follows Rodolphe's break-up, Emma believes she is dying, and sees her fading existence as a visible waft of burning incense: "il lui semblait que son être, montant vers Dieu, allait s'anéantir dans cet amour comme un encens allumé qui se dissipe en vapeur" ("it seemed to her that her being, rising toward God, would be annihilated in that love like a burning incense that dissipates into vapour"; 520). These words resonate once more when Charles visits Emma's body for the last time, as "[L]es herbes aromatiques fumaient encore, et des tourbillons de vapeur bleuâtre se confondait au bord de la croisée avec le brouillard qui entrait" ("The aromatic herbs were still smoking, and the spirals of bluish vapour blended at the window casement with the fog that was coming in"; 629). In addition to reinforcing Emma's bodily and perceptual connection to odours, this is one of many passages that, like the early portrait of Charles leaning on his windowsill, show him to be subtly connected to Emma, to have the stunted capacity to be the romantic hero she desired.

Attempting to demonstrate that Emma's beauty is provocatively por-trayed ("painted with a lascivious brush"), even in the most humble domestic scenes, Pinard quotes a passage dealing directly with fragrance: "Prenez Mme Bovary dans les actes les plus simples, c'est toujours le même coup de pinceau, il est à toutes les pages ... le mari se demande-t-il, en présence de cette femme sentant frais, si l'odeur vient de la peau ou de la chemise" ("Take Madame Bovary in the most simple acts, it is still the same brush stroke, it is on every page ... the husband wonders, in the presence of this fresh-smelling woman, if the odour comes from her skin or from her chemise"; 654–5). While the skin and chemise were the obvi-ously provocative elements of this passage, the intimacy of scent may have worked on the prosecutor, subliminally at least, as it did on Charles.

Emma's odour is all the more pleasant when juxtaposed to the more offensive smells of Charles's daily house calls. Once married, he is thrilled after a long day's work, to return home to a clean-smelling wife:

Il mangeait des omelettes sur la table des fermes, entrait son bras dans des lits humides, recevait au visage le jet tiède des saignées, écoutait les râles, examinait des cuvettes, retroussait bien du linge sale ; mais il trouvait tous les soirs un feu flambant, la table servie, des meubles souples, et une femme en toilette fine, charmante et sentant frais, à ne savoir même d'où venait cette odeur, ou si ce n'était pas sa peau qui parfumait sa chemise.

He ate omelets from farmhouse tables, reached under humid sheets, received the lukewarm spurt of blood-lettings in his face, listened to death rattles, examined basins, turned over a good deal of dirty linen; but every evening he found a blazing fire, a ready table, comfortable furniture, and a woman finely dressed, charming, and smelling fresh, and he couldn't even determine whence the odour came, or whether it was not her skin that perfumed her chemise. (380)

The novel's ironic juxtapositions, and its moral tension, are condensed in this montage of Charles Bovary's daily life as newlywed *officier de santé*, who mistakenly believes he is in a happy marriage. Those inelegant sensory encounters of a messy workday figure among the book's many gritty details. This vignette also encapsulates the novel's structure, which embeds the story of Emma within the often less captivating, but undeniably crucial story of Charles. The passage is one of many that will contrast Charles's marital bliss with Emma's dissatisfaction. Moreover, it represents the dangers of misinterpretation that accelerate Charles's and Emma's failures throughout the novel, whether misread gestures and cues, or indeed the misreading of books. Charles generally fails to read at all – he never even cuts the pages of his medical textbooks. For Emma, it is about dangerous novels contaminating her mind.[51]

The metonymic relationship between linens and Emma's skin finds later reinforcement in the depiction of her secretly sniffing a cigar case picked up from the road on the way home from la Vaubyessard. Though she initially threw it to the back of the cupboard, we later find the cigar case has been intentionally stored in the soft folds of Emma's own linens: "Souvent, lorsque Charles était sorti, elle allait prendre dans l'armoire, entre les plis du linge où elle l'avait laissé, le porte-cigares en soie verte. Elle le regardait, l'ouvrait, et même elle flairait l'odeur de sa doublure, mêlée de verveine et de tabac. À qui appartenait-il ?... Au Vicomte" ("Often, after Charles had gone out, she would take from the armoire, from between the folds of her linens where she had left it, the green silk cigar case. She would look at it, open it, and she even sniffed the odour of its lining, mixed with verbena and tobacco. To whom did it belong?... To the Viscount"; 377).

Later, this fragrance-fed fantasy of the Vicomte will be triggered by the scent of pomade in Rodolphe's beard, a smell that awakens Emma's desire for Léon as well, and becomes the first step towards her succumbing to Rodolphe's charms:

> elle sentait le parfum de la pommade qui lustrait sa chevelure. Alors une mollesse la saisit, elle se rappela ce vicomte qui l'avait fait valser à la Vaubyessard, et dont la barbe exhalait, comme ces cheveux-là, cette odeur de vanille et de citron; et, machinalement, elle entreferma les paupières pour la mieux respirer. Mais, dans ce geste qu'elle fit en se cambrant sur sa chaise, elle aperçut au loin, tout au fond de l'horizon, la vieille diligence *l'Hirondelle*...; puis tout se confondit, des nuages passèrent; il lui sembla qu'elle tournait encore dans la valse, sous le feu des lustres, au bras du vicomte, et que Léon n'était pas loin, qui allait venir ... et cependant elle

sentait toujours la tête de Rodolphe à côté d'elle. La douceur de cette sensation pénétrait ainsi ses désirs d'autrefois, et comme des grains de sable sous un coup de vent, ils tourbillonnaient dans la bouffée subtile du parfum qui se répandait sur son âme. Elle ouvrit les narines à plusieurs reprises, fortement, pour aspirer la fraîcheur des lierres autour des chapiteaux. Elle retira ses gants, elle s'essuya les mains; puis, avec son mouchoir, elle s'éventait la figure.

She smelled the perfume of the pomade that shined his hair. Then a weakness came over her, she recalled the Viscount who had waltzed with her at Vaubyessard, and the beard that exhaled, like this hair, an odour of vanilla and citron, and she mechanically half closed her eyes to better breath it in. But in making this gesture as she threw her shoulders back into her chair, she saw on the horizon the old diligence, the *Hirondelle…*; then everything mixed together, the clouds passed; it seemed to her she was spinning again in the waltz, under the light of the chandeliers, on the arm of the Viscount, and Léon was not far away, he was going to come back … and yet she still smelled Rodolphe's head next to her. The sweetness of this sensation penetrated her past desires, and like grains of sand in the wind, they whirled in the subtle gust of perfume that spread over her soul. She opened her nostrils wide several times to inhale the freshness of ivy around the capitals. She took off her gloves, she wiped her hands, then fanned her face with her handkerchief. (459–60)

This scene demonstrates the powerful effect odours have on Emma, and in so doing, it sets up the extreme reaction Rodolphe's apricot-scented break-up letter will later induce. At the same time, the association and repetition of smells, link past, present, and future episodes, and evoke the physical and figurative penetration of smells perceived by Emma and read in *Madame Bovary*.

The initial mention of damp linens in the Rouault farmhouse releases an iris sillage that the olfactorily attuned reader may attribute to Emma's chemise, to the scene of young Justin observing and touching Emma's undergarments as Félicité launders them (497), and to the folds of fabric that cradle the cigar case. The metonymic connection between Emma's body and the linens that touch it is made clear, as she stoically watches the tax collector and his witnesses paw through her most personal possessions: "Ils examinèrent ses robes, le linge, le cabinet de toilette; et son existence, jusque dans ses recoins les plus intimes, fut, comme un cadavre que l'on autopsie, étalée tout du long aux regards de ces trois hommes" ("They examined her robes, her linens, her dressing

room; and her existence, down to the most intimate corners, was, like
a cadaver being autopsied, spread out before the eyes of these three
men"; 594). Similarly, for the reader following the scent trail, the smell
of incense links young Emma's inappropriate daydreaming in church
to her illicit meeting with Léon in Rouen, her private reading and
perfume-burning, and the drawn-out, disturbing episode of her death.
Whether or not the reader is attentive to these smells, they permeate the
text, linking or confusing innocent and daring actions, thus creating an
equivocal sillage that some critics may have correlated, consciously or
not, with the novel's moral ambiguity.

From Iris-Scented Linens to *Pastilles du Sérail*

Charles cannot name the source of his wife's pleasant odour, but
Emma's ability to identify vanilla, verbena, and citron[52] attests to her
attention to taste and fashion, as do her proper use of iris in linen storage, her magazine reading, and her purchasing of cosmetic products
bearing the name of the capital on their labels. Many of the objects she
notices at the Vaubyessard ball (unspecified bouquets, pomegranate
blossoms, jasmine flowers, gloves, corsages, fans, little bottles dangling
from women's waists[53]) would have been recognized by contemporary
readers as both olfactory and visual signifiers. Her olfactory taste and
sensitivity also mark steps in her psychological decline. In the period
after the Vaubyessard ball, when neighbours begin to view her as capricious, Emma douses her arms with eau de Cologne instead of diluting a
few drops in water to wash her hands, as etiquette manuals of the day
prescribed. When Emma is seeing Rodolphe on the sly, her maid must
constantly launder linens, and she notices there is never enough cold-
cream for Emma's skin, nor enough patchouli for her handkerchiefs.
Later, during her wild fling with Léon, she passes those nights still
spent in her marital home reading novels with orgiastic and bloody tableaux, and enjoys the solitary pleasure of exotic fragrances: "Madame
était dans sa chambre. On n'y montait pas. Elle restait là tout le long du
jour, engourdie, à peine vêtue, et, de temps à autre, faisant fumer des
pastilles du sérail qu'elle avait achetées à Rouen, dans la boutique d'un
Algérien" ("Madame was in her bedroom. One didn't go up there. She
would stay there all day long, torpid, barely dressed, and, from time to
time, burning *pastilles du sérail* that she had purchased in Rouen, in an
Algerian's boutique"; 588).[54] The purchase of *pastilles du sérail* indicates
a shift in Emma's fragrance proclivities. Though there were many variations on the formula, the tablets and the popularity of incense burners for
the boudoir were associated with Orientalist trends. Piesse's 1865 recipe

includes sandalwood, benzoin, and Tolu, fragrances stronger and more complex than the iris and eau de cologne of her past. In this phase of her life, Emma's psychological state is depicted like fragrances interacting with the atmosphere, from evaporation to burning. She opens the window to drink in cold air, not to mitigate the effect of pastilles burning in the room, but rather, because she is "brûlée plus fort par cette flamme intime que l'adultère avivait" ("burning harder from this intimate flame that adultery revived"; 588–9).

For Emma, the linked pleasures of reading and perfuming accompany a painful demise. Before she was married, her fascination with *Paul et Virginie*, and with popular sentimental fiction,[55] stoked the flames of romantic desire that would forever haunt her. Later, as boredom, depression, and physical illness envelop her, she finds it difficult to focus on reading. Nonetheless, her mother-in-law, attributing Emma's illness and "airs évaporés" to bad books, books that make a mockery of religion (she mentions Voltaire), cancels Emma's lending library subscription (439–40). By the time Emma has moved along to orgiastic fiction and *pastilles du sérail*, alone and striking the lethargic pose of exotic clichés, she is deeply in debt and about to make several humiliating, futile attempts to borrow money before giving up.

Pinard expresses a similar concern for the book, *Madame Bovary*, and potentially vulnerable readers. The novel's "light pages" might fall into the wrong hands, "dans des mains de jeunes filles, quelquefois de femmes mariées. Eh bien! lorsque l'imagination aura été séduite, lorsque cette séduction sera descendue jusqu'au cœur, lorsque le cœur aura parlé aux sens, est-ce que vous croyez qu'un raisonnement bien froid sera bien fort contre cette séduction des sens et du sentiment?" ("in the hands of *jeunes filles*, sometimes married women. Well! once the imagination has been seduced, once this seduction will have descended all the way to the heart, once the heart will have spoken to the senses, do you think cold reasoning will be strong enough against this seduction of the senses and sentiment?"; 655). Cold reasoning was not enough to shut down publication of *Madame Bovary*, though the novel maintains its reputation as a banned book, and one that provokes uneasiness, perhaps less for what it shows than what it implies, about how easily one thing can contaminate and transform another. Realist evocations of sweat, blood, and filth infiltrate romantic tropes. Metaphors twist, turn, and end in clichés, rendering sentimental moments ironic. Cross-cut, competing dialogues intermingle, turning earnest conversations comic. When Emma reads fiction, her unleashed imagination competes with real life. The story of Emma's sillage encapsulates her characterization as a woman who is hygienically, socially, and mentally unstable, and echoes the many voices of the era who warn that perfume, like novels, can be dangerous for *jeunes filles* and married women. The fragrances of *Madame Bovary* do not counteract its miasmas, they mingle with them and become part of Emma's toxic brain fog.

Fragrances appear in metonymical and synecdochal portraits of Emma, beginning with the iris-scented linens in the farmhouse and ending in the miasmic sillage of her dead body, but they are also part of the novel's framing story. Winding its way to the cemetery, the funeral cortege passes rooftops covered with irises, accompanied by the unpleasant smell of wax candles and cassocks, heavy clerical clothing worn by male clergy; the sartorial opposite of a woman's chemise, its smell makes Charles feel faint. After Emma's death, the narrative focus returns to Charles, who once again takes on the romantic airs he assumed in his student days. He finds the fatal letter from Rodolphe, presumably now absent of apricot fragrance, that provoked Emma's near-suicide. As the narrator explains, Charles is not a person who gets to the bottom of things (638), yet he instinctively harbours a vague jealously of Rodolphe, which leads him to adopt habits Emma might have liked: using cosmetics, perfuming his mustache, buying shiny shoes and white ties, and paying with promissory notes that again put him in debt. His loss of Emma, and the vague knowledge of why she found Rodolphe attractive, motivates him to do things that would please her, and plunges him, as if it were contagious, into his own *bovarysme*, manifesting itself as: "un désir permanent, furieux, qui enflammait son désespoir et qui n'avait pas de limites, parce qu'il était maintenant irréalisable" ("a permanent, furious desire, which inflamed his despair and which had no limits, because it was now unrealizable"; 638).

Charles utters his last words just after indirectly revealing to Rodolphe that he knows about the affair, saying he doesn't blame him: "C'est la faute de la fatalité! ("It's the fault of fate!"; 644). This is nuanced dialogue, coming from the man whose conversation was earlier described as being flat as a sidewalk. Now the emotional subject of Rodolphe's smug gaze, as Emma once was, Charles has paraphrased the language Rodolphe used in his break-up letter: "Est-ce ma faute? O mon Dieu! non, non, n'en accusez que la fatalité!" ("Is it my fault? Oh, my God! No, no, blame only fate!"; 510). The death of Charles closes an ironic loop that has set him up as a surrogate Emma, suffering a true loss, rather than a loss of never attained desires. At the riverbank, the air thick with blooming lilies and jasmine (first mentioned in the Vaubyessard scene, and later a fragrant backdrop to Emma's trysts with both Rodolphe and Léon), Charles suffocates, "comme un adolescent sous les vagues effluves amoureux qui gonflait son Cœur chagrin" ("like an adolescent in the vague effluvia of love that filled his aching Heart"; 645). Rather than suffering a prolonged, painful, and grotesquely narrated death, Charles exits the novel like one of Emma's romantic heroes might have, with a lock of his love's hair in his hand, dying of a broken heart, in a heady sillage of lily and jasmine.

Chapter Seven

Decadent Perfuming

Jasmine, lily, narcissus, orange flower, rose: these were among the sweet aromas deemed dangerous to women if overused or over-sniffed.[1] *Jeunes filles* and *honnêtes femmes* were advised not to mask their soft and sweetly floral natural fragrance, as they were steered away from heady blooms, patchouli, musk, and amber. Proper perfume selection was a matter of choosing the right scent, using it in moderation, and avoiding mixtures, or *bouquets*. Madame Celnart's recommendations show that nearly any fragrance note, if applied with poor judgment, could signal bad taste:

> Les odeurs fortes, telles que le musc, l'ambre, la fleur d'orange, la tubé-reuse, et autres semblables, doivent être entièrement proscrites. Les par-fums suaves et doux de l'héliotrope, de la rose, du narcisse, etc., sont mille fois préférables ... les huiles et pommades au jasmin, à l'œillet, à la vanille, conviennent principalement: elles sont un intermédiaire entre ces derniers parfums et les premiers, qu'il faut vous interdire complètement.

> Strong odours, such as musk, amber, orange blossom, tuberose, and simi-lar scents, should be banned entirely. Suave and gentle perfumes like heliotrope, rose, narcissus, etc., are one thousand times preferable ... hair oils and pomades scented with jasmine, carnation, vanilla, are principally suitable: they are an intermediary between the former and latter, which must be banned completely. (15)[2]

As beauty consultants, physicians, criminologists, sexologists, and medical experts published cases of inappropriate fragrance usage, the popular press amplified titillating stories of excessive and deviant perfuming. Jean Fauconney wrote dozens of books loosely presented as serious studies of sexual phenomena, often under one of his many pseudonyms, the anagram Dr. Caufeynon.[3] His 1903 *La volupté des parfums* (*The Sensuous Pleasure of Perfumes*) includes several pages of targeted advertising, promoting illustrated novels (*romans passionnels*) on the subjects of incest, lesbianism, and various sexual adventures, and publicizing saucy illustrated weeklies like the *Rire et galanterie* and *La vie en culotte rouge*.[4] While the book's back matter indicates that *Volupté* is pleasure reading, the chapters themselves represent a pastiche of topics treated in more serious studies. Tackling subjects that had become the mainstay of osphresiology (the physiology and mechanics of smell, the history of perfume use, the toxic effects of fragrances, etc.), Caufeynon quotes extensively from other published material, but like many writers of his time, also absorbs into his own prose the unattributed words of others. The following sentence, for example, also appears in the 1896 French edition of Lombroso and Ferrero's *La femme criminelle et la prostituée*: "La civilisation provoqua la pudeur en supprimant la nudité, et les soins du corps affaiblirent l'odorat, état de la féminité qui attirait le mâle" ("Civilization brought about modesty by suppressing nudity, and bodily hygiene weakened odour, the state of femininity that attracted the male; 164).[5]

Though Caufeynon borrows from works ostensibly written to promote modesty and propriety, he adds a slight twist to accentuate that pleasing the senses of a sexual partner is the ultimate goal of perfuming. He reminds us that women "qui aime la société de l'homme" ("who like the company of men") know that perfume can augment the natural odour of the body, and they know not to wear too much, not to mix fragrances, and not to use artificial fragrance (196). In a passage heavily borrowed from a book published eighteen years earlier, Caufeynon recalls the popular image of a woman smelling a flower and its implicit evocation of the woman's natural smell, to illustrate the seductive power that even a woman who is not pretty can hold over a man, as long her odour delights him:

> Il en est de même du parfum des fleurs qu'on respire, mais qu'on ne voit pas, la jouissance n'en est pas moins exquise. N'est-ce pas l'habitude, du reste, de fermer les yeux lorsqu'on repose sur le sein d'une femme aimée, afin de ne pas avoir de distraction pour mieux savourer le parfum qui s'en dégage?
>
> N'est-ce pas encore qu'instinctivement, on ferme les yeux, lorsqu'on plonge le nez dans une rose épanouie?

It is the same for the scent of flowers that we breathe in, but that we do not see, the sensual pleasure is not less exquisite. Is it not customary, moreover, to close one's eyes when one is resting on the breast of a beloved woman, in order to avoid distraction and better savor the perfume that is released?

Isn't it true that instinctively, we close our eyes when we plunge our noses into an opened rose? (195)

The passage paraphrases a section called "La femme respirée est aimée" ("The inhaled woman is loved") from the 1886 *Le parfum de la femme et le sens olfactive dans l'amour: étude psycho-physiologique*, which, though never mentioned, seems to have been a primary source for Caufeynon's topic and material. The more credentialed Galopin[6] forewarns his delicate readers that they may find his book on this most intimate science a bit spicy (*pimentée*) here and there (xiii). Caufeynon nonetheless manages to turn up the heat in his recycling of Galopin and others. He presents personal odours according to gender, race, and class as a matter of educating the nose:[7] "le sens olfactif est susceptible d'éducation au même titre que les autres sens. Chaque classe n'a-t-elle pas une préférence marquée pour une certaine catégorie de parfums. Les gens de classe inférieure utilisent les parfums lourds; ylang-ylang, peau d'Espagne, patchouli. Ceux de la classe élevée préfèrent les parfums doux: héliotrope, violette, ambre, œillet, etc." ("the sense of smell is as susceptible to education as the other senses. And does not each class have a marked preference for a certain category of perfumes. People of the lower class use heavy perfumes: ylang-ylang, peau d'Espagne, patchouli. Those of high class prefer gentle perfumes: heliotrope, violet, amber, carnation, etc."; 9).[8] Caufeynon's classifications do not line up completely with those of other health and beauty writers, perhaps because accuracy is not the primary goal of his book; but in fairness, more legitimate sources do not always converge on the matter of which perfumes are acceptable.

If, in the interest of entertaining his readers, Caufeynon was able to repurpose more mainstream writing, this was in part because the topic of women's perfuming had long focused on intimacy, the skin, the body, and potential moral deviance. He is only repackaging familiar words when he states: "La femme qui abuse des parfums finit par perdre le sens physique et moral des odeurs et ceux qui les approchent ne manquent pas de méfier et de *flairer là-dessous* quelque parfum naturel désagréable, parmi tous ces bouquets artificiels d'un gout moins douteux" ("The woman who abuses perfumes ends up losing her physical and moral sense of odours and those who approach her do not fail to mistrust and *sniff out underneath* a disagreeable natural perfume, amidst all of these artificial bouquets of dubious taste" (Caufeynon, 197–8). If women are predisposed to use perfume they are also more likely to abuse it, says Caufeynon. Why? Because perfume is both an adornment and a temptation (9).

Galopin goes further in pathologizing overuse of perfume, identifying a toxic relationship between women, perfume, sexuality, and contagion that has been suggested throughout the century: "Que d'ivresses, et que d'orgies morales et physiques ont été engendrées et provoquées par l'abus des odeurs, avec autant d'énergie et d'incurabilité que par des liqueurs fortes" ("What drunkenness, and what moral and physical orgies have been engendered by the abuse of odours, with as much energy and incurability as by strong liqueurs'; 95–6). Comparing the overuse of intoxicating perfume to that of absinthe, ether, or chloroform, he declares that the woman who uses such toxins daily endangers herself and others: "La femme qui en abuse est bientôt saturée, sursaturée même, car ses tissus organiques sont aromatisés; elle est en quelques semaines, transformée en une boutique de parfumerie contagieuse et dangereuse" ("The woman who abuses it is soon saturated, oversaturated even, for her organic tissues are aromatized; in a few weeks, she is transformed into a contagious and dangerous perfume boutique"; 96).

By the *fin de siècle*, the perfumed woman was contagious enough to spread a proliferation of narratives about her malady, circulating its symptoms in medical tracts, novels, and erotica. Whether she naturally radiated a virginal violet, or had metamorphosed into an ambulatory perfume shop, the scented woman hovered close to a moral lapse, and it was the possibility of her fall that fascinated so many writers. The sillage of women occupied the male sniff by suggesting the presence of hidden, almost accessible skin, analogous to the visual tease of the chemise and other undergarments. Sillage represented the intimacy of the dressing room and the boudoir, and the idea of a woman's secret, perhaps excessive pleasures, made public. In descriptions of women who enjoyed perfume too much, metaphors of contagion and madness spawned analogies to drug and alcohol abuse, as in Galopin's commentary. At the same time, as we shall see, ether and potable alcohol did in fact provide unusual means of perfuming.

Depictions of women over-perfuming dwell on poor judgment and taste, but also label them as eccentric and elite. They become a social embodiment of the decadent aesthetics that, in literature, never fully neutralized the stenches of naturalism, but mingled them with intoxicating perfumes. The tenth chapter of Huysmans's *À rebours* has become

the best-known example of excessive perfuming in *fin-de-siècle* literature, but Goncourt's *Chérie*, published the same year, rivals Huysmans
in its attention to the insalubrious consequences of fragrance abuse.
Moreover, the story of a fragrance-crazed Chérie reads as an absurd
culmination of the physical, psychological, and moral degeneration of
the *jeune fille*, foreshadowed in the story of *Paul et Virginie*, and developed in the works of naturalist writers.

The Monograph of a Perfume-Crazed *Jeune Fille*

Naturalist and decadent works owe much of their appeal, as well as
their infamy, to an emphasis on odoriferous materials and smell. Balzac,
Baudelaire, and Flaubert set the stage for a *fin-de-siècle* aesthetic in which
characters and poetic personae show an uncommonly attuned olfactory
sense and a proclivity for perfume. The presence of aroma in modern
French fiction is most obvious in the realist and natural aesthetics that
produced evocations of muck, stench, death, disease, and debris (along
with perfume) in literary texts. It is not surprising, in light of this legacy,
that Edmond de Goncourt, in his preface to *Les frères Zemganno*, articulated his move away from naturalism in terms of odour: "Le Réalisme,
pour user du mot bête,... n'a pas en effet l'unique mission de décrier
ce qui est bas, ce qui est répugnant, ce qui pue; il est venu au monde
aussi, lui, pour définir dans de l'écriture artiste, ce qui est élevé, ce qui
est joli, ce qui sent bon" ("The sole mission of Realism, to use this stupid
term,... is not to decry what is base, what is repugnant, what stinks; it
came into the world, too, to define in artistic writing, what is elevated,
what is pretty, what smells good"; viii). Quoting from Goncourt's *La
Faustin* (1882), Nordau bolstered the claim that certain writers linger
on "bad odors," particularly the smell of women and their skin (501).
Yet Nordau does not mention Goncourt's *Chérie* (1884), a novel that
rivals Huysmans's *À rebours* in its portrayal of perfume fervour. Like
Des Esseintes, the doomed Chérie Haudancourt (whose name bears a
striking resemblance to that of the Hadancourt perfume house) would
seem to exemplify a "voluptuary" with a "sensitive nature yearning for
aesthetic thrills" (5). But Nordau's discussion of the male protagonist of
À rebours (304–10) undoubtedly better served his characterization of the
fin-de-siècle "mood" as "the impotent despair of a sick man" (3).

Although *Chérie* was a great success at the time of publication, the
novel was nearly forgotten in the twentieth century.[9] Following a
call for contributions embedded in the preface to his 1882 *La Faustin*,
Goncourt constructed his heroine's "monographie de jeune fille,"[10]
with a carefully manipulated (and much-embellished) compilation of

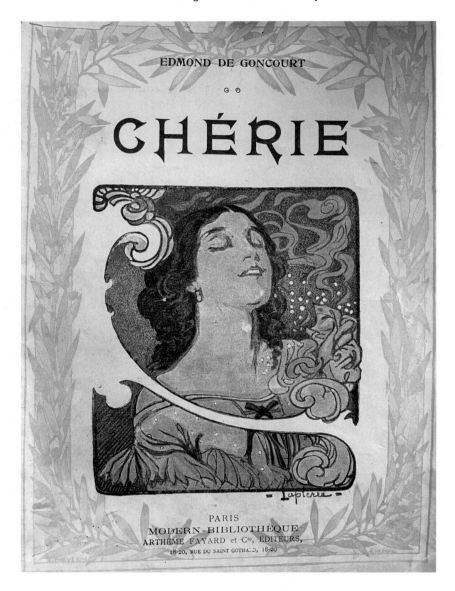

7.1. An early twentieth-century illustrated edition of Edmond de Goncourt's 1884 *Chérie*, with a cover inspired by episodes of extreme perfuming.

memoirs from at least four real women, none of whom seems to have been responsible for the passages on perfume.[11] The mosaic-like narrative, obviously and intentionally free of plot twists, offers episodes and commentary on the life of Chérie Haudancourt, granddaughter of a minister of justice. Chérie veers towards hysteria and untimely death, destined by heredity but also nurtured by a self-sabotaged libido, or as Goncourt explained in an interview, she is hystericized by her strong, unsatisfied desires (Cabanès, "La documentation dans le roman des Goncourt," 454). Although it is true that Chérie does not channel her sexual energy into marriage, she indeed finds other, less conventional outlets. Goncourt fictionalized the etiology of fragrance-enhanced hysteria in this "case study" of a woman whose autoerotic pleasure is stimulated by perfume.

Like Huysmans's Des Esseintes, Goncourt's Chérie shows an exaggerated fascination with smelling, wearing, and acquiring perfume. Des Esseintes is portrayed as an overzealous yet learned connoisseur capable of arranging his collection by category, of orchestrating his blends to harmonize with the rhythms of Baudelaire's poetry. In contrast, Chérie's messy, erotic obsession embodies the physicality, the smell, and the tactility of perfume – its liquidity, its tangible presence on fabric, paper, and skin. Both books dramatize the concept of degeneration that distinguishes these works, stylistically and theoretically, from earlier, related naturalist novels by the same authors.[12] Des Esseintes has lost his sexual appetite. Chérie dies a virgin. Yet Des Esseintes methodically orchestrates his physical and social withdrawal. The architecture of À rebours, a series of vignettes divided into framed chapters, contributes to a representation of Des Esseintes's eccentricities as carefully, consciously installed works of art. By comparison, Chérie's 105 chapters vary significantly in length and tone.[13] Their loose, uneven, unframed construction mimics the fluctuation of Chérie's hysterical symptoms, her excess and volatility.

Goncourt cultivated the structural disproportion of his novel as much as he did the psychological imbalance of his protagonist. After the death of his brother Jules, Edmond went on to write four more novels,[14] rejecting by increments the naturalist model for which, as Jules had predicted, the two would be remembered. Of these four works, Chérie – "pauvre dernier volume du dernier Goncourt" ("poor/pathetic last novel of the last Goncourt'; 51)[15] (as Edmond himself described it) – is probably the most unexpected (it deals with a wealthy heroine), and among the most experimental (it has been called a novel without a plot). Finding that novels rich in action and plot twists were exhausted early in the century by the likes of Soulié and Sue (41), Goncourt advocates, in the preface to *Chérie*, a constant rebirth of genre, through revolutionary renovation and negation of the status quo.[16] This modern novel would be a work without adventures, without intrigue and without base amusements (42).[17]

Chérie lives up to the claims of its preface by blending non-fiction narrative strategies with representations of decadent taste and practices. Literary reinvention meets documentary attention, particularly in the extensive passages on fragrance. Chérie's devotion to perfume and Goncourt's narrative interventions on the subject suggest that he, in the manner of his contemporaries Huysmans and Montesquiou, did significant research in the apothecaries and perfume manuals of his day. For example, his narrative interventions include the heavily circulated anecdote about the musk-crazed Empress Josephine (*la folle du musc*):[18] years after she had left, workers toiling to rid the Malmaison of Josephine's indestructible sillage reportedly passed out from the pervasive, musky, animalic odour (11–12).[19]

Cherié's taste for strong scents and her sensitivity to them is foreshadowed in the very name of her childhood home, a former convent called Nonains-le-Muguet, or le Muguet, for the property's abundance of lily-of-the valley. Chérie shows a sensitivity to the odour of natural plants and flowers, and the "neurotic" capacity to get high on substances inhaled or administered to the skin, at an early age. As a child suffering from a "délicatesse nerveuse," Chérie is treated with camphor compresses soaked in *eau de vie*. When she subsequently shows agitation and signs of delirium, the doctor concludes that, like many little girls and *jeunes filles* of a nervous nature, Chérie is drunk, her skin having absorbed the alcohol (*esprit de vin*, also used as a liquid perfume base) from her therapeutic compresses (88). The same doctor later points out that Chérie's sensitivity to cut hay, or hay fever ("fièvre des foins"), is comparable to "rose fever," and to her getting high via contact with camphor compresses (171). Chérie's skin once again absorbs sensorial pleasures when, on a hot summer day at le Muguet, she watches and listens to two scantily clad country girls cutting orange blossoms, sponging away the perspiration between each other's breasts, as they chatter in a familiar patois. In the "Oriental heat and odor of the of the day" (165), Chérie experiences these sights, sounds, odours, and observed touches, with the sweetness of a first kiss on the mouth. She lingers at the window taking in the synesthetic sensuality of the scene: "laissant entrer dans sa chair ouverte le gazouillement sensuel des deux fillettes, mêlé et confondu avec le brûlant midi du jour, avec les défaillantes senteurs des orangers" ("letting enter into her open skin/flesh, the little girls' sensual babbling, mixed and confused with the burning

noon day, with the swoon-inducing scents of the orange blossoms";
165). Later, Chérie knits on a *causeuse* (loveseat) with her head thrown
back, arms on her chest in a pretty pose of sluggishness (166), a posture
that reinforces the exoticist cliché suggested by the "oriental heat and
odour" mentioned earlier, and one she will assume again, with more
deliberately perfumed swooning. That evening, as her grandfather tries
to interest her in solving a rebus, she instead plays with a violet wood
fan, enjoying the fragrance created by pressing it with hands and fingers, and becoming almost immobile, save for some occasional nervous
extensions of the arm (167). In this and other episodes, Chérie's position shares elements of the poses featured in Charcot's iconography of
hysterics.[20]

Although Goncourt avoided balancing the novel's narrative arc,
he did present *Chérie* as the monograph of a little girl who reaches
marriageable age, a *jeune-fille* storyline favoured by male writers who
seem determined to plot their heroine's downfall via dashed dreams,
failed betrothments, moral decay, early death, solitary aging, or self-
destruction. The biological passage from girlhood to womanhood
marks a narrative turning point for doomed heroines like Virginie
and Chérie. Chapters 37–42, which deal with Chérie's physical and
moral "metamorphosis" (156) into young womanhood, culminate in
her first menstruation (chapter 39). This passage earned Huysmans's
praise and rivalled an episode in Zola's *La joie de vivre*.[21] Five con-
spicuous lines of uninterrupted elliptical marks fall between general
commentary on the onset of menstruation (a frightening event that,
according to the narrator, usually takes place in the night [151]), and
Chérie's internal monologue (occurring at her bedside in the morning), in reaction to her own presumably similar experience (152). The
visible ellipsis draws attention to the unsaid: the absent description of
the onset of menses. The series of dots also mark the page itself, evoking visually the blood that will not be described in words. In a sense,
the physical page of the book stands in for the fabric or skin on which
Chérie most likely discovered her blood. Here begins a downward
spiral, accelerated by Chérie's solitary sexual awakening, her love of
fiction and her attachment to perfume. At the age of fourteen, Chérie
takes to sneaking downstairs at night to read in the dark, "sollicitée
par une curiosité malsaine de vierge" ("solicited by an unhealthy virgin's curiosity"; 158).

Gustave Flaubert wrote against the grain of romantic aesthetics
in *Madame Bovary*, underscoring his own act of literary rebellion in
the description of Emma's reading practices, and casting Emma as a
would-be romantic heroine within a realist novel. Goncourt takes a

similar tack when he, in turn, writes against the naturalist novel; he arms his own Second Empire heroine [22] with a book from Emma's collection, Bernardin de St. Pierre's *Paul et Virginie*,[23] a novel also seen in the hands of Balzac's Véronique Sauviat (*Le curé de village*, 1855). Véronique's reaction to the novel illustrates that for some women, it does not take a man to awaken the "sixth sense," which is to say, to make them aware of sexual desire. Any number of sights, sounds, smells, or experiences, including reading, or a harmony of nature's perfumes (53), will do the trick:

> Véronique passa, pour aller dans la campagne, devant l'étalage d'un libraire où elle vit le livre de *Paul et Virginie*. Elle eut la fantaisie de l'acheter à cause de la gravure.... L'enfant passa la nuit à lire ce roman, l'un des plus touchants livres de la langue française.... Une main, doit-on dire divine ou diabolique, enleva le voile qui jusqu'alors lui avait couvert la Nature.... Pour toute autre, cette lecture eût été sans danger; pour elle, ce livre fut pire qu'un livre obscène.... Il est des natures vierges et sublimes qu'une seule pensée corrompt.... Son esprit exhala dès lors un parfum de poésie naturelle.... Sa toilette connut quelque recherche.

> Véronique passed, on the way to the countryside, a bookseller's stall where she saw a copy of *Paul et Virginie*. She had the fancy to buy it because of the engraving.... The child spent the night reading the novel, one of the most touching books in the French language.... A hand – should we say divine or diabolical? – raised the veil which until then had hidden Nature from her.... For any other [girl], this reading would not have been dangerous; for her it was worse than an obscene book.... There are natures chaste and sublime that a single thought corrupts.... From that time on, her spirit exhaled a perfume of natural poetry.... She paid close attention to her clothing and grooming. (52–5)

Unlike Véronique and Emma, Chérie consciously associates her reading with transgression: "Elle lisait, du feu monté aux joues, le cœur lui battant plus vite qu'à ordinaire, et prenant tout à coup d'adorables airs du coupable, quand on la surprenait dans la lecture, cependant autorisée, du livre de Bernardin de Saint-Pierre" ("She would read, her cheeks ablaze, her heart beating more quickly than usual, and suddenly taking on adorable airs of guilt, when she was caught in the nonetheless sanctioned reading of Bernardin de Saint-Pierre's book"; 160). In this way, Chérie is the literary descendant of the earlier hysteric Emma Bovary, whose sensibilities, as penned by Flaubert, were seen to render even the most innocent actions lascivious.

One obvious difference between Emma's and Chérie's identification
with *Paul et Virginie*, which Goncourt's narrator calls a love manual for
young girls (160), is Chérie's own eroticization of the book. Her physical response to reading (enhanced by her narrator's voyeuristic and
teasingly structured description of that response), is made possible by
liberal application of perfume not to her body or to linens, but to the
pages of the book:

> L'émotion intimement heureuse que la jeune fille éprouvait de la lecture
> de *Paul et Virginie*, ainsi que d'autres livres honnêtement amoureux, pour
> la faire plus complète, plus intense, plus entrante avant dans tout son être,
> devinerait-on jamais ce qu'elle avait imaginé? Le livre qu'elle lisait, elle le
> trempait, elle le plongeait dans des eaux de senteur, et l'histoire d'amour
> arrivait à son imagination, à ses sens, par les pages toutes mouillées, tout
> humides de parfums liquéfiés.

> The intimately happy emotion that the young woman would experience
> in reading *Paul et Virginie*, as well as other honorable love stories, to make
> it more complete, more intense, more penetrating in her whole being,
> can you guess what she thought up? The book that she was reading, she
> would drench it, she would drown it in scented waters, and the love story
> would reach her imagination, her senses, via these pages, all wet, all damp
> with liquefied perfumes. (160)

The porous, perfumed pages facilitate penetration of Chérie's mind
and body through dangerous reading.[24] Moreover, Chérie revises this
formerly "honorable" book by modifying the paper not with ink, but
with her own perfume. She saturates the pages as she might dip a handkerchief in violet water and, in so doing, writes into the book her signature scent. Earlier, Goncourt's elliptical marks on the printed page
placed ink where one might imagine blood. This later passage again
suggests a parallel between the body and the page. The emphatic and
drawn-out description of perfume's wetness reads metonymically as
an evocation of the body's natural, damp secretions. Fabricated perfume gradually mingles with and displaces natural fluids in this novel,
whose action dramatizes a move away from nature (and naturalism)
and towards decadence.

By embedding *Paul et Virginie* within *Chérie*, Goncourt reinforces his
objective – to create a new kind of fiction – and accentuates a novelistic
evolution with touchstones at 1787, 1857, and now 1884. The episode
marks, in liquid fragrance, the writer's deliberate alteration of what
had become naturalist norms. Goncourt's literary project involves a

conscious jettisoning of novelistic baggage – not just earlier romantic novels, but also a gritty brand of realism attributed to Flaubert and to the Goncourt brothers themselves. When Chérie drenches the pages of *Paul et Virginie* in perfume, she performs an act of hybrid reading closely related to Goncourt's hybrid writing. She renders romantic pages naturalist by giving them odour, while embellishing them with the artificial accessory of choice: perfume. Chérie's strange obsession with perfume – an over-determined awareness, an indulgence, perhaps a toxic addiction – marks a place where body and page commingle, where natural and unnatural desires converge, and where Goncourt articulates his new aesthetics against those of the past.

When Goncourt vicariously douses the pages of *Paul et Virginie* in perfume, and similarly marks his own pages with enumerated perfume materials (especially 264–8), he denounces, degrades, denaturalizes, and rebrands the novel. The earlier substitution of ink for blood seems to foreshadow Chérie's act of soaking her book's pages with the fabricated, partially synthesized odours of perfume. Cherie's dramatization of Goncourt's literary insurgence also functions as a pivotal episode in her life story. Perfume addiction is crucial to the documentation of her rapid psychological and physical decline:[25]

> Respirer dans l'atmosphère des exhalaisons entêtantes, dans une sorte d'embaumement écœurant de l'air, c'était devenu, pour Chérie, une habitude, une despotique habitude, et quand elle ne l'avait pas, cette atmosphère ambrosiaque, il manquait à sa vie quelque chose; elle ressemblait à un fumeur privé de fumer....
>
> À sentir le mouchoir trempé de ces bouquets, Chérie éprouvait du bonheur ayant quelque chose d'un très léger spasme. Il se faisait une détente de ses nerfs, une douce résolution de son moi, une sorte de contentement chatouilleux, un engourdissement à la fois jouisseur et un peu léthargique de son corps duquel, très souvent oublieuse des gens qui se trouvaient autour d'elle, Chérie se soulevait, pour aspirer de nouveau la senteur à pleines narines, frénétiquement, dans un renversement du buste où sa tête s'en allait un rien en arrière, avec des yeux se fermant de plaisir.

> Breathing in the atmosphere of heady exhalations, in a sort of nauseating embalming of the air, had become for Chérie, a habit, a despotic habit, and when she did not have it, this ambrosial atmosphere, something was missing from her life; she was like a smoker deprived of smoking....

By smelling her handkerchief soaked in bouquets, Chérie experienced happiness having something like a light spasm. There was a relaxing of her nerves, a gentle resolution of her self, a sort of ticklish contentment, a torpor in her body that was at once sensual and a little lethargic, out of which, very often forgetting the people around her, Chérie would get up, to breathe in deeply through her nostrils a new aroma, throwing back her chest with an ever so slight tilt of the head, with her eyes closed in pleasure. (265)

Chérie's erotic physical reaction to perfume echoes nasogenital reflex theories that trace a direct link from the nose to the "genital apparatus" via the olfactory nerve and spinal fluid,[26] along with symptoms of synesthesia associated with hysteria in medical writing. Perfume enables and enhances her withdrawal from society and expediates her entry into a toxic, private world of sensual pleasure. This may explain why perfume goes unmentioned in the many passages devoted to Chérie's attention to clothing, accessories, and toilette in preparation for social gatherings.[27] For Chérie, fragrance functions not in social ritual, but in solitary pleasure eventually reserved for the bedroom:

> Maintenant, tous les matins, à son premier réveil, la jeune fille se levait, et encore endormie, d'une main cherchant à tâtons, atteignait un vaporisateur, et se mettait à insuffler l'intérieur de son lit de la senteur de l'héliotrope blanc.
>
> Puis, aussitôt, elle se refourrait entre les draps parfumés, prenant soin de les ouvrir le moins possible. Et, la tête enfoncée sous la couverture jusqu'aux yeux, elle prenait une jouissance indicible à se sentir pénétrée et caressée, rafraîchie par l'humidité odorante de la vaporisation dans laquelle il lui semblait, son être encore mal éveillé, à demi s'évanouir, s'en aller, lui aussi, comme s'il était volatilisé, en parfum et en bonne odeur.
>
> À la fin elle se rendormait, trouvant une volupté dans un sommeil où il y avait un peu d'ivresse cérébrale et un rien d'asphyxie.

Now, each morning, upon awakening, the young woman would get up, and still drowsy, groping, would reach for a vaporizer, and would begin insufflating her bed with white heliotrope.

Then, right away, she would wrap herself between the perfumed sheets, taking care to move as little as possible. And, her head buried under the covers up to her eyes, she experienced inexplicable pleasure in feeling penetrated and caressed, refreshed by the fragrant dampness of the vaporization in which, it seemed to her, still not quite awake, half fainting, her very being itself was taking off, it too, as if it had been volatized in fragrance, in good odour.

Finally she would fall asleep again, finding voluptuousness in a sleep where there was a bit of cerebral inebriation and a dash of asphyxiation. (267–8)

Like the saturated pages of *Paul et Virginie*, the damply scented sheets provide a delivery system for perfume. They also expedite its unwholesome contact with the skin. Chérie's closing chapter takes the form of an obituary notice, with no narrative commentary and no cause of death reported – though suicide has been clearly foreshadowed in her final line of dialogue: "Adieu! – faisait Chérie, appuyant sur le mot" ("'Farewell!' – said Chérie, emphasizing the word"; 303). Perfume certainly plays a key role in the simultaneous degeneration of the naturalist novel and of its doomed protagonist. Death by perfume may well have been the decadent fate of Chérie, as it was of Goncourt's naturalism.

Though Chérie does not talk about the perfumes she collects, Goncourt sprinkles his novel's pages with perfume ingredients (264–8), interrupting the story at hand with detailed information on the social history and production of perfume, citing popular contemporary blends whose names could be read at a glance in magazine advertisements of the era. Chérie develops a taste for triple-odour extracts "à baptême anglais": Kiss Me Quick, Lily of the Valley, New Mown Hay (the list goes on), as well as the more complex "bouquet de l'Impératrice Eugénie."[28] Echoing some concerns about multiple notes in perfumes, voiced by medical doctors and etiquette specialists of the era, the narrator indicates that Chérie selects triple blends and bouquets – rather than less complicated, single-note fragrances – which envelop her in a "floating blend" of tuberose, orange flower, jasmine, vetiver, opoponax, violet, Tonka bean, ambergris, sandalwood, bergamot, neroli, rosemary, benzoin, verveine, and patchouli (299).[29] Like Emma Bovary before her, Chérie is compared to exotic women who pass their days in a near vegetative state, in the smoke of burning perfumes. The narrator compares her to Parisian women of a delicate, fragrance-loving nature who scent their clothing, skin, and hair with the nauseatingly strong vegetal and animalic notes (264); and like the Empress Josephine, she is crazy for musk (266). Chérie's desire to procure perfumes culminates in the acquisition of an authentic grain of musk from Tibet, a material representing the double seductive danger of animalic and exotic scents, and the final channel to her erotic perfume abuse. Chérie enacts an exaggerated refusal to follow the conventions of fragrance fashion: she enjoys blended bouquets, animalic notes, strong and oriental perfumes. These transgressions are not presented as hygienic or fashion-ably appealing. On the contrary, they are anti-social, pathological, destructive, and toxic.

The modest violet, so often cited in the century as the visual and aromatic correlative to the innocent *jeune fille*'s good virtue, is mentioned as part of Chérie's immoderate fragrance blend, hover-ing in Goncourt's enumeration of notes between stronger scents of opoponax and Tonka bean. Perfume has not corrupted Chérie; instead her eccentricities have corrupted the perfume. Later, as she prepares to attend her first ball in Paris, the dress designer Gentillat, a character based on couturier Émile Pingat,[30] recommends a cor-sage of violet and forget-me-nots for her gown (183, 287). But wear-ing violet bouquets does not restore Chérie to a state of innocence. By this time, the inevitability of Chérie's descent into a "nervous malady" (288) has been established. Chérie has not followed the advice of Madame Celnart, Baronne Staffe, or the other dispensers of hygiene and etiquette circulated at the time. *Chérie*'s inclusion of contemporary perfume names and industry jargon marks one of the ways in which the novel blurs fact and fiction, in the name of an idiosyncratic documentary truth. It also places perfume at the centre of a peculiar, feminized deviance or decadence that could be enacted nearby, behind closed doors, anywhere.

High on Perfume

On 1 October 1912, the *New York Times* ran the provocative report "Per-fume now Injected: Latest Fad in Paris. Skin Becomes Saturated with Aroma." Similar pieces had been circulating since at least 1891 when, under the heading "Her Point of View," a writer lamented the resur-gence of trendy perfume injections:

Some time ago paragraphs were printed everywhere telling that Paris-ian women exhaled a permanent perfume from their persons by inject-ing a few drops of scented liquid beneath the skin, thus odorizing the actual blood!"... The perfume-injecting fad was apparently nipped in the bud – only apparently however, for it has cropped out again, armed now with medical authority against its harmfulness.... And today, for 15s, in Bond Street, the whole outfit – essence, syringe, etc. – may be procured. Probably the kit is also on sale in New-York [*sic*], or, if not now, it soon will be.

It is to be hoped few women will take to the practice. The question of blood poisoning does not seem to be definitely settled, but aside from this consideration, there is something sickening in the idea of perfuming the blood! Good blood does not need it. Put plenty of red corpuscles in it by good air, cleanliness, and good living and the aroma of health will be the result—more wholesome and desirable than that of crushed roses or "violets three distilled." ("Her Point of View," 12)

One month later, on 18 July 1891, the *Chicago Daily Tribune* ran the same story with a new headline, "Injecting Perfume into the Blood," and the subtitle "The Whole Hypodermic Apparatus can be found for $8.95." Vague chronicles of perfume injection, presented alternatively as a new fad or a revival, appeared through the turn of the century. The strange account resurfaced in 1898, when the *New York Times* confirmed:

A Paris physician has nipped in the bud a habit which promised to be as dangerous as that of morphine. It appears that a well-known Parisienne had discovered that subcutaneous injections of certain perfumes gave their special fragrance to the skin, and that it was quite possible to exhale the lily, the rose, or any other floral scent. ("Injections of Perfumes," 10)

"Queer Fad of French Women" (*Los Angeles Times*, 5 March 1896) bemoans the news that, after a hiatus of unspecified duration, perfumes "have been restored to favor." While subcutaneous injection is "the latest freak of the Parisienne," most "Parisian whims find enthusiastic support here…, and it is very probable that with the American morphine fiend and cologne drinker we shall have the perfume faddist" (6). The author weaves commentary on the injection "freak" into discussion of more mundane perfume trends, specifying that lavender and violet are the most popular fragrances, while lamenting that "musk is being wafted abroad, and a new mixture of this scent is known as 'Frou-Frou' sachet." This perfume revival nonetheless has its limits. With obvious irony, the reporter applies the popular recommendation that women perfume their clothing, hair and accessories with a single, signature scent, to the absurdity of scent-coordinating perfume-injection paraphernalia: "there must be no mixing of odors. The contents of hypodermic syringes, sachet bags, atomizers, and toilet water bottles must be one familiar perfume" (6).

Was it an urban myth? Were Americans overreacting to quirks of continental fashion? Or were French women in fact infusing their bodies with perfume? As late as 1912, perfume injection was called "the latest trend" among Parisian women, though the *Los Angeles Times*

attributed its origins to an American in Paris, the "clever and popular society leader Mrs. Bobby McCreary" with her "charming little
flat, which looks right down upon l'Arc du triomphe [sic]" ("Perfume
Whim is Yankee Fad," 15 December 1912, ST2).[31] Loosely substantiated, and briefly recounted in a narrative tone that leans more towards
bemusement than outrage, the perfume-injection rumours provide
trans-Atlantic evidence of what Eugen Weber called a "showy perversity" (36), that was quickly sensationalized in the popular press at
the end of the century.[32] Yet as exaggerated or disingenuous as they
sometimes appear, titillating reports of perfume abuse reflect a more
earnest underlying message, overtly articulated in the popular press
and more learned discourse alike, in which olfaction and fragrance are
presented as deeply connected to moral depravity, social dysfunction,
emotional disturbance, physiological disorders and compromised
physical health. The idea of scent injection itself portends more serious and threatening meetings of the body and the needle that were
subjects of concern and fascination at the *fin de siècle*. Wilful puncturing of the skin recalls an algophilic behaviour that one turn-of-the-
century practitioner attributed to a "degenerate's fantasy" frequently
observed in hysterical women: sticking oneself with pins (Clérambault
2002, 29–30). The image of penetrating the body with scented liquid,
then exhaling chemical odours as a result, suggest fashionable drug
fads of the period as well: ether ingestion and injection, opium eating,
and morphine-shooting parties.[33]

In her discussion of morphine use in France between 1870 and 1916
(just before France passed a law restricting access to psychoactive substances), Susannah Wilson demonstrates that the figure of the morphine
addict (*morphinomane*) was most often depicted as a woman, and that in
the late 1880s, the more neutral word *morphinomane* was often replaced
by the neologism *la morphinée*, a term that better reflects the morphine
addiction as a female and feminine concept.[34] Visual and verbal representations of morphine abusers indeed correlated recreational use of
the substance with self-indulgence, lack of control, and a weakness of
character attributed to women or to failed masculinity; and overtly or
not, with exotic and Orientalist stereotypes of languid opium smokers.
An 1886 article in *Le Figaro* specifies that though there are few male
morphinomanes, morphine "a fait chez les femmes les mêmes ravages
que l'opium chez les Chinois" ("has wreaked havoc on women the way
opium has on the Chinese"; n.p.).[35] The article strengthens the bond
between *morphinomanie* and female self-indulgence by calling it a fashion (*une mode*), the difficulty of procuring the product only increasing its
desirability. The author explains that women under the influence either

7.2. Georges Moreau de Tours's *La morphine*, also called *Les morphinées*, 1886.

Image source: Wikimedia Commons

move like dazed, open-eyed sleepwalkers, or languidly sprawl on sofas, unable to resist the "triple ideal" of poetry, ecstasy, and consumption.

Georges Moreau de Tours's painting *La morphine*, exhibited in room 17 at the Salon of 1886, indeed echoes, or more likely influenced, the *Figaro*'s verbal portrait of women getting high on morphine (see Figure 7.2). The painting shows two women surrounded by lush fabrics (skirts, shawl, sashes, ruffles, ribbons, gathering, draping, pillows, curtains, upholstery, tassels), in two stages of morphine use. The woman on the left stares out at the viewer, or at nothing, as she injects her upper arm, the bump under her skin visible. Already under the influence, the woman on the right swoons in her chair, a fan and a book on her lap, the morphine kit and bottle (its shape and size resembling a perfume flacon) resting on a table to her left. Under the table lies a book whose blurred cover seems to read *Le paradis artificiel* [singular]/*Baudelaire*, as if to complete that triple ideal of ecstasy, poetry, and consumption, by suggesting that the woman has recently read Baudelaire's theory of reaching *L'idéal artificiel* via opium and hashish.[36] The text accompanying a colour reproduction of Moreau de Tours's painting in *Le petit journal, supplément illustré* (21 February 1891), again warns that morphine abusers will go the way of Chinese opium smokers, and that "notre belle race, si vaillante et si forte jadis, s'étiolera" ("our beautiful race, formerly so valiant and strong, will wilt"; 8). The description of the image closes by chastising the artist for not depicting the harm and ugliness this scene of morphine use will eventually cause, noting the image could have gone towards curing this "criminelle folie" (criminal folly) "en train de vicier le sang pur de la France" ("in the process of polluting the pure blood of France"; 8). While this brief text does not underscore the feminine nature of *morphinomanie* the way so much writing of the era does, a conscious or inadvertent revision of the painting's title appears in the article: no longer *La morphine*, a title that allows for the image to be interpreted as a personification of the drug, the women representing a living narcotic, the painting has now been renamed with a term that gained traction in the 1880s, one that only exists in a feminine form,[37] *Les morphinées*.[38]

While sensationalized anecdotes about perfume relate to practices regarded as unhealthy or perverse, they also suggest an underlying concern about medical treatments of the era. The 1891 article "Her Point of View" relates perfume injection to the increasingly widespread administration of subcutaneous injections for curative purposes: "And it is recited that the idea was discovered by a physician who, in using eucalyptus hypodermically as a remedy for phthisis, found that that the skin and breath of the patient became tainted with the pungent and disagreeable odor. So he tried perfume-injections to counteract this, with good results" (12). Indeed, the therapeutic use of hypodermic injection in nineteenth-century Europe and North America is well documented, as are its side effects of lingering tastes and odours. In his chapter on ether and alcohol, Roberts Bartholow observes that the smell of ether is noticeable on the breath within two or three minutes after injection (1882, 294).[39] He does not comment on the odour resulting from simultaneous injection of whiskey and brandy administered in cases of emergency, nor on the odour of ethyl bromide, which the French propose as a substitute for ether in subcutaneous administrations (294–5).

Substances like morphine, ether, and alcohol, ingestible therapeutically, or for recreational use and abuse, crossed over to cosmetics as well. Ethyl alcohol, used in compresses applied to the skin, also served as a base for liquid perfume (*esprit de vin*). Since the beginning of the nineteenth century, when Jean-André Chrestien published his treatise on the iatraliptic method,[40] physicians had been experimenting with delivery of medication via the skin.[41] Charles Hunter coined the term *hypodermic* in 1859 by compounding the Greek words for "under" and "the true skin." His goal was to standardize the language of an already prevalent practice, using a term whose etymology would distinguish the placement of medicine under the skin from other common procedures, such as inoculation (Bartholow 1882, 22).[42] Due to developments in medical procedures, the new word *hypodermic/hypodermique*, and the older *subcutaneous/soucutané* (derived from Latin in the seventeenth century) would have been quite familiar to readers in the United States and France in the second half of the nineteenth century. According to one practitioner, by the late nineteenth century the hypodermic needle would have been a fairly common sight in Europe and North America as well: "A physician of the present day without a hypodermic syringe in his pocket, or close at hand, would be looked upon as would have a physician fifty years ago, did he not own or use a lancet" (Kane 1880, 5).[43]

The development of subcutaneous medicinal treatments marks a way of thinking about the function of skin and pores that in a sense validates earlier, still lingering fears of upsetting the body's balance of energy and opening the inner organs to toxins.[44] If poisons could invade the body through the skin, then so could medications. The expanding industries of cosmetics and pharmaceuticals were also connected in more obvious ways, since some of their products were created in the same factories. In the preface to the first edition of his *Toilette d'une Romaine au temps d'Auguste et cosmétiques d'une Parisienne au XIXe siècle* (1865), Constantin James identifies the widespread use of chemicals as the source of poisonous agents in cosmetics, and the incentive for writing his book: "La chimie a fait dans ces derniers temps de tels progrès, que ses produits sont assez généralement passés dans le domaine de l'industrie. Malheureusement, parmi ces produits, bon nombre représentent des poisons véritables.... Qu'y a-t-il, en effet, qui se rattache plus directement à l'hygiène que les cosmétiques destinées à nos usages chaque jour?" ("Chemistry has made such progress that its products have generally entered the domain of industry. Unfortunately, among these products, a good number represent true poisons.... What is it, indeed, that relates more to hygiene than cosmetics destined for daily use?"; i).

In the nineteenth century, chemists and apothecaries were essentially one,[45] and perfumes were not only sold in pharmacies, they were manufactured in the same factories that produced pharmaceuticals. The medicinal use of aromatic materials, not yet called aromatherapy, had been established for centuries, and eau de Cologne in particular had been used as a skin tonic, an anti-neuralgic, and an emetic, rubbed into the skin, blended in soup, and perhaps injected.[46] Baudelaire groups together liqueurs, perfumes, opium, and hashish as similarly strong and mood-altering substances (*Les paradis artificiels*, OCI, 403), and some doctors list eau de Cologne, along with amyl nitrate and ether, as remedies for syncope (Boy-Tessier 1894, 19). But as Galopin warned, "[u]ne femme parfumée d'éther ou de chloroforme est un narcotique ambulant diurne et nocturne" ("[a] women perfumed with ether or chloroform is a daytime and nighttime walking narcotic"; 96).

The purported injection fad represents a peculiar breach of perfume-application etiquette in that it exemplifies to the extreme a strictly superfluous use of perfume, made possible by the medical, hypodermic needle. The perceived threat of invading women's skin and blood (and consequently, the space around them) with injected aroma links perfuming, in an unexpected way, to presumed causes of miasmic contagion that were only slowly discredited by germ theory in the second half of the century (see chapter 4). As late as 1882, Rimmel continued to voice the refuted premise that perfume was an antidote to miasma, business interests to promote perfume as both a luxury good and an object of utility.[47]

In a prurient way, stories of perfume injection echoed the tendency in learned discourse to discredit the salubrious properties of fragrance and, more radically, to deem perfume use potentially toxic and aberrant. But unlike the involuntary absorption of disease-ridden smells, or miasmas, fin-de-siècle perfume abuse (be it heightened sensitivity to odour or overzealous spritzing, huffing, injecting, or imbibing)[48] was considered a deviant behaviour rather than an environmental hazard, one – accurately or not – often ascribed to women, and linked to mental and emotional instability, in fiction as in medical literature of the era. The rumours of perfume injection in France relate to a peculiar concurrence of *fin-de-siècle* thought and practice around decadent portrayals of women and their bodily connection to fragrance, of which Goncourt's fictional *Chérie* serves as an extreme example, though her symptoms appear throughout medical literature of the era. Experts in various domains warned that no matter how artful, fine, or cultivated, the perfume wearer always drifted perilously close to a brush with excess and a fall from social grace: one must modulate grooming that acts against nature. Havelock Ellis focuses on many of the same fragrances singled out by earlier hygienists and beauty experts (including Celnart, whose advice carefully skirted all matters sexual), in his discussion of perfume, leather, and their sexual effects (91–106). After summarizing the influence of perfumes derived from the animal body (musk, ambergris, civette), and perfumed leather (*Peau d'Espagne*), he notes that women in particular take sexual pleasure from the smell of flowers, especially the heavy and penetrating gardenia, tuberose, and *frangipane* (102–3).

Charles Féré, chief medical officer at Hospice Bicêtre, claimed that even pleasant odours cause a range of maladies, including hemorrhoidal flux, and numerous digestive ailments. Abuse of odours provokes torpor, fatigue, and neurasthenia. Féré goes so far as to blame perfume, rather than imperialism or exoticism, for creating the stereotype of lethargic others: "Les parfums pourraient bien avoir contribué autant que les narcotiques à assoupir l'Orient" ("Perfumes may well have contributed as much as narcotics to lulling the Orient"; 176). Furthermore, perfume is addictive: "La difficulté qu'on éprouve à opérer le sevrage des parfums montre bien qu'ils sont devenus des excitants nécessaires au même titre que les poisons excitants et narcotiques ("The difficulty one experiences in weaning from perfumes shows well that they have become necessary stimulants in the same way as poisonous stimulants and narcotics"; 176).[49] Debay spelled out what other writers were suggesting: that the toxic effects of fragrance were triggered by certain individuals themselves, not the material they were sniffing. He cited the out-of-control imaginations and nervous systems of hysterical women and hypochondriacal men with adverse reactions: "les causes se trouvent plutôt dans la perversion nerveuse de l'individu que dans les propriétés des plantes" ("the causes are found more in the nervous perversion of the individual than in the properties of plants"; 127–841).

In 1909, Gaëtan Gatian de Clérambault reported an erotic physiological reaction to the smell of perfume among hysterical patients with kleptomania and silk fetishes (*Passion érotique des étoffes chez la femme*).[50] One diagnosed hysteric paired the pleasure of stealing silk with her use of cocaine, morphine, ether, and alcohol. She also described drinking Botot mouth rinse and eau de cologne, primarily to mask the odour of ether on her breath. According to Clérambault, women with sexual imbalances were particularly susceptible to *synesthésie génitale* (65–8), sexual arousal via sensorial stimuli, including smells. Since silk was a vehicle for the appreciation of perfume, it is possible that smell played a larger-than-acknowledged role in this fetish, generally associated with the touch and even the sound (a *froufrou* or *cricri*, according to one patient)[51] of silk fabric. Although his case studies reveal an underlying connection between the danger of odour sensitivity and the lure of products marketed to women (dresses and fabrics), Clérambault's observations never focus specifically on cosmetic perfume, nor do his case studies mention perfume injection.

Reports of perfume injection were substantiated by medical doctors in France, and the practice was dramatized in popular French fiction.[52] One case was reported by Antoine Combe, the doctor who so lamented the omnipresence of feminine sillage in Paris (see chapter 1). Combe saw perfume's entry into the domain of personal grooming (as opposed to religious ritual) as a trigger for abuse and debauchery. In the preface to his treatise, he cites examples of excessive perfuming from Ancient Greece, Rome, and Gaul, to Henri III and Madame de Pompadour. To punctuate his indictment of contemporary perfume practices, Combe comments on the perfume injection fad. He clarifies that while *la violet-tomanie* is not, as some would have it, "all the rage," he has encountered many women who tried and quickly renounced this form of "snobisme,"[53] because of a rather prolonged burning sensation left by subcutaneous perfume injections (13–14).[54] Combe concludes that injection is hardly the most serious example of contemporary perfume abuse:

> Et, de même que nos ancêtres ont fait des orgies de parfums, les sensuels d'aujourd'hui y cherchent de nombreuses jouissances. Nous ne parlons pas des éthéromanes qui se grisent en respirant de l'éther jusqu'à la narcose, mais de ceux qui "se saoûlent" en inhalant des parfums.

> And, just as our ancestors made orgies of perfume, today's sensualists seek all sorts of pleasures in it. We are not talking about ether addicts who intoxicate themselves to the point of unconsciousness by inhaling ether, but of those who "get drunk" by inhaling perfume. (14)

Combe then reports the self-observation kindly offered by a M. X, aged twenty-seven years, for whom 30 grams of Jicky (by Guerlain) induced hallucinations:

> Après quelques nouvelles inhalations, les objets voisins se transforment – (sensations un peu analogues à celles que fait éprouver le haschich) – et semblent entrer dans le monde des rêves. Je me souviens, en particulier, d'un abat-jour qui me semble être la coupole des Invalides.

> After a few more inhalations, neighboring objects transform – (sensations analogous to those caused by hashish) – and seem to enter into the world of dreams. I remember in particular a lampshade that seemed to me to be the dome of the Invalides. (14)

The selection of Jicky for this experiment in perfume huffing seems far from arbitrary. Created in 1889, Aimé Guerlain's groundbreaking, daringly unnatural fragrance does not recreate the scent of an identifiable flower or bouquet. Its blend of multiple synthetic and natural ingredients (including civet) renders the composition abstract rather than mimetic. Jicky is the sort of perfume made possible by what Combe describes as an industry once based on flowers, now taken over by chemists and synthetic processes (13).[55]

Nineteenth-century studies of neurology and physiology often focus on olfactory disorders and hypnosis via fragrance, and on reactions to smells of all kinds, including perfume.[56] As seen in his account of Jicky abuse, Combe further blends scientific inquiry and material culture by identifying the brand names of popular perfumes administered in studies of hysterical patients: "Violette (Viville, Paris) ... Peau d'Espagne (Viville)" (45). In setting up his studies, Combe makes no taxonomical distinction between the odours of perfume and the more noxious substances he administers: L'Héliotrope and Trèfle azuré (by Auber, Paris), chloroform, and above all, ether; all "produisent une crise à la première ou à la seconde inhalation" ("produce a fit at the first or second inhalation"; 45). Similarly, when experimenting on hysterics with odour sensitivities, Combe pays particular attention to subgroups of cosmetic perfume. Violet, heliotrope, white lilac, and Peau d'Espagne had no effect on one patient, but a few whiffs of chypre[57] threw her into a hypnotic trance (61–2). These product names and fashionable scents are reminders of the commodity status of perfume, its availability, and its recognizable presence. Like Huysmans's *À rebours* and Goncourt's *Chérie*, which mention contemporary perfumers by name and repurpose information from their manuals, Combe's medical writing is suffused with the sensorial, social, and consumer culture of perfume. By connecting extreme characters or hysterical patients with mainstream products, Huysmans, Goncourt, and Combe fuel the suggestion that that such extreme, or decadent, behaviours may be going on behind closed doors every day, corrupting women, softening men, and thus weakening France.

The Lance-Parfum Rodo

The perfume-abusing woman fictionalized in the character Chérie, and sensationalized in newspaper reports of women's injection parties, may also have been the target buyer for a gadget called the Lance-parfum Rodo (1896), now best remembered from a poster by Alphonse Mucha (see Figure 7.3).[58] Mucha's fluid style and carefully balanced compositions (often considered the foundation of Art Nouveau, though Mucha himself did not espouse the term)[59] hardly invoke the deliberate disharmony of Chérie's narrative forms. Yet the visual interpretation of solitary

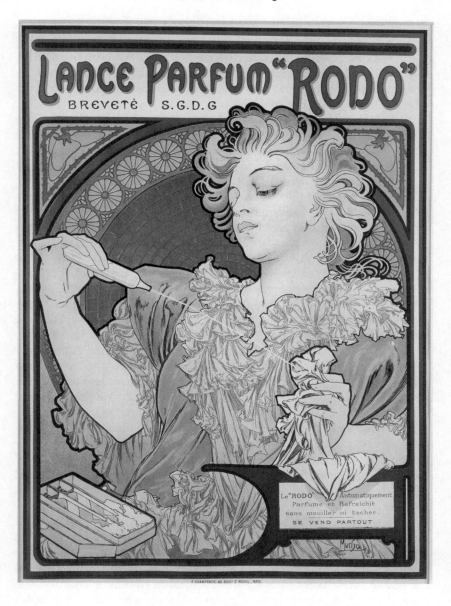

7.3. Poster for Lance Parfum "Rodo," 1896.

Image Source: Copyright © Mucha Trust 2022.

perfume bliss in the poster and logo (1896) could serve as an illustration for *Chérie*. In fact, a later illustrated edition of Goncourt's novel
features a cover design by Lapierre that seems to have been inspired by
Mucha's work. Eyes closed, head tilted back, nostrils visible, Lapierre's
Chérie holds what appears to be a slightly unfolded handkerchief, from
which perfumes rise in visible droplets and vapour swirls, enveloping,
entangling her, both reaching across the front of her body and wafting
behind her head (see Figure 7.1). The book-cover illustration shares a
visual language of olfactory representation with both Bouguereau (see
chapter 6) and Mucha, from the emphasis on the nose, to the intimacy
of the composition, to the woman's loose hair and clothing.

In Mucha's poster, the woman's eyes are lowered, directed towards,
though not quite focused upon, a visible jet of fragrance, leaving the
viewer outside a closed compositional circle that isolates the model and
her perfume in a moment of everyday decadence. She perceives the perfume's trajectory with lips sealed and eyes half shut, her vague glance
leading as much towards her nose as towards the Rodo or its perfume
spray. In fact, only the nostrils, clearly visible, open her face to the world,
her body to perfume. They contribute visually, and by association, to a
representation of olfactory experience. The woman's overt role in the
composition is to demonstrate how the Rodo works, yet the *mise en scène*
evokes pleasures beyond the joy of tidy perfume spritzing. A precursor
to women in fragrance advertisements of the twentieth and twenty-first
centuries, she conveys in both face and body a tension between surrender and control, enhanced by the suggestion of sensorial and sensual
delight.[60] While the hands show steady, and rather suggestive, manoeu-
vring – holding and aiming the Rodo and deftly catching its emissions –
the soft, loose clothing and hair indicate négligé and abandon. In contrast
to the purposeful movement of the hands (muscles engaged, the finger of
the right hand daintily arched),[61] the nearly blank facial expression and
heavy-headedness imply that operation of the Rodo is so simple it can be
performed inattentively, unconsciously, or in a daze.

The iconic *femme Mucha* is known for her flowing mane, often capped
in flowers or a bandeau, its lush tendrils unfurled in harmony with
organic and architectural background elements. Although the tousled
tresses of this bare-headed woman may at first appear to be cropped,
they have most likely escaped from a hidden ribbon or chignon, the
once crimped side curls now slackened. Unruly bed head contributes
to the portrayal of perfume application as an intimate indulgence.[62]
The suggestive shape of the Rodo itself – its handling and its action,
too – enhance this portrait of solitary, erotic perfume bliss. While perfume application may be a clean business (no wet spots, no stains),

it can also lead to secret, unwholesome pleasures and to unhealthy self-dispossession.

Although the image is much marketed today,[63] Mucha's poster has somewhat receded in chronicles of the artist's life and work.[64] The catalogue for the first public exhibition of Ivan Lendl's vast Mucha collection (2013) offers a rather vague description of the Rodo: "Mucha's beauteous maiden advertises a perfume spray – seemingly something of a novelty at the time, as the fact that the container dispenses the fragrance 'automatically' is stressed in the copy" (Rennet and Srp 2013, 112). What made the Rodo new and automatic? The Rodo advertisement illustrates speedy delivery of fragrance in a blade-like vaporous jet spray. The substance ejected by the Lance-parfum (a perfume thrower/flinger/launcher) darts at an angle in front of the woman's chest, into the rumpled but unsullied white cloth in her left hand (perhaps a handkerchief). Like Chérie's sheets, or the pages of her books, the fabric in the model's hand now bears the perceptible yet invisible signature of the woman's perfume. Draped over the advertisement copy below, the fabric draws attention to the words it justifies: "Le Rodo Automatiquement Parfume et Rafraîchit sans mouiller ni tacher. SE VEND PARTOUT" ("The 'Rodo' automatically perfumes and refreshes without dampening or staining. SOLD EVERYWHERE"). The claim is important, as *parfum liquide*, also called *parfum de mouchoir*, would indeed normally dampen, and potentially stain, fabric.

The poster serves as a reminder of how cosmetic fragrance was used and perceived in the late nineteenth century. Perfume was becoming more popular and easier to buy. The three-pack container on the left of the poster (reminiscent of travel sprays and *recharges* packs today) conveys practicality and portability that may connect the neologism Rodo (which reads as a reversal of odour) to the verb *rôder* (to wander, to roam – but also to loiter, to lurk) (Figure 7.4). The promise to provide dry, invisible scent is significant, since fragrance was applied to linens.[65] It is difficult to imagine, though, that the ample spray depicted would not have left some sort of temporary trace on white fabric.

While the advertisement claims that the Lance-parfum is sold everywhere, a search through histories of French perfume shows the Rodo device to be as elusive and resistant to commentary as the poster itself.[66] This may be because the Lance-parfum was as much a pharmaceutical product as a cosmetic. Patented in 1897[67] by chemical manufacturer the Société Chimique des Usines du Rhône (perhaps another link to the Rodo name), the Lance-parfum Rodo was the serendipitous reincarnation of an ethyl chloride dispenser called Kélène.[68] Records show ethyl chloride in surgical use as far back as 1831, but it was not until the 1880s that it

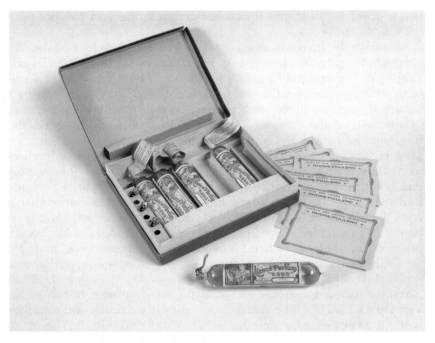

7.4. Alphonse Mucha, Set of Lance Parfum "Rodo" bottles in their original packaging.

Image Source: Copyright © Mucha Trust 2022.

was commonly administered, probably owing to previous difficulties experienced in packaging a volatile substance that vaporizes at room temperature. Enter the "Lance chlorure d'ethyle," its ether preserved in a liquid state until the seal was broken. The tubes, sometimes sold in multi-packs like the eventual perfume itself, allowed medical doctors to store and transport small doses of the anesthesia in little boxes similar to those used for morphine kits and travel perfumes (Figure 7.5).[69] The notion of using this appliance to propel perfume came by accident, and happens to be a story of violet perfume. The Société Chimique des Usines du Rhône manufactured both pharmaceuticals and synthetic perfume ingredients.[70] Violet fragrance spilled into ethyl chloride and an idea was born. Like its medical prototype, the Lance-parfum was a projection system for (now perfumed) ethyl chloride released automatically when the seal was broken: ethyl chloride meets warm air; liquid becomes vapour, hence the promise of dry, unstained, but scented fabric.

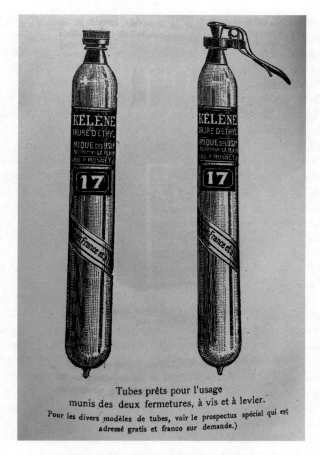

Tubes prêts pour l'usage
munis des deux fermetures, à vis et à levier.
Pour les divers modèles de tubes, voir le prospectus spécial qui est
adressé gratis et franco sur demande.)

7.5. Kélène tubes for portable anesthesia doses.

Source: *Le Kélène (chlorure d'éthyle pur) en anesthésie locale et en anesthésie générale*
(Paris: Société chimique des Usines du Rhone, n.d.), 35.

The Rodo device was eventually heavily marketed at the Carnival in
Rio de Janeiro, where users reportedly suffered intoxication, hallucination, and cardiac trouble. Some perished. Because of further reported
deaths related to Lance-parfum abuse, the product was finally out-
lawed in the 1960s.[71] A 1911 trade manual for perfumers summarizes
the chemistry and mechanics of generic lance-parfums. The author
highlights the refreshing sensation produced by solvents, including
ethyl chloride, but also deems the gadgets dangerous because they are

highly flammable ("Recettes et procédés utiles," 107–8). Perhaps the contents of the Rodo have influenced the artist or even the model, who languorously portrays the everyday decadence of inhaling (and presumably exhaling) fragrant anesthesia, as her skin and clothing remain dry and unstained.

Like the post-realist Chérie, and the fragrance-drenched pages of *Paul et Virginie*, the otherwise harmonious and decorative image of the Rodo user is transformed by a woman's decadent perfume. The Mucha poster and the Goncourt novel attest to an uneasy arousal provoked by the perceived moral and hygienic risks of perfuming a woman's body. Swooning on ethyl-chloride perfumes and Jicky-huffing may not have been widespread practices in France. Combe's loosely substantiated evidence suggests that many reports of perfume injection, if true, indeed amounted to a showy perversity of the fashionable few, quickly sensationalized in the popular press. Nonetheless, fascination with French fragrance breathers, drinkers, and shooters reflects a changing culture of perfume in the nineteenth century, made possible by a convergence of aesthetic innovation, marketing trends and medical discourse. Alterations of everyday health and beauty rituals are as antithetical to mainstream grooming as are decadent poetics to bourgeois taste. They are echoed, often amplified, in a range of texts and images, revealing a changing culture of women and perfume in nineteenth-century France. The cases of Chérie and the Rodo demonstrate that our reading of highly stylized literary and visual texts, in relation to what David Howes has called "an ever-shifting construction of the sensorium" (2003, xi), can expand understanding of the works themselves, and how they inevitably reflect, influence, form, and inform one another. Goncourt's *Chérie*, Alphonse Mucha's advertisement poster for the Rodo, and the surprisingly hazardous product itself, place women at the nexus of discourse on the social and literary implications of fragrant indulgences.

Cooked Apples and Exotic Perfumes

Concurrent feelings of desire and mistrust provoked by scented women, dramatized in the works of Balzac, Flaubert, Zola, Goncourt, and many others, are infused with a longstanding suspicion of odours and olfaction itself in Western civilization. Characterized as invasive, penetrating, lingering, masking, and displacing, smells were also more positively recognized for their capacity to conjure human presence, summon memories, unleash elation, incite mystery, or signal ephemerality. Both the appealing and insalubrious operations ascribed to aroma were frequently attributed to the perfume wearer as well, as a cause, a consequence, or a correlative manifestation of olfactive affiliation. Across the previous chapters, I have focused primarily on a male gaze, or male sniff, an olfactory perspective that influenced how the sillage of nineteenth-century women was interpreted, evaluated, and to some extent, controlled. I wanted to look closely at writers who co-created a code of perfuming by declaring its tenets, defining its terms, and setting its boundaries, often with a prurient interest in exploring what happens when women break the rules, when women smell too much. The stories of nineteenth-century perfume I have studied – fictional, factual, or in-between – disclose a collective, sometimes unconscious, correlation of perfume wearing to notions of the fascinating but disturbing other, in faraway lands or closer to home. Unfashionably pungent and animalic perfumes mark the presence of prostitutes in realist and naturalist novels. Physicians and fiction writers present the predominance of smell and sensitivity to perfume as symptoms of hysteria and neurosis. Patients and poets alike inhale perfume to alter time, space, and states of mind. In the following pages, I will begin to explore two related paths that my study has suggested: the voices of those who did not buy into the mainstreaming of perfume culture, and the persistent evocation of exoticism and Orientalism in the Western depiction of fragrant encounters.

Reclaiming the *Jeune Fille*

While so many writers adhere to a gendered representation of perfume use, aligning with and feeding perceptions of moral and psychological imbalance, I also recognize that there is a counter-discourse in French fiction. Novelists less attached to dominant literary movements hold a relationship to writing, culture, and perfume that is different from that of now-iconic men who plotted stories of "unstable" female protagonists. I have argued that the olfactory codes developed in the nineteenth century, often adopted by men and women, could nonetheless be subverted by those who rejected fashion trends and beauty advice. Similarly, not all writers sustained the olfactory status quo in their portrayals of women, gender, and aromas. Consider, for example, Rachilde's apples.

The best known of Rachilde's many published works, *Monsieur Vénus*, materializes in the sillage of novels like *Paul et Virginie*, *La joie de Vivre*, and *Chérie*, offering a fresh, often shocking take on the hysterical, doomed *jeune fille* of naturalist monographs.[1] Throughout the work, smells punctuate Rachilde's unique way of writing against gender normativity, naturalist aesthetics, and the *jeune-fille* plot. Maurice Barrès takes advantage of the era's fascination with ill-disciplined virgins in his preface to the 1889 edition of *Monsieur Vénus*. He insists that the novel is not autobiographical, all the while suggesting that Rachilde and protagonist Raoule de Vénérande share similar qualities, and referring to both the author and the protagonist as *jeunes filles*. After all, "[l]es jeunes filles nous paraissent une chose très compliquée" ("*jeunes filles* seem to us to be a very complicated thing"; 14).[2] The novel indeed complicates and questions the social and literary constructs of the *jeune fille*, through the development of not one, but two characters, Raoule and Jacques, who move along a spectrum of traditional male and female gender polarities. Dazzled by Jacques, Raoule finds herself feeling weak as a *jeune fille* in his presence. She lingers on those words, repeating them to herself, inviting the reader to shake them off with her: "Une jeune fille!... Non, non" (42, 41).[3] During their first encounter in Raoule's bedroom, after Jacques has just bathed using Lubin scented toilet water, his fleshy curves are compared to those of the Venus Callipyge. Raoule sometimes refers to herself as a boy (dubbed *nephew* even by her pious aunt), and Jacques at one point calls her *Monsieur* de Vénérande. In fact, protagonists Raoule and Jacques are both identified at different times as *he* and *she*, with Raoule finally taking on perhaps the closest thing to a gender neutral or inclusive pronoun at the time, a plural masculine *ils* ("they").[4]

Throughout the novel, Rachilde reclaims elements of earlier and contemporary *jeune-fille* plots, reshaping them to tell a new kind of story. Bernardin de Saint-Pierre's Virginie, Zola's Pauline, and Goncourt's Chérie are raised by one parent, relatives, and a grandfather respectively; the orphaned Raoule lives with her comically pious aunt Ermengarde.[5] *Paul et Virginie*, *La joie de vivre*, and *Chérie* each allude to the day the *jeune fille* becomes aware of her changing body, with descriptions of the confusion provoked by sexual feelings and by physical and emotional symptoms. The adults react quickly, discussing the need to marry her off. Rachilde connects this key event to Raoule's discovery of a book with an engraving. What Raoule reads and sees is reduced to an ellipsis, followed by the sentence "Vers ce temps, une révolution s'empara dans la jeune fille" ("About that time, there was a complete change [a revolution] in the *jeune fille*"; 26). This revolution manifests itself in the first of many symptoms Raoule will display. Shifting facial expressions, bursts of laughter or tears, fever, and hysteria are among the arsenal of nervous, *jeune-fille* attributes reframed in *Monsieur Vénus*. One could read the ellipsis in several ways: as marking a passage of time, as shielding the reader from words and images that transformed Raoule, or as an ironic demonstration of self-censorship, in a novel that has its share of shocking content, and that was itself censored. In each case, the ellipsis creates a space for the reader to fill in. In Balzac's *Le curé de village*, Véronique Sauviat picks up her copy of *Paul et Virginie* because of the engraving that catches her eye. She too is transformed after spending some time with the book. Zola's *La joie de vivre* casts illustrated anatomy books as dangerous reading for the *jeune fille*. If Raoule's book was indeed either of these, the ellipsis may signal the condensation of a trope so exhausted by the likes of Balzac, Flaubert, and Zola that it no longer bears repeating in Rachilde's "materialist" novel.[6]

Along with recontextualizing familiar literary touchstones, Rachilde effectively uses a verb frequently paired with smells in those earlier novels, which also, not surprisingly, alludes to sexual contact and entering the body: "pénétrer" and its derivatives. Rachilde overtly links these sexual-olfactory associations in *Monsieur Vénus* when, on their wedding night, Raoule urges her new husband – or wife – (Jacques) to let their love caresses penetrate every fibre of their boudoir, as the perfume from their incense burners already penetrates everything in the room: "pour que notre amour pénètre chaque objet, chaque étoffe, chaque ornement de caresses folles, comme cet encens pénètre de son parfum toutes les tentures qui nous enveloppent" ("so that our love shall permeate every object, every fabric every ornament, with its mad caresses, just as the perfume of this incense penetrates all the draperies that surround us"; 179).

Raoule is often depicted in acts that parallel Rachilde's own penetrating, opening, entering, and unlocking of the genre and gender expectations established by contemporary writers. The first episode of the novel shows Raoule groping her way through a narrow passageway, finding a door, turning the key, and entering the room that will reveal Jacques. The final passage finds Raoule, sometimes a woman dressed in mourning, sometimes a man in a black suit, eventually designated as *they*, entering a dark room, this time to visit the wax statue of the now defunct Jacques, an anatomical doll sporting the hair, teeth, and nails of the deceased lover. Raoule gains access to the Jacques figure not by turning a key in a lock, but by pushing or turning a spring inside the flanks, thus opening the mouth and thighs. Echoing the first passage in the last, this act belongs to a structural setup of satisfying repetitions that give the novel's background rhythm a sense of stability, or equilibrium, while its main plot and characters upset the apple cart.[7]

It is not perfume, but instead the smell of warm apples that provides an olfactory backdrop to the first episode of *Monsieur Vénus*, as by the dim light of a cigarette match, Raoule navigates a narrow hallway to the seventh-floor garret bearing the sign: *Marie Silvert, fleuriste, dessinateur*. Raoule's first perception of the flower designer's hovel is olfactory. Upon opening the door, she inhales a sickening blast of foreboding fruit: "Puis, la clef sur la porte, elle entra, mais sur le seuil une odeur de pommes cuisant la pris à la gorge et l'arrêta net. Nulle odeur ne lui était si odieuse que celle des pommes, aussi fut-ce avec un frisson de dégoût qu'avait de révéler sa présence elle examina la mansarde" ("Then, as the key was in the door, she entered, but the smell of apples cooking choked her and stopped her short at the threshold. No smell was more odious to her than of the apples, and so it was with a shiver of disgust that she examined the garret before revealing her presence"; 7–8).

Raoule's initial revulsion – "Cette odeur de pommes rissolées lui devenait insupportable" ("That smell of sautéed apples was becoming unbearable to her"; 11) – soon subsides. A long look at Jacques Silvert's body draped in a garland of fake flowers, facilitates Raoule's reconciliation with apple-infused air: "Cependant elle se trouvait mieux, les pommes avec leurs jets de vapeur chaude ne l'incommodaient plus; et, de ces fleurs éparses dans les assiettes sales, il lui semblait même se dégager une certaine poésie" ("But she was feeling better; the jets of hot steam from the apples no longer annoyed her, and the flowers scattered among the dirty plates even seemed to exude a certain poetry"; 12). Catching a glimpse of Jacques's tangled, golden chest hair: "Mlle de

Vénérande s'imagina qu'elle mangerait peut-être bien une de ces pommes sans trop de révolte" ("Mlle de Vénérande fancied that she might indeed eat one of those apples without much disgust"; 14).

To say that Raoule gives into temptation would be an understatement. The real apples and the artificial flowers that fill the room, aromatically for the fruit and visually for the blossoms, represent the first of many dichotomies constructed and quickly disassembled or reassembled. These oppositions most obviously concern nature and artifice, tropes easily associated with naturalism and decadence respectively. Amid this fog of cooked apple stench, Jacques appears to be sniffing a paper rose. The artificial flowers might take on the odour of apples, but that odour does not render them natural. The apples themselves seem to be overcooked, transformed from their natural state. Their smell, frying, steaming, or stewing, is not the same as that of fresh apples, after all. The symbolic power of those pluckable fruits and flowers, the apple and the rose, shift under the olfactory gaze of Rachilde, Raoule, and their readers.[8]

Considering Rachilde's apples in the context of other novels in which women are revolted by steamy, stewy foods that men find tolerable, even pleasant, I find this episode subversive in terms of genre as well as gender. Steaming, stewing, vaporous kitchen air will reappear throughout the novel, associated less with Jacques than with his sister Marie. Her memories of working as a *fille* are compared to "fumées malsaines" ("unhealthy fumes"; 31), and she walks in a sillage of the "cuisines nauséabondes" ("smelly kitchens"; 45) carried in the fabric of her dresses; steam cooking is, after all, her culinary technique of choice (32). Raoule's initial reaction of disgust at the smell of apples, and subsequent mentions of unpleasant kitchen odours, would at first seem to unite her with other protagonists who, in the presence of inadequately refined men, balked at the lowliness of steaming, stewing foods and their clinging odours. We recall both the lowly smell of steaming bouillons and kitchen sauces leaking through the walls and into Charles Bovary's examination room, and "le bon pot au feu" uttered by a husband who has no idea how much his wife longs for finer things, in Maupassant's *La parure*. But unlike Emma Bovary and Mathilde Loisel, Raoule de Vénérande's disgust for stewed foods wanes in proportion to her waxing desire, in this case, for flower-designer Jacques Silvert.

The apples appear six times in chapter 1. Their "atrocious odor" even wafts its way to chapter 2 in the book's 1889 edition.[9] As in the 1884 version, the second chapter shows Raoule back in her carriage, headed home, rather hot and bothered – what with the steaming apples and the steamy Jacques. The masturbation scene, rewritten to be even saucier in the 1889 edition, incorporates the smell of apples. The 1884 episode opens with the unembellished "Raoule évoqua Jacques Silvert" ("Raoule recalled Jacques Silvert"; 19, 18). In 1889: "Sans vouloir se rappeler l'escalier sinistre de la rue de la Lune, la fleuriste malade et sale, cette mansarde où régnait une odeur atroce de pommes, elle se mit à évoquer Jacques Silvert" ("Not wanting to remember the sinister stairway, on rue de la Lune, the sick and dirty florist, that garret where an atrocious odour of apple prevailed, she began to recall Jacques Silvert"; 1889, 33). Since the very denial of wanting to evoke the smell of the apples inevitably evokes it, the lingering memory of the smell serves as a backdrop to Raoule's solitary pleasure in the carriage, that private-within-public space so often related to sexual dalliance in French fiction.

When Jacques enters Raoule's world, cooked apples will be replaced by the aromas of tobacco, incense, and "Oriental perfume," the fragrant décor of Raoule's interiors. Her own lushly appointed room features a chandelier, a mink carpet, and an ebony bed, with "des coussins dont l'intérieur et les plumes avaient été imprégnés d'un parfum oriental embaumant toute la pièce" ("cushions whose insides and feathers are infused with an Oriental perfume that filled the whole room with balm"; 23, 22). The exoticism of Oriental perfume contrasts with the everyday, cooked apples stewing away. Raoule's incense burners attest to a certain style, to a luxury market targeting women and of course to the decorative landscape of exoticism and Orientalism. But like the rose and the apple, Oriental perfume had become, in literature by the 1880s, a popular but rather worn-out indicator of sexually desirable and usually available women. Rachilde's treatment of exotic motifs is ironic in its excess. The interior spaces to which Raoule introduces Jacques contain a hodge-podge of decorative items: Egyptian motifs, Greek statues, Japanese screens, Chinese screens, satins, velvets, brocades, and embroidered fabrics. Jacques is described as living the life of an Oriental woman in a harem. Though it is unlikely that Rachilde is confronting the notion of exoticism or Orientalism as imperialist ideologies (she was a fan of Claude Farrère, after all),[10] she does write against the grain of the authors before her, who defaulted to these exoticist tropes, as they did to the rose and to the apple.

At a later point in the relationship, we find Jacques dressed almost entirely in women's clothing, Raoule in menswear, both in a sillage of fragrant accessories that had themselves become gender-crossing scents. Raoule wears a gardenia, the male dandy's lapel choice, and she notices that Jacques has put *poudre à la Maréchale* in his hair.[11] Every nineteenth-century perfumer had a "maréchale" recipe in their book, though as Piesse noted, such blends had become a bit outdated.[12] In 1890, Fleury described a woman whose clothing, hair, and makeup were fashion-forward, modern, and bold, very *fin-de-siècle*, except for her *Maréchale* perfume, which constituted a throwback to the eighteenth century, a monstrous anachronism and failure of good taste that all the men notice (42). The remarkably heady fragrance of gardenia, the famously strong and old-fashioned scent of *Maréchale*, and the permeating aromas of incense and Oriental perfumes create an olfactory cacophony, recalling the greasy mess of Jacques's hovel, and the exotic mish-mash of Raoule's rooms. Beyond that, the busy smellscape lends an intermingling of odours to the intermingling of gender roles in this space.

The treatment of odour in this opening passage from *Monsieur Vénus* reveals and foreshadows how the senses, notably smell, play in the production and reception of literary texts in general, Rachilde's in particular. A series of sensual dichotomies, essential both to character development and to the depolarization of gender attributes, is set up from the first lines of the novel. The reader encounters Raoule de Vénérande via her embodiment, perception, and contemplation of sensation, beginning with the haptic sense of touch (Raoule's groping, a turning the key in a lock) and proprioception (the feeling of moving along a narrow, unlit passage). In this fin-de-siècle Garden of Eden, where the apples simmer and flowers have no scent, the cooking odours and Oriental perfumes that might lend verisimilitude to a different type of text, instead escape and intermingle. In so doing, they challenge the nature and artifice of binary gendering, and of overcooked olfactory tropes.

Visions of the Orient, Smells of Exoticism

New perfume notes and families have gained popularity over the years, among the most obvious, gourmand scents (offering foody notes like caramel, chocolate, coffee, candy floss, even sweet, cinnamoned apple), or the sea-breeze/marine note promoted especially in the 1980s and 1990s, and still featured in blends marketed as watery, cool, fresh, clean, and summery.[13] Other fragrances, including the esteemed soliflores of the nineteenth century – heliotrope, jasmine, rose, violet – have either remained popular, made nostalgic comebacks, or are recalibrated in updated blends. Peau d'Espagne, sold by many perfume houses in the nineteenth century, was originally used to scent gloves. Leather was the material that absorbed, diffused, but also altered the perfume with its own assertive scent. Now, gloves off, leather itself (like floral, citrus, chypre, fougère, and ambré/oriental) designates a family of perfumes. Though fans of leather fragrances may not know it, a whiff of their sillage connects us to centuries past. Brands like Maitre Parfumeur et

Gantier (founded in 1998) tap into a desire to access lost time through perfume, as do new versions of scents like Maréchale.[14]

By the turn of the century, and especially in the early 1900s, advertisers seized upon the potential power of establishing recognizable fragrance codes to target-market scents for specific tastes, moods, and activities: casual, daytime, seductive, innocent, fresh, professional perfumes; fragrance for the career woman, the active woman, the confident woman, the mysterious woman, the seductive woman, the cosmopolitan woman. The notion of finding a signature scent (mass produced or bespoke), to carve out a recognizable, fragrant identity that feels "like me," lives on in perfume culture, but so does the aspirational idea of using a perfume to try on a different way of being, to identify with a lifestyle depicted in advertisements.[15] Perhaps the most enduring legacy of nineteenth-century France's perfume culture, *oriental* perfume, and Orientalist marketing, continue to thrive, as in classic blends like Shalimar (1925) and Opium (1977), and their more recent flankers,[16] sequels, and prequels.[17]

A motif that surfaces in every chapter of my book is exotic perfume, from the materials themselves (Tonka), to their names (chypre), to their contributions to the language of perfume itself.[18] Exotic perfumes are present in countless texts and images: Mucha's illustration of Flaubert's *Salammbô,* in the patchouli-scented shawls of Balzac's *La cousine Bette,* in Camille Maupin's "Oriental taste," Emma Bovary's lounging in a cloud of *pastilles du sérail,* in Chérie's succumbing to "Oriental heat and odors," and in the perfume-infused upholstery of Raoule de Vénérande's bedroom. Orientalist tropes were developed in fiction and in beauty manuals at the same time. Antoine Le Camus's 1754 *Abdeker ou l'Art de conserver la beauté,* still popular in the nineteenth century, presented beauty advice in a hybrid narrative form, a two-volume "conte oriental galant" (7), a work of fiction attributed to a manuscript written in Arabic. Briefer exoticist anecdotes appear in introductory chapters of both perfume manuals and medical tracts, which seldom fail to include a section on the history of perfume in the Middle East and Asia, replete with orientalist clichés, and tales of perfume abuse in faraway places.

A term still used (to the surprise of many) in the industry today, *oriental* (also called *ambré*) refers to one of seven classic "families" of perfume.[19] The word attests to a collective, perhaps unconscious, yet persistent link between colonialism, travel, exoticism, imperialism, and the perfume industry. Exoticist tropes, still heavily marketed today, are apparent in advertising of the era and in a profusion of scents with names evocative of the Middle East and Asia, particularly in the early twentieth century. For example, Jacques Guerlain's classic 1919 perfume

Mitsouko recalls the heroine of Claude Farrère's 1911 novel *La bataille* [*The Battle*].[20] The story has obvious roots in Pierre Loti's *Madame Chrysanthème* (1887) and John Luther Long's *Madame Butterfly* (1898).[21] While Farrère's tale of war, love, lust, and loss in Japan does not withstand the test of time, its namesake Mitsouko lives on as a masterpiece of perfumery. A prolific and award-winning author, Farrère wrote travel fiction sporting such evocative names as *Trois histoires d'ailleurs*, *Fumée d'opium*, and *L'extraordinaire aventure d'Achmet Pacha Djemaleddine*. *La bataille* has relatively little to say about perfume, but in one episode an American woman, Mrs. Hockley, asks her "reader," Elsa Vane, to spray the air, the bed, and Hockley's entire body with perfume to counteract "a very Japanese odor" she has detected in the room (122). The scene recycles familiar tropes of perfuming behind closed doors that we have seen in Flaubert's *Madame Bovary* and Goncourt's *Chérie*, particularly a joining of erotic pleasure, reading, and sniffing. Hockley's lover Felze interrupts a scene in which an "indecently" dressed Elsa Vane reads aloud as Mrs. Hockley, wearing a transparent surah gown, lounges and strikes provocative poses in bed. A young woman of "ethereal charm" (68), Elsa Vane is identified as Mrs. Hockley's *lectrice* throughout the novel, though she "n'était officiellement que sa lectrice" ("was officially only her reader"; 68), and Hockley's "intime amitié" with Miss Vane has sparked Felze's jealousy (151). Once spritzed, Mrs. Hockley shows a physical reaction to vaporized scent similar to others we have seen in perfume-crazed protagonists. Her body tightens and arches, making her breasts yet more visible through her sheer gown, "under the caress" of this unnamed fragrance qualified only as fresh, presumably in contrast to the real or metaphorical odour she has identified as Japanese (122).

For decades, Guerlain's Mitsouko advertisements featured images of Asian women, alone or with a man, sometimes in close-up, often at enough distance to feature clothing Western consumers would readily identify as Japanese (see Figure E.1). The fragrance was marketed as exotic and Oriental, not only in name but in aroma. As one advertisement claimed: "In Mitsouko, Guerlain has captured all the romance and lure of the Orient – creating a romantic odeur [*sic*] of the occult and mystic enchantment."[22] In what has become the tradition in perfume advertising, this text does not mention ingredients or notes,[23] but as any perfume lover can detect, Mitsouko does not rely on components normally associated with *ambré* compositions. The name of Farrère's Japanese heroine clearly captured the imagination enough to lend itself to the marketing of a high-end perfume as feminine, exotic, and Asian, though in fact, the fragrance does not fit into the *oriental* scent

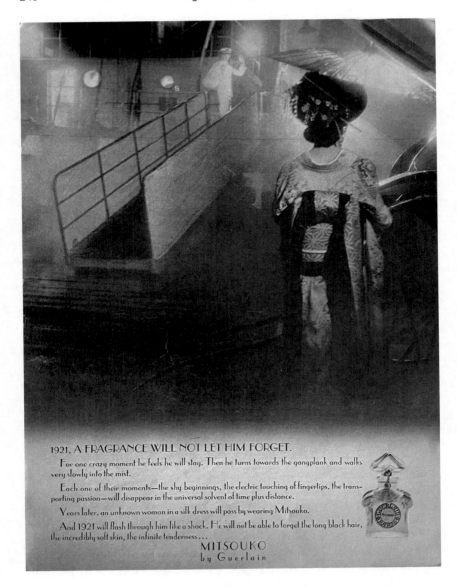

1921, A FRAGRANCE WILL NOT LET HIM FORGET.

For one crazy moment he feels he will stay. Then he turns towards the gangplank and walks very slowly into the mist.

Each one of their moments—the shy beginnings, the electric touching of fingertips, the transporting passion—will disappear in the universal solvent of time plus distance.

Years later, an unknown woman in a silk dress will pass by wearing Mitsouko.

And 1921 will flash through him like a shock. He will not be able to forget the long black hair, the incredibly soft skin, the infinite tenderness…

MITSOUKO
by Guerlain

E.1. A 1975 print advertisement blends nostalgia with orientalist tropes, as it weaves a brief story in which the scent of Guerlain's Mitsouko perfume triggers sensual memories from 1921.

family. Mitsouko is what many perfume lovers today deem the ultimate chypre.[24]

Before *oriental/ambré* came to designate a family of perfumes, specific ingredients were identified with faraway, seductive, dangerous places. Adolphe-Benestor Lunel, in his 1864 *Dictionnaire des cosmétiques et parfums*, identifies a toxic cluster of hypersensitivity to smell, the Orient, and women. He claims that "les Orientaux" were and remain even more avid perfume lovers than ancient Romans, for, generally speaking, warmer climates lead to sensitive nerves and an openness to sensual pleasures (156–7); strong and agreeable odours stir the brain and nerves, producing a sensation favourable to love; this is why women like fragrances so much and use perfume not only on their hair, but also in soaps, pastes, and elixirs (157). In her advice on perfumes to avoid, the Comtesse de Gencé clearly articulates a connection between contamination via oriental perfumes, sometimes expressed more subtly by other beauty mavens: "Défiez-vous surtout de ces bouquets exotiques…. L'Orient produit des essences qui sont de véritables poisons pour la pensée et presque aussi funestes que l'opium et le haschich" ("Be wary especially of those exotic bouquets…. The Orient produces essences that are veritable poisons for the mind and nearly as fatal as opium and hashish"; 1909a, 425).

By the time Gencé issued this warning, exotic and Orientalist themes had become established marketing tools for perfume and cosmetics (see Figures E.1–E.4). In the nineteenth century, novels and perfume advertising converged, in deploying the seductive alterity of exotic fragrances associated with transgressive characters like Balzac's Camille Maupin, Flaubert's Emma Bovary, and Goncourt's Chérie Haudancourt, and in offering a temporary, titillating whiff of danger and seduction to real-life consumers of fragrance products. Across the twentieth century, the perfume industry ramped up its exotic appeal by openly promoting perfume as a combination of danger and seduction. For example, print advertisements for Opium reappropriated and reframed the image of a woman alone and high on perfume, in photographs of glamourous, supine models and actresses, eyes closed, head thrown back,[25] their poses reminiscent of Emma Bovary's indolent lounging in a fume of *pastilles du sérail*, or Chérie's solitary swooning in perfume-infused bed sheets.

Exoticism and Orientalism became marketing tools in the nineteenth and early twentieth centuries, in real and fictionalized advertising campaigns for perfumes with names evocative of the Middle East and Asia. Balzac's protagonist perfumer César Birotteau (1836) builds his business on the invention of a "Double Paste of Sultans." Its selling

E.2. Poster for Crème orientale, poudre et savon pour la beauté et la santé de la peau. Parfumerie orientale, 1894.

Image source: gallica.bnf.fr / BnF.

points include a seductive fragrance formula and a bogus backstory about origins in Arabia.[26] In addition to such fictions, it is worth noting that France relied heavily on imported materials used in perfumery. Benzoin, Tolu, sandalwood styrax, and perfume-burners are among the imported goods included in reports of world fairs and colonial exhibitions in France.[27] If Chanel has reiterated that the costly jasmine in N°5 is grown in Grasse,[28] this is partly because so many fragrance products are cultivated outside the hexagon. Especially after the Prussian War, negative references to German perfumes appear in books and magazine articles. Because of the progress Germans had been making in synthesizing important fragrance molecules, it was easy to vilify artificial perfumes and the enemy in one breath. As we saw in chapter 1, Ernest Monin called upon women to show patriotism by avoiding

E.3. A 1913 print advertisement for Gueldy perfumes.

E.4. A 1917 print advertisement for Gueldy's Vision
d'Orient perfume offers a visual blend of
Orientalist and exoticist tropes.

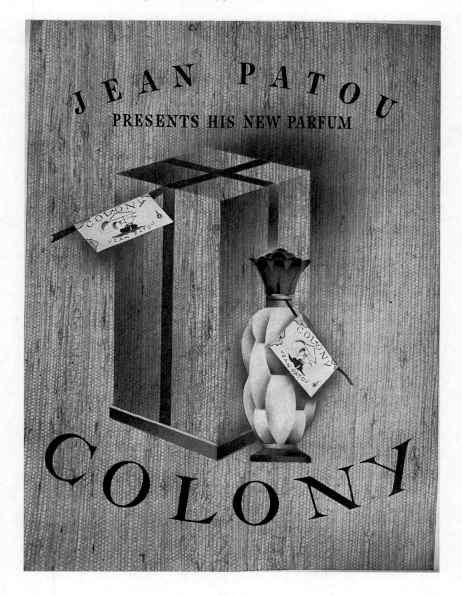

E.5. A 1937 print advertisement for Jean Patou's Colony perfume.

such chemical imports. In his 1895 *Nouveau manuel complet du parfumer*, Pradal steers readers away from perfumes made with an essence of rose recently produced in Germany and challenges French chemists to develop their essence from roses cultivated on French soil so that the Germans do not dispossess France of an industry thus far shared with the Orient (249–50). Pradal opens his volume with a nod to the importance of perfume production in England, recognizing London along with Paris as a fragrance capital, but he quickly points out the importance of Nice, Grasse, and Montpellier to perfume production. He underplays the importance of colonies, calling musk, myrrh, and benzoin, imported from Asia Minor, "confections" added to blends, and only after they have been processed in France (v). It is worth looking more closely at how colonial expansion and a trend for Orientalist-inspired perfumes intersect with the identity story of French perfumery, and with visual and literary art forms that link seduction to danger through exotic clichés. I think of *parfum exotique* as a subgenre of exoticism, a discursive field in and of itself, one that encompasses poetry, fiction, advertising, fine art, medicine, colonialism, travel, and more, a topic that will continue to draw critical attention.

The Story Continues

Perfume culture today has progressed in the wake of nineteenth-century France, still engaging with language, gender, exoticism, and fragrant materials, sometimes in surprisingly outdated ways, but often, quite creatively. The question of whether and how a limited lexicon of olfactory language can communicate the experience of smell is still debated. In the nineteenth century, a convergence of aesthetic, industrial, and medical experimentation brought perfume to the pages of books, magazines, and newspapers. Perfume was in the air, and it was documented, shaped, wielded, weaponized, and exploited via the written word. By the twentieth century, though the perception of a language–olfaction gap was still clear, French perfume publicists had more intentionally cultivated a relationship between books and fragrance that has since expanded. Guerlain's 1933 Vol de Nuit owes its name to the title of Antoine Saint-Exupéry's 1931 novel. Guerlain launched Chamade in 1969 following the publication of Françoise Sagan's 1966 book, and the subsequent release of a 1968 film adaptation starring Catherine Deneuve, who became the face of Chanel N°5 through the next decade.

Like Huysmans's Des Esseintes, though with less drama, twenty-first-century perfumers analogize the process of creating fragrance blends to composing in words. Though the inspiration for new perfume blends may come from scent memories, perfumers refer more often to a story. Francis Kurkdjian describes a creative process that begins with feelings and words, not raw materials: "anything can inspire me, as long as it becomes the beginning of a story that I can translate into a fragrance." He further specifies, "Once I have envisioned that idea, I translate it into a name that becomes the name of the fragrance. [The name] defines a frame for me to work within. A name is unswervingly tied to a fragrance. Once I have it, I dream about the actual scent and imagine the scent that goes with that name" (Benjamin 2020).

The title of Jean-Claude Ellena's 2017 memoir *L'écrivain d'odeurs* (*The Writer of Odors*) upholds his view that the process of creating a perfume is like that of writing a novel. Across Ellena's 2011 *Journal d'un parfumeur*, reading, writing, and smelling interact like the elements in a fragrance pyramid. He describes flankers (like Chanel N°5 Eau première) as a *rewriting* of their iconic ancestors. The perfumer's world comprises olfactory statements, olfactory poetry, olfactory declarations, and of course, olfactory compositions. Inspired by the Louvre's multidisciplinary exhibit *Le vertige de la liste* (with guest curator Umberto Eco), Ellena sorts through the peculiarities of the perfumer's everyday price lists, restricted materials lists, and perfume recipe lists. He highlights the interaction of words and smells, particularly in linguistic signs unrelated to the scent materials themselves. He owes to this alchemy of wordplay and smell ("olfactory semantics"), his liberation from natural representation in perfumery. In the journal's appendix, Ellena presents an *Abrégé d'odeurs*, a short list of odour juxtapositions blended to create the illusion of materials that are not present. These succinct descriptions encapsulate his signature word and fragrance alchemy, with the evocative restraint of Haiku. As much experimental writing as experimental perfumery, the *Abrégé d'odeurs* adds dimension to Ellena's earlier claim to being a writer of fragrance: "Je me suis toujours senti écrivain d'odeurs" ("I have always felt I was a writer of odours"; 12). Ellena claims to have reduced familiar scents – chocolate, fig, jasmine, olive, pistachio, etc. – to the level of a *sign* achieved by blending the minimum of materials. He invites the reader to play along with his semantic experiment: dip test strips in the materials listed. Smell separately. Then create a little fan, just slightly opened, and sniff the single sign they have become.[29]

Newer niche perfume houses have adopted names which underscore the connection between fragrance composition and the printed page. *Editions de parfum Frédéric Malle* (founded in 2000) promotes *auteur* perfumes. Its moniker and simple packaging were inspired by Éditions Gallimard books. Each bottle's label features the name of the *nez* (the perfumer, and therefore author) who composed the fragrance. The press kit for Histoires de Parfums (also founded in 2000) presents founder/ perfumer Gérard Ghislain as an author, armed with an "artisanal grammar" (1). Several perfumes, or tômes (volumes) in this line correspond to influential writers: the Marquis de Sade, George Sand, Jules Verne, Colette. The perfume bottle, nestled into a rectangular box, slips into a white case so that groups of bottles on a shelf resemble a library of Pléiade-like editions. Bookish marketing acknowledges that for perfume lovers, fragrance is a connection to the past, a means of self-expression, and a text to be interpreted or read.

The nineteenth-century perfumers who made the case for fragrance as an art would not have imagined that scent collections would become so esoteric, and at the same time so popular. The Osmothèque, based in Versailles, archives and recreates fragrances using orginal formulae dating to the first century CE. As their website states, this "living collection of existing but no-longer available perfumes protects the word's fragrance heritage." Scholars and enthusiasts may consult the Osmothèque library, book individual appointments with a perfumer/ osmocurator, or attend the archive's regularly scheduled workshops. As the Osmothèque carefully curates perfumes of the past, other online "scent libraries" allow customers to purchase the affordable, bottled scents of daily life and childhood memories: Kitten Fur, Waffles, Bonfire, Paperback, Petrichor. It is possible that some buyers wear these fragrances, but more often, I would guess, they collect them for the experience they offer, to consult them as one would peruse the books on a library shelf, or as Des Esseintes might relish his own collection.

As André Holler points out, creators of blended perfumes do not simply aim to reproduce pleasant smells, they seek out *interesting* odours (57). Surely it was this imaginative vision that led to some of the earliest nineteenth- and twentieth-century century mixes, including Fougère royale, Chypre, and the famously abstract, non-referential Jicky. The taste for not just pretty, but interesting perfume is evident today across the many web forums devoted to participants' discussion and reviews of perfume. Just a few minutes with any of these virtual communities shows how eager contributors are to put into words the feeling and phenomenon of fragrance. Similarly, books like Turin and Sanchez's *Perfumes: The Guide*,[30] though certainly helpful to perfume shoppers, serve more as a companion to sampling, discussing, contemplating, and enjoying perfumes. The book's evaluative descriptions, presented in an alphabetical series of witty verbal vignettes, is surprising not because of its often acerbic tone and unapologetic subjectivity, but because such tone and subjectivity are channelled into perfume reviews. *The Guide* and related fragrance media, show that perfume is worthy of appreciation, scrutiny, and debate; that perfume can be melancholic, fun, even funny; and that there is more to it than attracting a partner or finding your signature scent.

At Your Own Risk

Nineteenth-century hygienists grappled with the perils of perfuming, and twentieth-century marketers exploited those perceived dangers. In May 2012, a magazine promotion for Showtime's series *The Borgias* was released as a mock advertisement for Lucrezia perfume, complete with a scratchable scent sample. It is a marketing scheme in reverse, one that taps into the familiar concept of selling perfume for the entwined risk, danger, and eroticism it promises. Think Scandal, Shocking, My Sin, and, of course, Poison. But in this case, perfume was being used to sell something else as dangerous. The two-page spread features actress Holliday Grainger (Lucrezia Borgia) in medium close-up, a hand clutching her throat. Her nearly smiling lips and conspiratorial gaze recall a merging of surrender and control now familiar to those who have perused perfume advertisements. The image parodies cosmetics marketing so closely that one must turn the page to learn that Lucrezia was *not* the latest fragrance release. "Experience at your own risk" reads the ersatz ad copy, printed on the sealed fold of paper one must open to inhale the fragrance.

The allure of risk exploited in perfume advertising has become increasingly and more compellingly evident in the art of imaging and creating fragrance blends. Twenty-first-century perfumers continue to explore surprising perfume concepts, with names like Charogne ("Carrion") and Cambouis ("Motor Oil"). The definition of olfactory harmony, along with its relative value, has been expanded and sometimes achieved through an unexpected meeting of notes, like fig and caviar, or iris and white chocolate, a sort of fragrance grotesque that is simultaneously off-putting and alluring. And while even the earliest perfume advertising for blended fragrances emphasized image and ideas more than materials (a drawing of a woman at her dressing table sniffing her fragrance, but no list of its notes or ingredients) the twentieth and twenty-first centuries saw abstractions and scentless components built into the perfume pyramid. Director John Waters, who included odorama in the form of scratch-and-sniff cards for his 1981 film *Polyester*, has riffed on the idea of his own celebrity perfume, cleverly named Eau de Waters ("Waters Water"), "the smell of an obsessed film fanatic" (2010, 290); but in fact, some perfumes do define themselves as concepts blended with sniffable notes. Odeur 53 (Comme des Garçons 1998) includes "flash of metal" and "ultimate fusion" among its fragrance notes. Kenzo's Flower may be the best-known example of perfume containing a phantom note, or ghost flower,[31] the poppy featured in the bottle design and throughout ad copy, a beautiful, red, nearly scentless flower showcased as the heart of the creation.[32] It is a risky concept that worked, in part because the bottle itself is so appealing, but also because so many perfume lovers approach perfume discovery as a multi-dimensional experience, as sniffing, yes, but also seeing, touching, thinking, and communicating.

In 2018, UNESCO awarded World Heritage Status to both the art of perfumery and the city of Grasse, as part of the "Intangible Cultural Heritage of Humanity." This recognition affirms the image of modern perfume as distinctly French, an identity that was shaped by an evolving dialogue between literary invention, nonfiction writing about olfaction, and perfume marketing in the nineteenth century. Today multi-million-dollar advertising campaigns attest to a thriving international fragrance industry. An average of three perfumes per day were released in 2011. In 2012, Madonna's Truth or Dare eau de parfum went on the market only weeks before news of Pope Benedict XVI's exclusive, custom-designed cologne hit the press.[33] Although new fragrance launches dipped 42 per cent by the third quarter of 2020 due to obstacles related to COVID-19, production did not grind to a halt. The total number of fragrances released in France, Italy, the United Kingdom, and the United States in the third quarter slipped from 2,891 in 2019 to 1,669 in 2020, but by November 2020, the numbers were once again rising.[34]

A robust perfume industry, the far-from-subtle manipulation of consumers' scent preferences, and continued circulation of socially coded fragrance language, are inevitable descendants of the nineteenth century's pairing of perfume passion and scepticism. While aromatherapy for the mind and body, and home scenting with reed diffusers, cold-air misters, candles, and sprays are on the rise, so is recognition of those who are bothered by perfumes. As retailers and hotels pump fragrance out of doors and into lobbies to establish their brand's scented signature, a growing counter-current calls for fragrance-free zones, and for legislation protecting office workers from the toxic scent trails of their colleagues. Though physical reactions to fragrance, such as skin rash, headache, or lightheadedness, can now be identified as sensitivities or allergies, the mistaken belief persists that natural materials always provoke fewer such symptoms than synthetics. In 2017, the self-regulatory branch of the fragrance world, IFRA (International

Fragrance Association) banned scent molecules found in natural oak-moss, the beloved lifeblood note of chypre perfumes, because the material was found to cause skin rashes in 3 per cent of the EU population. Via online forums, perfume lovers continue to debate the wisdom of IFRA's increasingly rigid regulations, which have led to reformulations of countless perfumes.

During a year when IFRA "imposed a larger-than-usual number of bans, restrictions, and specifications" on perfume ingredients (Thrupkaew 2021), a very different story of smell made headlines. By May 2020, loss of taste and smell had been added to the World Health Organization's list of COVID-19 markers, and over one year later, some recovered COVID patients continued to experience smell distortions (Schoch 2021). Communications from link-sharing friends who knew I was working on this book accelerated during the pandemic months. The threat of anosmia had clearly prompted reconsideration of the too-often undervalued sense of smell. More than ever, it seemed, the popular press was devoting pages to the subject of olfaction and perfume. Or perhaps our heightened sensitivity to the topic made us more alert to such olfactory news and more appreciative of how much we rely on the sense of smell every day, for practical reasons, and for the pleasure of savouring a meal, discovering spring blooms, nuzzling our dogs and cats, or breathing in the scent of someone we love.

This raised awareness of the sense of smell is very much of the moment, yet it connects to an awakening that has been emerging in everyday life and academic studies for some time. As Karl Schlögel notes in *Scent of Empires: Chanel N°5 and Red Moscow*, though an "olfactory turn" already began in the 1980s with the publication Corbin's cultural history of olfaction *The Foul and Fragrant* and Süskind's novel *Perfume*, "the sense of smell is only gradually coming into its own in historiography" (23). The role of olfaction in literary studies, too, has gained momentum at a rather gentle pace, despite the important role smell plays in fiction and poetry across centuries. Just as one must listen to multiple voices in order to understand how the history of France's modern perfume culture was shaped and recorded, it has taken a convergence of interest from multiple fields, discourses, and modalities to develop the still emerging field of smell studies. The examples of Corbin and Süskind also remind us that academic and popular discourses did, and still do, inform one another. Media devoted to perfume today engages readers via online forums; in books about perfume, many cited across these chapters; and in more personal stories and memoirs such as Celia Lyttelton's *The Scent Trail* (2007), Bonnie Blodgett's *Remembering Smell* (2010), Alyssa Harad's *Coming to My*

Senses (2012), Denyse Beaulieu's *The Perfume Lover* (2013); and in novels like Timothy Schaffert's *The Perfume Thief* (2021). The expansion of the Osmothèque (International Perfume Conservatory) in France, and recent museum installations worldwide dedicated to scent as an art form, suggest that smell exploration will continue to test social and disciplinary boundaries as it changes the way we engage our senses and the way we read.

Notes

Introduction: Something in the Air

1 Antoine Combe, *Influence des parfums et des odeurs sur les névropathes et les hystériques* (Paris: Michalon, 1905), 13. Combe's credentials appear on the frontispiece: Aide-Major de 1ʳᵉ classe des troupes coloniales.

2 The word "sillage" is not used exclusively in relation to women today. Examples in published texts from the nineteenth century suggest that though the term was not by definition gendered, it cropped up initially as a way to characterize women's scent trails.

3 Elisabeth de Feydeau and Francis Kurkdjian created the formula based on the recipe found in the archives of Jean-Louis Fargeon, Marie Antoinette's perfumer. Emily Friedman discusses the logistics and desires that went into reviving Marie Antoinette's perfume in *Reading Smell in the Eighteenth Century* (Lewisburg: Bucknell University Press, 2016), 1–4. For more information on Fargeon, see Elisabeth de Feydeau, *A Scented Palace* (London: I.B. Tauris, 2006).

4 I am using the term "male gaze" as Laura Mulvey first defined it in relation to film, and as it has since been applied to other narrative media. See Laura Mulvey, "Visual Pleasure and Narrative Cinema," *Screen* 16, no. 3 (1975): 6–18, and later discussions of the power of the gaze, including bell hooks, "The Oppositional Gaze: Black Female Spectator," in *Black Looks: Race and Representation* (Boston: South End Press, 1992), 115–31, and Iris Brey, *Le regard féminin: une révolution à l'écran* (Paris: L'Olivier, 2020). By focusing on this male perspective, I am not suggesting that an alternative female gaze did not exist in the context of nineteenth-century perfume culture. On the contrary, the notion of the "female sniff" deserves equal focus and attention, but I am interested in first understanding the dominant discourse along with and against which it emerges.

5 I am using the term "smell culture" as Jim Drobnick conceptualizes it in his introduction to *A Smell Culture Reader* (Oxford: Berg, 2006), 1–2.

6 Key nineteenth-century works that define Corbin's "golden age of osphresiology" include Hippolyte Cloquet's *Traité des odeurs, du sens et des organes d'olfaction* (1821) and Dr. Ernest Monin's *Les odeurs du corps humain* (1885).

7 William Poucher, author of *Perfume, Cosmetics and Soaps* (released in nine editions from 1923 to 1997), is credited for introducing a three-tiered structure to map the volatility of perfume notes, using the terms "top notes," "middle notes," and "basic notes." Poucher organized fragrance notes classified by their rate of evaporation. His purpose was to provide a guide to help perfumers compose long-lasting blends knowing how the fragrant blends would develop over time. Poucher used the terms top notes, middle notes, and basic [*sic*] notes (Poucher, *Perfume, Cosmetics and Soaps*, vol. 2, 9th ed.), 53. See also Maurice Naurin, *La sagesse du créateur de parfum* (Paris: l'Œil neuf, 2006), 47. The pyramid is still frequently used in marketing today, though some perfumers subvert this traditional structure. Even perfumers who use the pyramid model to describe their creations acknowledge that this construct does not adequately depict the temporal development of perfume nor its dynamic spatial properties.

8 *Petrichor* derives from the Greek *petro* (earth) and *ichor* (a fluid that flows in the veins of the gods), or "tenuous essence," as Bear and Thomas define it in their study (993). See Isabel J. Bear and Richard G. Thomas, "The Nature of Argillaceous Odor," *Nature* 4923 (7 March 1964): 993–5.

9 *Ambre* (also called oriental) also designates one of seven classic perfume "families," the classification's name attributed to François Coty's 1905 Ambre Antique (Gobet and Le Gall, 98).

10 Perfumer Maurice Maurin defines an accord as at least three notes that together create a fourth more intense than the strongest of its individual components (40).

11 Guerlain's Jicky (1889) has been called the first abstract (as opposed to figurative) and the first modern perfume, for similar reasons: Jicky does not mimic a natural flower or bouquet (see Richard Stamelman, *Perfume*, 66–7, 98–9, and 184–5); see also Élisabeth Barillé, *Guerlain* (Paris: Assouline, 1999), 8–9.

12 Angus McLaren examines the pseudo-medical works (often deemed obscene) by the prolific author Dr. Fauconney, who also published under the anagram of this name, Dr. Caufeynon, and as Dr. Jaf (*Trials of Masculinity*, 137–57). See also Peter Cryle's discussion of the *fin de siècle*'s "remarkable extension of discourse beyond place of high specialization" by "doctors who did not hold positions at the Hôtel-Dieu or Salpêtrière" in "The Aesthetics of Spasm" (2008): 83–5. One such work is *La volupté et*

les parfums (*Sensual Pleasure and Perfumes*) by Jean Fauconney, published under one of his pseudonyms, Docteur Caufeynon (Paris: Offenstadt), 1905, discussed further in chapter 7.

13 On brand building in the nineteenth- and early twentieth-century French perfume industry, see Geoffrey Jones, *Beauty Imagined* (Oxford: Oxford University Press, 2010), 15–43.

14 Louis XV was said to have perfumed fabrics, furniture, fans, and himself, changing scents daily and even at different hours of the day. See Élisabeth de Feydeau, *Les parfums: histoire, anthologie, dictionnaire* (Paris: Laffont, 2011), 974.

15 Napoleon's use of eau de cologne has been described as immoderate, even obsessive. He is reported to have gone through a bottle each day during his Italy campaign: rubbing it into his skin, washing with it, and even sipping a bit, from long, thin bottles easily carried in a cavalier's boot (see Feydeau 2011, 1007).

16 See Jean-Alexandre Perras, "La Poudre et le petit maître en France et en Angleterre au XVIIIᵉ siècle: parfum de gloire, parfum de ruelle," in *Mediality of Smells/Médialté des odeurs*, edited by Jean-Alexandre Perras and Érika Wicky (Oxford: Peter Lang, 2022), 61–87.

17 Élisabeth de Feydeau discusses the history of men and perfume culture (practices, advice, attitudes, gender-focused and unisex marketing), from seductive uses mentioned in the Bible, to the nineteenth-century dandy who cultivated a perfume aesthetic (and his retrained bourgeois counterpart), to twentieth-century trends in sports perfumes and the recent popularization of oud fragrances by Yves Saint Laurent (featured in the 2002 M7) and niche houses like Kilian (*Les parfums: histoire, anthologie, dictionnaire*, 226–66; 1027).

18 The creation of perfumes deemed appropriate for men coincides with a growing suspicion of men who did not display "masculine" fashion. See Margaret Waller's "The Emperor's New Clothes: Display, Cover-Up and Exposure in Modern Masculinity," in *Entre Hommes: French and Francophone Masculinities in Culture and Theory*, ed. Todd Reeser and Lewis Seifert (Dover: University of Delaware Press, 2008), 115–42. On fragrance and homosexuality in the nineteenth century, see Sophie-Valentine Borloz, "Le parfum de l'inverti," *Littératures* 81 (2019): 131–42.

19 The text for Grandville's illustrations in *Les fleurs animées* was written by Taxile Delord, author of *La physiologie de la Parisienne* (1841); the book also includes an introduction by floriculturist Alphonse Karr.

20 The family of one of France's best-known dandies, Alfred Guillaume Gabriel Grimod, or Comte d'Orsay (1801–52), authorized the creation of the Parfums d'Orsay perfume line in 1908.

21 Over the decades, print advertisements for Le Dandy represent men,
    women, and by 1979, a woman wearing a white shirt, black jacket, and
    red bowtie, with the tagline "pourqoui pas?" ("why not?").
22 Though Balzac's *César Birotteau* is a perfumer, the novel focuses not so
    much on the sensorial nature of perfume as on the building of a cosmetics
    business, creation, branding and marketing of products, and on the
    economic risks of property speculation.
23 Translated as *The Ladies' Delight* or *The Ladies' Paradise*, the novel uses the
    name of the fictional department store as its title.
24 Zola based his fictional department store on the Bon Marché (1838)
    and the Grands Magasins du Louvre (1855). The character Grognet,
    who owns a small perfume shop, figures among the final victims of a
    neighborhood cleansing ("nettoyage," 428) attributed in the novel to the
    rapid expansion of large department stores that brutally destroyed small
    businesses.
25 See Janet Beizer's *Ventriloquized Bodies* (1994), Evelyne Ender's *Sexing
    the Mind: Nineteenth-Century Fictions of Hysteria* (1995), Michael Finn's
    Hysteria, Hypnotism, the Sprits, and Pornography (2009), Jann Matlock's
    Scenes of Seduction (1994), and Rachel Mesch's *The Hysteric's Revenge*
    (2006).

1. In a Violet Sillage

1 English perfumer George William Septimus Piesse (1820–82) was the
   co-owner of Piesse and Lubin perfumes, related to the French perfume
   house also called Lubin, originally called Au Bouquet des roses in
   1755 and Aux armes de France in 1861 (see Lheureux, *Une histoire des
   parfumeurs*, 23–5). Piesse's books on perfume for general audiences
   and specialists were reissued throughout the century in English and
   in French. Piesse's contemporary, Franco-English perfumer Eugène
   Rimmel (1820–87), wrote the highly successful *Book of Perfumes* (1865),
   also reissued in English and in French (*Le livre des parfums*). I refer to both
   authors throughout this book, usually citing them in French, though
   because of variations in the translated versions, I sometimes refer to the
   English editions. See Catherine Maxwell on Piesse's contributions to
   perfumery in *Scents and Sensibilites*, 22–7.
2 By 1935, the *Dictionnaire de l'académie française*, vol. 2, 589, expands the
   definition to include the figurative phrase *dans le sillage de* (influenced
   by, in the footsteps of) still much used today, but the relationship to
   perfumery is not yet mentioned.
3 Émile Zola, *Nana* [1880] in *Les Rougon-Macquart*, vol. 2, ed. Henri Mittérand
   (Paris: Gallimard, 1961), 1095–485. Translations my own.

4 Sybil de Lancey, "La Mode et les modes." *Les modes: revue mensuelle illustrée des arts décoratifs appliqués à la femme* 20 (9 August 1902): 16–22.

5 The double meaning of "wake" in English (a visually observable trail in the water, the air, a field, or a vigil for the dead) does not translate to French. Given that English was Vivien's first language, and that she was known for keeping a "constant cult of death" (Jay 1988, 19–20), it is reasonable to suspect Vivien was aware of the multiple *wakes* suggested in the title *Sillages*.

6 On Barney and Vivien's relationship, see Karla Jay, *The Amazon and the Page: Natalie Clifford Barney and Renée Vivien* (Bloomington: Indiana University Press, 1988), 38–54; and Marie-Ange Bartholomot Bessou, *L'imaginaire du féminin dans l'œuvre de Renée Vivien* (Clermond-Ferrand: Presses Universitaires Blaise Pascal, 2004), 41–9. On Barney's life, see also Melanie C. Hawthorne, *Women, Citizenship, and Sexuality: The Transnational Lives of Renée Vivien, Romaine Brooks, and Natalie Barney* (Liverpool: Liverpool University Press, 2021), 107–22.

7 The 9 March 1906 patent for Guerlain's Le Sillage appears in the supplement on soaps in Charles Thirion and Joseph Bonnet, *Revue générale de la propriété industrielle en France et à l'étranger: doctrine, législation, jurisprudence, chronique et bibliographie en matière de brevets d'invention* [etc.] (Paris: November 1906), 4–5.

8 Guerlain's Le Sillage was released for sale in 1907. The "Propos féminins" section of *Le figaro: journal non politique* (22 January 1931), 6, refers to "Sillage" as one of many enchanting Guerlain perfumes, including Jicky, Bouquet de faunes, Heure bleue, Djedi, and most recently, Ziu (perhaps a typographical error; Guerlain's popular Liu was released in 1929).

9 In the 28 January 1937 edition of *L'Atlantique: journal quotidien paraissant à bord des paquebots de la compagnie générale transatlantique: dernières nouvelles reçues par télégraphie sans fil*, a brief duo-language report, "Paris: City of Perfumes"/Paris: Cité des parfums," mentions fragrant sillage twice in the French, but circumlocutes to avoid the term in the English version (18).

10 For a history of the word *parfum* and its changing usage, see Magalie Gobet and Emmeline Le Gall, *Le parfum* (Paris: Champion, 2009).

11 Synthetic odour chemicals were used as early as 1837 (benzaldehyde, an almond odour), and drove trends in popular fragrances across the century. For example, coumarin (1868) is often described as the scent of new mown hay. Quinolines (1880) suggest smoke and leather. Ionone offers a violet note (1898). See Stamelman's detailed discussion of the use of synthetics in specific perfumes of the nineteenth century (96–9), as well as Annick Le Guérer's chapter "Vers la parfumerie industrielle'" in *Le parfum* (especially 181–90), and Luca Turin's *The Secret of Scent* (23–8).

12 Eugene Rimmel's *Le livre des parfums* offers examples of this approach to telling the history of perfume as a history of civilization. Although outdated (he has a chapter on "La toilette chez les sauvages," for example), his influential text is cited and paraphrased well into the twenty-first century. Elisabeth de Feydeau's 2011 *Les parfums* begins with an updated, more culturally sensitive articulation of this idea: "Raconter l'histoire du parfum, c'est dérouler toute l'histoire de l'humanité" ("To tell the story of perfume is to unfold the entire history of humanity," 3).

13 Especially in the last quarter of the nineteenth century, medical doctors and less specialized writers proposed typologies of women's odour based on race, hair colour, class, temperament, and character. See Augustin Galopin's *Le parfum de la femme et le sens olfactive dans l'amour* (Paris: Dentu), 1886; and Ernest Monin's *Essai sur les odeurs du corps humain dans l'état de santé et dans l'état de maladie* (Paris: Carré), 1885. Monin's subtitle, *Un nouveau chapitre de séméiologie*, attests to this interest in systematically reading olfactive signs. Jean-Alexandre Perras and Érika Wicky study the relationship between olfactive signs, the body, and nineteenth-century physiognomy in "La sémiologie des odeurs du XIXe siècle: du savoir médical à la norme sociale" in *Études françaises. La physiognomonie au XIXe siècle: transpositions esthétiques et médiatiques* 49, no. 3 (2013): 119–34.

14 Originally published in German, Süskind's novel was translated into more than forty languages. The novel was heavily influenced by Alain Corbin's *The Foul and the Fragrant: Odor and the French Social Imagination*. See Richard T. Gray, "Dialectic of 'Enscentment': Patrick Süskind's *Das Parfum* as Critical History of Enlightenment Culture," *PMLA* 108, no. 3 (May 1993): 489–505.

15 Enfleurage is a technique dating to ancient Egypt, in which fragrance is extracted from plants or flower petals pressed into animal fat or oil (olive, almond, etc.). The technique is still used today and on a large scale. For the history of this technique, see Nigel Groom, *The Perfume Handbook*, 2nd ed. (London: Blackie, 1997), 110–11.

16 On plague masks worn in Italy and France, see Augustin Cabanès, *La peste dans l'imagination populaire* (Paris: Société d'éditions scientifiques, 1901), 120–22.

17 See Corbin's third chapter, "Social Emanations" (35–56).

18 See Briot's analysis of these statistics on the expansion of the perfume industry in France in "From Industry to Luxury: French Perfume in the Nineteenth Century" (especially pages 275–8).

19 Focusing on the eighteenth century, Morag Martin provides a history of the guilds associated with perfume (these included wigmakers and mercers) in *Selling Beauty* (33–51). See also Reinarz's *Historical Perspectives on Smell* (53–84) and Stamelman's *Perfume* (57–9).

20 Originally from Montpellier, Fargeon was born into a family of perfumers. He opened an elegant boutique in Paris that served French nobility. He became Marie Antoinette's personal, exclusive perfumer for fourteen years. Fargeon survived the revolution and went on to open more branches of his perfume house. See Elisabeth de Feydeau's *A Scented Palace: The Secret History of Marie Antoinette's Perfumer* for the fascinating story of Fargeon's loyalty to the queen, to whom he continued to deliver fragrance products when she was in prison.

21 In the preface to his 1856 *Book of Perfumes*, Rimmel argues that books on perfumery fall into two categories: books of recipes "long disregarded by intelligent practitioners," and "others being what our neighbors call *réclames* ... terminating en *queue de poisson*, with the praise of some preparation made by the author" (vi). Claye's beauty manual indeed endorses Violet's products throughout.

22 In his discussion of the Grasse-based perfume firm Chiris, founded in 1768, Geoffrey Jones notes the importance of the company's acquisition of land in Algeria as early as 1836, then in other parts of Africa and Asia, including Madagascar, China, Vietnam, and the Philippines, in order to provide new raw materials (*Beauty Imagined*, 22).

23 See Rosine Lheureux's in-depth discussion of how the industry struggles with counterfeit perfumes in *Une histoire des parfumeurs* (Paris: Champ Vallon, 2016), 189–251.

24 Eugénie Briot shows how the identity of the luxury perfume market developed and defined itself in tandem with mass production and democratization in "From Industry to Luxury: French Perfume in the Nineteenth Century," *Business History Review* 85, no. 2 (Summer 2011): 273–94.

25 See Briot's discussion of how perfumers in nineteenth-century France promoted the use of synthetic fragrance in "Imiter les matières premières naturelles: les corps odorants de synthèse, voie du luxe et de la démocratisation pour la parfumerie du XIXe siècle," *Entreprises et histoire* 78 (2015): 60–73.

26 *Fougère* (from the French for *fern*) refers to a family of perfumes often described as green, featuring fresh, herbaceous notes on a base of oakmoss.

27 Coumarin, which smells of new mown hay, can be extracted from plants, but it is more often manufactured from coal tar today (see Groom 1997, 78). For further information on the history and chemical structure of early perfumes that use synthetic molecules, see Patricia de Nicolaï, "A Smelling Trip into the Past: The Influence of Synthetic Materials on the History of Perfumery," *Chemistry and Biodiversity* 5 (2008): 1137–46.

28 On Colette's fragrance beauty advice and work in the beauty industry, see Richard Stamelman, *Perfume*, 255–560; and Holly Grout, *The Force of Beauty*, 102–28.

29 The passenger is identified as a chemical engineer for Gabilla, a house that produced fragrances from 1910 to 1968. Founder Henriette Gabilla was a friend who helped Colette open her own cosmetics boutique in 1932 (see Feydeau, *Les parfums*, 907).

30 Cedrat, also called "citron" in English, still provides a citrus note in a wide range of perfumes.

31 See further discussion in chapters 2 and 4.

32 Perfume classification systems are discussed in chapter 3.

33 The idea that natural fragrance is less harmful than synthetics persists today, though this is not necessarily the case. For example, the International Fragrance Association (IFRA) heavily restricts the quantity of natural oakmoss (the signature note in modern chypre perfumes) because it causes contact skin rashes in some wearers, and ambrette seed (a plant-based source of musk scent) is banned since it was identified as a photoallergen.

34 In his 1857 edition of *The Art of Perfumery*, Septimus Piesse summarizes the use and popularity of patchouli: "The origin of the use of patchouly [*sic*] as a perfume in Europe is curious. A few years ago real Indian shawls bore an extravagant price, and purchasers could always distinguish them by their odor; in fact, they were perfumed with patchouly [*sic*]. The French manufacturers had for some time successfully imitated the Indian fabric, but could not impart the odor.

At length they discovered the secret, and began to import the plant to perfume articles of their make, and thus palm off homespun shawls as real Indian! From this origin the perfumers have brought it into use. Patchouly [*sic*] herb is extensively used for scenting drawers in which linen is kept; for this purpose it is best to powder the leaves and put them into muslin sack, covered with silk, after the manner of the old-fashioned lavender bag. In this state it is very efficacious in preventing the clothes from being attacked by moths" (50–1).

35 While the shawls go unmentioned in this episode (the scent of patchouli marking their presence, nonetheless), the inheriting, wearing, and exchanging of shawls are featured throughout the novel. Early on, we learn that even cousin Bette has been bitten by the current mania for shawls. See Susan Hiner's chapter on shawls and nineteenth-century "cashmere fever" in *Accessories to Modernity: Fashion and the Feminine in Nineteenth-Century France* (Philadelphia: University of Pennsylvania Press, 2010), 77–106.

36 The term "animalic" is used today both in reference to primary perfume materials derived from animals (the anal gland of the civet cat, the caudal

gland of the musk deer, the digestive secretion of the sperm whale) and to synthetic re-creations of these odours. The chemical compounds such as skatole, found naturally in feces, and flowers containing indoles (jasmine, for example) also lend an animalic quality to perfumes.

37 For an overview of shifting perfume preferences in France from the renaissance through the nineteenth century, see Robert Muchembled, *La civilisation des odeurs* (Paris: Les Belles Lettres, 2017), 161–234.

38 By the twentieth century, each decade tends to be associated with a dominant trend in perfumes that reflects the cultural zeitgeist through blockbuster fragrances. For example, the excess of the 1980s is distilled in opulent fragrances like Giorgio and Opium; the 1990s reacted – especially in the United States – with scents perceived as clean and fresh, such as cK One (see Turin and Sanchez, *Perfumes: The Guide*, 122). The 1990s also saw the beginning of a trend towards sweeter mixes that expanded in the early twenty-first century with fruity-floral perfumes and gourmands (blends with notes of chocolate, coffee, bubble gum, marshamllow, etc.).

39 Though not as trendy as in the nineteenth century, violet perfumes and blends remain successful today. The sweet scent is often described as candied, and it is quite different from the greener, fresher scent of violet leaf.

40 Beverly Seaton discusses the history of the phrase "language of flowers," which gained traction in the late eighteenth century and would have been commonly understood in Europe by 1809. Seaton notes that *language of flowers* is a Westernized version of the (misinterpreted) concept of the Turkish *sélam*. See chapter 4 in *The Language of Flowers A History* (61–79), where Seaton traces the origins of the language of flowers in France and discusses several nineteenth-century books on the topic.

41 M. Maryan and G. Béal, *Le fond et la forme: le savoir-vivre pour les jeunes filles* (Paris: Bloud & Barral, 1896), 108.

42 César Gardeton (1786–1831) was not a beauty expert. He wrote books, some of them humorous, on a variety of topics, including health and beauty, gastronomy, fasting, smoking and tobacco, marriage, and cuckoldry. His 1828 *Nouveau guide des dîneurs* reviews restaurants in Paris and beyond.

43 On the language of flowers, particularly violet, see *L'ancien et le nouveau langage des fleurs* (Paris: Le Bailly, 1858), 85; Cortambert, Madame Louis [Madame Charlotte de la Tour], *Le langage des fleurs* (Paris: Garnier frères, 1861), 150–2 ; Sirius de Massilie, *Le langage des fleurs* (Paris: Pontet-Brault, 1898), 101.

44 See Susan Hiner, "From *pudeur* to *plaisir*: Grandville's Flowers in the Kingdom of Fashion," *Dix-Neuf* 18, no. 1 (2014): 45–68.

45 In her 1829 *Manuel des dames*, Madame Celnart recommends violet (among other soft scents that are "peu pénétrants") for perfuming linens (53); she also recommends violet for handkerchiefs (56).

46 The marketing of new mown hay (or *foin coupé*) perfumes accelerated after 1868, when English chemist William Henry Perkin synthesized its key fragrance note, coumarin.

47 The play of vowels and consonants in *opulent opopanax* (sometimes spelled *opoponax*) suggest a fascination with not only the scent, but the word itself, which appeared in numerous works of the late nineteenth century. In his 1879 preface to Théodore Hannon's *Rimes de Joie*, Huysmans emphasized the sounds and musicality of Hannon's poem "Opopanax" and praised the poet for creating a poem that sings the libertine virtues of the perfume. For an analysis of how Monique Wittig reinvents the word in her 1964 *L'opoponax*, see Benoît Auclerc, "'On dit qu'on est l'opoponax": invention lexicale, innommé, nomination" in *Lire Monique Wittig aujourd'hui*, edited by Benoît Auclerc and Yannick Chevalier (Lyon: Presses Universitaires de Lyon, 2012), 257–79.

48 Huile antique (ancient oil) was used in hair and skin products, not as a stand-alone perfume. There is no standard formula for the scent, but Fleury specifies the choice of violet here.

49 René Fleury (René-Albert Fleury, 1877–1950) was a critic and poet whose publications include the poetry collection *Le cadavre et les roses* (Nevers: Cahiers nivernais, 1912).

50 An 1859 article offering a little course on the theory of elegance, defines the *je ne sais quoi* quality as innate and never showy; elegance is something one breathes in "comme on respire la violette; c'est un parfum" ("as one breathes in violet; it is a perfume"). See also Léo de Bernard, "Courrier de la mode," *Le monde illustré*, 17 December 1859, 394–5.

51 Eugénie Briot notes that between 1860 and 1910 every perfumer had a violent scent in their catalogue, and that Tiemann and Krüger synthesized ionone in 1893 in response to the fragrance's popularity in order to make it easier and less expensive to produce (Briot 2008, 3).

52 "Vogue of the Violet: From across the Seas Come Perfumes and Stories of Perfume." *The Washington Post* (26 June 1898), 25.

53 See M. Thévenot, "Modes, " *La mode illustrée* (14 June 1896), 191. See also discussions of violet being marketed as a fashionable prestige fragrance in Eugénie Briot, "Couleurs de peau, odeurs de peau: Le parfum de la femme et ses typologies au xixᵉ siècle," *Corps* 2, no. 3 (2007): 57–63; and in Beverly Lemire's *The Force of Fashion in Politics and Society* (London: Routledge, 2010), 97–113.

54 The 15 January 1893 edition of *La revue illustrée*'s "Courrier de la mode" recommends shopping for fragrance at Legrand, where one will find an array of violet-scented products (eau de cologne, soap, toothpaste) that "communiquent à toute personne ce délicat parfum le plus discret, le plus agréable que puisse souhaiter une femme distinguée" ("communicate

to every individual this delicate perfume, the most pleasant that a distinguished woman could wish for," n.p.).

55 Berthe de Présilly, "Carnet mondain," *La revue nouvelle* 67 (15 December 1890), 439–42.

56 Érika Wicky analyses how the traditional comparison of the *jeune fille* to a flower influences attitudes about the moral and biological significance of perfume (and vice versa) in her article "Ce que sentient les jeunes filles," *Romantisme* 165 (2014): 43–53.

57 See the anecdote in Colette's *Le pur et l'impur* describing Vivien, who appears to be drinking eau de toilette but may in fact be covering the scent of other substances on her breath (605).

58 See Gayle Levy, "'J'ai été très amusé(e)': Renée Vivien et l'(auto) mythologization à travers une lettre inédite," in *Renée Vivien à rebours: études pour un centenaire*, ed. Nicole G. Albert (Paris: Orizons, 2009), 129–40.

59 Maurice Martin du Gard describes a letter from Renée Vivien written on paper with a violet on the left of the page and signed in violet-coloured ink. See "Documents nouveaux sur Renée Vivien," *Nouvelles littéraires, artistiques et scientifiques* (2 January 1926), 1. See also Jeannette H. Foster's translation of aviator and journalist Louise Faure-Favier's "The Muse of the Violets" (reprinted in Margaret Porter and Catherine Kroger's *The Muse of the Violets* (Tallahassee: Naiad Press, 1982), 7–20. The text appeared in French in *Mercure de France* (1 December 1953), 633.

60 On the presence of Violet Shilitto in Renée Vivien's work, see Marie-Ange Bartholomot Bessou, *L'imaginaire du féminin dans l'œuvre de Renée Vivien* (Clermont-Ferrand: Presses Universitaires Blaise Pascal: 2004), 64–9.

61 See the summary of Marcelle Tinayre's *Une soirée chez Renée Vivien* and Gayle Levy's article "J'ai été bien amusé(e)," 133–40.

62 I am quoting from the excerpt of a 1953 article by Louise Faure-Favier first published in the *Mercure de France*, translated and reprinted in *The Muse of the Violets*, ed. Margaret Porter and Catharine Kroger (Tallahassee: Naiad Press, 1977), 7–20.

63 More recently, in her article on visiting Renée Vivien's grave, Melanie Hawthorne mentions an enduring little pot of plastic violets affixed to the grating on the left side of the tomb. See Melanie Hawthorne, "La Vie des Morts" in *Renée Vivien à rebours: études sur un centenaire*, ed. Nicole C. Albert (Paris: Orizons, 2009), 184.

64 See Nicole G. Albert, "Parfums de femmes: Variations sur les senteurs dans l'oeuvre poétique de Renée Vivien," in *Renée Vivien à rebours*, ed. Nicole G. Albert (Paris: Horizon, 2009), 174.

65 See Marie-Ange Bartholomot Bessou, *L'imaginaire du féminin dans l'œuvre de Renée Vivien: de mémoires en mémoire* (Clermont-Ferrand: Presses Universitaires Blaise Pascal), 2004.

66 Zola consulted a botany book and attended horticultural exhibitions
in order to experience the plants and flowers he evokes in *La faute de
l'abbé mouret* (see Mitterand's comments in the Pléiade edition, 1682–3).
Mitterand emphasizes that Zola attended horticulture shows in order to
see the plants and flowers, but the attention to aroma in the text suggests
that Zola's research focused on smelling the flowers as well. He also kept
an annotated, categorized list of plants (creeping, tall, flower-bed, etc.),
crossing them off one by one as he placed them in the novel (see p. 1696,
notes to pp. 1345 and 1346).

67 Jeanbernat's more humbly phrased sentence recalls Ronsard's verse on
the importance of gathering roses while they are fresh: "Puis qu'une telle
fleur ne dure/Que du matin jusques au soir!" ("For such a flower only
lasts/From morning to evening!")

68 Société de chimie médicale, "Alteration de la santé par les odeurs,"
Journal de chimie médicale, de pharmacie et de toxicologie 3, no. 2 (February
1867): 100–2.

69 See B.E., "Notices bibliographiques," *La revue de France* 14 (1875): 330–7.

70 See L.W. Tancock, "Some Early Critical Work of Émile Zola," *Modern
Language Review* 42, no. 1 (January 1947): 50–2.

71 Zola wrote a series of "Chroniques" for *l'événement illustré* between 23
April and 1 September 1868. F.W.J. Hemmings comments on the death-
by-flowers anecdote in "Zola's Apprenticeship to Journalism (1865–70),"
PMLA 71, no. 3 (June 1956): 350.

72 I am quoting from the reprint of Zola's "Chronique" on pp. 258–61 of
L'événement illustré. 23 Avril 1868 – 26 Août 1868, in *Œuvres complétes,
chroniques politiques (1863–1870)*, vol. 1, ed. Claude Sabatier, 251–337.

73 Sophie-Valentine Borloz discusses several examples of floral death
and murders in works of fiction in "'L'odorat a ses monstres': olfaction
et perversion dans l'imaginaire fin-de-siècle (1880–1905)" (PhD diss.,
University of Lausanne, 2020), 493–4, and note 282).

74 Here, Susannah Wilson discusses *volupté* and its feminine (or non-
masculine) connotations in relation to morphine abuse, a topic I will
discuss further in chapter 7.

75 Several artists were inspired to depict the scene of Albine's death. Léon-
François Comerre's *Albine morte* (*Albine Dead*), exhibited at the Salon
of 1882, recalls an identifiable episode in the narrative timeline where
Albine has already died. Her atheist Uncle Jeanbernat (contemporary
reviewers of the painting often misidentify him as Albine's father, who
died when she a child) holds an edition of Holbach (taken from the table
strewn with violets) that he has been reading all morning while watching
over Albine's body ("en veillant le corps d'Albine"). Nonetheless, some
viewers at the time who did not know Zola's novel reportedly found the

distinction between death and sleep in the painting to be unclear.
See "Visite au Salon 1882: Comerre, Léon" in *La coulisse* (22 May 1882):
n.p.; Goupil and Cie's illustrated *L'exposition des beaux arts: Salon de
1882* (Paris: Baschet, 1882) includes an engraved image of the painting
(50–1). See also "The Salon, Paris" in *The Anthenaeum* (10 June 1882),
737, in which the author (who also misidentifies Jeanbernat as Albine's
father) notes: "The idea of associating death with masses of flowers,
and of painting the corpse of a beautiful girl in a white bed surrounded
by splendidly colored blossoms, and thus setting off the warm and
cold whites of the room in which they appear, is thoroughly French."
Anaïs Beauvais's more voluptuous *La mort d'Albine dans le Paradou* was
displayed at the 1880 Salon; a reproduction appears in Gabriel Faure's
article on a pilgrimage to the estate outside of Aix that inspired Zola's
Paradou in "Le souvenir de Zola," *Chanteclair* 293 (March–April 1933):
245; and Albert-Émile Artigue's much reproduced *Albine* was published
in *L'estampe moderne, 1897–1898*.

76 See Charles Bernheimer, "The Decadent Subject," *Esprit Créateur* 32, no. 1
   (1992): 53–62.

77 Maupassant praised Zola for evoking odours that gave him the sensation
   of inhaling as he read (see the letter cited on page 1684 for the Pléiade
   edition). On the other hand, a reviewer for the *Revie de France* claimed
   the novel itself was as asphyxiating as Albine's flowers: "On étouffe dans
   cette atmosphère nauséabonde, ou les odeurs d'encens frelaté, de fleurs
   fanées, se mêlent aux émanations du fumier" ("One suffocates in this
   nauseating atmosphere, where the odours of contaminated incense, of
   wilted flowers, mingle with the emanations of manure"; B.E., "Notices
   Bibliographiques" *Revue de France* (1 January 1875), 335–6.

78 See Virginie A. Duzer's introductory essay ("Le Fruit défendu," 3–12) and
   the full special volume *Savoirs de jeunes filles, Romantisme* 165, 2014.

79 In *The Force of Fashion in Politics and Society*, Beverly Lemire analyses the
   impressive number of mentions of violet perfume in *Le petit messager
   des modes*, beginning in 1860 (see 106). See also Catherine Maxwell's
   discussion of violet fragrance and nineteenth-century English literature in
   Scents and Sensibilities (Oxford: Oxford University Press, 2017), 66–84.

80 Novelist and critic Jules François Felix Fleury-Husson (1821–89) is known
   by his pen name, Champfleury.

81 Champfleury's comments on Baudelaire's "excès de bizzarerie" and
   his taste for all things red, visually loud, sonorous, lacy, and capricious
   is cited in Eugène Crépet, *Charles Baudelaire biographique*, 3rd ed. (Paris:
   Vanier, 1908), 204, note 2.

82 The novel has fluctuated in popularity, even in Bernardin de Saint Peirre's
   lifetime. According to Jean-Michel Ricault, it gained and maintained the

status of a classic very quickly after publication, in part because abridged and redacted versions were widely used in teaching as early as 1837. See the introduction in Bernardin de St. Pierre, *Paulet Virginie* (Paris: LGF, 2019), 9. See also Bernard Bray, "*Paul et Virginie,* un texte variable à usages didactiques divers," *Revue d'histoire littéraire de la France* 5 (1989): 856–78. Today scholars are looking more closely at the novel's depiction of colonialism and slavery.

83 On women readers, see Danielle Bajomée, Juliette Dor, and Marie-Élisabeth Henneau, eds., *Femmes et livres* (Liege: l'Harmattan, 2007); and Belinda Jack, *The Woman Reader* (New Haven, CT: Yale University Press, 2012), especially chapter 9.

84 Gourmont's article is a response to an idea put forth by Léon Blum in *Du mariage.* Blum argues that there would be less adultery if both men and women postponed marriage until they had more experience of various kinds, particularly sexual.

85 This is how Edmond Goncourt describes the titular protagonist of his "monograph of a *jeune* fille" in the 1884 novel *Chérie,* whose doomed heroine is "plus une petite fille et pas encore une femme" (150).

86 All quotations are cited from Émile Zola, *La joie de vivre* [1884] (Paris: Gallimard, 1985). Translations my own.

87 In *La joie de vivre,* Lazare is linked to romantic tropes that no longer seem relevant in Zola's naturalist cosmos. His would-be ennui is more of a physical weakness and depression. Nature hardly reflects his emotion, and it does not provide inspiration for his short-lived goals to be a writer. Instead, he finds himself in a constant losing battle with the sea. His efforts to tame nature, by building jetties and breakwaters, and by extracting minerals from seaweed, fail tragically. Zola wrote of how he invested his own inner struggle in the depictions of a hopelessly pessimistic Lazare and an undauntedly optimistic Pauline (see Mittérand 1740).

88 Zola refers to individual characters' "odeur de femme" in this and other novels. On the wedding night of Louise and Lazare, Pauline, who is alone in her bedroom "respirait son odeur de femme, comme un bouquet épanoui dans l'attente de la fécondation" ("breathed in her [own] odour of woman, like a blooming bouquet waiting for fertilization," 294).

89 The novel is also rather isolated from the rest of the Rougon-Macquart series in that the action does not take place in the usual settings, and the family ties to other characters in the series are not explored.

90 See further discussion of novelistic accounts of menstruation in chapter 7.

91 In his chapter outline, Zola refers to Pauline's fate as the triumph of joy and abnegation. See Mittérand, 1762.

92 Charles Bernheimer discusses the obvious and more nuanced "Romantic notion of the prostitute's marginality" (35) in *Figures of Ill Repute*, chapter 2 (34–68).

93 In chapter 7, I discuss Maupassant's article on treatment of the *jeune fille* in Goncourt's *Chérie* and Zola's *La joie de vivre*.

94 See Sylvie Thorel-Cailleteau's discussion of the novel in *Joris-Karl Huysmans: Romans*, edited by Peirre Brunel and Sylvie Thorel-Cailleteau (Paris: Laffont, 2005), 1–10.

95 As Laure Katsaros specifies, "The second half of *La Fille Elisa* shows the horrendous effects of the penal 'code of silence,' imported from the Auburn Prison in New York State, which was then being imposed on inmates in some French prisons (most notably the Clermont-d'Oise women's penitentiary the Goncourt brothers visited in 1862). Under the Auburn system, the prisoners worked and ate together, but they were placed in individual cells and forbidden to speak to each other. The system was intended to make individuals reflect on their crimes and repent in isolation. More often than not, however, solitary confinement and continuous silence resulted in despair and insanity instead of the reflective state of repentance the system was trying to instill in its novices" (66).

96 The Goncourt brothers (who researched the novel together) read and took notes on Dr. Jules Brachet's *Traité de l'hystérie* (1847) in order to depict Élisa's manifestations of hysteria, and they attended Charcot's Tuesday lessons at the Pitié-Salpêtrière. For a detailed account of how the Goncourt brothers incorporated Brachet's work and other reported case studies of hysteria, see Robert Ricatte, *La genèse de* La fille Élisa. See also Laure Katsaros, "Goncourt's Dream: Night Terrors in *La fille Elisa*," *French Forum* 36, nos. 2–3 (2011): 62–78.

97 According to Ricatte, "[o]n sait que dans le roman l'hystérie d'Élisa est une consequence de sa vie de prostituée" ("[w]e know that in the novel Élisa's hysteria a consequence of her life as a prostitute"; 60). I would argue, though, that the novel presents Élisa as predisposed to hysteria through a combination of heredity and childhood experiences. Her nervous tendencies are nurtured and exacerbated first during her years as a prostitute, then by brutal prison conditions.

98 The spelling errors in the letter were intentional and may have been copied, all or in part, directly from real soldiers' letters to prostitutes, which the Goncourt brothers consulted (Ricatte 1960, 70–2).

99 Reported in Chandler Burr, *The Perfect Scent* (New York: Holt, 2007), 19.

100 See Harold McGee, *Nose Dive: A Field Guide to the World's Smells* (Penguin: New York, 2020), 465, for a discussion of how "dirty," animal, and "non-flowery" volatiles, including indole, skatole, and cresol, add dimension and appeal to fragrances such as jasmine and gardenia.

101 Coty's Chypre featured oakmoss, labdanum, patchouli, and bergamot, notes carried into variations of chypre perfumes today, though notably, the restricted use of natural oakmoss has altered the classic blend.

102 Tonka bean (also called Tonquin bean or tonka) is produced by two trees belonging to the Laburnum family and cultivated in Brazil, Guyana, Venezuela, Martinique, and West Africa (see Groom 1997, 329–30).

103 Like Piesse's 1857 formula, Pradal's 1895 recipe for Eau de Chypre does not mention oakmoss. Pradal blends (in order of quantity, high to low) eau de jasmine, bergamot, violet, and tuberose (1 liter each); esprit of ambrette (1/2 liter); Balm of Gilead, balm of storax, and essence of musk (30 grams) (147). In 1764, Antoine Hornot (publishing under the pseudonym Dejen) describes his "Autre manière de préparer la poudre de Chypre" (428–9) as starting with oakmoss gathered from the bases of trees in November, December, and January, then dried and pulverized. One of his recipes, Poudre de Chypre composée, does not call for oakmoss (427–8). His Eau de Chypre is distingued by ambergris and musk, blended with other materials according to the individual artist's taste (*Traité des odeurs*, 427–8 and chapter 14).

104 Nigel Groom discusses the history of oiselets de Chypre and Chypre perfumes in *The Perfume Handbook*, 65 and 289.

105 On these earlier Chypre recipes, see Elisabeth de Feydeau, *Les parfums*, 826–7.

106 See Sophie-Valentine Borloz's discussion of Nana's many odours and their relationship to contagion in "*Les femmes qui se parfument doivent être admirées de loin*" (23–46).

107 See Heidi Brevik-Zender, *Fashioning Spaces: Mode and Modernity in Late Nineteenth-Century Paris* (Toronto: University of Toronto Press, 2015), 123–42. Brevik-Zender analyses the metaphorical significance of spaces crowded with women's clothing, accessories, and other possessions in *Nana*.

108 Éléanore Reverzy discusses the integral role fragrance plays in the semiology of nineteenth-century French fictional characters, noting that Nana's use of violet perfume not only illustrates her acquired respectability but, via its heavy presence in her *hôtel particulier*, also masks the animal smell with which she had been associated. See "Parfums de (petites) femmes; pour une lecture olfactive," *Littérature: sociabilités du parfum* 185 (March 2017): 55–67.

109 Manet's 1877 painting was completed before the last instalments of Zola's *Nana* were published, but the two men knew one another and most likely discussed their work. As Charles Bernheimer notes, "Zola may have found inspiration in Manet's image, and the scene of Count Muffat's visit to Nana's dressing room may owe something to Manet's depiction" (231).

110 See further discussion of perfume injection in chapter 7.

111 Combe is of course referring to the smell of violets, but the colour, too, was implicated in discussions of excess in fin-de-siècle France; both the scent and the colour hover near other fin-de-siècle *manies*. Impressionist painters were praised but also panned by critics for their use of violet and other hues associated with women and fashion. See Laura Anne Kalba, *Color in the Age of Impressionsism: Commerce, Technology, and Art* (University Park: Pennsylvania State University Press, 2017), 85–6; see also Oscar Reutersvärd, "The 'Violettomania' of the Impressionists." *The Journal of Aesthetics and Art Criticism* 9, no. 2 (1950): 106–10. In 1891, it was widely reported in French and English scientific journals that M.P. Cazeneuve had created a dye for fabrics called *le violet de morphine* (violet morphine, sometimes morphine blue). See Louis Figuier, *L'année scientifique et industrielle* (Paris: Hachette, 1891), 437–8, and "Violet Color Matter Derived from Morphine" in *The Journal of the Chemical Society* 60, no. 2 (London: Gurney and Jackson, 1891), 1120–1.

112 Hammond, William A., "The Odor of the Human Body as Developed by Certain Affections of the Nervous System." In E.C. Seguin, ed. *Transactions of the American Neurological Association*, vol. 2 (New York: Putnam's and Sons, 1877), 17–23. Hammond also refers briefly to two other cases.

113 See Annick Le Guérer's section on the odour of sanctity in *Smell: The Essential and Mysterious Powers of Smell* (New York: Kodansha, 1992), 120–7.

114 Hammond's case study is cited in Ernest Monin's *Essai sur les odeurs du corps humain dans l'état de santé et dans l'état de maladie* (Paris: Carré, 1886), 17–18. Hammond's study is summarized on page 279 under "Miscellany" in *The London Medical Record* (15 June 1878): 278–80. Augustin Cabanès refers to Hammond's case in *Les Cinq Sens* (Paris: Le François, 1926), adding that the skin of a hypocondraic also emits a violet odour (246).

115 George Dumas expands on Hammond's thesis in "L'odeur de Sainteté" in *La Revue de Paris* (November–December, 1907): 531–52.

2. The Language of Flowers and Silent Things

1 All translations of Baudelaire's work are mine unless otherwise indicated. I try to maintain the French syntax as often as possible. The original reads: "Heureux …/ Celui dont les pensers, comme des alouettes, / Vers les cieux le matin prennent un libre essor, / – Qui plane sur la vie, et comprend sans effort/ Le langage des fleurs et des choses muettes!"

2 I refer to "A to Z" names rhetorically, but the number of French fiction writers known for their attention to odours indeed covers an alphabetical

spectrum. In his discussion of Apollinaire's poem "Cortège," Richard
Stamelman argues that after sight, smell is "the most powerful faculty
in [Apollinaire's] sensory arsenal" (191). Émile Zola's nose was deemed
famous (and infamous) during his lifetime due to the abundant smell
references in his novels. In 1889, Léopold Bernard studied odours in
Zola's work (*Les odeurs dans les romans de Zola*). It was widely reported
after a series of experiments conducted by Jacques Passy that Zola's sense
of smell was not quantitatively above average, but that his scent memory
was most precise (Toulouse 163–78).

3 Edward Sagarin (1913–86) co-edited *Cosmetics Science and Technology* with
M.S. Balsam in 1957. An American who worked in the cosmetics industry
and was associated with Givaudan Corporation and Standard Aromatics,
Sagarin is now better known for his pioneering book *The Homosexual in
America* (1951), written under the pen name Donald Webster Cory.

4 On the history of odour used as a medical diagnostic tool, see Wilson
and Baietto, "Advances in Electronic-Nose Technologies Developed for
Biomedical Applications," *Sensors* (19 January 2011): 1105–76.

5 See Declan Butler, "Joan of Arc's Relics Exposed as Forgery," *Nature* 446
(5 April 2007): 593; and Jean Etienne, "La Relique de Jeanne d'Arc était un
morceau de momie égyptienne," *Futura* (5 April 2007): n.p.

6 The term *nez* (*nose*) is used to signify a professional perfume creator.

7 Arthur C. Aufderheide discusses medicinal use of mummy powder in
The Scientific Study of Mummies (Cambridge: Cambridge University Press,
2003), 516–18.

8 The phrase "[o]dors are surprisingly difficult to name" appears in the
abstract of Jonas K. Olofsson, Robert S. Hurley, Nicholas E. Bauman,
et al., "A Designated Odor-Language Integration System in the Human
Brain," *The Journal of Neuroscience* (2014): 14864–73. These words echo
Plato who like Aristotle attributed the paucity of olfactory vocabulary in
part to the primarily emotional reaction humans have to odours: "[t]he
varieties of smells have been born nameless, since they don't come from
forms either definite in number or simple. But let them be spoken of here
in a twofold way – the 'pleasant' and the 'painful' – the only pair of terms
that applies to them with any clarity" (68).

9 For references to the silence of olfaction, see especially "Le Sens sans
parole" by anthropologist David Howes, and Joël Candau, *Mémoires et
expériences olfactives: anthropologie d'un savoir-faire sensoriel* (Paris: PUF,
2000).

10 See Joël Candau and A. Jeanjean, "Des odeurs à ne pas regarder…"
Terrain 47 (2006): 51–68.

11 See Olofsson (et al.). Their study and its bibliography attest to a surge of
research on the anatomy and physiology of smell–language connections.

12 See Chantal Jaquet, *Philosophie de l'odorat* (Paris: PUF, 2010), 1–13, as well as chapter 6, "Les modèles philosophiques olfactifs" (351–425), in which she analyses the complexity of olfactive paradigms in Lucretius, Condillac, and Nietzsche. See also "The Philosophical Nose" in Annick Le Guérer, *Scent: The Mysterious and Essential Powers of Smell* (2013), 141–203.

13 Freud, note 1 in chapter 4 (78–9).

14 See Ewelina Wnuk and Asifa Majid, "Revisiting the Limits of Language: The Odor lexicon of Maniq," *Cognition*, 131 (2014): 125–38. Jonathan Reinarz discusses differences in the language, appreciation, and perception of smell in the "Alternative Cultures of Smell" section of *Past Scents* (107–12).

15 Linguist Rémi Digonnet offers a detailed study of metaphorical language and odour in *Métapohore et olfaction: une approche cognitive* (Paris: Champion, 2016).

16 See Holly Dugan's *The Ephemeral History of Perfume*. On metaphor, see also George Lakoff and Mark Johnson, *Metaphors We Live By* (Chicago: University of Chicago Press, 1980); Susan Stewart, *Poetry and the Fate of the Senses* (Chicago: University of Chicago Press, 2002); and Paul Rodaway, *Sensuous Geographies: Body, Sense and Place* (London: Routledge, 1994), 71–4.

17 Sophie David argues that the linguistic limitations of smell language should be taken into consideration by those issuing instructions and evaluating verbal responses in psychology experiments. See "Linguistic Expressions for Odors in French" in Rouby et al., 82–99.

18 See Georges Kleiber and Marcel Vuillaume, "Pour une linguistique des odeurs: présentation," *Langages* 181 (2011): 3–15 ; and Joël Candau and Olivier Wathelet, "Les catégories des odeurs en sont-elles vraiment?" *Langages* 181 (2011): 37–52. The journal volume, edited by Armand Colin, is devoted to the language of olfaction.

19 See Constance Classen, *Worlds of Sense: Exploring the Senses in History and across Cultures* (London: Routledge, 1993), 50–76.

20 See Anne Theissen, "Sentir: les constructions prédicatives de l'olfaction," *Langages* 181 (2011): 109–25.

21 Wicky's use of the verb *sentir* (to smell, to feel, to sense, to understand) of course opens the title to further interpretations, but her article focuses on olfaction and fragrance.

22 For further discussion of headspace technology, see Groom, *The Perfume Handbook* (152) and Ellena, *Perfume: The Alchemy of Scent* (25–6). Ellena also describes the "more portable and practical" solid-phase microextraction (SPME) method of capturing fragrance, an extraction technique that requires no solvents.

23 According to Passy, an odour is strong if even the smallest dose can be perceived. Benzine, camphor, and lemon are strong. Iris and vanilla are weak. Intensity is a relative measure. When two odours are present at the same time, the more intense odour will mask the other (386–7).

24 For a history of the word *parfum* and its changing usage, see Gobet and Le Gall (2011). The entire book is dedicated to the word *parfum* and its derivatives, and to the naming of perfumes. See also Schnedecker's study of the semantics of the word *parfum* in "Quand la sémantique se met au parfum," *Langages* 181 (2011): 89–107.

25 These examples can be found in "Femmes damnées Delphine et Hippolyte" ("leurs parfums affreux"/"their atrocious perfumes"), "Le chat" ("un dangereux parfum"/"a dangerous perfume"), "La chevelure" ("parfum chargé de nonchaloir"/"perfume charged with nonchalance"), and "Les veuves" ("un parfum de hautaine vertu"/"a perfume of haughty virtue").

26 Translations consulted: Aggeler (1954), Dillon (1936), Leclerq (1958), Martin (1997), Scott (1909), Shanks (1931), Wagner (1974), Roy Campbell (1952), Francis Cornford (1976), Allen Tate (1924), and Richard Wilbur (1955), which appear in Clark and Sykes, *Baudelaire in English* (14–19).

27 These two meanings of *parfum* – a flavour or a smell – remind us that taste and olfaction are closely linked, and flavour relies on more than the taste buds. As Harold McGee explains, our fifty or so taste receptors offer "a handful of taste sensations…. Smell is more versatile than taste. It's more open-minded, broader, more specific, and more sensitive. And it's much more informative. Because things in the world are made up of many different kinds of molecules – far more than the dozens that taste can notice" (xx–i) (*Nose Dive: A Field Guide to the Word's Smells*, 2020).

28 See Richard Stamelman's discussion of John Singer Sargeant's *Smoke of Ambergris* in *Perfume* (38–9).

29 I discuss Mucha's perfume posters at greater length in chapter 7.

30 The *cassolette*, or *brûle-parfum* (incense burner), shows up in numerous nineteenth-century novels, both the object itself and its perfume marking exotic and orientalist themes, episodes, and imagination. See Elizabeth Emery's study of the *brûle-parfum* in Georges Clemenceau's 1901 play "*Le voile du bonheur*: le brûle-parfum, objet de sociabilité à la fin du XIX siècle," *Littérature* 185 (March 2017): 81–96.

31 Perfumes, scents, and aromas abound in Flaubert's *Salammbô*. The passage I have paraphrased reads: "dans les quatre coins s'élevaient quatre longues cassolettes remplies de nard, d'encens, de cinnamome et de myrrhe" (*Œuvres complètes* I: 746).

32 In French, *Les fleurs du mal* and *Petits poèmes en prose*. Baudelaire did not settle on a definitive title for his prose poem volume, which has been

published posthumously, often with the alternative title *Spleen de Paris*, translated as *Little Prose Poems* or *Paris Spleen*.

33 In *The Production of Space*, Henri Lefebvre posits that "if there is any sphere where, as a philosopher might say, an intimacy occurs between 'subject' and 'object,' it must surely be in the world of smells and the places where they reside" (197).

34 On movement in perfume, see Jean-Claude Ellena's *The Diary of a Nose* (14–15).

35 Pichois discusses the relationship between *Marginalia* and "Mon Cœur mis à nu" in OCI, 1490–1.

36 At the time of publication, Baudelaire's "Correspondance" was understood as a poetic representation of Emanuel Swedenborg's concept of correspondence. Kevin T. Dann discusses how, only later in the century and after the publication of Rimbaud's "Voyelles," Baudelaire's sonnet was read as a "founding document on sensory correspondences" (1998, 41).

37 American poet Rod McKuen published his bestselling collection *Listen to the Warm* in 1967.

38 As Evans points out, there is a syntactical and functional difference between the first six appearances of the word (introductions of comparisons that create connections and open up paths of interpretation) from the seventh, which "simply introduces a list of scents" (153).

39 Ambergris, benzoin, incense, and musk remain popular perfume notes today, though more often than not in synthetic form. Ambroxide is most often used to convey an ambergris note.

40 In chapter 91 of Melville's *Moby Dick*, sailors chop up a sperm whale to see if they might be lucky enough to find ambergris within: "now that I think of it, it may contain something worth a good deal more than oil … Dropping his spade, he thrust both hands in, and drew out handfuls of something that looked like ripe Windsor soap, or rich mottled old cheese; very unctuous and savory withal. You might easily dent it with your thumb; it is of a hue between yellow and ash colour. And this, good friends, is ambergris, worth a gold guinea an ounce to any druggist. Some six handfuls were obtained; but more was unavoidably lost in the sea, and still more, perhaps, might have been secured were it not for impatient Ahab's loud command to Stubb to desist, and come on board, else the ship would bid them good bye" [303]. Further discussion of the substance and its odour appears in chapter 92, "Ambergris" (303–5).

41 In 2011, a 40 kg mass of ambergris found on a South Wairarapa Beach in New Zealand was eventually sold to a bidder in France for an undisclosed price, estimated as between $10 and $40 per gram. See "Whale 'Rewards' Wairarapa Maori." See also Kemp, *Floating Gold* (xi–xiii).

42 The seven traditional perfume classifications or "families" recognized
    by the Osmothèque are citrus, floral, fougère, chypre, woody, amber/
    oriental, and leather, each with subgroups (*Classification officielle
    des parfums et terminologie*). Not all perfumers agree on this general
    classification. Michael Edwards, for example, divides perfumes into four
    main groups (fresh, floral, oriental, woody) (*Fragrance of the World*, 6). In
    each case, categories or subcategories are added regularly to account for
    new directions in perfumery.

43 Caressing the cat's head and back in "Le Chat" (XXXIV) makes the poet
    "see [his] woman," Jeanne Duval. The second titular cat (LI) belonged
    to Baudelaire's lover Marie Daubrun. Both poems seem to read as
    evocations of the women themselves, though some critics reject the
    double meaning.

44 Catherine Maxwell defines the *olfactif* as "a cultivated individual with a
    refined sense of smell" (4) in several sections of *Scents and Sensibility*.

45 The same phrase appears in Léopold Bernard's 1889 *Les pdeurs dans les
    romans de Zola* (8).

46 Steve Murphy discusses and cites the many critiques of Baudelaire's
    poetic smelliness in *Logiques du dernier Baudelaire: lectures du* Spleen de
    Paris (Paris: Champion, 2007), 77–8.

47 Grasset uses the word "névrose," a term designating various
    manifestations of neurosis deemed less severe than hysteria but
    sometimes applied to men whose symptoms would have been
    characterized as hysteria in women. The term was used by Pinel and
    Charcot, for whom it "had come to denote a psychological, or functional
    abnormality of the nervous system not attended by any discernable
    anatomical lesion" (Goldstein 1987, 334).

48 In this passage, Nadar has just reported Baudelaire's detailed description
    of Jeanne Duval's hair as smelling atrocious, abominable, and rancid
    (20). As Robin Mitchell argues, Nadar (like Baudelaire and other men
    in his social circle) vacillates between fascination with and denigration
    of Jeanne Duval. What little information is known of her life comes
    primarily from biographies and tributes to Baudelaire by those who
    knew him, and from Baudelaire's letters. Duval's grandmother is
    believed to have been born in Saint-Domingue and of African descent,
    her mother was described as a "negress" (Mitchell 2020, 44), and
    Baudelaire and his friends called Duval the Vénus noire (black Vénus).
    See Robin Mitchell, *Vénus noire: Black Women and Colonial Fantasies in
    Nineteenth-Century France* (Athens: University of Georgia Press, 2020),
    42–29 and 105–33.

49 Grasset uses Lombroso's term for decadent writers, *mattoïdes littéraires*,
    from the Italian *matto*, mad.

50 The line from which Lombroso embellished reads: "Il est des parfums frais comme des chairs d'enfants" ("There are perfumes/smells as fresh as children's flesh").

51 In *Esotérisme de Baudelaire*, Paul Arnold traces the nineteenth-century fascination with synesthesia in France.

52 For further discussion of the poem's reception in Baudelaire's time, see Bandy and Pichois, *Baudelaire devant ses contemporains* (145–7) and Pichois's *Œuvres complètes* I, 889.

53 Fragrant philocome pomades were marketed to men and women as treatments for various hair conditions. Dr. Adolphe Benestor Lunel's philocome pomade calls for a blend of cinchona, rose oil, bergamot oil, beef marrow, and balsam of Peru, rubbed into the scalp to fight hair loss (1860, 35). Women were encouraged to use the product to achieve soft, shiny hair. They were warned to buy high-quality philocome pomades with smooth, sweet, fresh, and healthy fragrances that, unlike "ordinary" perfumes, would not cause mgraines ("Mode et Fashions," *Journal des couturières et modistes*, 30 September 1848, 48). An 1866 do-it-yourself beauty manual offers a recipe of beef marrow, hazelnut oil, and almond oil (*Recueil des recettes pour faire soi-même* …,1866, 42).

54 Baudelaire's verse was indeed eventually marketed with high-end and niche perfumes, including État Libre d'Orange's 2007 "Charogne." Black Phoenix Alchemy Lab carries, among its many Baudelaire-inspired concoctions, Le Léthé, Le Serpent qui danse, and Sed non satiata. The online ad copy for *Byredo's Baudelaire eau de parfum* quotes the second stanza "Parfum exotique," a section that does not mention smell directly: "a lazy isle to which nature has given / singular trees, savory fruits, / men with bodies vigorous and slender, / and women in whose eyes shines a starling candor" (from https://byredo.com/catalog/product /view/id/24/s/baudelaire-eau-de-parfum-50-ml/category/6/). Serge Lutens's De profundis (2011) recalls Oscar Wilde's 1897 letter, and for readers of Baudelaire, the poem "De profundis clamavi" comes to mind.

55 The letter reads: "Il m'est pénible de passer pour le Prince des Charognes. Tu n'as sans doute pas lu une foule de choses de moi, qui ne sont que musc et que roses" (CI, 574).

56 Much of the discussion of "Une Chargone" in this chapter appeared in my article "The Scent Trail of 'Une Charogne,'" *French Forum* 38, nos. 1–2 (2013): 51–68.

57 "Rappelez-vous l'objet que nous vîmes, mon âme / Ce beau matin d'été si doux; / Au détour d'un sentier une charogne infâme / Sur un lit semé de cailloux" (Remember the thing we saw, my dear / That beautiful, so sweet summer morning / At a path's bend a vile carcass / On a bed of strewn pebbles [OCI, 31]).

58 Ainslee McLees argues that Baudelaire applies the aesthetics of caricature to poetic expression in "Une Chargone," with the last lines playing a key structural role, both visual and rhetorical: "Also allying 'Une charogne' with caricature is the graphic layout of the poem's two thematic parts. The first nine stanzas are descriptive, sketching the scene and suggesting its curious effect on the observer. The final three stanzas function as a caption which delivers the ironic punchline" (119).

59 See Corbin's preface to *L'Avènement des loisirs: 1850–1960* (9–18).

60 As the British sanitary reformer Chadwick said to Napoleon III: "Sir, it was said of Augustus that he found Rome brick and left it marble. May it be said of you that you found Paris stinking and left it sweet." Quoted in Barnes, chapter 3.

61 I discuss the notion of smellscapes in Baudelaire's prose poems in the 2012 article "Flâneur Smellscapes in *Le Spleen de Paris*."

62 See Emily-Jane Cohen's article "Mud into Gold," which studies several of Baudelaire's works in relation to discourse on public and private hygiene.

63 Chambers challenges the divide between poetry and cultural studies, arguing that Baudelaire plays a crucial role in the poetic form's "becoming-essay-like." He deals specifically with urban settings in his discussion of fetishization of the everyday (seeing the ordinary as *insolite*, and thus beautiful) in three "Tableaux parisiens." I believe his work, on the "manifestations of beauty that arise as a consequence of the everyday's ability to become strange and to impose the shock of knowing" (252), sheds light on "Une Charogne" as well, particularly if we see the discovery of the carcass as displacement of a relatively ordinary phenomenon.

64 There are, no doubt, still countless smell references that could easily go unnoticed. For example, in this line from "Femmes damnées": "Il en est, aux lueurs des résines croulantes" ("There are some who by the light of crumbling resin"). As we have seen, resin was burned especially for its scent, as translator Roy Campbell understood. His translation reads: "Some by the light of resin-scented torches…" (Campbell 1952). Still, most translators do not emphasize the reference to odour implicit in the word *résine*. For example, Walter Martin's translation reads: "There are some who, to the resin's shaking glimmer."

3. Confused Words?

1 Milk sickness in humans is caused by consumption of milk containing snakeroot, on which cattle have grazed.

2 Dr. Sharples did attempt to describe the odour of milk sickness on the breath: "The odor has been compared to that of ptyalism [excessive

production of saliva], also to the odor arising from fresh excrement of cow" (Sharples, "Milk Sickness," *The Medical World*, 28).

3 See the table on pages 1109 and 1110 of Wilson and Baietto's article "Advances in Electronic-Nose Technologies Developed for Biomedical Applications," showing aroma descriptors historically related to specific diseases and conditions.

4 See more current discussions of the cultural relativity of smell preferences in Pascal Lardellier's edited volume *À Fleur de peau* (especially David Le Breton's chapter on the smell of others, 115–28); in Jim Drobnick's *The Smell Culture Reader* (especially pages 13–81); and in David Howes's *Sensual Relations* (2003).

5 Later, in *Les odeurs du corps humain, dans l'état de santé et dans l'état maladie*, 2nd ed. (1886), Ernest Monin makes clear that in 1855 Bertrand de Saint-Germain was speaking "sans métaphore" ("without metaphor") when he wrote that in old age the skin exhales an odour of dry leaves (16).

6 The passage in the Moncrieff and Kilmartin translation of *In Search of Lost Time* reads: "all night long after a dinner at which I had partaken of them, they played (lyrical and coarse in their jesting like one of Shakespeare's fairies) at transforming my chamber pot into a vase of aromatic perfume" (vol. 1, *Swanns's Way*, 169).

7 As was often the case at the time, Monin's "clinical observations" included a great deal of anecdotal evidence.

8 The corpse flower is rare and short-lived enough to make the news when it blooms. See information about their blooms at https://www.huntington .org/corpse-flower and a report by Alixandra Caole Vila in *Nature World News*, http://www.natureworldnews.com/articles/22571/20160519 /rare-giant-corpse-flower-blooms-in-texas-what-makes-them-smell-like -rotting-cadavers.htm.

9 The classes of odours Zwaardemaker presented in 1895 combine Linnaeus's seven with Lorry's ethereal (perfume, beeswax) and Haller's empyreumatic (tobacco smoke, roasted coffee). See Stanley Finger, *Origins of Neuroscience: A History of Explorations into Brain Function* (Oxford: Oxford University Press, 1994), 78–9.

10 Augustin Galopin devoted an entire book to *Le parfum de la femme et le sens olfactif dans l'amour, étude psycho-physiologique* (1886). See also a lighter treatment of the topic in *La volupté et les parfums* (1903) by Jean Fauconney, who also wrote under the acronym Caufeynon and the pseudonym Jaf. Like many Offenstadt publications, *La Volupté* offers a titillating blend of medicine and erotica. See further discussion in chapter 7.

11 Eugénie Briot's discussion of this and other contemporary works devoted to the *odor di femina* appears in the article "Couleurs de peau, odeurs de peau: le parfum de la femme et ses typologies au XIXe siècle" (2007). Carol

Mavor questions the traditional gender lines drawn in nineteenth-century psychiatry that associate men with vision and women with the other senses, in her 1998 article "Odor di Femina: Though You May Not See Her, You Can Certainly Smell Her."

12 On various classification systems for perfume and smells, see Reinartz *Historical Perspectives on Smell* (7–18); Tony Curtis, "The Development of Odor Language between Professionals in the Aroma Trades Industry," in *Sense and Scent: The Exploration of Olfactory Meaning*, edited by Bronwen Martin and Felizitas Ringham (London: Philomel, 2003), 57–78.

13 References to Linnaeus in self-help books and perfume manuals of the era are inconsistent. In the *Nouveau manuel complet du parfumeur* (1845), Madame Celnart credits him for coming up with four categories: balsamic, aromatic, fragrant, and ambrosial (55). See discussions of Linnaeus's treatment of olfaction in Holly Dugan's *The Ephemeral History of Perfume* (182–3), and Paul Rodaway's *Sensuous Geographies* (64–5).

14 The literary term "synesthesia" (from *together* and *sensation*), used to describe the mixing of words from different sense modalities, also refers to the involuntary neurological condition in which stimulation of one sense leads to the experience of another.

15 Scent pyramids appear in print materials and web pages that advertise specific perfumes. Some perfumers nonetheless see this as an inaccurate way of conceptualizing the dimension of a perfume. See Jean-Claude Ellena on "the error of dividing up a perfume into head, heart, and base" (2011b, 49).

16 In the context of perfumery, *citron* (*cédrat* in French) refers to a fragrant citrus fruit classified as *citris medica*. It resembles the lemon but is much larger with a thicker rind. It is easily confused with *lemon*, called *citron* in French.

17 Catherine Maxwell traces the history of Piesse's virtual odophone, so named by his son Charles. See *Scents and Sensibility: Perfume in Victorian Culture* (Oxford: Oxford University Press, 2017), 23–5.

18 The classification of perfumes was part of a larger drive towards classification in the nineteenth century, in all fields, though the connection to sound and colour is especially intriguing. While perfumers used sound and colour analogies to sort their scents, chemists including Michel-Eugène Chevreul devised systems for categorizing colours. See Laura Anne Kalba, *Color in the Age of Impressionism*, 14–40.

19 Pisano and Wicky argue that the theory of odour waves functioning like sound waves motivated interest in creating the first olfactory concerts (see "Concerts olfactifs fin-de-siècle: parfums," 2022). Sergej Rickenbacher shows that nineteenth-century literature drove the creation

of technologies that made scent organs a reality in the twentieth century (see "L'invention de l'orge à senteurs," 2022).

20 In 1895, a breezy history of perfume printed in *Le petit Parisien: supplément littéraire illustré* invokes the metaphor of the musical scale, without going into detail, and without citing specific perfumers: "il y a des gammes de parfums comme la gamme en musique, et toutes les notes ne concordent pas entre elles" ("this is a scale of perfumes like the scale in music, and not all notes harmonize with one another"). See Jacques Lefranc, "Le Courrier de la semaine," *Le petit Parisien* (6 January 1895), 138.

21 See "Spice-Jars, Pot-Pourri and Rose-Jars," *The Art Interchange: A Household Journal* (17 July 1886), 19–22.

22 Joseph Grasset discusses the relationship between intellectual superiority and literary madness in *Leçons de clinique médicale faites à l'hôpital Saint-Éloi de Montpellier* (706–7).

23 See chapter 4 for further discussion of perfume and olfaction in the tenth chapter of *À rebours*.

24 Huysmans is reported to have consulted the catalogue from Maison Violet perfumes; the *Catalogue des produits de l'industrie française admis à l'exposition publique, rapport du jury central sur les produits de l'industrie française* (Paris: Fain et Thunot), 1834; and Gaston Vassy's *Reine des fleurs, légende hindoue: articles spéciaux et recommandés de la maison* (published by the perfumer L.T. Piver). See notes in the following critical editions of *À rebours*: Brunel, 671; Fumaroli, 420; Fortassier, 337.

25 French quotations are from J.-K Huysmans, *À rebours*, ed. Pierre Brunel in *Joris-Karl Huysmans: Romans I* (Paris: Laffont) 2005, 529–762. English translations are from *Against Nature*, translated by Margaret Mauldon (Oxford: Oxford University Press, 1998).

26 Piesse seems to be referring to Scottish agricultural chemist James Finlay Weir Johnston, whose *Chemistry of Common Life* vol. 1 was published in 1855, also the year of Johnston's death. Piesse is referring to the categories of "smells we dislike" and "odors we enjoy," using them to express his own opinion about the smell of styrax, a scent Johnston does not name. The 1877 French edition of Piesse's *Des odeurs des parfums, et des cosmétiques* also, regrettably, refers to Johnston as being "de regrettable mémoire" instead of "de regrettée mémoire." Piesse's 1965 *Art of Perfumery* also refers to Johnston in the very similar passage on styrax (also called storax).

27 See further discussion of the frangipane episode in chapter 4.

28 There is a variety of *syringa* known as "mock orange blossom" in English. The *Nouveau dictionnaire encyclopédique universel illustré* (1885–91) describes the orange-flower-like fragrance of *philadelphus coronarius* as stunningly odorous, a scent that will go to your head if you get too close (Trousset,

vol. 5, 263). *Syringa* is also called the *"jasmin des poètes"* (jasmine of poets) in France, not be confused with *syringa vulgaris*, or lilac, which looks and smells quite different. The *Larousse pour tous: nouveau dictionnaire encyclopédique*, vol. 2 (1907–10) offers a succinct description of *seringa/ seringat* along with an illustration (723).

29   Barthes explains that the phenomenon of tmesis occurs even in the reading of novels more obviously plot-driven than *À rebours*: "Yet the most classical narrative (a novel by Zola, Balzac, Dickens, or Tolstoy) bears within it a sort of diluted tmesis: we do not read everything with the same intensity of reading…; our very avidity for knowledge impels us to skim or to skip certain passages (anticipated as 'boring') in order to get more quickly to the warmer parts of the anecdote (which are always its articulations: whatever furthers the solution to the riddle, the revelation of fate): we boldly skip (no one is watching) descriptions, explanations, analyses, conversations" (1975, 10–11).

30   Janice Carlisle redirects the focus from lexicon towards the ways in which characters encounter and interpret odours, when she analyses smell in high-Victorian fiction (*Common Scents*, 2004).

4. The Osmazome of Literature

1   The feminine noun *une fleur* means flower. The masculine *un fleur*, not as commonly used, signifies odour. As we will see later in this chapter, Huysmans uses *un fleur* once, possibly twice, in chapter 10 of *À rebours*.

2   Maurice de Fleury (1860–1931) also wrote under the name Horace Bianchon. Among his many published works are books on insomnia, neurasthenics, and criminality.

3   Fleury cites perfumers Atkinson, Piesse, and Rimmel as specialists whose books on perfume are notable.

4   Fleury names Francis Poictevin and Goncourt as having contributed to the valorization of perfume, under the influence of Huysmans and Loti.

5   As Veysset notes, the term "cyclothymic" was coined in 1882 by German psychiatrist Karl Ludwig Kahlbaum (21). Cyclothymic disorder, with symptoms similar to bipolar disorder, is characterized by unpredictable mood swings.

6   Several early studies of *À rebours* focus specifically on how to inventory the novel's unwieldy grammar and vocabulary. See Marcel Cressot, *La phrase et le vocabulaire de J.-K. Huysmans* (Paris: Droz, 1938); E. Frey, "La langue chez J.-K. Huysmans," in *Mélanges de philologie offert à Ferdiand Brunot* (Paris: Société nouvelle de librairie et d'édition: 1904), 163–88 ; André Guyaux, "Huysmans et le lexique baudelairien," *Cahiers de AIEF*

60 (2008): 301–11; Hubert Phalèse, *Comptes À rebours: l'œuvre de Huysmans à travers les nouvelles technologies* (Paris: Nizet, 1991).

7 All quotations from *À rebours* are from the 2005 Laffont edition (edited by Pierre Brunel), with English translations from the 1998 Oxford World's Classics edition.

8 On stylistic similarities in Zola and Huysmans, see also Jean-Louis Vissière, "L'Art de la phrase dans *l'Assommoir*," *Les cahiers naturalistes* 11 (1958): 455–64.

9 Bernheimer traces this "mutual imbrication" by analysing the production of decadent moments in a selection of novels that blur the line between naturalism and decadence: Émile Zola's *La Faute de l'abbé Mouret*, J.-K. Huysmans's *En Rade*, Thomas Hardy's *Tess of the d'Urbervilles*, and Octave Mirbeau's *Le jardin des supplices*.

10 See Jens Lohfert Jørgensen, "The Bacteriological Modernism of Joris-Karl Huysmans's *Against Nature*." *Literature and Medicine* 31, no.1 (Spring 2013): 91–113; and Debra Segura, "The Dream of the Hermetic Utopia: *À rebours* as Allegory for the World after Germ Theory," *Discourse* 29, no. 1 (2007): 49–76.

11 A closer translation would read: "in an atmosphere of a washhouse." Public laundries were notoriously smelly, often associated with filth rather than cleanliness. Zola's *L'assommoir* repeatedly refers to the stench of fetid humanity wafting from dirty linen in the washhouse, an odour of soiled linens, harsh chemicals, and working women, hanging heavily in the damp air and rivalling the many other stenches of Paris: slaughtered animals, the wastewater from a dye shop, foul human breath, the smell of death. In the first chapter of the novel, many of these smells are introduced through protagonist Gervaise's perception of them; in the novel's final chapter, Gervaise's dead body is discovered because of its strong odour.

12 Amy B. Trubek discusses the history and importance of the Maison Chevet to French haute cuisine in *Haute Cuisine: How the French invented the Culinary Profession* (39).

13 See L. Montigny, "Le Passage des Panoramas en 1826, " in Simond, 556–9.

14 The report does not fail to mention the memorable odours of Chevet, noting that both father and son died in the kitchens they loved: "The soul of the great cook, like that of his father before him, had passed away from the things of earth on the savory fumes of his own kitchen" (175).

15 See the discussion of Briquet's work in Françoise M. Mai and Harold Merskey, "Briquet's Concept of Hysteria: An Historical Perspective," *The Canadian Journal of Psychiatry* 26, no. 1 (1981): 57–63.

16 The 1821 *Bazar parisien* includes an entry on the Chardin-Hadancourt Parfumerie located at No. 3 rue Saint André des Arts: "L'Ancienneté

de cette maison la recommande autant que la qualité des parfums"
(Malo 1821, 87). Chardin-Hadancourt and Massignon are credited
with contributing to the French edition of Piesse's *Chimie des parfums et
fabrication des essences* (v) and *Des odeurs, des parfums, et des cosmétiques*
(1877, vii).

17 See Pierre Brunel, "*À rebours*: du catalogue au roman," in *Huysmans: une
esthétique de la décadence*, edited by Guyaux and Kopp (Geneva: Slatkine,
1987), 13–21. Marcel Cressot's 1938 *La phrase et le vocabulaire de J.-K
Huysmans* (reprinted in 2014) is devoted entirely to the classification of
Huysmans's vocabulary, syntax, and punctuation.

18 New mown hay gained popularity in France and England around
1870. Though perfumers had their own formula for new mown hay, the
common denominator was coumarin, derived from Tonka bean. See
Charles H. Piesse, *The Art of Perfumery*, 5th ed. (1891), 298–9; and Mandy
Aftel, *Essence and Alchemy: A Natural History of Perfume* (Salt Lake City:
Gibbs Smith, 2001), 37.

19 In his 1877 *Des parfums, des odeurs, et des cosmétiques*, Piesse explains that,
although fragrance may be extracted from the heliotrope flower by
maceration or enfleurage, any heliotrope extract purchased in Paris or
London department stores is created by following a formula analogous
to his own, which contains vanilla, rose, orange blossom, ambergris,
and almond (124–5). In 1905, Piesse adds that when perfumers
compose a heliotrope factice, they often use artificial heliotropin
(*Histoires des parfums et hygiène de la toilette*, 140). In his *Chimie des
parfums* section on artificial fragrances, Piesse describes heliotropin
as a mixture of vanillin and piperanol (217). See also Charles Sell, *The
Chemistry of Fragrance from Perfumer to Customer*, for a detailed history
of synthetic perfumes.

20 Balsam of Peru (also called Balm of Peru, Indian Balsam, and Black
Balsam), originating in San Salvador and shipped from Peru, is
described as cinnamon-like (see Groom 1997, 27–8).

21 Debay offers more formulae in his *Les parfums de la toilette et les cosmétiques
les plus favorables...*" (140 and 161).

22 The manuscript, housed at the Bibliothèque nationale de France
Département des manuscrits, is available online as well. For its history,
see Guyaux and Jourde (1553–4) and Montmorillon-Boutron (7–41).

23 Pâte d'avelines (Pradal 1863, 86–7) was used traditionally for perfuming
gloves, but also in oils and pastes for the skin: "on sait avec quelle faveur
la pâte d'avelines rosée a été reçue du public en 1827, et combien les
savons roses plaisent généralement" ("we know with what favor rose-
scented pâte d'avelines was received in 1827, and how much roses please
in general"; Celnart 1854, 115).

24 In her *Nouveau manuel du parfumeur* (1845), Madame Celnart includes
the patented formula for Dissey and Piver's "Serkis du Sérail," "Poudre
favorite des sultanes, importée de l'Achaïe, pour blanchir la peau, et ôter
les taches de rousseur" ("Powder favored by sultanas, imported from
Alchaia, to lighten the skin and remove freckles"; 109–10). The powder
was sold in little octagonal boxes, to be mixed with a pink-coloured paste
(probably aveline). Celnart also advocates its use in *Manuel des dames*
where she attests to its skin-softening and whitening properties (56–7).
See Morag Marin's discussion of images used to advertise Serkis du Sérail
in "French Harems: Images of the Orient in Cosmetic Advertisements,
1750–1815," in *Proceedings of the Western Society of French History* 31 (2003):
125–37.

25 I use the French *frangipane*, rather than the English *frangipani*, throughout
this discussion for the sake of clarity, and because Piesse and other
perfumers maintain the French spelling in the English editions of their
books.

26 In both his 1857 *The Art of Perfumery* and his 1905 edition of *Histoire des
parfums et hygiene*, Septimus Piesse refers to *maréchale* and *bouquet de roi*
as outdated ("parfums qui ont eu aussi leur temps"/"perfumes that
have had their day"; 137; 213). He attributes the character of *maréchale*
fragrance to vetiver, and perhaps based on Piesse's writing, others do
as well (see Reutter de Rosemont, 288 and 438–42). However, *maréchale*
blends published in French manuals predating Piesse do not tend to
include vetiver, as contributor E.G. demonstrates in a two-page article
on the complicated history of the *marchale* formulae beginning in the
early seventeenth century. Focusing on both its "paternity" (documented
recipes by male perfumers) and its "maternity" (the woman – or
women – who wore the fragrance and for whom it was named), E.G.
asserts that there is no strict formula, that "artistes" have always added
their own touches, but that English perfumer Atkinson has gotten it all
wrong by using cassie, orange rind, and mint. Moreover, E.G. points out
anachronistic errors in Piesse's ("another English perfumer") historical
summary of the blend, and takes him to task for Piesse in stating that
vetiver was ever a part of the blend (*La parfumerie moderne*, April 1914,
25–6). It is worth noting that this article appears as a critical response to
maréchale recipes perfumer Floriane published in the January 1914 issue
of *La parfumerie moderne* (17–18), one of which, clearly described as a
modern version of the blend, indeed uses vetiver. Perfume manuals of
the nineteenth and twentieth centuries trace the creation of powder *à la
Maréchale* to 1611, named for the Maréchele d'Aumont, and note that as a
fragrance, parfum à la Maréchale remained a success for three centuries.
Piver's report on French perfume for the 1900 *Exposition Universelle*

singles out Frangipane and Poudre à la Maréchale as emblematic of
seventeenth-century French fragrances (19). In the article cited in this
chapter's epigraph, Maurice de Fleury reports that a modern woman
smelling of Maréchale in 1890 is a noticeable, monstrous anachronism
and a failure of taste (42). See further discussion of *maréchale*, as
mentioned in Rachilde's *Monsieur Vénus*, in the epilogue.

27 *Cassie* (not to be confused with *cassia* or with *bourgeons de cassis*, which
smell quite different) is the yellow bud of the *acacia farnesiana*, known
more commonly in France as *mimosa*. It was considered an especially fine
odour and often used in handkerchief perfumes.

28 Andrew Kettler aptly refers to a "confused timeline" in his discussion of
how *Plumeria alba/frangipani* got its name(s). See "Making the Synthetic
Epic: Septimus Piesse, the Manufacturing of Mercutio Frangipani, and
Olfactory Renaissance in Victorian England," *The Senses and Society* 1,
no. 1 (2015): 13–14.

29 Dominique Paquet discusses the figurative power of frangipane in this
episode, arguing that "[f]rangipané et névrosé," Des Esseintes is pursued
by the odour of the world and the odour of himself in this episode (225).

30 The Spanish verb *oler* does not have a French homonym.

31 Each word is used in chapter 10 as follows: souffle 1; baume(s) 5;
haleine 1; fumet 2; aromate 1; bouquet(s) 5; effluence 1; émanation(s)
3; exhalaison (exhalée, exhalait) 3; fleur(s) 16 (once – though I argue
this was meant to be twice – as a masculine noun); flair 3 (once in
verb form); fragrance 2; fumée (not used); odoration (not used); oler
(not used); répandre une odeur (not used); odeur(s)12; olfactoire (not
used); odorant/e/s 5; montant 1 ("un vague montant d'essence de
bergamote"); vapeur 3; émaner (not used).

32 Hubert de Phalèse counts one hundred occurrences of just seventeen
selected, generic smell words in *À rebours* (*nez, odeur, odeurs, odorante,
odorantes, odorants, odorat, parfum, parfumé, parfumerie, parfumeries,
parfumeurs, parfums, senteur, senteurs, sentir, sentit*), forty-seven of the
one hundred appearing in chapter 10 (*Comptes* À rebours: *l'œuvre de
Huysmans à travers les nouvelles technologies*, Paris: Nizet [1991], 58–61). As
Huysmans's own list shows, there are many other lexical fields associated
with smell in the novel. In addition, as we have seen, the novel is rich in
references to specific fragrant materials (frangipane, musk, etc.) that are
not counted in Phalèse's study.

33 My reading of this correction in the manuscript is confirmed in
Montmorillon-Boutron's critical edition, *À rebours* (Paris: Garnier, 2011),
241 and 431 (note 1). The 1884 Charpentier edition of *À rebours*, on
which subsequent translations and critical editions are based (up to and
including the 2019 Pléiade edition) does not incorporate this correction.

34 Baudelaire makes frequent appearances in *À rebours*. Des Esseintes has
   framed copies of "l'Ennemi," "La Mort des amants," and "Any where
   [*sic*] out of the world – N'Importe où hors du monde" (chapter 1). In
   chapter 5, we learn that Des Esseintes compares Gustave Moreau's work
   (which he finds to have no real predecessor in the visual arts) to the
   works of Baudelaire: "Il y avait dans ses œuvres désespérées et érudites
   un enchantement singulier, une incarnation vous remuant jusqu'au fond
   des entrailles comme celles de certains poèmes de Baudelaire" ("There
   was a singular enchantment in his erudite, despairing paintings, a magic
   which stirred you to the depths of your soul [entrails], like that of certain
   poems of Baudelaire's"; 630, 49). In chapter 12, where Des Esseintes
   browses his home library, Flaubert, Edmond de Goncourt, Zola, and
   Baudelaire are named.

5. Perfumed Letters and Signature Scents

1 The original French in Staffe's popular etiquette book reads: "Une jeune
   femme fut gravement indisposée pour avoir reçu une lettre fortement
   imprégnée d'un parfum violent" (334). A number of beauty manuals
   appeared at the turn of the century penned by self-titled aristocrats,
   among them the Comtesse de Norville, the Comtesse de Tramar, the
   Comtesse de Gencé, the Vicomtesse Nacla, and the Baronne Staffe. Holly
   Grout notes that "these Beauty Countesses had little real connection to
   the aristocracy. Among the aforementioned authors, only the Comtesse
   de Tramar … was a certifiable French noble woman" and the "humble
   origins of the Baronne Staffe (Blanche Soyer) are well documented" (63).
2 In the 1901 essay "Fashion," Georg Simmel identified the tension between
   self-expression and conformity as a basic dialectic of fashion.
3 Eugénie Briot discusses the rise of the French perfume industry in
   nineteenth-century France in "From Industry to Luxury: French
   perfume in the nineteenth century" (2011), and in her book *La fabrique
   des parfums: naissance d'une industrie de luxe* (2015). See also the first
   chapter of Geoffrey Jones's *Beauty Imagined* (15–43), and Rosine
   Lheureux's *Une histoire des parfumeurs: France 1850–1910* (Céyzérieu:
   Champ Vallon, 2016).
4 Though Roland Barthes has shown that the language of fashion always
   implicitly signifies more than just stated functionality ("Le bleu est à
   la mode cette année,"), I am referring to a blurry distinction between
   hygiene and fashion that was addressed explicitly by experts in perfume
   and etiquette during the nineteenth century.
5 On the construction of feminine identity through accessories, see
   Susan Hiner's 2010 *Accessories to Modernity: Fashion and the Feminine in*

Nineteenth-Century France, and Holly Grout's 2015 *The Force of Beauty: Transforming French Ideas of Femininity in the Third Republic.*

6 On letters in Balzac's novels, see Patrick Berthier, "Balzac romancier épistolaire"; and Rose Fortassier, "Balzac et le roman par lettres." Patricia Reynaud-Pactat studies the composition of Rodolphe Boulanger's break-up letter to Emma Bovary in "La lettre de rupture de Rodolphe à Emma Bovary: l'énonciation parle l'économie," *Nineteenth-Century French Studies* 19, no. 1 (1990): 83–94.

7 The term *distinction* also appears in etiquette manuals, including the Baronne Staffe's *Cabinet de toilette*. Roland Barthes points out the specificity of the word *distinction* in his 1962 *Dandysme*. Pierre Bourdieu further theorizes about the relationship between distinction and social power in his *La distinction: critique social du jugement* (Paris: Minuit, 1979).

8 See, for example, Algirdas Griemas's *La Mode en 1830* and Balzac's 1842 *Autre étude de femme.*

9 See Geneviève Fontan's illustrated article "Les étiquettes de parfumerie" in *Parfum art et valeur* 18 (November–December 1993): 8–12.

10 Geneviève Fontan presents an illustrated catalogue of French perfume cards in *Cote générale des cartes parfumées* (1997). The second chapter of Richard Stamelman's *Perfume* includes photographs of perfumed objects used for advertising in the nineteenth through the early twentieth century, among them, cards, labels, calendar pages, fans, and posters (52–99). Perfumer Septimus Piesse provides instructions for perfuming bookmarks in his 1865 *Des odeurs, des parfums, et des cosmétiques* (289).

11 See discussions of Rimmel in Stamelman's *Perfume* (86–7), de Feydeau's *Les parfums* (1064–5), Reinarz's *Past Scents* (53–4), and Maxwell's *Scents and Sensibilities* (21–3).

12 In his 1889 psycho-physiological study of the smell of women, Augustin Galopin points out that certain odours (tobacco, musk, assa foetida) are preserved so well in paper and linens that for months they awaken the sensitivity of the *muqueuse olfactive* (olfactive mucus membrane) (2).

13 Celnart also devoted a section of her 1829 *Manuel du fleuriste artificiel* to creating paper flowers (32–4).

14 In her 1837 *Nouveau manuel complet d'économie domestique*, Celnart recommends scenting sealing wax with an odour that harmonizes with its colour (179).

15 The original French reads: "Tu exhales, pour moi, le parfum le plus enivrant qu'une femme puisse avoir." See Balzac's January 1834 letter to Madame Hanska in *Lettres à l'étrangère*, 110–11.

16 The letter to Madame Hanska is dated 9 September 1833 (*Lettres à l'étrangère* 40–1).

17 See Flaubert's letter of 20 September 1846, written at 10:00 p.m. (*Correspondence* I, 353–4).

18 Peau d'Espagne was cut into pieces about four inches square and highly perfumed. Madame Celnart offers instructions for making Peau d'Espagne in her 1845 *Nouveau manuel complet du parfumeur*, where she suggests that the scent is out of fashion: "Cette peau, autrefois fort en usage, très-forte en odeur, se portait comme sachet, et se place dans les armoires, corbeilles, etc., pour parfumer le linge, les hardes, et autres objets" ("This skin, formerly in high demand, very strong in odour, was used as a sachet, and is placed in wardrobes, baskets, etc., to scent linens, old clothing, and other items," Clenart 1854, 211). Her words are repeated in Pradal's 1863 *Nouveau manuel complet*, vol. 1, 281.

19 Extracted from the glands of civet cats, *civette* has been almost completely replaced by synthetics today. Rimmel described techniques for obtaining and using civet in his *Livre des parfums*, where he calls the raw odour hardly appealing, but in homeopathic doses, almost floral (251–2). When Piesse includes civet in his recipes for liquid perfume, he notes that its purpose is to add longevity to the blend (207).

20 Mandy Aftel discusses the history of Peau d'Espagne in *Essence and Alchemy: A Natural History of Perfume* (35–6). Piesse names neroli, rose, sandalwood, lavender, verbena, bergamot, cloves, cinnamon, benzoin, civet, and musk in his Peau d'Espagne blend. In the last decade of the nineteenth century, Baronne Staffe (quoting an unnamed *grande dame*) suggests that Peau d'Espagne is no longer the height of fashion: "Quelques personnes, amoureuses du siècle dernier, choisissent *la peau d'Espagne*" ("Some people, lovers of the last century, choose *Peau d'Espagne*"; *Cabinet de toilette* 1891, 299).

21 Maryn and Béal similarly advise in their *Form et fond: savoir vivre pour les jeunes filles* (1896), that while it is not in bad taste to use scented sachets for writing paper, only light and discreet (and discrete) fragrances like iris and violet should be used; musk and patchouli, above all, are to be avoided (252).

22 These words appear again in Feydeau's 1873 book, *L'art de plaire: études d'hygiène, de goût et de toilette*. Feydeau's "theory of perfumes," written with humour and exaggeration, reflects (and lampoons) less playful writers who suggest that perfumes be light and floral, and that specific fragrances be selected according to hair colour and complexion.

23 See Comtesse de Gencé, *Le code mondain de la jeune fille* (Paris: Bibliothèque des ouvrages pratiques, 1909), 80.

24 The question of blends (bouquets) versus single-note (soliflore) perfumes comes up often in nineteenth-century discussions of taste, fashion, and hygiene. Writers focused on health and medicine direct women towards

simple fragrances, while perfumers understandably show greater appreciation for blends. Ernest Feydeau, the novelist who, though not a perfumer, showed a great (and often ironic) interest in fashion, proposed an ingenious approach to the bouquet perfume. A woman should not smell like a flower, says Feydeau. Instead, she should unite masses of odours by perfuming each part of her "person" with a different scent (154–5).

25 This tension is central to Georg Simmel's theory of fashion. As Roland Barthes later writes in his essay on "Le Dandysme et la mode," "La Mode est en effet imitation collective d'une nouveauté régulière; même lorsqu'elle prend pour alibi l'expression d'une individualité, d'une 'personnalité', c'est essentiellement un phénomène massif … une dialectique toute pure entre l'individu et la collectivité" ("Fashion is in fact collective imitation of a constant novelty; even when it uses the expression of individuality, of 'personality' as an alibi, it is essentially a mass phenomenon … a pure dialectic between the individual and the collective" (*Le bleu est à la mode cette année et autres articles*, 101).

26 Gustave Flaubert, [1869], in *Œuvres*, vol. 2, Paris: Gallimard, 1952 (11–457). All citations are from this edition. Translations my own.

27 See further discussion of the scent of iris in chapter 6.

28 Balzac, *Béatrix* [1836], in *La comédie humaine*, vol. 2 (Paris: Gallimard, 1976). All citations are from this edition. Translations my own.

29 *Béatrix* was a success at the time of publication largely because contemporary readers enjoyed its *roman à clef* depiction of Franz Liszt and Marie d'Agoult's love affair. It soon fell into relative obscurity, despite its wry humour and playful characterization of George Sand's avatar Camille Maupin (Félicité des Touches).

30 "Oui, Mlle Des Touches est George Sand," wrote Balzac in a letter to Madame Hanska. See *Lettres à Mme Hanska*, vol. 1 (665).

31 The request appears in a long letter written on 12 May 1834. The patchouli should be purchased at Leblanc, rue Sainte-Anne. Musset should be careful not to be overcharged (Decori 1904, 69).

32 Septimus Piesse discusses the use of patchouli for fabrics, shawls, and perfumes on pages 153–4 of *Des odeurs, des parfums, et des cosmétiques* (1865). See discussion in chapter 1.

33 See the discussion of fictional prostitutes Marthe, Élisa, and Nana in chapter 1.

34 It would be difficult to pinpoint the smell of the fatal letter, since it is misidentified as belonging to stationery used by members of the elite Jockey Club (frequented by several characters in Balzac's *Comédie humaine*). Several perfumes called Jockey-club (or Jockey Club) were bottled and sold in the nineteenth and early twentieth centuries. Piesse

deems the mixed (*bouquet*) perfume Jockey-club very much in style in 1865, formulated in a base of wine alcohol and iris root (118). Piesse offers a different formula for French and English Bouquet de Jockey Club based on the fact that the alcohol bases used in France and England (grape alcohol and corn alcohol respectively), alter the quality of other ingredients (269). Piesse's blend of rose, tuberose, cassie, and civet would have been one of many formulae circulating under the name Jockey-club.

35 "Flaubert had a special device which may be called the *counterpoint method*, or the method of parallel interlinings and interruptions of two or more conversations or trains of thought" (143). An often-cited example is the conversation between Rodolphe and Emma at the Agricultural Fair, cross-cut with speeches from members of the community.

36 All quotations from *Madame Bovary* are from the Pléiade edition of Gustave Flaubert's *Œuvres completes*, vol. 1 (Paris: Gallimard, 1951); translations my own.

37 Examples of such metaphors include: "La conversation de Charles était plate comme un trottoir de rue, et les idées de tout le monde y défilaient dans leur costume ordinaire" ("Charles's conversation was as flat as a sidewalk, and everyone's ideas trooped through it in their everyday garb," 362); "sa vie était froide comme un grenier dont la lucarne est au nord, et l'ennui, araignée silencieuse, filait sa toile dans l'ombre à tous les coins de son cœur" ("her life was cold as an attic with a window facing north, and boredom, a silent spider, was weaving its web in the shadows in every corner of her heart," 366); and pleasures have so trampled Rodolphe's heart, like schoolboys on a courtyard, that "rien de vert n'y poussait, et ce qui passait par là, plus étourdi que les enfants, n'y laissait pas même, comme eux, son nom gravé sur la muraille" ("nothing green grew there, and those who passed through it, more thoughtless than children, did not even leave, like them, their names carved on the wall," 510).

38 See further discussion of Emma Bovary's perfuming habits in chapter 6.

39 Apricot kernels, found inside the pit, are now widely known to contain cyanide, a detail that renders the scene even more ominous for today's reader, since Emma will eventually ingest poison (arsenic).

40 Larry Duffy analyses the sources of much of Homais's monologues on chemistry, pharmacy, and medicine in "*Madame Bovary* and the Institutional Transformation of Pharmacy" (2011).

41 See Robert J. Niess's analysis of Homais's discourse style in "On Listening to Homais" (1977).

42 Hartshorn was a material used for smelling salts, derived from oil of hartshorn (deer horn and bones), noted for its strong ammonia or urine-like odour.

43 Dr. Jean-Baptiste Mège cites not only cases of syncope, but also of death by odour in his *Alliance d'Hygie et de la Beauté, ou l'art d'embellir* (1818), 119–20. In this title, *Hygie* refers to the Greek goddess of health.

44 André Levret, *Essai sur l'abus des règles générales et contre les préjugées qui s'opposent aux progrès de l'art des accouchements* (Paris: Prault, 1766).

45 Levret mentions that women are becoming increasingly nervous and irritable. He argues that this is a problem specific to *Dames* (Ladies) and those who imitate them, that is, women who overuse perfume; this is not a problem for country women (73).

46 See Beizer, *Ventriloquized Bodies* (132–68).

47 In "The Aesthetics of the Spasm" (2008), Peter Cryle analyses in depth a nineteenth-century fascination with spasm related to epilepsy and hysteria, as presented in fiction, medical writing, and works of medical vulgarization. Juliette Azoulai studies intersections of nineteenth-century medical writing on hysteria and Homais's discourse in "Le Savoir medical dans la scène des abricots" (2009).

6. Smelling (of) Iris

1 Flaubert submitted the novel in instalments to the *Revue de Paris*, where editors urged him to suppress and modify certain passages. Flaubert subsequently had the *Revue* print a disclaimer. As Christine Haynes suggests, "maybe because of the conflict between Flaubert and his editor, the publication of *Madame Bovary* attracted the attention of the authorities, and the author, the editor, and the printer, were brought to trial" (3). See discussions of the trial in Christine Haynes, "The Politics of Publishing during the Second Empire: The Trial of *Madame Bovary* Revisited," *French Politics, Culture, and Society* 23, no. 2 (2005): 1–27; William Olmsted, *The Censorship Effect* (Oxford: Oxford University Press, 2016); Elisabeth Ladenson, *Dirt for Art's Sake* (Ithaca, NY: Cornell University Press, 2007); and Dominick LaCapra, *Madame Bovary on Trial* (Ithaca, NY: Cornell University Press, 1982).

2 See Ladenson's discussion of how realism was invoked, both in the prosecution and defence of the novel in *Dirt for Art's Sake*, 17–46.

3 Pinard lost the case against Flaubert but prevailed in the trial against Baudelaire.

4 Flaubert is known for his use of indirect free discourse, or *style indirect libre*, though he was far from the first novelist to use the technique. See Vahid Ramazani's analysis of free indirect mode (his preferred term) in *The Free Indirect Mode: Flaubert and the Poetics of Irony* (Charlottesville: University Press of Virginia, 1988).

5 Neither Baudelaire nor Flaubert defined themselves as realists, but the
   term was in the air and quickly applied to painting and fiction that was
   seen as scandalous.

6 On the approach to Yonville, the narrator notes that the area produces
   the worst Neufchatel cheeses and that farming is costly because so
   much manure is needed for the poor soil (389). At the agricultural
   fair, discussions of manure's virtues (by Homais, and by the prefect
   representative, Monsieur Lieuvain) are the crude audio backdrop to
   Rodolphe and Emma's flirtation. Twice their conversation is undercut
   by the word, first exclaimed as if to call out Rodolphe's insincerity, then
   "Flemish fertilizer" is heard just after a gust of wind ruffles a tablecloth,
   an indirect, comical linking of the word to the odour. Walking arm-in-arm
   with Léon to see Emma's baby and wet nurse, Emma and Léon traverse
   a landscape revealing pigs on a manure heap. At the height of her affair,
   when Emma has never seemed as beautiful, a potentially flattering
   description uses manure figuratively to represent the experiences and
   illusions that have nourished her (self-deceiving) feeling of fulfilment.

7 See the discussion of olfactory lexicon, primarily in relation to
   Baudelaire's poetry, in chapter 2.

8 The French text reads: "Au point de vue hygiénique, on peut favoriser
   les parfums, pour leurs propriétés stimulantes et rafraîchissantes, mais
   il ne faut jamais en abuser, la santé et le bon goût réclameraient" (Staffe,
   Cabinet de toilette, 1891). The advice is repeated in the 1897 and 1899
   editions of Staffe's *Cabinet de toilette*.

9 Some medical practitioners also advised against perfuming the hair. In
   his 1836 treatise on hygiene, Dr. Joseph Briand asks his readers to abstain
   from using scented pomades (a practice he attributes largely to coquettes
   and dandies), warning that such products may cause problems in those
   with high nervous susceptibility, due to the strong odour that alters the
   warmth of the head, and the mingling of hair products with transpiration.
   See *Manuel complet de l'hygiène* (Brussels: Tircher, 1836), 129.

10 By the 1920s and 1930s, women were advised to apply perfume directly
   to their skin for two reasons often cited today. A 1937 *Marie Claire* article
   reminds women that the warmth of the skin brings the fragrance to life,
   and that perfume damages clothing. Though "[l]a discretion dans le
   parfum est une règle pour la femme qui travaille" ("discretion in perfume
   is a rule for women who work"), women should apply perfume to their
   skin with a vaporizer, especially behind the ears and in the palm of the
   hands. See "Votre parfum … c'est vous" (*Marie Claire*, 10 December 1937,
   18–19).

11 The author can attest that when a client purchases a scent at the Guerlain
   boutique on the Champs Élysées, the sales associate ends the transaction

298   Notes to pages 180–8

by offering to perfume the buyer. This perfuming constitutes a generous spray of the clothing from scarf to shoes.

12 Dufaux's target reader, the well-bred young woman, would likely have understood the concept of wearing perfume "on herself" as using scented skin and hair products, or accessories carried or worn very close to the body, or as scenting one's clothing.

13 See "Variétés" in *Gazette de France* (4 September 1818), 1033–6.

14 In chapters 13–15 of *Le propre et le sale*, Vigarello focuses on changes in the perceived relationship between bathing and cleanliness. He recounts changes in attitude regarding the function of skin and its relation to water and disease, emphasizing that prevailing theories were not always reflected in daily practice. See also Corbin (260–6).

15 David Jouysse, *Bref discours de la préservation et de la cure de la peste* (Amiens: Hubault, 1668), 3. As cited in Le Guérer, *Le parfum* (Paris: Odile Jacob, 2005), 133.

16 Érika Wicky discusses the contradictory advice on bathing directed to women in the nineteenth century in "Parfum de bonté et odeur de sainteté: Les enjeux de l'olfaction dans l'éducation religieuse des jeunes filles au xixᵉ siècle," *Arts et savoirs* 11 (2019): 11–13.

17 Joseph Briand, for example, devotes a full chapter to baths and lotions in his much cited 1836 *Manuel complet d'hygiène* (116–28).

18 On hydrotherapy in nineteenth-century France, see Mary Donaldson-Evans, *Medical Examinations: Dissecting the Doctor in French Narrative Prose, 1857–1894* (Lincoln: University of Nebraska Press, 2000).

19 The "Hygie" of Mège's title refers to the Greek goddess of health.

20 There were (and are) very real dangers associated with some cosmetic products and clothing manufacturers. See Alison Matthews David, *Fashion Victims: The Danger of Dress Past and Present* (London: Bloomsbury, 2015).

21 Recipes for *lait virginal* rely mostly on a tincture of benzoin, but lead and mercury were often added to this and other milky cosmetic products. See *Wood's Medical and Surgical Monographs*, vol. 8 (New York: Wood, 1890), 364–5.

22 In 1894, the Comtesse de Norville reveals awareness of germs when she recommends that the sponge used for cold-water bathing be stored in water mixed with lemon juice or ammonia, "afin de prévenir la naissance de microbes" (41).

23 Comtesse de Norville, *Les coulisses de la beauté* (Paris: Ampleman,1894), 41.

24 See the discussion of this passage from *Éducation sentimentale* in chapter 5.

25 This is not the only reference to spaces smelling of iris in *À la recherche du temps perdu*. In *Combray*, Marcel glimpses the castle-keep tower of Roussainville from his perch in *le petit cabinet sentant l'iris*." He mentions

this view (and odour) again in *Albertine disparue*. In *Le côté des Guermantes*, Marcel mentions another iris-scented air freshener, this time in a hotel. And in the posthumously published collection of essays *Contre Sainte-Beuve*, Proust recalls the petit cabinet of his youth that inspired the passage in Combray. Here, he gives a bit more visual context for the presence of iris: "Mais à douze ans, quand j'allais m'enfermer pour la première fois dans le cabinet qui était en haut de notre maison à Combray, où les colliers de grains d'iris étaient suspendus, ce que je venais chercher, c'était un plaisir inconnu, original, qui n'était pas la substitution d'un autre" ("But at age twelve, when I was going to lock myself for the first time in the water closet that was on the top floor of our house in Combray, where the garlands of ground iris root were hanging, what I was seeking was a pleasure unknown, original, which was not a substitution for another," 54). See Marie Miquet's comments on how some of these iris references related in "Le Séjour à Doncières" dans *Le côté des Guermantes: avant-textes et texte*," *Semen* 11 (1999). Luzius Keller studies the novel's network of *petits cabinets, cabinets d'aisances*, and *petites pieces* in "L'Installation du petit cabinet sentant l'iris: De toutes sortes de pièces et petites pièces proustiennes," *Marcel Proust: la fabrique de combray* (Zoe: Carouge-Geneva, 2006), 161–90.

26 On iris versus violet, see Eugène Rimmel, *Le livre des parfums* (Paris: Dentu, 1870), 391, and Septimus Piesse, *Chimie des parfums* (Paris: Baillière, 1897), 126–7.

27 See further discussion of violet in chapter 1. The ionone molecule has been identified as a common denominator that links orris (iris root) to the violet flower. Tiemann and Krüger developed synthetic ionone in 1893. See Berndt Scheafer, *Natural Products in the Chemical Industry* (New York: Springer, 2014), 51, 62–4.

28 See the discussion of Hammond's case study in chapter 1.

29 The *iris germanica* is most likely a hybrid of the purple *iris pallida* and the yellow *iris variegata*. See W.-R. Dykes, "L'Hybridation chez les Iris," in *Les iris cultivés. Actes et comptes rendus de la première conférence internationale des iris, tenue à Paris 1922* (Paris, 1923) 68–75.

30 See discussion of the *iris gigot* (*iris foetidissam, stinking iris*, or *roast-beef plant*) in M.F. Laplace, "Historique de l'introduction, de l'hybridation et des variétés d'iris du groupe apogon," in *Les iris cultivés. Actes et comptes rendus de la première conférence internationale des iris, tenue à Paris 1922* (Paris, 1923), 123.

31 M.S. Mottet, "Classification des variétés d'iris des jardins," *Les iris cultivés. Actes et comptes rendus de la première conférence internationale des iris, tenue à Paris 1922* (Paris, 1923), 100–20.

32 In the United States, varieties such as the "Grape Soda" tall bearded iris, hybridized by Robert Annand in 2000, have been bred to feature the

fragrance more prominently. The volatile molecule responsible for the grape scent is methyl anthranilate. See Ohler, Guidet, et al., "Aggregation of *Thaumatomyia glabra* (Diptera Chloropidae) Males on *Iris* spp. Flowers releasing Methyl Anthranilate," *Environmental Entomology* 45, no. 6 (December 2016): 1476–9.

33 Although each of these flowers has a distinctive fragrance, they share the methyl anthranilate molecule responsible for grape candy and soda flavouring. In her chapter on the development of imitation grape flavour, Nadia Berenstein reports that the American chemist Gilbert Hurty "was riding an Indianapolis streetcar when he caught a whiff of destiny in a fellow rider's perfume. It smelled just like ripe Concord grapes" (122). He tracked down the methyl anthranilate responsible for that smell, known in perfumery since the late nineteenth century, and used it to create imitation grape flavouring. See Nadia Berenstein, *Flavor Added: The Sciences of Flavor and the Industrialization of Taste in America* (PhD diss., University of Pennsylvania, 2018), 198–256.

34 Hippolyte Cloquet, *Osphrésiolgie ou traité des odeurs, du sens et des organes* (Paris: Méquignon-Marvis,1821), 55.

35 Dane Mitchell's 2017 exhibition *Iris, Iris, Iris,* curated for the Auckland Art Gallery, NZ, features an ongoing process of molecule extraction, called gas chromatography mass spectrometry, headspace technology, filling the gallery space with the scent of iris petals. See photographs and commentary athttps://www.aucklandartgallery.com/whats-on /exhibition/iris-iris-iris?q=%2Fwhats-on%2Fexhibition%2Firis-iris-iris.

36 Piesse situates iris root on the spectrum at "mi," between musk and heliotrope.

37 Earlier in the century, iris (named for the Greek goddess, messenger to the gods) signified news or good news. By the early twentieth century, the depiction of women with iris flowers on postcards was accompanied with the words *confiance* or *confiance et attachement* (trust and affection).

38 See M. Petit, *Les parfums* (Paris: Demarson, Petit & Co., 1858), 46.

39 See the formula for tablets containing iris in Espelly and Le Febvre, *Ordonnances de M. Espelly* (Amiens: Hubault, 1668), 5. See recipes for products including iris tablets to treat asthma, coughs, and to clear phlegm from the brain and the chest in Nicolas Lemery, *Pharmacopée universelle*, vol. 1, 5th ed. (Paris: Saillant, 1763–4), 412–14.

40 See Alfred Franklin, *La Civilité, l'étiquette, la mode, le bon ton du XIIIe au XIXᵉ siècle*, vol. 2 (Paris: Émile-Paul, 1908), 41.

41 Piesse notes that iris was not perceived to have the stand-alone olfactory beauty of violet (*The Art of Perfumery*, 1857, 48–9). See also Piesse's *Des odeurs, des parfums, et des cosmétiques* (Paris: Baillière, 1865), 115–16.

42 See René Cerbelaud, *Formulaire des principales spécialités de parfumerie et de pharmacie* [1908] (Paris: Cerbelaud, 1920), 732–8.

43 Perfume advertisements of the late nineteenth and early twentieth centuries use similar compositional elements in depictions of women smelling flowers and bottled perfumes. See my discussion of Alphonse Mucha's Lance Parfum Rodo in chapter 7.

44 See also Christina Bradstreet, "Wicked with Roses: Floral Femininity and the Erotics of Scent," *Nineteenth-Century Art Worldwide* 6, no. 1 (2007): n.p. In her study of English and American paintings, Bradstreet demonstrates that depictions of women smelling flowers were abundant from the mid-nineteenth through early twentieth centuries, and that such images "defined femininity not only through body language and the representation of the physical gesture of smelling but also with reference to contemporary popular and scientific ideas about odor, olfaction and female sexuality" (20).

45 See Érika Wicky, "Ce que sentent les jeunes filles," *Romantisme* 3, no. 165 (2014): 43–53.

46 Despite his tremendous success, Bouguereau's infamous male gaze has managed, since his lifetime, to offend viewers by being both shocking and sappy.

47 The left-hand finger positions in Bouguereau's *Woman with Iris* are much like that of Botticelli's *Venus*, and Bouguereau uses it in other paintings.

48 Janet Beizer discusses Emma Bovary's "vaporish airs" and similar characterizations of "Emma, her imagination, her perceptions (and including evaporation, vapor, haze, fog, clouds, mist) diffused throughout the narrative discourse" (1994, 154). See also Tony Tanner, *Adultery in the Novel: Conduct and Transgression* (Baltimore: Johns Hopkins University Press, 1979).

49 Critics have observed that despite the remarkable presence of food in *Madame Bovary*, the heroine is seldom shown eating. Anna Igou notes: "Even the most extensive criticism touching on the alimentary motif in *Madame Bovary* fails to expose the utter emptiness that characterizes food in the novel…: on mange beaucoup. Emma does not, however, eat a lot. In fact, the actual act of eating is kept decidedly vague despite the bounty of food in the text" (36). See Anna Igou, "Nothing Consumed: The Dangerous Space of Food in *Madame Bovary*," *French Forum* 38 (December 2013): 35–50.

50 See the discussion of the apricot episode in chapter 5.

51 On a "social fabric where we find women, reading, and hysteria knotted into the texture of time" (55), see Beizer, *Ventriloquized Bodies*, especially pages 55–73. See also Sarah Hurlburt, "Educating Emma: A Generic Analysis of Reading in *Madame Bovary*," *Nineteenth Century French Studies* 40, no. 1 (2011–12): 81–94.

52 Emma does not speak the names of these odours, but they are revealed from her perspective.

53 Later, when Emma sees ladies (*dames*) in Rouen wearing charms attached to their watches, she buys her own. The sight of the charms attached to a watch chain may have reminded her of the chatelaines (more often called an *armoire* or an *escarelle* in French) that she saw at la Vaubyessard, where several women wore perfume bottles dangling from a belt worn around the waist. The trendy belt chatelaines were parodied in cartoons depicting women with household items (brooms, tea kettles) and children attached. See illustrations in Genevieve Cummins and Nerylla D. Taunton, *Chatelaines: Utility to Glorious Extravagance* (Aberdeen: Antique Collectors Club, 1994), 78–81.

54 Turkish motifs are mentioned several times in *Madame Bovary*, including the large bed with a cotton canopy depicting Turkish men, which Charles spots shortly before encountering the smell of iris sheets, a foreshadowing of the Orientalist taste that Emma develops. As Jennifer Yee points out, "the Orientalist 'pastilles du sérail' (where the seraglio evoked is the imperial seraglio of the Ottoman empire) is undercut by the fact that she has bought them in the local provincial capital in a shop run by an early colonial immigrant, probably a French colonist returning from Algeria" (118). See Jennfier Yee, *The Colonial Comedy: Imperialism in the French Realist Novel* (Oxford: Oxford University Press, 2016).

55 *Paul et Virginie* is often cited as a novel that influenced Emma Bovary at an early age, but Emma also read several works by women. See Margaret Cohen, "Flaubert lectrice: Flaubert Lady Reader," *MLN* 122, no. 4 (September 2007): 746–58.

7. Decadent Perfuming

1 See Auguste Debay, *Les parfums et les fleurs* (Paris: Dentu, 1861), 121.

2 This quotation from Celnart's 1829 *Manuel de dames ou l'art de la toilette* appears in subsequent editions throughout the century.

3 Caufeynon published between 1901 and 1950. The BnF lists the following pseudonyms for Jean Fauconney: Docteur Caufeynon, Docteurs Caufeynon and Jaf, Docteur Fauconney, Jehan Fauconney, Docteur Jaf, and Docteurs Jaf et Caufeynon.

4 Among the dozens of titles appearing under the name of Doctor Caufeynon are *L'hermaphrodite au couvent* and *Les Vénus impudiques ou la prostitution à travers les âges*, *La ceinture de chasteté: son histoire, son emploi autrefois et aujourd'hui* and *La masturbation et la sodomie féminines*.

5 Césare Lombroso and Guglielmo Ferrero, *La femme criminelle et la prostituée* (Paris: Alcan, 1896), 112.

6 The cover page of *Le parfum de la femme* lists Galopin's credentials
   as: "Professeur de Physiologie Générale; Directeur de l'Hygiène
   contemporaine; Lauréat des hôpitaux de l'École de Médecine et
   de L'Association française; Membre correspondant de l'Académie
   Christophe Colombe, de Marseille, etc." The book is written for
   non-specialists, with a preface addressing "mes lecteurs" and "nos
   intelligentes lectrices" (10). Across the chapters, Galopin addresses his
   readers in a chummy tone.
7 Ernest Monin referred to "educating the nose" in his 1886 *Odeurs du corps
   humain*, 24. See discussion in chapter 3.
8 As outdated as nineteenth-century coding of scents according to class,
   gender, race, ethnicity, and nationality may be, a recent study shows
   that twenty-first-century perfume buyers attribute similar meanings to
   fragrances. See Karen A. Cerulo, "Scents and Sensibility: Olfaction, Sense-
   Making, and Meaning Attribution," *American Sociological Review* 83, no. 2
   (2018): 361–89.
9 On the popularity of *Chérie* (6,000 of the 8,000 copies released sold in one
   day) see Ashley (2005, 19–20) and Fosca (1941, 339). As Ashley notes,
   Chérie was nearly forgotten in the twentieth century, but finally re-edited
   in 2002 by Cabanès and Hamon. The novel has attracted renewed
   critical attention for its relationship to perfume culture. See, for example,
   Stamelman, *Perfume*, 297–8; Krueger, "Decadent Perfume: Under the Skin
   and through the Page"; and Oberhuber and Wicky, "Du mauvais usage
   des parfums, Chérie empoisonnée par le musc et l'héliotrope?"
10 On 27 April 1884, Guy de Maupassant's article "La Jeune Fille" appears
   on the front page of *Le gaulois*. Maupassant lauds Goncourt and Zola for
   their treatment of the delicate topic of the *jeune fille* in *Chérie* and *La joie de
   vivre*.
11 The four women whose letters and memoirs contributed to the volume
   were: Mlle Abbatuccci (daughter of a French Minister of Finance),
   Julia Daudet (see *L'enfance d'une Parisienne*), Catherine Junges (niece
   of Tolstoy), and Pauline Zeller (lady-in-waiting to Princess Mathilde
   Bonaparte). See the discussion of these sources in Ashley (2005, 127–45).
   Bayle reprints letters that arrived in response to Goncourt's call in *Chérie
   d'Edmond de Goncourt* (84–93).
12 Examples of the Goncourts' naturalist novels include *Germinie Lacerteux*
   (1865), *Manette Salomon* (1867), and *Madame Gervaisais* (1869). Huysmans
   wrote *Marthe, histoire d'une fille* (1876), *Les sœurs Vatard* (1879), *En ménage*
   (1881), and *À vau-l'eau* (1882) (and many other works) before rejecting the
   Naturalist school.
13 See Ashley (2005, 149–74) and Bayle (1983) for analysis of plot structure in
   Chérie.

14 The four novels Edmond de Goncourt published after his brother's death are: *La fille Elisa* (1877), *Les frères Zemganno* (1879), *La Faustin* (1882), and *Chérie* (1884).

15 All quotations of *Chérie* are from the Cabanès and Hamon 2002 critical edition. Translations are my own, unless otherwise attributed. I have retained original sentence structure whenever possible, particularly in Goncourt's winding sentences.

16 See Ashley's chapter on the complicated interplay of prefaces in Goncourt's works (2005, 51–67), and on how it came to pass that the preface to *Chérie* contains the preface to the Goncourt journal (62–3).

17 In chapter 2, "Words" (19–54), Christopher Lloyd discusses *écriture artiste*, a term the Goncourts first coined to describe their own writing, but which was eventually applied to other literary prose of the late nineteenth century. Lloyd observes that the Goncourts "in fact write fiction that is deliberately unreadable, in the sense this term has when applied to practitioners of the 'nouveau roman' a century later. In other words they subvert the reader's habitual conception of what makes an acceptable novel in the realist tradition" (28). Though Lloyd does not include *Chérie* in this discussion, his argument applies.

18 Various reports of Empress Josephine's inordinate use of musk, some indicating that the Malmaison still smelled of musk fifty years after Joséphine's death, appear in publications including: Jean Alesson, "Musc," *La femme* (14 May 1888), 75; Piesse, *Des odeurs, des parfums et des cosmétiques* (1865), 225; *Reports of the Paris Exhibition, 1867*, vol. 2 (1868), 569; and Robert de Montesquiou-Fézensac, *Pays des aromates* (11–12). Montesquiou published *Pays des aromates* and *Musée rétrospective de la classe 90: parfumerie* in the same year. They contain much of the same material, with differences in the first section. The Comtesse de Gencé refers to the anecdote in her *Le cabinet de toilette d'une honnête femme* (418).

19 The term *animal/animale* is still used in perfumery, although the materials themselves are now usually synthetic. The animal note in perfumery is often described as smelling of a horse stable or a barnyard. Use of natural animal products (traditionally ambergris, castoreum, civet, and musk) in perfumery today is for the most part banned, or at the very least highly regulated (see de Guérer *Le Parfum* [263–70] on the use of animal products in perfume). In the nineteenth century, however, animals were hunted for the perfume materials they supplied. See further discussion in chapter 1.

20 See discussion of Charcot's iconography and nosology in the French novel, in Janet Beizer, *Ventriloquized Bodies*, and in Rachel Mesch, *The Hysteric's Revenge*, 119–43.

21 In a letter dated 21 April 1884, Huysmans thanks Goncourt for his copy
of *Chérie*. He delivers his praise in detail, stating that the passage on
menstruation amazed him ("Puis les règles me stupéfient"). The full
letter is quoted in Lambert and Cogny (76–9). This passage was a source
of rivalry between Goncourt and Zola, stirred up by Alphonse Daudet
and documented in a fascinating exchange of letters. Daudet reported
that Goncourt thought Zola had seen the passage from *Chérie* at some
point and incorporated a similar episode in *La joie de vivre*. Zola wrote
to confirm that he had not seen Goncourt's chapter drafts. Goncourt
in turn maintained that he understood the similarity in their pages on
menstruation to be a coincidence, and that Daudet had been mistaken.
His only concern was that since he worked more slowly than Zola
(starting his own novel earlier, but finishing it later), and since Zola
enjoyed more public favour, readers would think Goncourt had been
"inspired" by Zola's work (Lambert and Cogney 78–9). Huysmans,
Goncourt, and Zola had already published potentially rival novels about
prostitutes. See the discussion in chapter 1.
22 *Madame Bovary* was written between 1851 and 1857. The action, however,
takes place a bit before and during the July Monarchy (1830–48). As
Cabanès and Hamon point out, protagonist Chérie's lifespan (1851–70)
invites a meta-reading of the text. The years cover the Second Empire and
mark both the starting date of the brothers' *Journal*, and the end of their
collaboration, with the death of Jules in 1870 (7–8).
23 Though Paul reads and discusses more novels than Virginie, she is not
seen as exempt from being tainted by fiction. When Virginie expresses her
desire to leave France and return to her island home, her aunt accuses her
of being a silly girl whose head has been ruined by novels.
24 On the education of women and women readers in this and other
Goncourt novels, see Anne-Simone Dufief, "Devenir femme? L'éducation
des filles dans l'œuvre des Goncourt," *Cahiers Edmond et Jules de Goncourt*
15 (2008): 123–41.
25 Giraud discusses Chérie's illness in detail, linking the symptoms, attributed
to hysteria at the time, to current etiologies of depression and anorexia
nervosa.
26 On the nasogenital reflex see Combe (46–7), and Harrington and Rosario
(1992), who also offer a detailed account of olfaction in medical thinking
in the nineteenth century. These include pervasive theories of olfaction
in relation to evolution, nasal reflex neuroses, olfactory and neurological
disorders, smell and brain function, and olfaction and sexual deviance.
Annick Le Guérer studies the importance of odour and the nose in the
history of psychology in "Le Nez d'Emma," and on smell and civilization
in *Scent*, especially chapter 8 (188–93). See a summary and recent links

to a revival of interest in the nasogenital reflex in Alexander C. Chester, "The Nose and Sex: The Nasogenital Reflex Revisited," *Journal of the Royal Society of Medecine* 100, no. 11 (2007): 489–90.

27 Though her own perfume is not mentioned, Chérie visits a shop in which the dressmaker, M. Gentillat, is described as a victim of second-hand fragrance, suffering from neuralgia caused by exposure to the smells of perfumed women clients (181).

28 Piesse's formula for "Bouquet de l'impératrice Eugénie" includes musk, vanilla, Tonka, neroli, geranium, rose triple (a blend of rose essence and rectified alcohol), and sandalwood (*Des odeurs, des parfums, et des cosmétiques* 1865, 293).

29 The list of perfume notes filling the air around Chérie may seem exaggerated, but Goncourt's fictional perfume blend is in fact very much on trend, even prescient. Guerlain's 1889 Jicky included top notes of bergamot, rosemary, lavender, and rosewood; heart notes of jasmine, geranium, and rose; and base notes of Tonka bean, vanilline, coumarin, and opoponax (see description in de Feydeau 948–9).

30 Cabanès and Hamon note that the nod to Pingat in this passage contributes to an undertow of erotic pressure in Chérie, since Pingat was known to dress demi-mondaines (179, note 1).

31 The *San Francisco Call* likewise reported that Mrs. "Bobby" McCreary gave vogue to hypodermic perfuming when she shared this "latest wrinkle in personal perfumery" with women she was entertaining in her Paris flat. See "Perfumes Self with Hypodermic: American Woman Introduces Latest Toilet Craze for Paris Smart Set," *San Francisco Call* (15 December 1912), 53. The article also appears that month in the *Honolulu Star Bulletin*, *The Birmingham Age-Herald*, and in another edition of the *San Francisco Call*.

32 In chapter 2, "Transgressions" (27–50), Weber discusses the appeal of other sorts of racy stories circulated in the popular French press. It is, of course, worth examining perfume injection reports in the context of American cultural discourses as well.

33 See also "Injecting Perfume into the Blood" (*Chicago Tribune*, 1891), as well as "Injections of Perfume (*The New York Times*, 1898) and "Injections of Perfume" (*The Washington Post*, 1898), both attributed to the *London Chronicle*.

34 On the concept of morphine abuse as a feminine vice, see Arnould de Leidekerke, *La Belle Époque de l'opium* (Paris: Éditions de la Différence, 2001), 114–22. See also Jesper Vaczy Kagh, "Women, Men, and the Morphine Problem, 1870–1955" (2014).

35 See Georges de Labruyère, "Les Morphinomanes," *Le Figaro*, 1 June 1886.

36 In *Les paradis artificiels*, Baudelaire identifies opium and hashish as being among the drugs best for creating *l'idéal artificiel*, noting that liqueurs and strong perfumes are not as effective because the former leads to a material fury, dragging down the spiritual force, while the latter renders man's imagination more subtle but gradually weakens his strength (OCI, 403).

37 See Susannah Wilson's discussion of the neologism *morphinée* and related terminology in "Morphinisé/morphinomane/morphinée," 342–6.

38 The 1886 Salon's *Catalogue illustrée* clearly identifies Moreau de Tours's painting as "La Morphine" (129) in various reports on the exhibition that year.

39 See, for example, Mourneville and Bricon, *Manuel des injections sous-cutanées* (1883); and "Vade-Mecum pour les injections hypodermiques" in Lutaud, *Nouveau formulaire thérapeutique* (1884), 220–37. In an article on the use of hypodermic injections of an iodine formula for tuberculosis patients, Dr. Charles Wilson Ingraham mentions that the taste and odour of menthol (eliminated via the lungs) are noticeable for several hours after each daily injection (483).

40 The iatraliptic method involves healing by rubbing lotions or ointments into the skin. Chrestien is interested in both the salubrious effects of rubbing the skin, and in how the skin's absorption of materials may be therapeutic for the treatment of internal maladies.

41 On the history of hypodermic treatment and technologies in Europe and the United States, see Kane's *The Hypodermic Injection of Morphia* (1880, 13–33) and Bartholow's *Manual of Hypodermic Medication* (1882, 2–19). Chrestien's treatise is cited in Bartholow (2) and throughout medical literature of the nineteenth century.

42 In the 5th edition of his *Manual* (1891), Bartholow explains that all scholars agree on the terminology, pointing out that "hypodermatic" would be the appropriate term, but "hypodermic" is "so firmly established, and in such universal use, that the substitution of the correct term can be accomplished only by combined effort.... The word *subcutaneous* expresses the same idea and is in all respects appropriate" (27).

43 According to Dr. Harry Hubbell Kane, Dr. Alexander Wood of Edinburgh is credited with the first use of subcutaneous injection in 1843 (written up in 1855). However, Drs. Taylor and Washington claim to have used this method as early as 1839, saying they had read about subcutaneous injection of morphine in a provincial French journal (13–14). See also the chapter on "History of Subcutaneous Injection" in Bartholow (17–30).

44 In chapters 13–15 of *Le propre et le sale*, Vigarello recounts changes in attitude regarding the function of skin and its relation to water and

disease, emphasizing that prevailing theories were not always reflected in daily practice. See also Corbin (260–6).

45 For a detailed discussion of how the fields of pharmacy and chemistry developed in the nineteenth century, see Larry Duffy, "*Madame Bovary* and the Institutional Transformation of Pharmacy," *Dix-Neuf* 15, no. 1 (2011): 70–82.

46 See Élisabeth de Feydeau, *Les parfums* (873), and the unattributed article "Les Buveuses d'eau de Cologne," *Le véteran* (14 February 1904), 14.

47 See further discussion of fumigation in the introduction.

48 On the dangers of perfume drinking, see "New Fad in Drinking: Perfume Habit Is the Latest Form of Dipsomania: Cocktail of Peau d'Espagne" (1899) and "Perfume in Liquor: Hysterical Woman Taken to Receiving Room Is Esthetic in Her Indulgence" (1910), and "Perfume as a Drink Is Fatal" (1910). Clérambualt also mentions that one of his patients with erotic silk fetishes sometimes drank eau de cologne, among other things (ether, rum, white wine, mouthwash) (50).

49 Charles Féré, *Le travail et le plaisir: nouvelles études experimentales et psycho-mécanique* (Paris: Alcon, 1904).

50 See Peta Allen Shera's analysis of Clérambault's studies in "Selfish Passions and Artificial Desires: Rereading Clérambault's Study of 'Silk Erotomania,'" *Journal of the History of Sexuality* 18, no. 1 (2009): 158–79.

51 Clérambault uses the verb crier (to cry [out]) to identify the sound of silk. In 1910, forty-nine-year-old Marie D. explains, "La masturbation à elle seule ne me fait pas grand plaisir, mais je la complète en pensant au chatoiement et au bruit de la soie" ("Masturbation on its own does not give me great pleasure, but I supplement it by thinking of the tickle and the sound of silk"; 105).

52 See Sophie-Valentine Borloz's discussion of the short story "La Piqure" in her doctoral thesis "'L'odorat a ses monstres': Olfaction et perversion dans l'imaginaire fin-de-siècle (1880–1905)" (PhD diss., 2020, 364–5). See Borloz's discussion of perfume shooting and the narcotic effect of perfume on pages 421–40.

53 Snobbery is a characteristic of degeneration, according to Nordau (5).

54 Combe quotes in full an anecdote from a humour column entitled "Les gaietés de la médicine," published in *Le mouvement thérapeutique et médical* (1 June 1897), a monthly trade paper for practitioners, edited by Dr. E. (seemingly the same Dr. E. Monin who wrote more than a dozen hygiene manuals, including *Hygiène de la beauté* (discussed earlier), and *Les odeurs du corps humain*) (13).

55 The oldest perfume in continuous production today, though the formula has inevitably morphed over the years, due in part to evolving industry standards, Jicky is still considered unique and modern. On the history

and reception of Jicky, see de Feydeau (948–9), Fellous (36–64), Gobet and Le Gall (117), and Stamelman (184–5).

56 On perfume and hypnosis, see Combe (49–62). For a more thorough discussion of hypnosis in nineteenth-century France, see Silverman, chapter 5, "Psychologie nouvelle" (106).

57 One of seven classic perfume families today, *chypre* is named for Coty's iconic 1917 Chypre (no longer in production), and generally composed as variations on a basic structure of bergamot, labdanum, patchouli, and oakmoss (*Classification officielle des parfums* [7]; see also Feydeau [870]). Eau de Chypre dates to the Middle Ages. Louis XIV's perfumer, Simon Barbe, includes a recipe for poudre de Chypre in his 1693 Le Parfumeur François, in a section called "Poudre de mousse chêne: autrement dit cipre [*sic*]" (7). Mousse de chêne (oakmoss) is one of the natural ingredients now highly restricted by the International Fragrance Association's self-regulatory Code of Practice, which increasingly introduces measures to protect consumers from potential allergic reactions. Perfumes called Chypre were widely available in the late nineteenth century, but their formulae were not necessarily precursors to Coty's Chypre.

58 Note that use of the hyphen in lance-parfum is inconsistent: it appears in citations of trademark and patent applications but not on the product label or advertisements. Both Alphons and Alphonse are used for Mucha's first name.

59 For discussion of Mucha's influence and influences, see Rennet and Srp (17–33); the artist's biography by Jiri Mucha; Gaillemin (11–15); Lipp (10–21); and Mucha's own *Lectures on Art*.

60 Dana's 1995 "Blame It on Tabu" campaign (printed in Reichert 2003, 285) provides an example of equivocally eroticized images of women, as does the more recent tongue-in-cheek print promo for Showtime's series *The Borgias*, which parodies a perfume advertisement, complete with a scent strip insert for an as yet fictional Lucrézia perfume. The spoof advertisement appears in *Vanity Fair* (May 2012): 131. For commentary on depictions of women in Mucha's advertisements, see Dolores Mitchell (1991, 4) and Thompson (161–4).

61 Mucha's 1898 poster for printer Ferdinand Champenois shows a woman's similarly posed, right hand turning the page of a large book.

62 See Carol Rifelj's discussion of immodesty and immorality associated with women *en cheveux* in the nineteenth century (68–74). For an analysis of hairstyles and their signification, see especially chapter 1, "The Language of Hairstyles" (32–82).

63 Reproductions of Mucha's Rodo advertisement are widely available today on posters, key chains, mugs, tote bags, and most recently, rather ironically, face masks.

64 In *Alphonse Mucha: The Complete Graphic Works* (1980), Lance Parfum
   "Rodo" is catalogued as poster A5. The Rodo itself is identified as "a
   perfume spray" rather than a "perfume sprayer" (152). The Rodo was, in
   a sense, both. The Mucha Foundation features a reproduction at its online
   gallery, along with a brief description: "This poster advertises a perfume
   produced by the Société des Usines du Rhône in Lyon." Stamelman's
   Perfume includes a nearly full-page reproduction (80).
65 See Stamelman's discussion of perfume-wearing and bottle and label design
   in Perfume (49–90). Along with the full-page reproduction (80), a cropped
   image of the Rodo is used to demonstrate its application to fabric (171).
66 A website created by Christian Richet presents a number of Rodo labels
   and a photograph of the sprayer itself: http://richet.christian.free.fr
   /mode/modpat.html.
67 See labels for the Lance-parfum Rodo box designed in 1897 and 1912
   in Thierry Lefebvre and Cécile Raynal, "Le Lance-parfum. Un matériel
   médical devenu accessoire de carnaval," *Revue d'histoire de la pharmacie*
   95, no. 357 (2008): 69.
68 See detailed information on the development and patenting of the
   Lance-parfum Rodo in Lefebvre and Raynal.
69 An account of how ethyl chloride tubes and ether cans were used together
   in surgery appears in the article "Ethyl Chloride-Ether Anesthesia by a
   Simplified Method," *International Journal of Surgery* (March 1909): 75.
70 As Lefebvre and Raynal point out, the pharmaceutical and synthetic
   perfume industries have always been closely connected, their products
   often created in factories serving both sectors. Coumarin (synthesized
   by William Henry Perkin in 1867) was used both as a fragrance note
   and a venotonic; a synthetic musk produced in 1889 was used for its
   antispasmodic and emmenagogic properties (63).
71 The "Lança-Perfume" name and material did not disappear from Rio
   after the 1960s. Brazilian rock singer Rita Lee's song "Lança perfume"
   was released in 1980 and has since been covered by many other artists.
   In 2010, police seized more than 1,400 flasks of the drug, which was used
   much like poppers or whippets. See Meredith Melnick, "What Is lança-
   perfume? The Drug from Rio's Bust You've Never Heard Of," *Time*,
   2 December 2010. https://healthland.time.com/2010/12/02/whats-lanca
   -perfume-the-biggest-drug-in-rio-youve-never-heard-of/.

Epilogue: Cooked Apples and Exotic Perfume

1 Diana Holmes situates Rachilde's novels in relation to earlier realist
   works as well as naturalist and other contemporary genres in *Rachilde:
   Decadence, Gender and the Woman Writer* (Oxford: Berg, 2001), 91–112.

2 See the preface, "Complications d'amour" in Rachilde, *Monsieur Vénus* [1889] (Paris: Flammarion, 1977), 5–21.

3 Quotations from *Monsieur Vénus* in French and English are taken from Melanie Hawthorne's French MLA editions, and the Hawthorne and Constable English MLA edition. Pagination is sometimes identical in the two volumes, in which case I cite the page number only once.

4 In *Before Trans*, Rachel Mesch's discussion of pronouns in *Monsieur Vénus* leads to deeper analysis of language challenges, and of Rachilde's representations of gender plurality and fluidity, in her life and in the novels (see especially 149–64).

5 The name Ermengarde is replaced by Elisabeth in the 1889 edition.

6 As Melanie Hawthorne explains, the 1884 novel originally carried the subtitle "Un Roman matérialiste," a term used before "decadent" had gained wide acceptance. According to Hawthorne, materialism "shared many of the properties of literary naturalism" but "rejects the implicitly moralizing tone of naturalism" (Rachilde [1889] 1977, 89).

7 There are many examples of such parallels. Aunt Ermengarde is introduced in the second chapter as having just entered the convent, the doors nearly closing behind her, when she had to leave to raise her orphaned niece, Raoule. But at the end of the novel, fed up with Raoule's behaviour, Ermengarde returns to the convent. In the first chapter, Jacques's mouth, from Raoule's perspective, is like the healthy mouths that have not yet been saturated with the virile perfume of tobacco smoke. Later, Jacques complains when confronted with the smell of tobacco. Jacques is wearing a garland of artificial flowers when Raoule first sees him. Raoule will offer him a series of real bouquets, she will wear a real gardenia in the lapel of her men's suit, and she will wear real orange blossoms in her hair on their wedding day.

8 As Constance Classen points out in *The Color of Angels*, "apples and roses, symbols of women and of Venus, combine to identify Jacques as a male Venus" (124). See analysis of the apples' symbolic value in Nathalie Buchet Rogers, *Fictions du scandale: corps féminin et réalisme romanesque au dix-neuvième siècle* (West Lafayette: Purdue University Press, 1988).

9 See Melanie Hawthorne's publication history of *Monsieur Vénus* in Rachilde ([1889] 1977, 88–100) and in her critical edition *Monsieur Vénus* (xxvi–xxx). Two nearly identical versions of the book were published in Belgium in 1884. An 1889 French edition appeared with obvious revisions.

10 Farrère considered Rachilde's review of his *Les civilisés* in the "Romans" section of *Mercure de France* (15 November 1905, 260–1) crucial to his being awarded the Prix Goncourt (see Quella-Villéger, 21–38).

11 See Piesse, *Des odeurs, des parfums et des cosmétiques* (1865), 190.

12 See further discussion of *maréchale* fragrance in chapter 4. The word
    Maréchale refers to the fragrance, not the substance – which can be
    powder, paste, toilet water, cologne, and so on. Maréchale is considered
    the first perfume named after a celebrity of sorts, Madame la maréchale
    d'Aumont, in 1675. It was marketed in the eighteenth and nineteenth
    centuries for its tenacity, and in powders for its white colour, which
    would probably have lent, along with its penetrating odour, a silvery
    tone to Jacques's red hair.

13 In *Perfumery: Techniques in Evolution*, Arcadi Boix Camps notes that calone
    (methylbenzodioxepinone or watermelon ketone) was virtually unknown
    until 1978 (69). It is a key component of the watery and sea-breeze
    perfumes made popular in the 1980s and 1990s.

14 Crown Perfumery released a (now discontinued) Maréchale perfume in
    1994, based on a 1669 formula.

15 It is in the interest of perfume producers to promote the quest for a
    signature scent, while also encouraging consumers to wear more than
    one fragrance. Anne Archibald, who wrote a chatty monthly column,
    rich in product placement, for *Theatre Magazine*, devoted her March 1922
    instalment of "The Vanity Box" to perfume parties and the purchase of
    multiple miniature bottles. One perfume-sniffing hostess said, "I think
    it's dull, don't you, to have only one perfume and to be known by that
    alone? Like having only one dress, or one mood…. It was these miniature
    bottles, I might add, that inspired me to the party" (190).

16 Flankers, called *les flankers* in French, are new iterations, versions, riffs,
    or *déclinaisons*/declensions, as Élisabeth de Feydeau puts it in *Les
    parfums* (896), of an existing fragrance. Flankers are not reformulations
    (those occur all the time, often under the radar, especially when
    perfumers adapt to new industry restrictions). A flanker generally
    uses the same name as the original perfume (say, Shalimar), with
    a descriptor (*souffle de parfum, souffle intense, cologne, intense, power,
    hypnotic, noir, light*, etc.).

17 I use the term *prequels* for what I think of as a sub-category of flankers,
    new variations of classic perfumes with starter adjectives (*premier, initial*)
    in their names.

18 See discussion of the language of perfumes in chapter 1.

19 On perfume families or classifications, see chapter 2, note 41.

20 Claude Farrère (the pen name for Frédéric-Charles Bargone, 1876–1957),
    won the third Prix Goncourt and was admired by writers, including
    Rachilde and Colette. See Alain Quella-Villéger, *Le cas farrère, du Goncourt
    à la disgrâce* (Paris: Presses de la renaissance, 1989).

21 Though Alain Quella-Villéger, quoting Rachilde (Mercure de France, 6
    March 1909, 313–14), called *La bataille* "un anti-*Madame Chrysanthème*"

(74–5), others have argued that, while showing more awareness of its own exoticism and *japonisme*, the novel still owes a great deal to Loti. See Akame Kawakami's discussion of *La bataille* in *Travellers' Visions of Japan in French Literature, 1881–2004* (63–72).

22 The Guerlain advertisement appears in *Theatre Magazine* 36, no. 261 (December 1922): 407.

23 Even today, though scent notes may be listed in detailed descriptions of perfumes, marketing campaigns rely more on image, mood, and ideas. It is rare to find a mainstream advertising campaign that highlights or describes a perfume's smell. Ingredients, the least alluring of perfume's sellable elements, appear in small print on packaging that the buyer will likely ignore.

24 Released two years after Coty's groundbreaking 1917 Chypre, Mitsouko was not the first to define this genre, or family of perfumes, but has garnered enduring praise from perfume lovers and critics, including Luca Turin and Tania Sanchez, who deem it the "reference chypre" and a "masterpiece whose richness brings to mind the mature chamber music of Johannes Brahms" (2008, 245–6).

25 See Richard Stamelman's analysis of several *Opium* print advertisements in *Perfume* (301–3).

26 Jennifer Yee discusses the democratization of exotic products during the nineteenth century, Orientalist marketing, and fakes, in *The Colonial Comedy: Imperialism and the French*, 86–112.

27 See Eugène Charbot, *Les productions végétales des colonies françaises* (Paris: Callamel, 1908), 46–7; and Eugene Rimmel, *Recollections of the Paris Exhibition of 1867* (London: Chapman & Hall, 1867), 141–3.

28 See Tilar J. Mazzeo's history of jasmine and its legendary role in Chanel N°5 in *The Secret of Chanel No.5: The Intimate History of the World's Most Famous Perfume* (New York: HarperCollins, 2010).

29 This section on Ellena overlaps with my longer review of Ellena's book written for *Now Smell This* in 2011.

30 First published in hardback in 2018, *The Guide* has been reissued in paperback (as *Perfumes: The A-Z Guide*, 2009), and electronically, and it has spawned its own flanker, *The Little Book of Perfumes: The Hundred Classics* (2011).

31 Perfume critic Chandler Burr uses the expression ghost flowers to designate any perceived floral notes in perfume that are not derived from the flower itself, often because it is nearly impossible to do so. Lily-of-the valley is the chief example of a ghost flower, a note that Edmond Roudniska successfully and synthetically brought to Diorissimo in 1956. I use the term phantom note for the fragrance notes, floral or not, that are primarily ideas or illusions.

32 Kenzo does include other floral notes, including rose and violet.

33 See Phoebe Natanson, "Pope Benedict Has Custom-Designed Cologne: Silvana Casoli Makes Heavenly Scent for Pope Benedict," *ABC News*, 15 March 2021. https://abcnews.go.com/International/pope-benedicts-custom-made-cologne/story?id=15927330.

34 In the 2020 newsletter *Quarterly Insights*, Michael Edwards reports that the impact of COVID-19 was toughest on niche and independent fragrances. Definitions of the category have been debated, but niche fragrances include smaller-batch artisanal perfumes, and more generally, perfumes that are harder to find in department stores that sell designer and luxury products.

Bibliography

Fiction, Poetry, Essays, Memoirs, and Letters

Balzac, Honoré de. *Le curé de village* [1841]. Paris: Gallimard, 1975.
– *Béatrix* [1839]. General editor Pierre-Georges Castex, 601–941. Vol. 2 of *La comédie humaine*. Paris: Pléiade, 1976a.
– *Le curé de Tours* [1832]. Paris: Gallimard, 1976b.
– *Histoire de la grandeur et de la décadence de César Birotteau* [1837]. General editor Pierre-Georges Castex, 37–312. Vol. 6 of *La comédie humaine*. Paris: Pléiade, 1977a.
– *La cousine Bette* [1846]. General editor Pierre-Georges Castex, 55–451. Vol. 7 of *La comédie cumaine*. Paris: Pléiade, 1977b.
Baudelaire, Charles. *The Flowers of Evil*. Translated by Cyril Scott. London: Mathews, 1909.
– *Flowers of Evil*. Translated by Lewis Piaget Shanks. New York: Washburn, 1931.
– *Flowers of Evil*. Translated by George Dillon and Edna St. Vincent Millay. New York: Harper, 1936.
– *Flowers of Evil*. Translated by Geoffrey Wagner. Cambridge, MA: New Directions, 1946.
– *Poems of Baudelaire: A Translation of* Les fleurs du mal. Translated by Roy Campbell. New York: Pantheon, 1953.
– *The Flowers of Evil*. Translated by William Aggeler. Fresno: Academy Library Guild, 1954.
– *Flowers of Evil*. Translated by Jacques Leclerq. Mount Vernon: Peter Pauper Press, 1958.
– *Œuvres complètes*. Edited by Claude Pichois. 2 vols. Paris: Pléiade, 1975–6.
– *Baudelaire in English*. Edited by Carol Clark and Robert Sykes. New York: Penguin, 1997a.

– *The Flowers of Evil*. Translated by Walter Martin. Exeter: Carcanet Press, 1997b.
– *Complete Poems*. Translated by Walter Martin. Manchester: Carcanet, 2006.
Beaulieu, Denyse. *The Perfume Lover: A Personal Journey of Scent*. New York: St. Martin's, 2013.
Bernardin de Saint-Pierre, Jacques-Henri. *Paul et Virginie* [1788]. Paris: GF, 2019.
Blodgett, Bonnie. *Remembering Smell: A Memoir of Losing – and Discovering – the Primal Sense*. Boston: Houghton Mifflin Harcourt, 2010.
Colette. *Le pur et l'impur*. In *Œuvres complètes* vol. 3. General editor Claude Pichois, 441–653. Paris: Gallimard, 1991.
– "Parfums," in *Paysages et portraits*, edited by Marie-Françoise Berthu-Courtivron, 147–58. Paris: Flammarion, 2002.
Daudet, Julia. *L'enfance d'une Parisienne* [1883]. Paris: Alphonse Lemerre, 1892.
Decori, Félix, ed. *Correspondance de George Sand et d'Alfred de Musset*. Brussels: Deman, 1904.
Farrère, Claude. *La Bataille* [1909]. Tours: Arrault, 1947.
Flaubert, Gustave. *Madame Bovary* [1857]. In *Œuvres* vol. 1. General editors Albert Thibaudet and René Dumesnil, 291–611. Paris: Pléiade, 1951a.
– *Salammbô* [1862]. In *Œuvres*, vol. 1. General editors Albert Thibaudet and René Dumesnil, 707–994. Paris: Pléiade, 1951b.
– *Education sentimentale* [1869]. In *Œuvres* vol. 2. General editors Albert Thibaudet and René Dumesnil, 31–457. Paris: Pléiade, 1952.
Goncourt, Edmond de. *Les frères Zemganno*. Paris: Charpentier, 1879.
– *La Faustin*. Paris: Charpentier, 1882.
– *Chérie*. Edited by Jean-Louis Cabanès and Philippe Hamon. Jaignes: La Chasse au Snark, 2002.
– *La fille Élisa* [1877]. Paris: Zulma, 2004.
Goncourt, Edmond de, and Jules de Goncourt. *Germinie Lacerteux* [1865]. Paris: Crès, 1921.
– *Madame Gervaisais* [1869]. Paris: Gallimard, 1982.
– *Manette Salomon* [1867]. Paris: Gallimard, 1991.
Gozlan, Léon. *Le notaire de Chantilly*. 2 vols. Paris: Dumont, 1836.
Hannon, Théodore. *Rimes de joie*. Brussels: Gay et Doucé, 1881.
Harad, Alyssa. *Coming to My Senses. A Story of Perfume, Pleasure, and an Unlikely Bride*. New York: Penguin, 2012.
Huysmans, Joris-Karl. *À rebours* [1881–3]. Manuscript. Bibliothèque nationale de France, Département des Manuscrits, NAF 15761.
– *À rebours*. Paris: Charpentier, 1884.
– *Croquis Parisiens, a vau-l'eau, un dilemme*. Paris: Plon, 1908.
– *Lettres inédites à Edmond de Goncourt*. Edited by Pierre Cogny. Paris: Nizet, 1956a.
– *Lettres inédites à Edmond de Goncourt*. Edited by Pierre Cogny. Paris: Nizet, 1956b.

– *À rebours* [1884]. Edited by Marc Fumaroli. Paris: Gallimard, 1977.
– *À rebours* [1884]. Edited by Rose Fortassier. Paris: Imprimerie nationale, 1981.
– *Against Nature.* Translated by Margaret Mauldon. Oxford: Oxford University Press, 1998.
– *À rebours* [1884]. In *Joris-Karl Huysmans: Romans I.* General editor Pierre Brunel, 529–762. Paris: Laffont, 2005a.
– *À vau-l'eau* [1882]. In *Joris-Karl Huysmans: Romans I.* General editor Pierre Brunel, 477–525. Paris: Laffont: 2005b.
– *En ménage* [1881]. In *Joris-Karl Huysmans: Romans I.* General editor Pierre Brunel, 285–475. Paris: Laffont, 2005c.
– *Les sœurs Vatard* [1879]. In *Joris-Karl Huysmans: Romans I.* General editor Pierre Brunel, 67–220. Paris: Laffont, 2005d.
– *Marthe, histoire d'une fille* [1876]. In *Joris-Karl Huysmans: Romans I.* Directed by Pierre Brunel, 3–68. Paris: Laffont, 2005e.
– *À rebours* [1884]. In *Romans et nouvelles.* General editors André Guyaux and Pierre Jourde, 535–917. Paris: Pléiade, 2019.
Lambert, Pierrre, and Pierre Cogny, eds. *Lettres inédites à Edmond de Goncourt.* Paris: Nizet, 1956.
Leroux, Gaston. *Le parfum de la dame en noire* [1908]. Paris: Gallimard, 1974.
Maupassant, Guy de. *Boule de suif.* Paris: Albin Michel, 1957a.
– "La Parure" [1885]. In *Boule de suif*, 169–83. Paris: Albin Michel, 1957b.
Melville, Herman. *Moby Dick* [1851]. New York: Norton, 2018.
Proust, Marcel. *À la recherche du temps perdu* [1913–27]. 4 vols. General editor Jean-Yves Tadié. Bibilothèque de la Pléiade. Paris: Gallimard, 1987–9.
– *In Search of Lost Time.* Translated by C.K. Scott Moncrieff and Terence Kilmartin. New York: Modern Library, 2003.
Rachilde. *Monsieur Vénus* [1889]. Paris: Flammarion, 1977.
– *Monsieur Vénus* [1884]. Edited by Melanie Hawthorne and Liz Constable and translated by Melanie Hawthorne. New York: MLA, 2004.
– *Monsieur Vénus* [1884]. Translated by Melanie Hawthorne. New York: MLA, 2004.
Sand, George. *Indiana* [1832]. Paris: Gallimard, 1984.
Schaffert, Timothy. *The Perfume Thief.* New York: Penguin, 2021.
Süskind, Patrick. *Perfume: The Story of a Murder* [1985]. New York: Vintage, 2001.
Vivien, Renée. *Une femme m'apparut.* Paris: Lemerre, 1904.
– *Sillages* [1908]. Paris: Sansot, 1921.
– Vivien, René. *The Muse of the Violets: Poems by Renée Vivien.* Translated by Margaret Porter and Catherine Kroger. Tallahassee: Naiad Press, 1982.
– *A Crown of Violets.* Translated by Samantha Pious. Sequim, WA: Headmistress Press, 2015.
Wittig, Monique. *L'opoponax.* Paris: Les Éditions de Minuit, 1964.
Zola, Émile. "Livres d'aujourd'hui et de demain." *L'Évenement*, 20 March 1866.

– *La Faute de l'abbé Mouret* [1875]. In *Les Rougon-Macquart: histoire naturelle et sociale d'une famille sous le Second Empire*, vol 1. Edited by Henri Mittérand, 1213–527. Paris: Gallimard, 1961a.

– *Les Rougon-Macquart: histoire naturelle et sociale d'une famille sous le Second Empire*, vol 2. Edited by Henri Mittérand. Paris: Gallimard, 1961b.

– *Nana* [1880]. In *Les Rougon-Macquart: histoire naturelle et sociale d'une famille sous le Second Empire*, vol 2. Edited by Henri Mittérand, 1093–485. Paris: Gallimard, 1961c.

– *Au Bonheur des dames* [1883]. Paris: Gallimard, 1980.

– *La joie de vivre* [1884]. Paris: Gallimard, 1985.

– *L'Eévénement illustré. 23 avril 1868 – 26 août 1868*. In *Œuvres complétes, Chroniques politiques (1863–1870)*, vol. 1. Edited by Claude Sabatier, 251–337. Paris: Garnier, 2018.

Secondary and Non-Fiction Works

Académie française. *Dictionnaire de l'académie Française*, vol. 2 [J–Z]. Paris: Firmin Didot Frères, 1835.

Ackerman, Diane. *A Natural History of the Senses*. New York: Vintage, 1990.

Aftel, Mandy. *Essence and Alchemy: A Natural History of Perfume*. Salt Lake City: Gibbs, 2001.

Albert, Nicole G. *Renée Vivien à rebours: études pour un centenaire*. Paris: Orizons, 2009.

The Anthenaeum. "The Salon, Paris." 10 June 1882, 737.

Archibald, Anne. "The Vanity Box." *Theatre Magazine*, March 1922, 190.

Arnaud, Sabine. *On Hysteria: The Invention of a Medical Category between 1670 and 1820*. Chicago: Chicago University Press, 2015.

Arnold, Paul. *Esotérisme de Baudelaire*. Paris: Vrin, 1972.

Ashley, Katherine. "Policing Prostitutes: Adaptations and Reactions to Edmond de Goncourt's *La Fille Elisa*." *Nineteenth-Century French Studies* 33, nos. 1–2 (2004–5): 135–46.

– *Edmond de Goncourt and the Novel: Naturalism and Decadence*. Amsterdam: Rodopi, 2005.

Atkinson, George William. *Perfumes and Their Preparation*. New York: Henley, 1892.

Auclerc, Benoît. "'On dit qu'on est l'opoponax": invention lexicale, innommé, nomination." In *Lire Monique Wittig aujourd'hui*, edited by Benoît Auclerc and Yannick Chevalier, 257–79. Lyon: Presses Universitaires de Lyon, 2012.

Auclerc, Benoît, and Yannick Chevalier, eds. *Lire Monique Wittig aujourd'hui*. Lyon: Presses Universitaires de Lyon, 2012.

Aufderheide, Arthur C. *The Scientific Study of Mummies*. Cambridge: Cambridge University Press, 2003.

Axenfeld, A. *Traité des névroses*, 2nd ed. Paris: Baillière, 1883.

Azoulai, Juliette. "Le savoir médical dans la scène des abricots." In *Madame Bovary et les savoirs*, edited by Pierre-Louis Rey and Gisèle Séginger, 231–41. Paris: Presses Sorbonne Nouvelle, 2009.

B.E. "Notices bibliographiques." *La Revue de France* 14 (1875): 330–7.

Bader, Jean-Michel. "Le relique de Jeanne d'Arc est une momie d'Egypte." *Le Figaro*, 5 April 2007. https://www.lefigaro.fr/sciences/2007/04/05/01008 -20070405ARTFIG90024-la_relique_de_jeanne_d_arc_est_une_momie_d _egypte.php.

Bajomée, Danielle, Juliette Dor, and Marie-Élisabeth Henneau, eds. *Femmes et livres*. Liege: l'Harmattan, 2007.

Balsam, Marvin S., and Edward Sagarin, eds. *Cosmetics Science and Technology*. 3 vols. 2nd ed. New York: Wiley, 1972.

Bandy, W.T., and Claude Pichois. *Baudelaire devant ses contemporains* [1957]. Paris: Klincksieck, 1995.

Barbe, Simon. *Le parfumeur françois*. Lyon: Amaulry, 1693.

Barillé, Élisabeth. *Guerlain*. Paris: Assouline, 1999.

Barnes, David S. *The Great Stink of Paris and the Nineteenth-Century Struggle against Filth and Germs*. Baltimore: Johns Hopkins University Press, 2006.

Barthes, Roland. "L'Effet de réel." *Communications* 11 (1968): 84–8.

– *The Pleasure of the Text*. Translated by Richard Miller. New York: Hill and Wang, 1975.

– "Le Dandysime et la mode" [1962]. In *Le bleu est à la mode cette année et autres articles*, 97–103. Paris: Éditions de l'Institut français de la Mode, 2001.

Bartholow, Roberts. *A Manual of Hypodermic Medication: The Treatment of Diseases by the Hypodermic Method*, 4th ed. Philadelphia: Lippincott, 1882.

Bayle, Marie-Claude. *'Chérie' d'Edmond de Goncourt*. Naples: Edizioni scientifiche italiane, 1983.

Bear, Isabel J., and Richard G. Thomas. "The Nature of Argillaceous Odor." *Nature* 4923 (7 March 1964): 993–5.

Beizer, Janet. *Ventriloquized Bodies: Narratives of Hysteria in Nineteenth-Century France*. Ithaca, NY: Cornell University Press, 1994.

Benjamin, Mark. "Francis Kurkdjian, Hitting the Right Notes." *Rain*, 17 July 2020. https://rain-mag.com/francis-kurkdjian-hitting-the-right-notes/.

Bérard, P.-H. "Olfaction." *Dictionnaire de médecine*, 2nd ed., vol. 22. Paris: Béchet, 1840, 11–22.

Berenstein, Nadia. "Flavor Added: The Sciences of Flavor and the Industrialization of Taste in America." PhD diss., University of Pennsylvania, 2018.

Bernard, Léo de. "Courrier de la Mode." *Le monde illustré*, 17 December 1859, 394–5.

Bernard, Léopold. *Les odeurs dans les romans de Zola: conférence faite au cercle artistique*. Montpellier: Coulet, 1889.

Bernheimer, Charles. "The Decadent Subject," *Esprit Créateur* 32, no. 1 (1992): 53–62.

– *Figures of Ill Repute: Representing Prostitution in Nineteenth-Century France*. Durham, NC: Duke University Press, 1997.

Berthier, Patrick. "Balzac romancier épistolaire." *Revue belge de philologie et d'histoire* 70, no. 3 (1992): 641–53.

Bertrand, Antoine. *Curiosités esthétiques de Robert de Montesquiou*. Geneva: Droz, 1996.

Bertrand, C.F. *Le parfumeur impérial*. Paris: Brunot-Labbé, 1809.

Bessou, Marie-Ange Bartholomot. *L'imaginaire du féminin dans l'œuvre de Renée Vivien*. Clermont-Ferrand: Presses Universitaires Blaise Pascal, 2004.

Best, Kate Nelson. *The History of Fashion Journalism*. London: Bloomsbury, 2017.

Billot, Marcel, and F.V. Wells. *Perfumery Technology: Art, Science, Industry*. New York: Halsted, 1975.

Bloy, Léon. *Sur la tombe de Huysmans*. Paris: Curiosités Littéraires, 1913.

Blum, Léon. *Du mariage* [1907]. Paris: Albin Michel, 1947.

Borloz, Sophie-Valentine. *"Les Femmes qui se parfument doivent être admirées de loin": les odeurs féminines dans* Nana *de Zola.* Notre Cœur *de Maupassant et* l'Eve future *de Villiers de L'Isle-Adam*. Lausanne: Archipel, 2015.

– "Le parfum de l'inverti." *Littératures* 81 (2019): 131–42.

– "'L'odorat a ses monstres': olfaction et perversion dans l'imaginaire fin-de-siècle (1880–1905)." PhD diss., University of Lausanne, 2020.

Bourdieu, Pierre. *Distinction: A Social Critique of the Judgement of Taste*. Cambridge, MA: Harvard University Press, 1984.

Bourneville, Désiré Magloire, and Paul Bricon. *Manuel des injections sous-cutanées*. Paris: Delahaye, 1883.

Boy-Tessier. "De l'angine de poitrine symptomatique...." *Revue internationale de bibliographie médicale, pharmaceutique, et vétérinaire*. 5, no. 2 (10 January 1894): 19.

Bradstreet, Christina. "Wicked with Roses: Floral Femininity and the Erotics of Scent." *Nineteenth-Century Art Worldwide* 6, no. 1 (2007). http://www.19thc-artworldwide.org/spring07/144-qwicked-with-rosesq-floral-femininity-and-the-erotics-of-scent.

Brey, Iris. *Le regard féminin*. Paris: l'Olivier, 2020.

Briand, Joseph. *Manuel complet de l'hygiène*. Brussels: Tircher, 1836.

Bridges, Ann, ed. *Alphonse Mucha: The Complete Graphic Works*. New York: Harmony, 1980.

Brieude, Jean-Jaques. *Mémoire sur les odeurs que nous exhalons, considérés comme signes de la santé et des maladies: histoire de la société royale de médecine*. Paris: l'École de santé de Paris, 1789, xlv–lxv.

Briot, Eugénie. "Couleurs de peau, odeurs de peau: le parfum de la femme et ses typologies au XIXᵉ siècle." *Corps* 2, no. 3 (2007): 47–63.

– "De l'eau impériale aux violettes parfum du Czar: le jeu social des élégances olfactives dans le Paris du XIXᵉ siècle." *Revue d'histoire moderne et contemporaine* 55, no. 1 (2008): 28–49.

– "From Industry to Luxury: French Perfume in the Nineteenth Century." *Business History Review* 85, no. 2 (2011): 273–94.

– "Imiter les matières premières naturelles: les corps odorants de synthèse, voie du luxe et de la démocratisation pour la parfumerie du XIXᵉ siècle." *Entreprises et Histoire* 1, no. 78 (2015a): 60–73.

– *La Fabrique des parfums: naissance d'une industrie de luxe.* Paris: Vendémiaire, 2015b.

Briquet, Pierre. *Traité clinique et thérapeutique de l'hystérie.* Paris: Baillière, 1859.

Brunel, Pierre. "*À rebours*: du catalogue au roman." In *Huysmans: une esthétique de la décadence*, edited by André Guyaux, Christian Heck, and Robert Kopp, 13–21. Geneva: Slatkine, 1987.

Bullen, F. St. John. "Olfactory Hallucinations in the Insane." *The British Journal of Psychiatry* 190 (July 1899): 513–33.

Burr, Chandler. "Ghost Flowers." *The New York Times*, 25 February 2007. https://www.nytimes.com/2007/02/25/style/tmagazine/25tghost.html.

– *The Perfect Scent: A Year Inside the Perfume Industry in Paris and New York.* New York: Holt, 2007.

Butler, Delcan. "Joan of Arc's Relics Exposed as Forgery." *Nature* 446 (5 April 2007): 593. https://www.nature.com/articles/446593a.

Cabanès Augustin. *Grands névropathes. Malades immortels.* Vol. 3. Paris: Albin Michel, 1930–5.

– "Un chaptire de physiologie littéraire. Le nez dans l'œuvre de Zola." *La Chronique médicale* 46 (15 November 1895): 680–5.

– *La peste dans l'imagination populaire.* Paris: Société d'éditions scientifiques, 1901.

– *Les cinq sens.* Paris: Le François, 1926.

Cabanès, Jean-Louis, ed. *Les frères Goncourt: art et littérature.* Bordeaux: Presses Universitaires de Bordeaux, 1997.

Cabanès, Jean-Louis, and Philippe Hamon. "Preface." In *Chérie*, edited by Jean-Louis Cabanès and Philippe Hamon, 7–37. Jaignes: La Chasse au Snark, 2002.

Camps, Arcadi Boix. *Perfumery: Techniques in Evolution*, 2nd ed. Morrisville, NC: Lulu Press, 2017.

Candau, Joël. *Mémoire et expériences olfactives: anthropologie d'un savoir-faire sensoriel.* Paris: PUF, 2000.

Candau, Joël, and Agnès Jeanjean. "Des odeurs à ne pas regarder...." *Terrain* 47 (2006): 51–68.

Candau, Joël, and Olivier Wathelet. "Les catégories d'odeurs en sont-elles vraiment?" *Langages* 181 (2011): 37–52.

Carlisle, Janice. *Common Scents: Comparative Encounters in High-Victorian Fiction*. Oxford: Oxford University Press, 2004.

Catalogue des produits de l'industrie française admis à l'exposition publique, rapport du jury central sur les produits de l'industrie française. Paris: Fain et Thunot, 1834.

Caufeynon, Docteur [Jean Fauconney]. *La volupté et les parfums*. Paris: Offenstadt, 1903.

Cazenave, Alphée. *De la décoration humaine. Hygiène de la beauté*. Paris: Daffis, 1867.

Celnart, Madame. *Manuel des dames, ou art de la toilette*. Paris Roret, 1827.

– *Manuel du fleuriste artificiel, ou l'art d'imiter d'après la nature*. Paris: Roret, 1829.

– *Manuel des dames, ou l'art de l'élégance*. 2nd ed. Paris: Roret, 1833.

– *Nouveau Manuel complet d'économie domestique*. 3rd ed. Paris: Roret, 1837.

– *Nouveau Manuel complet du parfumeur*. Paris: Roret, 1854.

Cerbelaud, René. *Formulaire des principales spécialités de parfumerie et de pharmacie* [1908]. Paris: Cerbelaud, 1920.

Cerulo, Karen A. "Scents and Sensibility: Olfaction, Sense-Making, and Meaning Attribution." *American Sociological Review* 83, no. 2 (2018): 361–89.

Cevasco, G.A. *The Breviary of the Decadence: J.-K. Huysmans's* À Rebours *and English Literature*. New York: AMS, 2001.

Chambers, Ross. "Modern Beauty: Baudelaire, the Everyday, Cultural Studies." *Romance Studies* 26, no. 3 (2008): 249–70.

Chavant, Ferdinand, *La peste à Grenoble 1410–1643*. Lyon: Storck, 1903.

Chicago Daily Tribune. "Injecting Perfume into the Blood." (18 July 1891): 16.

– "About Perfume and Its Abuse." (12 May 1908): 10.

– "Perfume as a Drink Is Fatal." (14 May 1910): 5.

Chrestien, Jean André. *De la méthode ïatraleptique, ou observations pratiques sur l'efficacité des remèdes administrés par la voie de l'absorption cutanée dans le traitement de plusieurs maladies internes et externes*. Paris: Crouillebois, 1811.

Classen, Constance. *Worlds of Sense: Exploring the Senses in History and across Cultures*. London: Routledge, 1993.

– *The Color of Angels: Cosmology, Gender, and the Aesthetic Imagination*. London: Routledge, 1998.

Classen, Constance, David Howes, and Anthony Synnott. *Aroma: The Cultural History of Smell*. London: Routledge, 1994.

Classification officielle des parfums et terminologie. Versailles: Comité français du parfum, 2010.

Claye, Louis. *Les talismans de la beauté*. Paris, 1861.

Clérambault, Gaëtan Gatian de. *Passion érotique des étoffes chez la femme* [1908 and 1910]. Edited by Yves Edel. Paris: Les Empêcheurs de penser en rond, 2002.

Cloquet, Hippolyte. *Osphrésiologie ou traité des odeurs, du sens et des organes de l'olfaction*, 2nd ed. Paris: Méquignon-Marvis, 1821.

Cohen, Emily-Jane. "Mud into Gold: Baudelaire and the Alchemy of Public Hygiene." *Romanic Review* 87, no. 2 (March 1996): 239–56.

Combe, Antoine. *Influence des parfums et des odeurs sur les névropathes et les hystériques*. Paris: A. Michalon, 1905.

Comtesse Xila. "Les Parfums." *La Grande Dame: revue de l'élégance et des arts*, vol. 1, 1893. 221–4.

Corbin, Alain. *Le miasme et la jonquille: l'odorat et l'imaginaire social, XVIIIe-XIXe siècles*. Paris: Aubier Montaigne, 1982.

– *The Foul and the Fragrant: Odor and the French Social Imagination*. Cambridge, MA: Harvard University Press, 1986.

–, ed. *L'avènement des loisirs: 1858–1960*. Paris: Flammarion, 2001.

"Corpse Flower (*Amorphophallus titanium*)." *The Huntington*. https://www .huntington.org/corpse-flower.

Cory, Donald Webster [Edward Sagarin]. *The Homosexual in America: A Subjective Approach*. New York: Greenberg, 1951.

"Courrier de la Mode." *La revue illustrée* 171 (15 January 1893).

Crépet, Eugène. *Charles Baudelaire biographique*, 3rd ed. Paris: Vanier, 1908.

Cressot, Marcel. *La phrase et le vocabulaire de J.-K Huysmans*. Paris: Droz, 1938.

Cryle, Peter. "The Aesthetics of Spasm." In *Sexuality at the Fin de Siècle: The Makings of a "Central Problem,"* edited by Peter Cryle and Christopher E. Forth, 77–92. Newark: University of Delaware Press, 2008.

Cryle, Peter, and Christopher E. Forth, eds. *Sexuality at the Fin de Siècle: The Makings of a "Central Problem."* Newark: University of Delaware Press, 2008.

Culler, Jonathan. "Intertextuality and Interpretation: Baudelaire's 'Correspondances.'" In *Nineteenth-Century French Poetry*, edited by Christopher Prendergast, 118–37. Cambridge: Cambridge University Press, 1990.

Cummins, Genevieve, and Nerylla D. Taunton. *Chatelaines: Utility to Glorious Extravagance*. Aberdeen: Antique Collectors Club, 1994.

Curtis, Tony. "The Development of Odor Language between Professionals in the Aroma Trades Industry." In *Sense and Scent: The Exploration of Olfactory Meaning*, edited by Bronwen Martin and Felizitas Ringham, 57–78. London: Philomel, 2003.

Dann, Kevin T. *Bright Colors Falsely Seen: Synesthesia and the Search for Transcendental Knowledge*. New Haven, CT: Yale University Press, 1998.

David, Sophie. "Linguistic Expressions for Odors in French." In *Olfaction. Taste, and Cognition*, edited by Catherine Rouby et al., 82–99. Cambridge: Cambridge University Press, 2002.

Debay, Auguste. *Nouveau manuel du parfumeur chimiste*. Paris: Dentu, 1856.

– *Les parfums et les fleurs*. Paris: Dentu, 1861.

– *Les parfums de la toilette et des cosmétiques les plus favorables à la beauté sans nuire à la santé*. Paris: Dentu, 1884.

Dechembre, A. *Dictionnaire encyclopédique des sciences médicales*, vol. 3. Paris: Asselin/Masson, 1865.

– *Dictionnaire encyclopédique des sciences médicales*, vol. 5. Paris: Asselin/Masson, 1866–9.

De Flers, Robert. *Ilsée, Princesse de Tripoli*. Paris: Piazza, 1897.

Delord, Taxile. *Physiologie de la Parisienne*. Paris: Aubert, 1841.

Delzant, Alidor. *Les Goncourt*. Paris: Charpentier, 1889.

De Man, Paul. "Anthropomorphism and Trope in the Lyric." In *The Rhetoric of Romanticism*, 239–62. New York: Columbia University Press, 1984a.

– *The Rhetoric of Romanticism*. New York: Columbia University Press, 1984b.

Desmarais, Jane. *Monsters under Glass: A Cultural History of Hothouse Flowers from 1850 to the Present*. London: Reaktion, 2018.

Dictionnaire de médecine, 2nd ed., vol. 22. Paris: Béchet, 1840.

Digonnet, Rémi. *Métaphore et olfaction: une approche cognitive*. Paris: Champion, 2016.

Donnard, Jean-Hervé. *Balzac. Les réalités économiques et sociales dans* La comédie humaine. Paris: Colin, 1961.

Drobnick, Jim, ed. *The Smell Culture Reader*. Oxford: Berg, 2006.

Duchesne, Alphonse. "Echos de Paris." *Figaro: Journal non politique* 11 (18 June 1859): 6.

Dufaux de la Jonchère, Ermance. *Le savoir-vivre dans la vie ordinaire et dans les cérémonies civiles et religieuses*. Paris: Garnier, 1883.

Duffy, Larry. "Madame Bovary and the Institutional Transformation of Pharmacy." *Dix-Neuf* 15, no. 1 (2011): 70–82.

Dufief, Anne-Simone. "Devenir femme? L'éducation des filles dans l'œuvre des Goncourt." *Cahiers Edmond et Jules de Goncourt* 15 (2008): 123–41.

Dugan, Holly. *The Ephemeral History of Perfume: Scent and Sense in Early Modern England*. Baltimore: Johns Hopkins University Press, 2011.

Dumas, F.-G. *Catalgue illustrée du salon*. Paris: Baschet, 1886.

Dumas, Georges. "L'odeur de sainteté" in *La revue de Paris* (November–December 1907): 531–52.

Dupuis, Danielle. "*César Birotteau*: de la publicité à la littérature." *L'année balzacienne* 9 (2008): 283–300.

Dussauce, Hippolyte. *A Practical Guide for the Perfumer: Being a New Treatise on Perfumery the Most Favorable to Beauty without Being Injurious to the Health.* London: Trübner, 1868.

Duzer, Virginie A. "Le fruit défendu." *Romantisme* 165 (2014): 3–12.

Eco, Umberto. *Le vertige de la liste.* Paris: Flammarion, 2009.

Edwards, Michael. *Quarterly Insights.* October–December 2020.

Ellena, Jean-Claude. *Journal d'un parfumeur.* Paris: Wespieser, 2011a.

– *Perfume: The Alchemy of Scent.* Translated by John Crisp. New York: Arcade, 2011b.

– *The Diary of a Nose: A Year in the Life of a Perfumer.* New York: Rizzoli, 2013.

– *L'écrivain d'odeurs.* Nez-Le Contrepoint, 2017.

Emery, Elizabeth. "*Le voile du bonheur*: Le brûle-parfum, objet de sociabilité à la fin du XIXe siècle en France." *Littérature* 185 (March 2017): 81–96.

Encyclopédie méthodique. Médecine vol. 2. Paris: Pancoucke, 1790.

Ender, Evelyne. *Sexing the Mind: Nineteenth-Century Fictions of Hysteria.* Ithaca, NY: Cornell University Press, 1995.

Espelly and Le Febvre, *Ordonnances de M. Espelly.* Amiens: Hubault, 1668.

Etienne, Jean. "La relique de Jeanne d'Arc était un morceau de momie égyptienne." *Futura Sciences* 5 April 2007. https://www.futura-sciences .com/sciences/actualites/recherche-relique-jeanne-arc-etait-morceau -momie-egyptienne-10634/.

Evans, David. "Forests of Symbols and Patterns of Meaning: Reading Poetry through Baudelaire's 'Correspondances.'" In *Critical Insights: The Poetry of Baudelaire,* edited by Tom Hubbard, 39–156. Amenia, NY: Grey House, 2014.

Evans, Martha Noel. *Fits and Starts: A Genealogy of Hysteria in Modern France.* Ithaca, NY: Cornell University Press, 1991.

Fauconney, Jean. *See* Caufeynon.

Faure, Gabriel. "Le souvenir de Zola." *Chanteclair* 293 (March–April 933): 245.

Fellous, Colette. *Guerlain.* Paris: Denoël, 1989.

Féydeau, Elisabeth de. *A Scented Palace: The Secret Story of Marie Antoinette's Perfumer.* London: I.B. Tauris, 2006.

– *Les parfums: histoire, anthologie, dictionnaire.* Paris: Laffont, 2011a.

– *La grande histoire du parfum.* Paris: Larousse, 2019.

Feydeau, Ernest. *L'art de plaire.* Paris: Lévy, 1873.

Figuier, Louis. *L'année scientifique et industrielle: ou exposé annuel des travaux scientifiques, des inventions et des principales applications de la science à l'industrie et aux arts, qui ont attiré l'attention publique en France et à l'étranger.* Paris: Hachette, 1891.

Finger, Stanley. *Origins of Neuroscience: A History of Explorations into Brain Function.* Oxford: Oxford University Press, 1994.

Finn, Michael. *Hysteria, Hypnotism, the Sprits, and Pornography: Fin-de-siècle Cultural Discourses in the Decadent Rachilde*. Newark: University of Delaware Press, 2009.

Fleury, Maurice de. "Le Paris des Parisiens: l'art des parfums," I and II. *Le Figaro. Supplément littéraire*, 15 March 1890, 41–2, and 22 March 1890, 46–7.

Fleury, René [René-Albert]. "L'art des parfums." *La Vogue*, 15 January 1900, 38–46.

– *Le cadavre et les roses*. Nevers: Cahiers Nivernais, 1912.

Fliess, Wilhelm. *Les relations entre le nez et les organes génitaux féminins présentés selon leurs significations biologiques* [1896]. Translated by Patrick Ach and Jean Guir. Paris: Seuil, 1977.

Fontan, Geneviève. "Les étiquettes de parfumerie." *Parfum Art et Valeur* 18 (November–December 1993): 8–12.

– *Cote générale des cartes parfumées*. Toulouse: Arfon, 1997.

Fortassier, Rose. "Balzac et le roman par lettres." *Cahiers de l l'AIEF* 29 (1977): 205–21.

Fosca, Françis. *Edmond et Jules de Goncourt*. Paris: Albin Michel, 1941.

Franklin, Alfred. *La civilité, l'étiquette, la mode, le bon ton du XIIIe au XIXe siècle*, vol. 2. Paris: Émile-Paul, 1908.

Freud, Sigmund. *Civilization and Its Discontents*. Translated by James Strachey. New York: Norton, 2010.

Frey, E. "La Langue chez J.-K. Huysmans." In *Mélanges de philologie offert à Ferdinand Brunot*, 163–88. Paris: Société nouvelle de librairie et d'édition, 1904.

Friedman, Emily. *Reading Smell in Eighteenth-Century Fiction*. Lewisburg, PA: Bucknell University Press, 2016.

Gacon-Dufour, Marie. *Manuel du parfumeur*. Paris: Roret, 1825.

Gallais, Jean-Pierre. *Mœurs et Caractères du XIXe siècle*, vol 1. Paris: Belin-Le Prieur, 1817.

Gallemin, Jean Louis. "Line and Form – the 'Mucha Style.'" In *Alphonse Mucha*, edited by Agnes Husslein-Arco, Jean Louis Gaillemin, Michel Hilaire, and Christiane Lange, 11–15. Munich: Prestel, 2009.

Galopin, Augustin. *Le Parfum de la femme et le sens olfactif dans l'amour*. Paris: Dentu, 1886.

Gardeton, César. *Dictionnaire de la beauté ou la toilette sans dangers*. Paris: Cordier, 1826.

– *Nouveau guide des dîneurs*. Paris: J. Breauté, 1828.

Gazette de France. "Variétés." (4 September 1818): 1033–6.

Geczy, Adam. *Fashion and Orientalism: Dress, Textiles and Culture from the 17th to the 21st century*. London: Bloomsbury, 2013.

Gencé, Comtesse de. *Cabinet de toilette d'une honnête femme*. Paris: Albin Michel, 1909a.

– *Code mondain de la jeune fille*. Paris: Albin Michel, 1909b.

Genlis, Stéphanie Félicité (comtesse de). *La botanique historique et littéraire*. Vol. 1. Paris: Maradan, 1810.

Gibbons, Boyd. "The Intimate Sense of Smell." *National Geographic* 170, no. 3 (September 1986): 324–61.

Gilbert, Avery. *What the Nose Knows: The Science of Scent in Everyday Life*. New York: Crown, 2008.

Giraud, Barbara. *L'héroïne goncourtienne. Entre hystérie et dissidence*. Bern: Peter Lang, 2009.

Gobet, Magalie, and Emmeline Le Gall. *Le parfum*. Paris: Champion, 2011.

Goldstein, Jan. *Console and Classify: The French Psychiatric Profession in the Nineteenth Century*. Cambridge: Cambridge University Press, 1987.

González, Julio, Alfonso Barros-Loscertales, Friedemann Pulvermüller, Vanessa Meseguer, Ana Sanjuán, Vincente Belloch, and César Ávila. "Reading *Cinnamon* Activates Olfactory Brain Regions." *Neuroimage* 32, no. 2 (2006): 906–12.

Goupil and Cie. *L'exposition des beaux arts: salon de 1882*. Paris: Baschet, 1882.

Gourmont, Rémy. "Les jeunes filles" [1907]. In *La culture des idées*, 730–3. Paris: Laffont, 2008.

Grandville, J.J., and Alphonse Karr. *Les fleurs animés*. 2 vols. Paris: Gabriel de Gonet, 1847.

Grasset, Joseph. "La supériorité intellectuelle et la névrose." In *Leçons de clinique médicale faites à l'hôpital Saint-Éloi de Montpellier avril 1898 à décembre 1902*, 683–723. Montpellier: Couet et Fils, 1903a.

– *Leçons de clinique médicale faites à l'hôpital Saint-Éloi de Montpellier: Avril 1898 à Décembre 1902*. Montpellier: Coulet et Fils, 1903b.

Gray, Richard T. "Dialectic of 'Enscentment': Patrick Süskind's *Das Parfum* as Critical History of Enlightenment Culture." *PMLA* 108, no. 3 (May 1993): 489–505.

Green, John P. "Cosmetics and Conflicting Fictions in Balzac's *César Birotteau*." *Neophilologus* 83, no. 2 (1999): 197–208.

Grimod de La Reynière, Alexandre. "Promenade d'un Gourmand au Palais-Royal." In Simond, *La vie parisienne à travers le XIX siècle: Paris de 1800–1900*, vol. 1, 50–2. Paris: Plon, 1900.

Grout, Holly. *The Force of Beauty: Transforming French Ideas of Femininity in the Third Republic*. Baton Rouge: Louisiana State University Press, 2015.

Guerlain. Advertisement. *Theatre Magazine*, December 1922, 407.

Guyaux, André. "Huysmans et le lexique baudelairien." *Cahiers de AIEF* 60 (2008): 301–11.

Hammond, William A. "The Odor of the Human Body as Developed by Certain Affections of the Nervous System." In *Transactions of the American*

Neurological Association for 1877, vol. 2. edited by E.C. Seguin, 17–23. New York: G.P. Putnam's Sons, 1877.

Hamon, Philippe. "Autour de *Chérie*." Jean-Louis Cabanès 275–85.

Harrington, Anne, and Vernon Rosario. "Olfaction and the Primitive: Nineteenth-Century Thinking on Olfaction." In *Science and Olfaction*, edited by Michael J. Serby and Karen L. Chobor, 3–27. New York: Springer-Verlag, 1992.

Havelock Ellis. *Studies in the Psychology of Sex: Sexual Selection in Man*, vol. 4. Philadelphia: Davis, 1905.

Hawthorne, Melanie. "La vie des morts." In *Renée Vivien à rebours: Études sur un centenaire*, edited by Nicole C. Albert, 181–91. Paris: Orizons, 2009.

– *Women, Citizenship, and Sexuality: The Transnational Lives of Renée Vivien, Romaine Brooks, and Natalie Barney*. Liverpool: Liverpool University Press, 2021.

Hemmings, F.W.J. "Zola's Apprenticeship to Journalism (1865–70)." *PMLA* 71, no. 3 (June 1956): 340–54.

Hiner, Susan. *Accessories to Modernity: Fashion and the Feminine in Nineteenth Century France*. Philadelphia: University of Pennsylvania Press, 2010.

– "From *pudeur* to *plaisir*: Grandville's Flowers in the Kingdom of Fashion." *Dix-Neuf* 18, no. 1 (2014): 45–68.

Holler, André. "Les trois piliers de l'art du parfum." In *L'Art olfactif contemporain*, edited by Chantal Jaquet, 55–61. Paris: Garnier, 2015.

Holmes, Diana. *Rachilde: Decadence, Gender and the Woman Writer*. Oxford: Berg, 2001.

hooks, bell. *Black Looks: Race and Representation*. Boston: South End Press, 1992.

Hornot, Antoine. *See* Dejean.

Howes, David. "Le sens sans parole: vers une anthropologie de l'odorat." *Anthropologie et sociétés* 10, no. 3 (1986): 29–45.

– *Sensual Relations: Engaging the Senses in Culture and Social Theory*. Ann Arbor: University of Michigan Press, 2003.

Hubbard, Tom. *Critical Insights: The Poetry of Baudelaire*. Ipswich, MA: Salem Press, 2014.

Husslein-Arco, Agnes, Jean Louis Gaillemin, Michel Hilaire, and Christiane Lange, eds. *Alphonse Mucha*. Munich: Prestel, 2009.

Igou, Anna. "Nothing Consumed: The Dangerous Space of Food in *Madame Bovary*." *French Forum* 38, nos. 1–2 (2013): 35–50.

Ingraham, Charles Wilson. "A Practical Mode of Administering Iodine Hypodermically in the Treatment of Pulmonary Tuberculosis." *Medical Record* 54, no.14 (1898): 483–4.

Jack, Belinda. *The Woman Reader*. New Haven, CT: Yale University Press, 2012

James, Constantin. *Toilette d'une Romaine au temps d'Auguste et cosmétiques d'une Parisienne au XIXe siècle*. Paris: Hachette, 1865.

Jaquet, Chantal. *Philosophie de l'odorat*. Paris: PUF, 2010.

–, ed. *L'art olfactif contemporain*. Paris: Garnier, 2015.

Jarvis, Brooke. "What Can Covid-19 Teach Us about the Mysteries of Smell?" *The New York Times Magazine*, 28 January 2021. https://www.nytimes.com /2021/01/28/magazine/covid-smell-science.html.

Jay, Karla. *The Amazon and the Page: Natalie Clifford Barney and Renée Vivien*. Bloomington: Indiana University Press, 1988.

Johnston, James. *The Common Chemistry of Modern Life*. Vol. 1. New York: Appleton, 1855.

Jones, Geoffrey. *Beauty Imagined: A History of the Global Beauty Industry*. Oxford: Oxford University Press, 2010.

Jørgensen, Jens Lohfert. "The Bacteriological Modernism of Joris-Karl Huysmans's *Against Nature*." *Literature and Medicine* 31, no. 1 (Spring 2013): 91–113.

Journal des couturières et modistes. "Mode et Fashions." (30 September 1848).

Jouysse, D. *Bref discours de la préservation et de la cure de la peste*. Amiens: Hubault, 1668.

Kalba, Laura Anne. *Color in the Age of Impressionism: Commerce, Technology, and Art*. University Park: Pennsylvania State University Press, 2017.

Kane, Harry Hubbell. *The Hypodermic Injection of Morphia: Its History, Advantages, and Dangers (Based on the Experience of 360 Doctors)*. New York: Bermingham, 1880.

Katsaros, Laure. "Goncourt's Dream Night: Terrors in *La Fille Elisa*." *French Forum* 36, nos. 2–3 (2011): 61–78.

Kawakami, Akane. *Travellers' Visions: French Literary Encounters with Japan*. Liverpool: Liverpool University Press, 2005.

Keller, Luzius. *Marcel Proust: la fabrique de combray*. Geneva: Zoe, 2006.

Kemp, Christopher. *Floating Gold: A Natural (and Unnatural) History of Ambergris*. Chicago: University of Chicago Press, 2012.

Kettler, Andrew. "Making the Synthetic Epic: Septimus Piesse, the Manufacturing of Mercutio Frangipani, and Olfactory Renaissance in Victorian England." *The Senses and Society* 10, no. 1 (2015): 5–25.

Kiernan, James G. "Ozolagny." *The Urologic and Cutaneous Review*, 26, no. 7 (July 1922): 413–17.

Kleiber, Georges, and Marcel Vuillaume. "Pour une linguistique des odeurs: présentation." *Langages* 181 (2011): 3–15.

Kragh, Jesper Vaczy. "Women, Men, and the Morphine Problem, 1870–1955. In *Gendered Drugs and Medicine: Historical and Socio-Cultural Perspectives*, edited by Teresa Ortiz-Gómez and Maria Jesús Santesmases, 177–98. London: Routledge, 2016.

Krause, Virginia, and Christian Martin. "'Une charogne' or *Les Amours* Decomposed: Corpse, *Corpora and Corpus*." *Romanic Review* 89, no. 3 (1998): 321–31.

Krueger, Cheryl. "Flâneur Smellscapes in *Le spleen de Paris*." *Dix-neuf* 16, no. 2 (2012): 181–92.

- "The Scent Trail of 'Une Charogne.'" *French Forum* 38, nos. 1–2 (2013): 51–68.
- "Decadent Perfume: Under the Skin and through the Page." *Modern Languages Open* (20 October 2014): 1–33.
- "Lettres parfumées, correspondances fatales." *Littérature* 185 (2017): 39–54.

Labruyère, Georges de. "Les morphinomanes." *Le Figaro*, 1 June 1886.

LaCapra, Dominick. *Madame Bovary on Trial*. Ithaca, NY: Cornell University Press, 1982.

Lacey, Simon, et al. "Metaphorically Feeling: Comprehending Textural Metaphors Activates Somatosensory Cortex." *Brain and Language* 120, no. 3 (2012): 416–21.

Ladenson, Elisabeth. *Dirt for Art's Sake: Books on Trial from* Madame Bovary *to* Lolita. Ithaca, NY: Cornell University Press, 2007.

Lancey, Sybil de. "La mode et les modes." *Les modes: revue illustrée des Arts décoratifs appliqués à la femme* 20 (August 1902): 16–22.

L'ancien et le nouveau langage des fleurs. Paris: Le Bailly, 1858.

Laplace, M.F. "Historique de l'introduction, de l'hybridation et des variétés d'iris du groupe apogon." In *Les iris cultivé: actes et comptes rendus de la première conférence internationale des iris, tenue à Paris 1922*. Paris: Au siège de la Société, 1923, 121–9.

Lardellier, Pascal, ed. *À fleur de peau: corps, odeurs et parfums*. Paris: Belin, 2003.

Larousse, Pierre. *Grand dictionnaire universel du XIXe siècle, 1866–1877*, vol. 14. Paris: Administration du Grand Dictionnaire Universel, 1875.
- *Le larousse pour tous: nouveau dictionnaire encyclopédique*, vol. 2. Paris: Larousse, 1907–10.

Lasowski, Patrick Wald. "Le faux Joris-Karl Huysmans." *Revue des Sciences Humaines* 170–1 (1978): 158–72.

Laurent, Émile. *La poésie décadente devant la science psychiatrique*. Paris: Maloine, 1897.

Le Breton, David. "Les mises en scène olfactive de l'autre ou les imaginaires du mépris." In *À fleur de peau*, edited by Pascal Lardellier, 115–28. Paris: Belin, 2003.
- *La saveur du monde. Une anthropologie des sens*. Paris: Métailié, 2015.

Le Camus, Antoine. *Abdeker, ou l'art de conserver la beauté* [1754]. Edited by Alexandre Wenger. Millon: Grenoble, 2008.

Lefebvre, Henri. *The Production of Space*. Translated by Donald Nicholson-Smith. Oxford: Blackwell, 1991.

Lefebvre, Thierry, and Cécile Raynal. "Le Lance-parfum. Un matériel médical devenu accessoire de carnaval." *Revue d'histoire de la pharmacie* 95, no. 357 (2008): 63–79.

Lefranc, Jacques. "Le courrier de la semaine." *Le Petit Parisien: supplément littéraire illustré* (6 January 1895): 138.

Le Guérer, Annick. *Scent: The Essential and Mysterious Powers of Smell*. New York: Kodansha, 1992.

– "Le Nez d'Emma. Histoire de l'odorat dans la psychanalyse." *Revue internationale de psychopathologie* 22 (1996): 339–85.

– *Le parfum: des origines à nos jours*. Paris: Odile Jacob, 2005.

Leidekerke, Arnould de. *La Belle Époque de l'opium*. Éditions de la Différence, 2001.

Lemery, Nicolas. *Pharmacopée universelle*, vol. 1, 5th ed. Paris: Saillant, 1763–4.

Les iris cultivés. Actes et comptes rendus de la première conférence internationale des iris, tenue à Paris 1922. Paris: Au siège de la société, 1923.

Le Véteran. "Les Buveuses d'eau de Cologne." (14 February 1904): 4.

Levy, Gayle. "'J'ai été très amusé(e)': Renée Vivien et l'(auto)mythologization à travers une lettre inédite." In *Renée Vivien à rebours: études pour un centenaire*, edited by Nicole G. Albert, 129–40. Paris: Orizons, 2009.

Lheuruex, Rosine. *Une histoire des parfumeurs: France 1850–1910*. Ceyzérieu: Champ Vallon, 2016.

Lipp, Ronald. "Alphonse Mucha: The Message and the Man." In *Alphonse Mucha*, edited by Mucha, Sarah Mucha, 10–21. London: Frances Lincoln, 2011.

Littré, Émile. *Dictionnaire de la langue française*, vol. 4. Paris: Hachette, 1875.

Livi, François. *J.-K. Huysmans: à rebours de l'esprit décadent*. Paris: Nizet, 1991.

Lombroso, Cesare. *The Man of Genius*. London: Scott, 1891.

Lombroso, Cesare, and Guglielmo Ferraro. *La femme criminelle et la prostituée*. Translated by Louise Maille. Paris: Alcan, 1896.

Loomis, Jeffrey B. "Of Pride and the Fall: The Allegorical *À Rebours*." *Nineteenth-Century French Studies* 12/13, nos. 1–2 (1984): 147–61.

Los Angeles Times. "Queer Fad of French Women." (5 March 1896): 6.

– "Perfume Whim Is Yankee Fad: My Lady Uses Hypodermic Needle to Scent Herself." (15 December 1912): ST2.

"Lucrézia." Advertisement. *Vanity Fair*, May 2012, 131.

Lunel, Adolphe-Benestor. *Traité des maladies des cheveux et de tout le système pileux… suivi d'un formulaire général des préparations en usage pour combattre ces maladies*. Paris, 1860.

Lutaud, Dr. *Nouveau formulaire de thérapeutique*. Paris: Journal de médecine de Paris, 1884.

Lyu, Claire Chi-ah. *A Sun within a Sun: The Power and Elegance of Poetry*. Pittsburgh: University of Pittsburgh Press, 2006.

Mackenzie, J.N. "The Production of So-called 'Rose Cold' by Means of Artificial Rose." *American Journal of the Medical Sciences* 91 (1886): 45–57.

Magnard, Francis. "Paris au jour le jour." *Figaro: journal non-politique* (14 July 1872): 3.

Malo, Charles. *Bazar Parisien ou annuaire raisonnée de l'industrie*. Paris: Bazar Parisien, 1821.

Majid, Asifa, and Niclas Burenhult. "Odors Are Expressible in Language, as Long as You Speak the Right Language." *Cognition* 130, no. 2 (February 2014): 266–70.

Marcelin. "Revue comique de France 1957. *Le monde illustré* (30 January 1858): 72–3.

Martin, Bronwen, and Felizitas Ringham, eds. *Sense and Scent: The Exploration of Olfactory Meaning*. London: Philomel, 2003.

Martin, Morag. "French Harems: Images of the Orient in Cosmetic Advertisements, 1750–1815. *Proceedings of the Western Society for French History* 31 (2003): 125–37.

– "Doctoring Beauty: The Medical Control of Women's *Toilettes* in France, 1750–1820." *Medical History* 49, no.1 (2005): 351–68.

Maryan, M. and G. Béal. *Le fond et la forme: le savoir-vivre pour les jeunes filles*. Paris: Bloud & Barral, 1896.

Masque de Velours. "La vie mondaine, le vernissage au salon des Champs-Élysées." *La revue illustrée* 179 (1 June 1893): 403–4.

– "Le vernissage aux Champs-Élysées." *La revue illustrée* 179 (1 June 1893): 403–4.

Matlock, Jann. *Scenes of Seduction: Prostitution, Hysteria, and Reading Difference in Nineteenth-Century France*. New York: Columbia University Press, 1994.

Maupassant, Guy de. "La jeune fille." *Le gaulois* (27 April 1884): 1.

Maurin, Maurice. *La sagesse du créateur de parfum*. Paris: L'Œil neuf, 2006.

Mavor, Carol. "Odor di femina: Though You May Not See Her, You Can Certainly Smell Her." *Cultural Studies* 12, no. 1 (1998): 51–81.

Maxwell, Catherine. *Scents and Sensibility: Perfume in Victorian Literary Culture*. Oxford: Oxford University Press, 2017.

McGee, Harold. *Nose Dive: A Field Guide to the World's Smells*. New York: Penguin, 2020.

McLees, Ainslie Armstrong. "Baudelaire's 'Une charogne:' Caricature and the Birth of Modern Art. *Mosaic* 21, no. 4 (1988): 111–22.

Mège, Dr. Jean-Baptiste. *Alliance d'Hygie et de la Beauté, ou l'art d'embellir, d'après les principes de la physiologie: précédé d'un discours sur les caractères physiques et moraux de la femme, ses prérogatives et ses devoirs, et sur les mœurs et les coutumes des anciens*. Paris: Eberhart, 1818.

Melnick, Meredith. "What Is Lança-Perfume? The Drug from Rio's Bust You've Never Heard Of." *Time*, 2 December 2010. https://healthland.time .com/2010/12/02/whats-lanca-perfume-the-biggest-drug-in-rio-youve -never-heard-of/.

Merleau-Ponty, Maurice. *Phenomenology of Perception* [1945]. Translated by Colin Smith. London: Routledge, 2005.

Mermet, Émile. *La publicité en France: guide pratique annuaire 1879.* Paris: Chaix et Cie, 1879.

Mesch, Rachel. *The Hysteric's Revenge: French Women Writers at the Fin de Siècle.* Nashville: Vanderbilt, 2006.

– *Before Trans: Three Gender Stories from Nineteenth-Century Paris.* Stanford, CA: Stanford University Press, 2020.

Millet, Jules. *L'audition colorée.* Paris: Octave Doin, 1892.

Minnelli, Vincente, dir. *Madame Bovary.* MGM, 1949.

Miquet, Marie. "Le séjour à doncières dans *le côté des Guermantes*: avant-textes et texte." *Semen* 11 (1999). http://journals.openedition.org/semen/2855.

Mitchell, Dolores. "The 'New Woman' as Prometheus: Women Artists Depict Women Smoking." *Woman's Art Journal* 12, no. 1 (1991): 3–9.

Mitchell, Robin. *Vénus Noire: Black Women and Colonial Fantasies in Nineteenth-Century France.* Athens, GA: University of Georgia Press, 2020.

Monéry, André. *L'âme des parfums: essai de psychologie olfactive.* Paris: Quillet, 1924.

Monin, Ernest. *Hygiène et traitement des maladies de la peau.* Paris: Société d'Éditions Scientifiques, 1883.

– *Les odeurs du corps humain dans l'état de santé et dans l'état maladie.* Paris: Carré, 1886.

– *Hygiène de la beauté.* Paris: Doin, 1890.

– *Les odeurs du corps humain, causes et traitements.* Paris: Doin, 1903.

Montesquiou, Robert de. *Musée rétrospective de la classe 90: parfumerie (matières premières, matériel procédés et produits) à l'exposition universelle de 1900 à Paris.* Saint-Cloud: Berlin Frères, 1900a.

– *Pays des aromates: commentaire descriptif d'une collection d'objets relatifs aux parfums suivi d'une nomenclature des pièces qui la composent ainsi que du catalogue d'une bibliothèque attenante et orné d'un portrait.* Paris: Floury, 1900b.

– *Le chef des odeurs suaves.* Paris: Georges Richard, 1907.

Montigny, L. "Le passage des panoramas en 1826." I. *Paris de 1800 à 1900* vol.1, edited by Charles Simond, 556–9. Paris: Plon, 1900.

Montmorillon-Boutron, Benoîte, ed. *À rebours: édition du manuscrit.* Paris: Garnier, 2011.

Mottet, M.S. "Classification des variétés d'iris des jardins." *Les iris cultivés: actes et comptes rendus de la première conférence internationale des iris, tenue à Paris 1922* (Paris: Au siège de la Société, 1923): 100–20.

Mucha, Alphonse. *Lectures on Art.* London: Academy Editions, 1975.

Mucha, Jiri. *Alphonse Mucha: His Life and Art.* London: Heinemann, 1966.

Mucha, Sarah. *Alphonse Mucha.* London: Frances Lincoln, 2011.

Muchembled, Robert. *La civilisation des odeurs.* Paris: Les Belles Lettres, 2017.

Mulvey, Laura. "Visual Pleasure and Narrative Cinema." *Screen* 16, no. 3 (1975): 6–18.

Murphy, Steve. *Logiques du dernier Baudelaire: lectures du* Spleen de Paris. Paris: Champion, 2007.

Musset, Danielle, and Claudine Fabre-Vassas, eds. *Odeurs et parfums*. Paris: CTHS, 1999.

Nabokov, Vladimir. *Lectures on Literature*. Edited by Fredson Bowers. New York: Harvest, 1980.

Nadar. *Charles Baudelaire intime: le poète vierge*. Paris: Blaizot, 1911.

Natanson, Phoebe. "Pope Benedict Has Custom-Designed Cologne: Silvana Casoli Makes Heavenly Scent for Pope Benedict." *ABC News*, 15 March 2021. https://abcnews.go.com/International/pope-benedicts-custom-made-cologne/story?id=15927330.

National Magazine. "A Dynasty Not Mentioned in History." vol. 3 (1858): 175–6.

New York Times. "Her Point of View." 28 June 1891, 12.

– "Injections of Perfumes." 21 August 1898, 10.

– "Perfume Now Injected: Latest Fad in Paris – Skin Becomes Saturated with Aroma." 1 October 1912, 5.

Nicolaï, Patricia de. "A Smelling Trip into the Past: The Influence of Synthetic Materials on the History of Perfumery." *Chemistry and Biodiversity* 5 (2008): 1137–46.

Niess, Robert J. "On Listening to Homais." *The French Review* 51, no. 1 (1977): 22–28.

Noël, Eugène. *Rouen, rouennais, rouenneries*. Rouen: Schneider frères,1894.

Nordau, Max. *Degeneration* [1895]. Lincoln: University of Nebraska Press, 1993.

Norville, Comtesse de. *Les coulisses de la beauté*. Paris: Ampleman, 1894.

Oberhuber, Andrea, and Érika Wicky. "Du mauvais usage des parfums, Chérie empoisonnée par le musc et l'héliotrope." *Cahiers Edmond et Jules Goncourt* 23 (2016): 131–40.

Ockman, Carol, and Kenneth E. Silver. *Sarah Bernhardt: The Art of High Drama*. New York: The Jewish Museum, 2005.

Ohler, Bonnie J., Christelle Guédot, et al. "Aggregation of *Thaumatomyia glabra* (Diptera Chloropidae) Males on *Iris* spp. Flowers Releasing Methyl Anthranilate." *Environmental Entomology* 45, no. 6 (December 2016): 1476–9.

Olmsted, William. "Immortal Rot: A Reading of 'Une Charogne.'" In *Understanding* Les Fleurs du Mal, edited by William J. Thompson, 60–71. Nashville: Vanderbilt, 1997.

Olofsson, Jonas K., Robert S. Hurley, Nicholas E. Bowman, et al. "A Designated Odor-Language Integration System in the Human Brain." *The Journal of Neuroscience* (4 November 2014): 14864–73.

Ortiz-Gómez, Teresa, and Maria Jesús Santesmases. *Gendered Drugs and Medicine: Historical and Socio-Cultural Perspectives*. London: Routledge, 2016.

Paquet, Dominique. "L'Impérialisme olfactif chez Joris-Karl Huysmans." In *Odeurs et parfums*, edited by Danielle Musset and Claudine Fabre-Vassas, 221–7. Paris: CTHS, 1999.

Parfumerie moderne. "Recettes et procédés utiles: lances-parfums." August 1911, 107–8.

– "Parfum à la Maréchale" (April 1914): 46–7.

Paris Exposition 1900: guide pratique du visiteur de Paris et de l'exposition. Paris: Hachette, 1900.

Passy, Jacques. "Revue générale sur les sensations olfactives." *Année psycholologique* 2 (1895): 363–410.

Paul, Tanya, and Stanton Thomas, eds. *Bouguereau and America*. New Haven, CT: Yale University Press, 2019.

Perras, Jean-Alexandre. "La Poudre et le petit-maître en France et en Angleterre au XVIIIe siècle: parfum de gloire, parfum de ruelle." In *Mediality of Smells/Médialité des odeurs*, 61–87. Edited by Jean-Alexandre Perras and Érika Wicky. Oxford: Peter Lang, 2022.

Perras, Jean-Alexandre, and Érika Wicky. "La sémiologie des odeurs du XIXe siècle: du savoir médical à la norme sociale." In *Études françaises. La physiognomonie au XIXe siècle: transpositions esthétiques et médiatiques* 49, no. 3 (2013): 119–34.

– *Mediality of Smells/Médialté des odeurs*. Oxford: Peter Lang, 2022.

Perrot, Philippe. *Le travail des apparences: le corps féminin XVIII-XIX siècle*. Paris: Seuil, 1984.

Phalèse, Hurbert de. *Comptes* à rebours: *l'œuvre de Huysmans à travers les nouvelles technologies*. Paris: Nizet, 1991.

Pierre, Arnauld. "Musical Ecstasy and Fixing the Gaze: Mucha and the Culture of Hypnosis." In *Alphonse Mucha*, edited by Agnes Husslein-Arco, Jean Louis Gaillemin, Michel Hilaire, and Christiane Lange, 25–9. Munich: Prestel, 2009.

Piesse, Charles. *The Art of Perfumery*, 5th ed. London: Piesse and Lubin, 1891.

Piesse, G.W. Septimus. *Art of Perfumery and the Methods of Obtaining the Odors of Plants*, 2nd American Edition. Philadelphia: Lindsay and Blakiston, 1857.

Piesse, G.W. Septimus. *Des odeurs, des parfums et des cosmétiques*. Paris: Baillière, 1865.

– *The Art of Perfumery and the Methods of Obtaining the Odors of Plants*. 4th ed. Philadelphia: Lindsay and Blakiston, 1880.

– *The Art of Perfumery*. Philadelphia: Lindsay and Blakiston, 1867.

– *Des odeurs, des parfums et des cosmétiques*. Paris: Baillière, 1877.

– *Chimie des parfums et fabrication des essences*. Paris: Baillière, 1897.

– *Chimie des parfums et fabrication des essences*. Paris: Baillière, 1903.

– *Histoire des parfums* et *hygiène de la toilette*. Paris: Baillière, 1905.

Pisano, Giusy, and Érika Wicky. "Concerts olfactifs fin-de-siècle: les parfums entre vibrations et matières." In *Mediality of Smells/Médialités des odeurs*, edited by Jean-Alexandre Perras and Erika Wicky, 341–56. Oxford: Peter Lang, 2022.

Piver, L.-T. *Rapports du Jury International. Classe 90. Parfumerie.* Paris: Imprimerie nationale, 1901.

Plato. *Timaeus.* Translated and edited by Peter Kalkavage. Indianapolis: Focus, 2016.

Pommier, Jean. *La mystique de Baudelaire.* Paris: Les Belles Lettres, 1932.

Poncelet, Polycarpe. *Chimie du goût et de l'odorat, ou principes pour composer facilement, et à peu de frais, les liqueurs à boire, et les eaux de senteurs.* Paris: Le Mercier, 1755.

Porteous, J. Douglas. "Smellscape." In *A Smell Culture Reader*, edited by Jim Drobnick, 89–106. Oxford: Berg, 2006.

Poucher, William. *Perfume, Cosmetics, and Soaps*, vol. 2, 9th ed. New York: D. Van Nostrand, 1993.

Pradal, P., and F. Malpeyre. *Nouveau manuel complet du parfumeur.* 2 vols. Paris: Roret, 1863.

– *Nouveau manuel complet du parfumeur.* 2 vols. Paris: Roret, 1895.

– *Nouveau manuel complet du parfumeur.* 2 vols. Paris: Roret, 1918.

Prendergast, Christopher. *Nineteenth-Century French Poetry: Introductions to Close Readings.* Cambridge: Cambridge University Press, 1990.

Présilly, Berthe de. "Carnet mondain." *La Revue Nouvelle* 67 (15 December 1890): 439–42.

"Propos féminins." *Figaro: journal non-politique* (22 January 1931): 5–6.

Quella-Villéger, Alain. *Le cas Farrère: du Goncourt à la disgrace.* Paris: Presses de la renaissance, 1989.

Rachilde. "Les Romans." *Mercure de France* (15 November 1905): 260–1.

Ramazani, Vahid. *The Free Indirect Mode: Flaubert and the Poetics of Irony.* Charlottesville: University Press of Virginia, 1988.

Raynaud, Ernest. "Les écrivains de filles." *Mercure de France* (July 1890): 231–8.

Reade, Brian. *Art nouveau and Alphonse Mucha.* London: Her Majesty's Stationery Office, 1967.

Recueil de recettes pour faire soi-même tout ce qui est nécessaire à l'entretien de la beauté.... Paris: Prost, 1866.

Reeser, Todd, and Lewis Siefert. *Entre Hommes: French and Francophone Masculinities in Culture and Theory.* Newark: University of Delaware Press, 2008.

Reichert, Tom. *The Erotic History of Advertising.* Amherst, NY: Prometheus, 2003.

Reinarz, Jonathan. *Past Scents: Historical Perspectives on Smell.* Urbana: University of Illinois Press, 2014.

Rennet, Jack, and Karel Srp. *Ivan Lendl: Alfons Mucha.* Translated by Adrian Dean. Bratislava: Richard Fuxa Foundation and Nakladatelstvi Slovart, 2013.

Reutersvärd, Ocar. "The 'Violettomania' of the Impressionists." *The Journal of Aesthetics and Art Criticism* 9, no. 2 (1950): 106–10.

Reutter de Rosemont, Louis. *Histoire de la pharmacie à travers les âges. Tome II: du XVIIe siècle jusqu'à nos jours*. Paris: Peyronnet & Cie, 1932.

Rey, Pierre-Louis, and Gisèle Séginger. *Madame Bovary et les savoirs*. Paris: Presses Sorbonne Nouvelle, 2009.

Reynaud-Pactat, Patricia. "La lettre de rupture de Rodolphe à Emma Bovary: l'énonciation parle l'économie." *Nineteenth-Century French Studies* 19, no. 1 (1990): 83–94.

Ricatte, Robert. *La genèse de* La fille Élisa. Paris: PUF, 1960.

Richet, Christian. "Photographs of the Lance-parfum and Its Labels." http://richet.christian.free.fr/mode/modpat.html.

Rickenbacher, Sergej. "L'invention de l'orgue à senteurs: sur l'interdépendance de la littérature et de l'objet technique." In *Mediality of Smells/Médialités des odeurs*, edited by Jean-Alexandre Perras and Erika Wicky, 357–8. Oxford: Peter Lang, 2022.

Rifelj, Carol. *Coiffures: Hair in Nineteenth-Century French Literature and Culture*. Newark: University of Delaware Press, 2010.

Rimmel, Eugene. *The Book of Perfumes*. London: Chapman and Hall, 1865.
– *Le livre des parfums*. Paris: Dentu, 1870.

Rindisbacher, Hans J. *The Smell of Books: A Cultural-Historical Study of Olfactory Perception in Literature*. Ann Arbor: University of Michigan Press, 1992.

Rodaway, Paul. *Sensuous Geographies: Body, Sense and Place*. New York: Routledge, 1994.

Rouby, Catherine, Benoist Schaal, Danièle Dubois, Rémi Gervais, and A. Holley, eds. *Olfaction, Taste, and Cognition*. Cambridge: Cambridge University Press, 2002.

Sagarin, Edward. *The Science and Art of Perfumery*. New York: McGraw Hill, 1945.

San Francisco Call. "Perfumes Self with Hypodermic. American Woman Introduces Latest Toilet Craze for Paris Smart Set." 113 (15 December 1912): 53.

Schaefer, Bernd. *Natural Products in the Chemical Industry*. Berlin: Springer, 2014.

Schlögel, Karl. *The Scent of Empires: Chanel N°5 and Red Moscow*. Cambridge: Polity, 2020.

Schnedecker, Catherine. "Quand la sémantique se met au parfum." *Langages* 181 (2011): 89–107.

Schoch, Deborah. "Distorted, Bizarre Food Smells Haunt Covid Survivors." *The New York Times*, 15 June 2021. https://www.nytimes.com/2021/06/15/health/covid-smells-food.html.

Seaton, Beverly. *The Language of Flowers: A History*. Charlottesville: University Press of Virginia, 1995.

Seguin, E.C., ed. *Transactions of the American Neurological Association for 1877*. New York: G.P. Putnam's Sons, 1877.

Segura, Debra. "The Dream of the Hermetic Utopia: *A rebours* as Allegory for the World after Germ Theory." *Discourse* 29, no. 1 (2007): 49–76.

Serby, Michael J., and Karen L. Chobor, eds. *Science of Olfaction*. New York: Springer-Verlag, 1992.

Serres, Michel. *The Five Senses: A Philosophy of Mingled Bodies* [1985]. Translated by Margaret Sankey and Peter Cowley. London: Continuum, 2008.

Serval, Maurice. "*Autour de Balzac*. César Birotteau." *Revue d'histoire littéraire de la France* 37, no. 2 (1930): 196–226.

Sharples, Dr. H. "Milk Sickness." *The Medical World* 6, no. 1 (January 1888): 28.

Shera, Peta Allen. "Selfish Passions and Artificial Desires: Rereading Clérambault's Study of 'Silk Erotomania.'" *Journal of the History of Sexuality* 18, no. 1 (2009): 158–79.

Silverman, Deborah L. *Art Nouveau in Fin-de-Siècle France: Politics, Psychology, and Style*. Berkeley: University of California Press, 1989.

Simond, Charles, ed. *La vie parisienne à travers le XIX siècle: Paris de 1800 à 1900*. Vol. 1. Paris: Plon, 1900.

Sirius de Massilie. *Le langage des fleurs*. Paris: Pontet-Brault, 1898.

Société de chimie médicale. "Alteration de la santé par les odeurs." *Journal de chimie médicale, de pharmacie et de toxicologie* 3, no. 2 (February 1867): 100–2.

"Spice-Jars, Pot-Pourri and Rose-Jars." *The Art Interchange: A Household Journal* (17 July 1886): 19–22.

Srp, Karel, and Lenka Bydzovska. "A Delicate Eden." In *Ivan Lendl: Alfons Mucha*, edited by Jack Rennet and Karel Srp, 17–33. Bratislava: Richard Fuxa Foundation and Nakladatelstvi Slovart, 2013.

Staffe, Baronne. *Le cabinet de toilette*. Paris: Havard, 1891.

– *Usages du monde: règles du savoir-vivre dans la société moderne*. Paris: Havard, 1891.

– *Le cabinet de toilette*. Paris: Havard, 1897.

– *Le cabinet de toilette*. Paris: Havard, 1899.

Stamelman, Richard. *Perfume: Joy, Obsession, Scandal, Sin: A Cultural History of Fragrance from 1750 to Present*. New York: Rizzoli, 2006.

Summers, Claude J. *Gay and Lesbian Literary Heritage*. 2nd ed. London: Routledge, 2002.

Symons, Arthur. *Figures of Several Centuries*. London: Constable and Company, 1916.

– *The Symbolist Movement in Literature*. New York: Dutton, 1919.

Tancock, L.W. "Some Early Critical Work of Zola." *Modern Language Review* 42, no. 1 (January 1947): 43–57.

Tanner, Tony. *Adultery in the Novel: Contract and Transgression*. Baltimore: Johns Hopkins University Press, 1979.

Tessereau, Auguste. *Cours d'hygiène*. Paris: Garnier, 1855.

Thévenot, M. "Modes." *La mode illustrée* (14 June 1896): 191.

Theissen, Anne. "Sentir: les constructions prédicatives de l'olfaction." *Langages* 181 (2011): 109–25.

Thirion, Charles, and Joseph Bonnet. *Revue générale de la propriété industrielle en France et à l'étranger: doctrine, législation, jurisprudence, chronique et bibliographie en matière de brevets d'invention [etc.], Supplément au no. 5* (1 November 1906): 1–4.

Thompson, Jan. "The Role of Woman in the Iconography of Art Nouveau." *Art Journal* 31, no. 2 (1971–2): 158–67.

Thompson, William J. *Understanding* Les Fleurs du Mal. Nashville: Vanderbilt, 1997.

Thorel-Cailleteau, Sylvie. *La tentation du livre sur rien: naturalisme et décadence*. Mont-de-Marsan: Éditions Universitaires, 1994.

Thrupkaew, Noy. "The Big Stink in the World of Perfume." *The Washington Post Magazine*, 21 April 2021.

Tiersten, Lisa. *Marianne in the Market: Envisioning Consumer Society in Fin-de-Siècle France*. Berkeley: University of California Press, 2001.

Toulouse, Édouard. *Enquête medico-psychologique sur les rapports de la supériorité intellectuelle avec la névropathie: Émile Zola*. Paris: Flammarion, 1896.

Trousset, Jules. *Nouveau dictionnaire encyclopédique universel illustré: répertoire des connaissances humaines*. Vol. 5. Paris: à la librairie llustrée, 1885–91.

Trubek, Amy B. *Haute Cuisine: How the French Invented the Culinary Profession*. Philadelphia: University of Pennsylvania Press, 2000.

Tucker, Cynthia Grant. "Pétrarchisant sur l'horrible: A Renaissance Tradition and Baudelaire's Grotesque." *French Review* 48, no. 5 (April 1975): 887–96.

Turin, Luca. *The Secret of Scent: Adventures in Perfume and the Science of Smell*. New York: Harper Perennial, 2006.

Turin, Luca, and Tania Sanchez. *Perfumes: The Guide*. New York: Viking, 2008.

– *Perfumes: The A-Z Guide*. New York: Penguin, 2009.

– *The Little Book of Perfumes: The Hundred Classics*. New York: Viking, 2011.

Vassy, Gaston. *La reine des fleurs, légende hindoue: articles spéciaux et recommandés de la maison*. Paris: Piver, 1874.

Veysset, Georges. *Huysmans et la médecine*. Paris: Les Belles Lettres, 1950.

Vigarello, Georges. *Le propre et le sale: l'hygiène du corps depuis le Moyen Âge*. Paris: Seuil, 1985.

Vila, Alexandra Caole. "Rare Giant Corpse Flower Blooms in Texas, What Makes It Smell Like Rotting Cadavers?" *Nature World News*, 19 May 2016. https://www.natureworldnews.com/articles/22571/20160519/rare -giant-corpse-flower-blooms-in-texas-what-makes-them-smell-like-rotting -cadavers.htm.

"Violet Color Matter Derived from Morphine." In *Journal of the Chemical Society* 60, no. 2 (1891): 1120–1.

"Visite au salon 1882: Comerre, Léon-Albine morte-une étoile." *La Coulisse* (22 May 1882): n.p.

Vissière, Jean-Louis. "L'art de la phrase dans *l'Assommoir*." *Les Cahiers Naturalistes* 11 (1958): 455–64.

Voivenel, Paul. *Littérature et folie: étude anatomo-pathologique du génie littéraire.* Toulouse: Gimet-Pisseau, 1908.

"Votre Parfum … c'est vous." *Marie Claire* (10 December 1937): 118–19.

Waller, Margaret. "The Emperor's New Clothes: Display, Cover-up and Exposure in Modern Masculinity." In *Entre Hommes: French and Francophone Masculinities in Culture and Theory*. Edited by Todd Reeser and Lewis Seifert, 115–42. Dover: University of Delaware Press, 2008.

Washington Post. "Vogue of the Violet: From across the Seas Come Perfumes and Stories of Perfume." (26 June 1898): 25.

– "Injections of Perfumes." (28 August 1898): 21.

– "New Fad in Drinking: Perfume Habit Is the Latest Form of Dipsomania. A Cocktail of Peau d'Espagne." (16 July 1899): 26.

Waters, John, dir. *Polyester*. New Line Cinema, 1981.

– *Role Models*. New York: Farrar, Strauss and Giroux, 2010.

Watson, Janell. *Literature and Material Culture from Balzac to Proust*. Cambridge: Cambridge University Press, 1999.

Weber, Eugen. *France: fin de siècle*. Cambridge, MA: Harvard University Press, 1986.

"Whale 'Rewards' Wairarapa Maori." *NZ Herald*, 9 May 2011. https://www .nzherald.co.nz/nz/whale-rewards-wairarapa-maori/EUA2VHBATFRBT 77E7F3VAF4FG4/.

Wicky, Érika. "Ce que sentent les jeunes filles." *Romantisme* 3, no. 165 (2014): 43–53.

– "Parfum de bonté et odeur de sainteté: les enjeux de l'olfaction dans l'éducation religieuse des jeunes filles au xixᵉ siècle." *Arts et Savoirs* 11 (2019): 11–13.

Williams, Rosalind H. *Dream Worlds: Mass Consumption in Late Nineteenth-Century France*. Berkely: University of California Press, 1982.

Wilson, Alphus D., and Manuela Baietto. "Advances in Electronic-Nose Technologies Developed for Biomedical Applications." *Sensors* 11, no. 1 (2011): 1105–76.

Wilson, Michael L. "'The Despair of Unhappy Love'": Pederasty and Popular Fiction in the Belle Époque." In *Sexuality at the Fin de Siècle: The Makings of a "Central Problem,"* edited by Peter Cryle and Christopher E. Forth, 109–22. Newark: University of Delaware Press, 2008.

Wilson, Susannah. "Morphinisé/Morphinomane/Morphinée: Cultural Representations of a French Opioid Crisis, 1870–1940." *Contemporary French Civilization* 44, no. 4 (2019): 333–57.

Wnuk, Ewelina, and Asifa Majid. "Revisiting the Limits of Language: The Odor Lexicon of Maniq." *Cognition* 131, no. 1 (2014): 125–38.

Wood's Medical and Surgical Monograph. Vol. 8. New York: Wood, 1890.

Yee, Jennifer. *The Colonial Comedy: Imperialism in the French Realist Novel.* Oxford: Oxford University Press, 2016.

Index

Gautier, Judith, 150; *Livre de Jade*, 150

Gautier, Théophile, 98, 139

Gazette de France (newspaper), 184

Gencé, Comtesse de (Marie Louise Poyollon), 162, 194, 247; *Cabinet de toilette d'une honnête femme, Le,* 162, 304n18

geranium, 142, 147, 306n28, 306n29

germs, awareness of, 298n22

Ghislain, Gérard, 254

ghost flower (Burr), 256, 313n31

Gibbons, Boyd, 79, 110

Gilbert, Avery, 80

ginseng, 150

Gobet, Magalie, 263n10, 278n24

"golden age of osphresiology", 32; Corbin on, 9, 260n6

Goncourt, Edmond de, 132, 237, 247, 272n85, 286n4, 303n12, 304n14; *Chérie,* 6, 20, 56, 63, 211–21, 227, 230, 232, 236, 238, 239, 245, 272n85, 303n9; *Faustin, La,* 211; *Fille Élisa, La,* 61, 62, 64; *Frères Zemganno, Le,* 211

gourmand (fragrance classification), 243, 267n38

Gourmont, Remy de, 56, 272n84

goût auditif (auditory taste), 99, 132

Gozlan, Léon, 51

Grainger, Holliday, 255

Grand Dictionnaire universel du XIXe siècle, 1866–1877, 22, 86, 93

grape soda, 191, 299–300n32

Graphic, The (newspaper), 52

Grasset, Joseph, 96, 98, 99, 126, 285n22

Gray, Richard T., 264n14

Griemas, Algirdas, 292n8

Grimod, Alfred Guillaume Gabriel, 261n20

griserie, intoxication, excitation, 23

Groom, Nigel, 264n15, 265n27, 274n102, 274n104, 277n22, 288n20

grotesque (in fragrance), 255

grotesque (in literature), 107, 126

Grout, Holly, 266n28, 291n1, 292n5

Gueldy perfumes, advertisement, 249

Gueldy's Vision d'Orient perfume, advertisement, 250

Guerlain, 72, 77; boutique, 297–8n11; Jicky, 34, 229; Le Sillage, 25–6, 263n7, 263n8; Mitsouko, 245, 246, 247; Mouchoir de Monsieur, 73; Vol de Nuit, 252

Guerlain, Aimé, 229

Guerlain, Jacques, Mitsouko, 244–5, 247

guild system, 32, 264n19

gutta-percha, 126

Guyaux, André, 286n6, 288n22

Hammond, William A., 28, 72–3, 275n112, 275nn114–15

handkerchief(s): fragrance vehicle, 152; perfumed, 172–3; print advertisement, 31; scented, 159

Hannon, Théodore, 268n47

Harad, Alyssa, 257

Hardy, Thomas, 287n9

hartshorn, 175, 176, 295n42

hashish, 225, 227

Haussmannization of Paris, 103

Havelock Ellis, Henry, 96, 117, 159, 227; *Studies in the Psychology of Sex,* 129

Hawthorne, Melanie, 263n6, 269n63, 311n3, 311n6, 311n9

Haynes, Christine, 296n1

headnotes, fragrance pyramid, 9, 10

headspace technology, 81–2, 191, 277n22, 300n35

rosewood, 306n29
rotten, term, 107
Roudniska, Edmond, 313n31

Sabatier, Claude, 270n72
Sade, Marquis de, 254
saffron, 146, 147
Sagan, Françoise, 252
Sagarin, Edward, 75–6, 114, 276n3;
 Science and the Art of Perfumery,
 The, 75
Saint-Exupéry, Antoine, 252
Saint-Germain, Bertrand de, 283n5
Salammbô (Flaubert), 83, 85, 278n31
Salammbô (Mucha), 83, 85, 244
Salomé (Moreau), 149
Sanchez, Tania, 254, 267n38, 313n24
Sand, George, 19, 163, 167, 254
sandalwood, 204, 220, 293n20,
 306n28
sandalwood styrax, 248
San Francisco Call (newspaper),
 306n31
sarcanthus, 150
Sargent, John Singer, 83, 84, 86,
 278n28
scented letters: Béatrix (Balzac), 153,
 177; Madame Bovary (Flaubert),
 153, 177; perfume on page, 154–5
scented matter, 7
scent of a woman, odor di femina,
 116, 117
Scent of Empires (Schlögel), 257
Scent Trail, The (Lyttelton), 257
scent trails, 3; literary, 7
Schaffert, Timothy, 258
Scheafer, Berndt, 299n27
Schlögel, Karl, 257
Science and the Art of Perfumery, The
 (Sagarin), 75
science cosmétique (cosmetic
 science), 188

scrofula, 76
Seaton, Beverly, language of flowers,
 41, 267n40
Second Empire, 216, 305n22
secret affinities, 114
Seguin, E.C., 275n112
Segura, Debra, 287n10
Seifert, Lewis, 261n18
Sell, Charles, 288n19
sentant l'iris, 188, 189, 191, 192, 194,
 298–9n25
Sentimental Education (Flaubert), 6
sequel (perfume), 244, 312n17
seringa, 126, 129
serkis du harem, 145, 289n24
Serres, Michel, 77
sewer, term, 107
Shalimar, perfume, 244
Sharples, H., 110, 282–3n2
shawls, patchouli and, 40, 266n34,
 266n35
Shera, Peta Allen, 308n50
Shilitto, Violet, 47, 269n60
showy perversity, Weber on, 223,
 306n32
silence continu (code of silence), 62,
 273n95
sillage: dangerous, 68–9; discussions
 of women and fashion, 23, 24;
 emergence as fragrance term, 74;
 fille and, 60–8; fragrant, 263n9;
 intimacy of dressing room and
 boudoir, 210; jeune fille and, 55–60;
 linguistic, 18; noun, 22; poem
 language, 95; pronunciation,
 3; repurposing of, 11; scent
 movement, 4; term, 26; translation,
 3; variation on odiferous, 72–4;
 violet, 17; word, 259n2
Sillage (fragrance), Guerlain, 26
Sillages (Vivien), 23, 47
Simmel, Georg, 291n2, 294n25

Vivien, Renée, 17, 23, 46–7, 268nn
 58–60, 268nn63–4; *Une femme
 m'apparut*, 47
Viville, 72; advertisement, 30
volupté: French concept of, 52;
 morphine, 270n74; perfume
 abuse, 52
*Volupté des parfums, La (The Sensuous
 Pleasure of Perfumes)* (Caufeynon), 208
Vuillaume, Marcel, 80, 277n18

Waffles (perfume), 254
wake, double meaning of, 263n5
Waller, Margaret, 13, 261n18
washhouse, atmosphere of, 135,
 287n11
Washington Post (newspaper), 45
Waters, John, 255–6
Wathelet, Olivier, 277n18
wave theory (odour waves), 115, 119,
 121, 142, 146, 150, 284n19
WD-40, iconic scent, 80
Weber, Eugen, 223, 306n32
white lilac, 230
Wicky, Érika, 81, 192, 264n13,
 269n56, 298n16; verb *sentir*, 81,
 277n21
Wilde, Oscar, 133, 281n54
Williams, Rosalind H., 13
Wilson, Susannah, 223, 270n74,
 307n37
wintergreen, 186
Wittig, Monique, 268n47
Wnuk, Ewelina, 277n14
Woman with an Iris
 (Bouguereau), 190

women, perfumed products for, 11–12
Wood, Alexander, 307n43
words: confused and corresponding,
 88–96; Huysmans's word list,
 143–9; smell of, 76–81
wordscapes, Baudelaire's,
 87–8
word-smell correlations, 109
World Health Organization, 257
World Heritage Status, 256
World's Fair (1900), 15, 27
writing paper: perfuming, 41;
 scented, 159

Xila, Comtesse, 180

Yee, Jennifer, 302n54, 313n26
yellow fever, 76
ylang-ylang, 119, 191
Yves Saint Laurent, 261n17

Zeller, Pauline, 303n11
Zola, Émile, 98, 114, 132, 134,
 237, 262n24, 270n66, 276n2,
 305n21; artist depiction of
 death scene, 52, 270–1n75; *Au
 Bonheur des dames*, 15; *Faute
 de l'abbé Mouret, La*, 48–50,
 51–4, 270n66, 287n9; fictional
 department store, 262n24; *Joie
 de vivre, La*, 57–60, 215, 238,
 239, 272n87, 305n21; *Nana*,
 6, 22–3, 63, 67–8, 167, 262n3;
 Terre, La, 115
Zwaardemaker, Hendrik, 82, 115,
 283n9